THE BUSINESS COMMUNICATOR

THE BUSINESS COMMUNICATOR

ROBERT E. SWINDLE, D.B.A.

Phoenix College

Prentice-Hall, Inc.
Englewood Cliffs, New Jersey 07632

Library of Congress Cataloging in Publication Data

Swindle, Robert E
  The business communicator.

  Includes index.
  1. Communication in management.   2. Commercial
correspondence.   3. Business report writing.   I. Title.
HF5718.S9   658.4'53   79-9523
ISBN   0-13-091819-9

© 1980 by Prentice-Hall, Inc., Englewood Cliffs, N.J.   07632

Printed in the United States of America

10   9   8   7   6   5

PRENTICE-HALL INTERNATIONAL, INC., *London*
PRENTICE-HALL OF AUSTRALIA PTY. LIMITED, *Sydney*
PRENTICE-HALL OF CANADA, LTD., *Toronto*
PRENTICE-HALL OF INDIA PRIVATE LIMITED, *New Delhi*
PRENTICE-HALL OF JAPAN, INC., *Tokyo*
PRENTICE-HALL OF SOUTHEAST ASIA PTE. LTD., *Singapore*
WHITEHALL BOOKS LIMITED, *Wellington, New Zealand*

CONTENTS

ONE MOMENT, PLEASE!

Before turning to the first chapter, take just a minute or two to consider two important aspects of business communications and three impressive reasons for committing yourself to this book.

Essential skill. If you were an employment manager, would you hire a college graduate who couldn't write a simple business letter or report? Probably not, and neither would most employment managers. Businesses do not, for example, hire accountants and secretaries solely on the basis of their accounting or secretarial skills. Businesses prefer to employ accountants who can communicate well in meetings, on the telephone, and through written documents; and they hire secretaries who can, in addition to performing shorthand and typing functions, compose letters and converse intelligently.

Yes, people who communicate effectively are the ones who generally land the good jobs; they are also the ones who invariably achieve the higher-paying managerial positions. Business managers spend as much as 80 percent of their time each day communicating—talking, listening, writing, and reading—which makes communicative skills an essential qualification for promotion.

Universal application. Contrary to what you may now believe, business people are leaders in transactional correspondence. As they have shifted from the flowery writing styles of the past to today's more concise and direct approach, other segments of our society have followed. Accordingly, the crisp and lucid style of business writing is equally applicable in educational, governmental, medical, social, and other types of environments.

Fresh approach. For the past ten years or so, many high school and college instructors have emphasized the importance of creative writing, often neglecting instruction in the fundamentals of oral and written communications. In essence, students were told to forget about the rules and to just let their natural creative juices flow. With benefit of the 20-20 vision of hindsight, academicians, business managers, government leaders, parents, and students themselves can now observe the adverse consequences of this neglect: an entire generation of people, who, on the average, cannot communicate very well.

This book represents a direct response to the resulting clamor for a "return to the basics" by presenting a concise (but comprehensive) coverage of basic grammar and punctuation. Rather than discussing such nonessentials as past-perfect participles, idiomatic possessives, or predicate complements, however, *The Business Communicator* presents a no-frills approach to learning that will enable you to master, quickly and completely, the fundamentals of our English language. Don't neglect this section, because it may represent your last practical opportunity to learn which words to capitalize, which numbers to spell, how to write interesting sentences and paragraphs, where to place commas and semicolons, and other details that are essential to everyday communications and success in business.

Stimulating materials. Subsequent sections of the book introduce you to the intricacies of interoffice memos, letters, and telegrams—including current methods of communicating electronically and exciting developments in word-processing systems. An entire section is devoted to various psychological techniques that you may utilize to motivate others to respond in the manner you desire. Another section surveys current developments in telephone communications, face-to-face communications with people inside and outside your organization, the impact of graphic aids in selling your ideas, and the importance of nonverbal communication. The final two sections of the book instruct you in the preparation of business reports and methods for promoting yourself effectively when seeking employment.

Constructive challenge. I have heard many people, including some excellent speakers, complain with anguish, "I just can't write." Don't ever make such a statement to yourself or to anyone else, because it just isn't true. If you can talk, you can write; and the better you can talk, the better you can write. Give it a good try by reading the book thoroughly, attending class regularly, and completing all assignments. The rewards should be well worth the effort.

Acknowledgments. Like most books, *The Business Communicator* represents the combined efforts of many people. John Duhring, Greg Hubit, and Victoria Nelson contributed immeasurably to the final product. I am also grateful to the several business people who made direct contributions to the book, and to the following educators who reviewed the original manuscript and offered invaluable suggestions: Hilda F. Allred, University of Rhode Island; Jimmie Lee Burrows, Florida Junior College; George N. Freedman, Dutchess Community College; Judith R. McFatter, Rockland Community College; Marie A. Messer, Phoenix College; Dr. Willie Minor, Phoenix College; and Judith R. Rice, Eau Claire, Wisconsin. A special thanks is reserved for Elizabeth (my wife, chief critic, and advisor) and for my students, past and present.

Robert E. Swindle

THE BUSINESS COMMUNICATOR

PART ONE
MODERN BUSINESS COMMUNICATIONS

If you believe that business communications consist solely of letters and reports, prepare yourself for a surprise. Chapter 1 outlines the many ways that business people communicate with one another inside the organization and with people outside their companies. Business communications flow in several directions; sometimes they travel one way, sometimes two ways, sometimes at a distance, and sometimes face to face. To appreciate how totally communications pervade business, consider the following statement by a manager in a leading corporation:

Kellogg Company attempts to communicate effectively with federal, state, and local governments; educators; professional people; and other interested groups.

We communicate through personnel contact and correspondence. For example, we provide both oral and written information to the more than 200,000 people who tour our main plant each year, and we utilize the print and broadcast media to communicate a wide range of carefully prepared information to the general public—information ranging from policy to nutrition, to breakfast facts, to the contents of products. Additionally, we communicate regularly with our many employees through company publications, bulletin boards, meetings, and question-and-answer sessions.

Kellogg managers recognize the importance of communicative skills when considering which job applicants to hire. We consider communication so important, in fact, that we require regular face-to-face performance reviews between supervisors and their subordinates; we conduct in-house training sessions for improved oral and written communications; and we encourage employees to attend outside training-and-development programs through a company-wide education reimbursement plan. We also encourage employee participation in community activities and the acceptance of speaking engagements.

Rolfe Jenkins
Corporate Publications Manager
Kellogg Company

Let's begin our discussion of business communications by facing a very important fact: Communicating effectively in business or any other environment is *not* an easy task. We sometimes wonder why other people don't understand us, even though we have said precisely what we meant; and others experience similar frustrations when communicating with us. Even worse, some people seem to ignore completely our efforts to communicate with them. Why do these communication breakdowns occur? How can we overcome them? Chapter 2 discusses different types of communication barriers and offers several methods that you may use to counter them.

1

PROFILE OF BUSINESS COMMUNICATIONS

When we think of business communications, most of us imagine employees communicating with one another in a retail outlet, such as the local grocery store. But the grocery store is probably one of many stores that are owned and operated by a single company. It is not at all unusual, in fact, for one corporation to operate thousands of stores and employ several thousand people.

In this perspective, the communication challenge is obvious: How do business managers communicate effectively with all those people? Just as important, perhaps, how do the employees communicate with management? Additionally, management and other employees must communicate with many people and organizations outside the company.

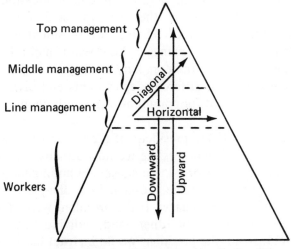

Figure 1-1   Internal communication flows

Figure 1-1 presents a graphic illustration of communication flows within an organization. An example of **downward communication** is when a top manager sends a message to the lower-level managers or the workers. An example of **upward communication** is when the workers or a lower-level manager conveys a message to top management.

Horizontal communication occurs when one employee relates to another employee on the same level, such as when one middle manager in one area of the company talks with a middle manager in another area of the company. **Diagonal communication** occurs when people on different levels relate to one another, such as when a line manager in the production department talks with a middle manager in the finance department.

Now hear this!

DOWNWARD COMMUNICATIONS

Now place your imaginary self at one of the upper levels of management and try to answer these key questions: How can we tell all our employees exactly what we are thinking? How, for instance, can we get word to them that the company desperately needs their support? That 300 employees are to be furloughed? That we are adding a new product line? Fortunately, we have a choice of several vehicles for communicating such messages.

Interoffice memos. **Interoffice memorandums** (commonly called **memos**) are the most common form of written communication within a business. Memos are like letters, except they exclude such formalities as "Dear Mr. Brown" and "Sincerely yours." When a vice president wants to send a written message to the distribution manager, he doesn't mail a letter to him; instead, he sends a memo through the company mail system. We use memos to correspond with employees in different departments and divisions of the company, but memos are never used for communicating with people outside the company.

Bulletin boards. If the president of a company wishes to direct a written message to all middle managers, he would normally send individual copies of a bulletin or memo. To inform the managers of an impending legal problem, for example, he might outline the problem in a one-page or multipage bulletin and send a copy to each manager. If the president wants to make an announcement to all employees, on the other hand, individual communications become too expensive. Instead, the president would instruct his assistants to have copies of the bulletin posted on **bulletin boards.**

But who reads bulletin boards? Nearly everyone, if they are strategically placed and properly controlled. We should place bulletin boards near food and coffee areas, where employees normally form waiting lines, and near elevators, where short waits are common. Conversely, we should avoid placing bulletin boards at the entrances to buildings or near time clocks, places where people usually hurry past and where any unnecessary congestion should be avoided.

The most effective bulletin board the author has witnessed was placed in a company cafeteria. As office employees waited their turns at the coffee urns, there was a natural tendency for them to read whatever was on the bulletin board. But the feature that made this board so very effective was that it was usually blank. The board was under a glass cover that was locked, and the personnel director was the only person with a key. When an announcement did appear on the board, therefore, employees knew that the message was important, timely, and official.

Company publications. Most medium-sized and large companies communicate regularly with their employees through company **newsletters** and **magazines.** Top management often uses newsletters to keep middle and line managers aware of events that are important to company operations. Monthly magazines, on the other hand, are directed at all employees—from top management to the most recently hired clerk.

Do most employees read company magazines? The answer is yes. Do most employees applaud the effort and costs that are involved in these publications? The answer is a resounding no; an informal survey conducted by the author suggests that most employees view company magazines as "corny," "full of company propaganda," and a "waste of time." So why do employees bother to read them? Company magazines typically include much factual data (such as promotions, replacements, retirements, marriages, deaths, transfers, and recreational activities) that hold some interest for employees. The major complaint seems to be that the publications do not come to grips with major issues.

So what is it that employees want to read about? Besides the factual data already mentioned, employees are interested in key issues confronting their companies. Because their futures are dependent on the survival and success of the company, employees seek related information: Is the company profitable? How profitable? Did the company win that important government contract? How successful or unsuccessful is the new product offering? How well is the company competing in the marketplace?

Won't knowledge of company earnings cause employees to seek more lucrative wage settlements? Probably not, because experience shows that most employees have the false impression that their companies are earning four or five times their actual rates of profit. But shouldn't this type of information be kept secret? Not at all. A few enlightened business managers, recognizing that they already disseminate a wide range of financial and operational data to investors and the general public through annual stockholder reports, are now preparing annual reports for their employees.

Employees also demonstrate a vital interest in salary negotiations and working conditions. Ironically, some labor unions communicate much better with employees on these gut issues than the companies do. As one disgruntled employee commented, "Our union leaders talk to us about the real issues, while the company keeps telling us what a nice, happy family we all are."

Some companies are striving to overcome this communication gap by being more candid in their publications. Several European companies have taken an additional step in this direction by agreeing to publish any employee complaint. The agreement also stipulates that management may respond to the complaint in the same issue. Sounds like an effective arrangement, doesn't it? Management may take corrective action on valid complaints or explain their reasons for not doing so. They can put out the small brush fires before they become roaring forest fires.

Spouse-grams. Would it be practical to mail some messages directly to employees' homes? Are spouses actually interested in the company? Again, the answer is yes. Most spouses are highly concerned with the welfare of their partners, and the future of the family is often directly correlated with the future of the company. Recognizing the influence that a spouse can have on the employee's attitude toward the company, many firms mail company magazines, bulletins, and newsletters directly to employees' home addresses.

Video programs. Several large corporations keep employees informed of current events that affect their companies by airing their own closed-circuit television programs. Exxon, Travelers Insurance, Bell Telephone, John Hancock, and several other large companies are using their own facilities and personnel to prepare regular newscasts. Rather than having employees receive what might be one-sided news coverage, especially of negative events involving the company, management presents employees with both sides of the story.

Public address systems. Business use of public address systems usually is reserved for paging key employees and for emergency announcements. An important exception was noted at the Boeing plant in Seattle. Several years ago, when survival of the company seemed dependent on construction of a supersonic aircraft, Boeing managers used their public address system to keep employees informed of related events in Washington, D.C., as they happened. Employee response to this direct form of communication was dramatic and positive.

Employees viewing WGO ("what's going on") television program (Photo courtesy Dremel Manufacturing Division, Emerson Electric Corp.)

Is anyone up there listening?

UPWARD COMMUNICATIONS

If business executives are to know what is happening at all levels of their companies, they must utilize several methods of upward communication. They must also depend on upward communication for important **feedback,** to assess accurately the reaction of employees to management's downward communications. Upward communications are more difficult to initiate and control than downward communications, because rank-and-file employees are often reluctant to express their views to superiors. It is imperative, therefore, that management pay special attention to the following methods of upward communication.

Interoffice memos. Yes, memos are also effective in the upward direction. For example, the warehouse manager might write a memo to the traffic manager concerning the number of outbound shipments that are scheduled. The traffic manager, in turn, might send a memo to the vice-president of sales concerning information that relates to a new sales program. Memos normally move in several directions: downward, upward, and (as you will see later in this chapter) horizontally and diagonally.

Formal reports. **Reports** are the most widely used form of upward communication. Many kinds of reports flow upward from all segments of a company: sales reports, production reports, quality control reports, inventory reports, shipping reports, wage-and-salary reports, insurance reports, financial reports, and many others. Managers at all levels of a business rely on reports to measure the performance of employees under their direction, and they compare current reports with those for earlier periods to measure company progress.

Reports at lower levels of management are quite detailed. They are progressively condensed, however, as they filter upward through successive layers of management personnel. At the upper levels of management, as a way of controlling their vast companies, managers use what is called **exception reporting,** concerning themselves only with those aspects of the business that are exceptions to normal operating procedures. They might study the operations at a particular factory, for example, only if profits there decline beyond a preestablished norm.

Grievance systems. Formal **grievance systems** normally exist within unionized companies. Employees, however, should have some way of communicating their complaints to upper-level managers even when they are not unionized. Management should be aware of the concerns of employees so that any sparks of discontent may be extinguished before they become major problems.

When unionized employees have complaints, they usually discuss them with their immediate supervisor. If the problem cannot be resolved by the supervisor, or if the supervisor is part of the problem, employees inform their union representatives. Union stewards discuss the problem with people in the personnel department; if the problem still cannot be resolved, an arbitrator is called in to decide what should be done. A decision by an arbitrator is binding on both management and employees.

Suggestion programs. Ford Motor Company advertises that when someone has a better idea Ford will put it on wheels. Now who do you suppose that someone is? The chairman of the board? The president? A vice-president? Very doubtful, because top managers often are so busy controlling their giant companies that they don't have much time to be creative. Workers at the lower levels of corporations, the people who deal directly with the machinery and products, often have excellent suggestions to make if given the chance.

These types of upward communication seldom happen naturally; management must give them a pull. Workers generally withhold their ideas from management if they believe that others will steal the credit. An effective **suggestion system** enables employees to communicate their thoughts directly to top management without having to push the messages through several layers of managers.

If a suggestion system is to be successful, however, top management must respond promptly to all suggestions—explaining why certain suggestions cannot be used and rewarding employees for those ideas that will benefit the company.

Monetary rewards are not uncommon for ideas that result in huge savings, but the publication of a useful idea also can be rewarding to its creator. Most people are motivated by a pat on the back, especially when witnessed by their peers.

Eastman Kodak official presenting George Whetan with a $50,000 (yes, $50,000) award for suggesting that cameras be packed with batteries just prior to shipment. (Photo courtesy Eastman Kodak Company)

Attitude surveys. But what about morale? How do employees feel about procedures? Their work environment? The company in general? Most managers are surprised to learn that their employees know more about them than they know about their employees. Most of us spend quite a lot of time studying the characteristics and thought patterns of our superiors. We want to please them or, at the least, avoid offending them. Managers, on the other hand, rarely expend the time or effort necessary to gain insight into the personalities of subordinates. Even when managers try to understand their employees, the superior-subordinate relationship often prohibits the intimate discussion that would be required for meaningful insight.

As a way of adjusting this imbalance, many companies encourage **attitude surveys.** If a manager volunteers to have such a survey conducted, representatives of the personnel department administer a questionnaire. They assure the employees being questioned that they will not be identified with their responses, so that they may be completely honest without fear of reprisal by the boss. The questionnaire is designed to elicit candid answers to questions concerning attitudes toward fellow employees, work, place of work, and a wide range of company policies. Representatives of the personnel department tabulate the information and discuss the results with the manager and other interested officials, with the objective of overcoming any deficiencies in the supervisor's method of operation or company policy.

Exit interviews. Key people in the personnel department solicit similar information from employees leaving the company. They conduct **exit interviews** at the time of departure to hear the employee's side of the story. Management may learn from such interviews that an inordinate number of people are transferring to other companies to earn higher pay, or that several people have experienced difficulty with a particular manager.

Experience has shown, however, that during exit interviews people often withhold the true reasons for their departure for fear of jeopardizing their chances of receiving favorable references for their next jobs. In an attempt to accumulate more accurate information, therefore, many companies mail **questionnaires** to employees two or three months after they have left the company. People who have had time to recover from the trauma of leaving a job, and especially those who are securely settled in new positions, are willing, even eager, to lay it on the line—to state exactly their reasons for leaving and their true thoughts about the company.

Can't we talk it over?

TWO-WAY COMMUNICATIONS

Thus far, we have concentrated on **one-way communications,** those situations where any feedback that may be received is a delayed communication. To learn the response of others to our letters, for example, we must wait several days for replies. When we use **two-way communications,** the response is instantaneous.

Telephone. The telephone is usually more effective than written communications, because it is a form of two-way communication. The caller receives an immediate response from the person on the other end of the line, and the exchange that follows might require several letters and many weeks of waiting for replies. Unlike written communications, however, telephone calls often interrupt the person being called, and once the conversation has ended there is no record of what was said.

But some people claim that telephone calls, even long-distance calls, are less expensive than letters. Such assertions are no doubt true, if we are speaking of three-minute calls. When a company is paying the phone bill, however, employees often talk on and on with little regard for cost.

Millions of work hours each day are devoted to telephone conversations—so much so that some companies now have "thinking rooms" where employees can momentarily escape the continual ring of telephones and other disturbances. Telephone conversations may be initiated in any direction: Bosses may phone their employees; employees may phone their bosses. Rank-and-file employees use telephones many times each day to confer with one another, and high-level managers feel free to call any employee at almost any time. Businesses may still run on the mails, as the old saying goes, but they would certainly be hard pressed to operate without the use of telephones.

Business meetings. Videophones will be in general use in the foreseeable future, providing us with two-way, face-to-face communications with the push of a few buttons. We can now realize this most effective form of communication only when we are actually in the presence of others. Businesses often benefit from face-to-face communication through business meetings. When those in authority assign several people to work together on a project, we say that a **committee** has been formed; and businesses have many types of committees in effect most of the time. When these people gather to discuss issues, we say that they are conducting **committee meetings**. Although meetings are often time consuming, they do provide effective communication. Participants may ask questions and offer answers until major points have been clarified, and each person may assess both the verbal and nonverbal behavior of all other participants.

Employee counseling. As an effective two-way exchange of ideas and opinions, many organizations encourage periodic consultation between all employees and their immediate superiors. For example, the credit manager might call departmental employees into her office individually to discuss their progress on certain projects that she has assigned or their work in general. The employees respond to questions asked them and often seek answers to questions of their own. These sessions are generally confined to work-related subjects, however, with separate sessions being held for wage-and-salary counseling.

Social events. Many companies provide regularly scheduled social events: company night at the ball park, a golf tournament, the Christmas party. Why do they go to all the trouble? Why do they endure the expense? Management's desire to maintain high employee morale is a main objective, certainly. But these activities also elicit a lot of valuable downward and upward communication between employees at all levels of management. When people are socializing, they tend to be more talkative. Lower-level employees talk with company officials they would normally hesitate to approach, and officials converse with employees they would not otherwise encounter. So long as such events are well planned and controlled, they provide a healthful, communicative outlet for all participants.

Managerial visibility. Employer-employee communications should be regular, however, not just at social functions and not only when a crisis is at hand. In an attempt at establishing open lines of communication, some company executives publicize an **open-door policy,** assuring employees that their doors are always open to them. But imagine the courage it takes for a filing clerk to enter the president's office! It is almost impossible for a lower-level employee to go upstairs and walk by several departments and secretaries en route to the president's office without being conspicuous, and the employee's immediate superior soon will learn of the occasion and wonder why the employee bypassed his own supervisor by going directly to the president.

Other questions arise in the minds of employees about an open-door policy. Will the president be busy? Will he be receptive, or will he think that what I have to say is ridiculous? How will I express my thoughts? How will my fellow employees react if they learn that I went to see the "big boss"?

A more effective approach to managerial visibility, therefore, is for the president and other high officials to walk out their office doors and mingle with employees. Employees may be ridiculed by others for seeking out company officials, but no one can criticize them for relating to officials who have stopped by their workplaces to talk.

Tell them yourself, Rachel

HORIZONTAL AND DIAGONAL COMMUNICATIONS

Not all business communications travel between managers and their subordinates. As a way of speeding communications, employees often bypass their bosses and go directly to the source of information. If you were working as a shipping clerk in a large corporation, for example, you might go directly to the credit department for a credit approval rather than bothering your boss with the transaction. Communications between employees who are on the same level as each other, but who work in different functional areas of the company, are called horizontal communications.

If you went instead to the credit manager, who holds a higher position than you do, we refer to the exchange as diagonal communication. Most managers encourage horizontal and diagonal communications, knowing that communications are generally much less efficient when management insists that all communications "go through regular channels."

Rumors are flying.

INFORMAL COMMUNICATIONS

Memos, reports, company publications, video programs, and meetings are examples of formal communications. Informal messages, on the other hand, are communicated on the company **grapevine**. The grapevine is often more effective than management's formal communications because almost every employee participates in one or more grapevines. Dave in data processing learned from an executive secretary during coffee break that all office employees are to receive an extra day off during the Christmas holiday. Dave passed the information to members of his grapevine, which included three other people in data processing and Thelma in the traffic department. Thelma communicated the good news to members of her grapevine, which included four people in her own department and two guys at the warehouse. And each of these employees passed the information to others.

Practically everyone in the company offices learned of the extra day off before an official bulletin could be posted on the cafeteria bulletin board. Although the grapevine mainly operates on rumors, studies indicate that rumors usually turn out to be accurate.

Hello, out there!

EXTERNAL COMMUNICATIONS

So far, we have talked only of communications that take place inside business organizations. But let's not overlook that big world outside the company. As shown in Figure 1-2, businesses communicate with a variety of groups.

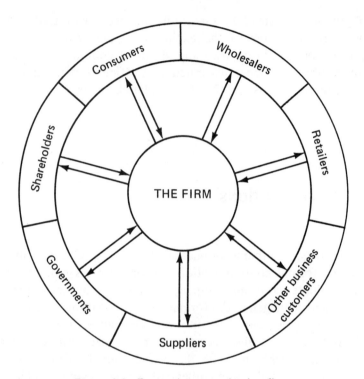

Figure 1-2 External communication flows

Some businesses sell directly to retailers and wholesalers. They communicate with you and me, the final consumers of products and services; they report to their shareholders; they deal with suppliers; and, of course, a large volume of correspondence is exchanged each year between businesses and government.

One-way communications. If you were working in a business and wanted to send a routine message to just one person (an employee in another business, perhaps, or a consumer), you would write a **letter;** or you could send a **telegram.** To communicate with whole groups of people, such as stockholders and potential investors, businesses undertake mass mailings of **quarterly** and **annual reports.** These reports generally include statements by the chief executive officer concerning important aspects of the business: new products and programs, levels of profitability, long-term trends and projections.

When any business activity might be of general interest to the public, public relations employees submit **news releases** to the news media. News releases permit businesses to keep the names of their companies before the public when favorable news is concerned and to counter publicity that would be detrimental to the company.

Businesses utilize the broadcast media (television and radio), print media (newspapers and magazines), and other types of advertising to communicate with their customers. In doing so, they often employ the services of advertising agents who are skilled in these highly specialized types of communication.

Two-way communications. The telephone is the most widely used medium for communicating with people outside the firm. You may save money and establish a record of your conversation, however, by using Telex or TWX, two teletypewriter services offered by Western Union that are discussed in Chapter 11. Businesses may also benefit from face-to-face communications. Salespeople are generally the source of valuable product and customer information because of their daily contacts with purchasing managers. And the managers of most companies arrange direct encounters with their owners at **annual stockholder meetings.** Some annual meetings are dull, admittedly, but the give-and-take atmosphere at many meetings can be electrifying and productive.

There you have it, a profile of communication methods in modern businesses. Before moving on to, Chapter 2, however, you should test your comprehension of the preceding materials by answering the following questions. In being thorough as you progress through the book, you will become a competent communicator by the time you reach the last page.

DISCUSSION AND REVIEW QUESTIONS

1. List the various means of downward and upward communication in business.

2. How do interoffice memos differ from letters?

3. Why is the location of bulletin boards an important consideration?

4. How can a bulletin board that has little or nothing posted on it most of the time be of any value?

5. What suggestions could you offer your company for improving company publications?

6. Why do some companies undertake the expense of producing television programs for employees?

7. Which type of communication flow is more difficult to achieve and control, upward or downward? Why?

8. What is exception reporting?

9. Should a company bother with a grievance system when there is no union to force them to do so? Why?

10. In what ways can employees be motivated to submit to management any good ideas they may have?

11. How may top management determine the true feelings that employees have about the company?

12. What are the possible shortcomings of exit interviews, and how may these be overcome?

13. What methods of business communication are two-way communications?

14. If an accountant told you that the cost to the company for your writing a letter would be $4.50, would you make a phone call rather than write?

15. Do social events provide favorable environments for employer-employee communications? Explain.

16. What is managerial visibility? How is it accomplished?

17. After reading this chapter, how would you react to the following statement by a company president: "All employees, from the lowest to the highest level of the company, are invited to drop into my office at any time to chat a while."

18. Provide examples of horizontal and vertical communications. From management's point of view, are these types of communication desirable?

19. Are you part of a school or company grapevine? Explain.

20. List the outside groups with which most businesses communicate.

21. How would you communicate the following messages?
    a. You seem to be the only person who is aware of a raging fire that endangers a crowded office building.
    b. The company has just been awarded a lucrative government contract, and you are charged with informing all employees of the good news.
    c. James Walters, who was District Sales Manager, has been appointed General Sales Manager. Notify all office employees and the outside community.
    d. Company offices were closed for Veteran's Day on October 24 last year but are to be closed on November 11 this year—the original date of the holiday. Notify all office personnel.

2

BARRIERS TO EFFECTIVE COMMUNICATION

Having learned in Chapter 1 of the several methods of communicating within and outside a company, you are probably eager to start doing just that—communicating. Before we get into the specifics of speaking and writing, however, let's consider some common barriers to communication. Becoming aware of communication flows and methods is necessary, but an awareness of the influences that may distort our communicative efforts is equally important. Once we have identified these potential barriers to effective communication, we will be better prepared to cope with the behavior of others and to correct any of our own deficiencies.

But isn't that what I said?

LANGUAGE DIFFICULTIES

We Americans are fortunate to be using the most widely spoken language in the world: English. As with any other language, however, English is distorted by regional and ethnic variations within our culture. Many English words have several meanings, and we have added a wide variety of slang terms to our everyday communications. When we interact with people in other countries, our language difficulties become even more pronounced.

Ignorance of rules. Many people, including some business leaders, pervert the English language. They mispronounce and misspell words. They use plural verbs with singular subjects, and they sometimes interject a double negative or two. What makes their situation even more hopeless is that they often do not recognize that their communications are substandard.

Although we might expect people entering business today to be more literate than earlier arrivals because more of them have attended college, this is not always the case. Many older people have only had high school educations, it is true, but elementary and high schools used to place much more emphasis on grammar, reading, and writing than most schools or teachers have recently. Consequently, many business leaders complain that their new employees cannot write coherent paragraphs—not to mention letters, bulletins, or reports. They are looking to colleges and universities for a reversal of this undesirable trend, and educators are responding with renewed emphasis on language skills.

Deliberate confusion. Some people seem to spend a lot of time and effort trying to confuse, impress, or intimidate others. As an example of what has been called "federalese," consider the following statement by a top government economist:

> Thus once the inflation genie has been let out of the bottle it is a very tricky policy problem to find the particular calibration and timing that would be appropriate to stem the acceleration in risk premiums created by falling incomes without prematurely aborting the decline in the inflation-generated risk premiums. This is clearly not an easy policy path to traverse but it is the path which we must follow.

You may have trouble with this statement even if you are an economics major. What is says is this: It is difficult to reduce unemployment without increasing the rate of inflation. So why didn't he say so?

Administrative officials are not the only offenders in this respect. To illustrate what has been called "legelese," the following lines are verbatim from a routine legal notice:

> YOU ARE COMMANDED that all and singular business and excuses being laid aside, you appear and attend in person, for the purpose of having your deposition taken, at the offices of Biaette & Bahde, 1400 Luhrs Tower, 45 West Jefferson, Phoenix, Arizona, on the 28th day of September, 1978, at 2:00 p.m., then and there to testify, and to have your deposition taken upon oral interrogatories, in the above-entitled matter now pending in said Superior Court, on the part of the plaintiffs.

Why didn't they shorten this long sentence by just telling the person to come to the address shown and make a statement about what he or she witnessed?

Unfortunately, the business community is not immune to this noncommunicative style of writing. The following statement, which appeared in the annual report of a large corporation, provides an example of what we might call "commercialese."

> Furnishing each requesting shareholder with a list of the individual recipients of charitable contributions and the amount donated to each, as the resolution provides, would inevitably result in the general availability of the list and consequently impose an enormous administrative burden on the Corporation's management to defend specific contributions criticized for purely partisan reasons and to respond to solicitations from competing institutions and shareholders advocating or requesting donations to be made to them or their favorite charities, as the case may be, in addition to or instead of the recipients included in the list.

Try reading that sentence without coming up for air at least twice. Better still, try comprehending the intended message without reading the sentence several times.

Can't we write such documents as court orders, insurance contracts, sales agreements, and loan agreements in language that the average person can understand? The answer to this question is an emphatic "yes"; legal and quasilegal documents can and are being written in everyday language. Several leading companies are rewriting their legal forms voluntarily, and the State of New York recently passed a law requiring that businesses write consumer contracts in nontechnical language. Additionally, the President of the United States has directed all administrative agencies to write future regulations in what he termed "plain English for a change."

Semantics. Semantics is the study of the meaning of words. Although our dictionaries provide us with the popular meanings of tens of thousands of words, we tend to attach different shades of meanings to many of the same words. Words are symbols for people, places, animals, and things. The word *dog* is not actually a dog, of course; it is a collection of three letters that enable us to refer to our four-legged friends without actually having to point at one. But if someone mentions the word *dog,* you might imagine a German shepherd and I might think of a cocker spaniel. Similarly, if someone mentions the word *liberal,* you might picture a politician and my mind might focus on an acquaintance's spending habits.

To illustrate further, suppose that the owner of a business announces that she expects a noticeable increase in efficiency this coming month. Is she alluding to the fact that some employees have been arriving late the last few mornings? Is she concerned with the length of their coffee breaks? Is she implying that the employees have been careless with their work? Does she want them to reduce costs? Or is she talking about increasing profits? Only the owner herself knows for sure.

Words such as *efficiency, achievement, courteous, morale,* and *loyalty* are abstract words; they have different meaning for different people. Recognizing the potential problems of semantics, we can strive to overcome such barriers to communication by being more explicit. Rather than telling someone that we expect more efficiency and letting it go at that, we should be specific in our directions by stating whether we are speaking of punctuality, neatness, costs, or profits; and we may even ask the other person to explain his or her understanding of our directions so that we may be certain that we have communicated the intended message.

Cultural differences. Our language difficulties are generally compounded when we transact business with foreigners. Even when they speak English or we speak their language, we may misunderstand one another. Foreigners are often astonished at our "Let's get at it" approach to business, preferring to spend about half the time leading up to the main point of discussion. If an American says, "That's one hell of a deal," a foreigner would probably not realize that the American is speaking well of the transaction. Conversely, if a Japanese businessman responds to an American's offer of a business transaction with the comment, "Oh, that would be *very* difficult," the American probably would continue to negotiate, not realizing that this is the Japanese way of offering a polite but definite no.

The Chinese respond to a compliment by denying that they deserve it, and they expect us to be just as humble. Similarly, the French would be appalled if we were to respond to a compliment with the usual "thank you," and they would be offended if called by their first names. We must also consider cultural barriers to communication when sending flowers to foreigners or presenting them with gifts. The situation becomes so sensitive, in fact, that many companies have their employees schooled in foreign etiquette before sending them abroad.

So I sometimes exaggerate a little.

EXCESSIVE SUBJECTIVITY

We sometimes accuse others of being evasive; they ramble on and on without providing us with any concrete information. People tend to fall into this pattern of noncommunication for one or more of the following reasons.

Insufficient information. As with most segments of society, the business world has its share of bluffers. When managers or their employees fail to acquaint themselves with essential information, they often try to hide their shortcomings by talking around the subject. This type of evasive behavior, which soon becomes obvious to others, can be overcome only through diligent preparation.

Personal biases. We all have our personal biases, of course—educational, political, religious, and social. Once having recognized these biases, we should avoid making broad statements that we cannot support with facts. We should not criticize all union leaders, for example, just because we read that one large union has been infiltrated by mobsters. Neither should we castigate all corporate leaders just because a relatively few have been found guilty of criminal acts. In short, we should not stereotype any segment of our society unless the behavior of some members is truly representative of an entire segment.

Glowing generalities. Business people, especially, should avoid broad generalities. Company managers should not respond with meaningless statements to inquiries from concerned employees. Rather than telling employees that an impending crisis has been averted, for example, management should be specific. Tell them how the problem was contained. Tell them exactly what is being done to prevent a recurrence. The same statement applies to management's communications with people outside the company. As greater numbers of Americans acquire higher education and an increasing ability to recognize evasiveness, they expect more direct and more honest responses to their questions.

Credibility gap. When the employees of a business do not believe the managers, a credibility gap exists. We begin doubting the credibility of others when they do not appear knowledgeable in their subject area, when they try to infect others with their personal biases, and when they speak in generalities rather than facts. Credibility gaps often exist between businesses and their outside contacts as well: customers, suppliers, and government. When management's credibility is questioned by any of these factions, all future efforts to communicate are impaired.

But what I have to say is important—this time.

OVERCOMMUNICATION

Let's interrupt all this talk about ways of communicating and consider the possibility that we might be *over*communicating. Do you ever monopolize conversations? Do you sometimes say things you wish later you had kept to yourself? Do you write memos and reports that few people bother to read?

Talking incessantly. One of the students in a night class the author taught a few years ago couldn't stop talking. He asked questions. He offered comments. He challenged. He rebutted. He was offensive to the point that the class applauded his absence from class. Even when the author managed to minimize the student's talking, his presence and the author's efforts to contain him made it difficult for students to concentrate on the intended subject.

Listening to this student before, during, and after each class, the author learned that he had talked himself into and out of one job after the other. He was basically intelligent, but he would not take even a direct request to stop talking so much. As a consequence, people not only stopped listening to what he had to say, they even tired of his presence.

Foot-in-the-mouth syndrome. Marie Antoinette presented history with a classic example of foot-in-the-mouth syndrome. In response to appeals for bread from a group of starving peasants, she is reported to have said, "Let them eat cake." News of the comment further angered the mob, and Marie was guillotined during the revolution that followed.

Although business managers aren't in danger of losing their heads, their off-the-cuff remarks sometimes get them into trouble. When the president of a large airline company publicly referred to the company's pilots as "overpaid flight jockeys," the company lost many dollars in the work slowdown and wage demands that followed. Similar remarks, though sometimes made in jest, have been known to alienate customers and members of the general public. Even the failure of several presidential campaigns have been blamed on inappropriate comments by candidates. When we try to be amusing, therefore, we should select our words carefully.

Memo mania. So you like the idea of being promoted and earning more money than you are now receiving. But how, you ask yourself, can you cause management to notice you among all those other people? Maybe just doing a good job would do the trick, but that approach could take years.

Some employees try to spread their names around a company by writing one memo after another. They look for even the slightest excuse to write memos—sending copies to as many key people as possible. Memos represent an excellent means of internal communications, as we saw in Chapter 1, but you should use them only when you have something to say that cannot be communicated in person or on the telephone. If your memos lack substance, others will soon catch on and tune you out.

Reports, reports, reports. Businesses have long relied on many types of reports, as indicated earlier, but the number of reports issued in some companies has recently multiplied faster than a pen of healthy rabbits. With computers that can manipulate figures at lightning speed and print reports faster than 1,000 lines per minute, business's capacity to prepare reports often exceeds the ability of managers to absorb them.

Is it possible that some managers fail to read reports that have been sent to them? A middle manager at a Midwest manufacturing firm decided to determine the number of people who were actually reading a monthly report he prepared. He placed the picture of a well-known manager on one page of the report and offered a prize to anyone who identified the manager. From the responses that followed, he learned that only 12 percent of the recipients were reading the report, and of those who were reading it several were not authorized to do so.

Why, then, don't the managers who are not reading a report direct the sender to remove their names from the mailing list? One answer is that they just don't get around to reading all the reports that they receive, no matter how good their intentions. Another is that certain reports become status symbols to some managers; these people are broadcasting to anyone who may notice that they are important enough to receive such reports, whether they read them or not.

They won't be able to blame this one on me.

DEFENSIVE COMMUNICATION

We sometimes must overcommunicate as a way of penetrating the psychological barriers that people erect against the excess verbiage to which they have become accustomed. We also rely on the written word to protect us against official sanctions and criticism.

Selective perception. Humans are limited in their ability to receive messages. When two or three people begin talking to us at the same time, for example, we usually throw up our hands in despair and ask them to lay it on us one at a time.

We can't tell advertisers to approach us one at a time, unfortunately, so we are bombarded daily by thousands of newspaper and magazine ads, radio and television commercials, and many types of outdoor advertisements. We are confronted at work with a barrage of phone calls, letters, telegrams, memos, and reports; and our friends and relatives are not without comment. To avoid being overwhelmed with the sheer volume of communications directed at us each day, we become selective in what we receive. We briefly analyze the type of messages sent and accept only a select few for serious consideration. We give attention only to certain ads, and we read only those documents that are important to our personal lives or our work.

In attempting to communicate with others, therefore, we should realize that we are competing for attention. If we are to penetrate the protective barriers that people erect for themselves, we must make certain that our communications seem relevant to their interests.

Emotional reaction. Some managers and supervisors rant and rave when things go wrong. In doing so, they generally complicate things for themselves and for others. Imagine a supervisor storming into an office and shouting, "What idiot caused the king-sized foul-up this time?" Since only an idiot would respond to such a question, the supervisor must begin a long series of unproductive and unpleasant interrogations.

We all have self-images, liking to think of ourselves as conscientious and capable employees; and we generally react defensively when anyone threatens this self-image. This defensive mechanism is so strong, in fact, that the person challenged often fails to listen closely to what the other person is saying.

Imagine the apprehension that could have been avoided and the time that could have been saved if the supervisor had approached the problem calmly. He would have communicated much more effectively if he had assumed an understanding and helpful attitude. Although it is true that the supervisor might have frightened employees to the point that they would be careful to avoid such mistakes, frightened employees seldom possess the self-confidence essential to top performance.

Self-protection. To protect themselves from false accusations, business people tend to overcommunicate. They write memos to confirm their conversations with employees and customers. They send copies of their communications to people who can serve as witnesses if their actions should later be questioned. They establish a written record of almost everything they do. By all means, business people should record conversations and actions that are of great importance, but when they record almost every transaction, their defensiveness becomes a formidable barrier to effective communication.

So what can be done? Management may alleviate this problem by creating a work environment that is less threatening to the participants. When employees realize that the sky isn't going to fall in every time something goes wrong, they will probably worry less and work more.

Defensive language. Business people may look to government for some classic examples of defensive language. Rather than suffering the criticism for taking frequent recesses, Congressional representatives now refer to this free time as "nonlegislative periods." To avoid criticism from reformers and foreign governments over the plight of poor families in the United States, the Agriculture Department now refers to poor people as "limited-resource families."

Defensive language also includes efforts to talk around the problem, as a university president illustrated with the following statement:

> We will divert the force of this fiscal stress into leverage energy and pry important budgetary considerations and control out of our fiscal and administrative procedures.

This statement, which appeared in a recent issue of *Time* magazine, suggests that university administrators spent more money than they had, but they will try to do better in the future. Businesses do not have to search for such devious means of self-defense. Why? Haven't you noticed that businesses seem able to blame most problems on computer breakdowns or malfunctions?

Conditioned mistrust. Business managers sometimes fret over declines in employee loyalty, and they brood over reports of public mistrust of business. Are we, the American people, unduly skeptical of business leaders, or have these leaders fostered our mistrust? Is the continual conflict between management and labor, and between management and government, an inherent part of our free enterprise system, or have the business leaders themselves created these confrontations?

No one can answer these questions with certainty. What we do know, however, is that trust is usually the result of consistently fair treatment among the parties concerned. When we learn from the news media that businesses have violated our laws, however, we tend to question the behavior of all business people. We also know that trust is usually a mutual relationship; when we demonstrate our trust of others, they are more likely to trust us.

So how can business managers establish a feeling of mutual trust among employees, consumers, and the general public? The first step they must take, and certainly the most difficult one, is to behave in a responsible manner—realizing that laws have been established over the years not only to regulate businesses, but also to protect them. Second, management may establish a mutual trust between themselves and their employees by removing symbols of distrust such as dress codes, secret salaries, and time clocks. Once the barrier of distrust is removed, a free flow of communication becomes possible.

I'm not going to listen, because I might learn something.

POOR LISTENING HABITS

We may blame many of our communication problems on language difficulties and defensiveness, but often we fail to communicate simply because we don't listen properly.

Feelings toward speaker. We sometimes seem unwilling to listen to what another person has to say because we don't approve of the person. We reason that the person is "just another macho male" or "only a woman," too young or too old, too liberal or too conservative. By rejecting the person, we "tune out" the message.

Preconceived notions. We have all been frustrated at one time or another when encountering people who are rigid in their thinking, people who espouse an attitude of "My mind is made up, so don't bother me with facts." Such thinking is manifested in such comments as "Everyone knows that the earth is flat"; "This is my country, right or wrong"; and "I wouldn't vote for anybody but a Democrat." We all have opinions, of course, but when we become so opinionated that we refuse to listen to others, we will never know how our thoughts compare with their views.

Rebuttal formation. If we listen attentively to what the other person is saying, we may gain a new perspective. We sometimes become so involved in the subject under discussion, however, that we fail to respond effectively. We spend too little time listening and too much time planning our next verbal assault. The added hazard of this type of one-sided conversation is that our rebuttals often do not account for key points already made by the other person.

Daydreaming. Since we can listen to what people say at a much faster rate than they can say it, we are sometimes tempted to daydream. While others pour out their hearts to us, our minds skip from one subject to the other, pausing briefly from time to time to utter an "Oh?" or an "Uh, huh" designed to fool the other person into thinking that we are still tuned in. Not only is this type of nonlistening unproductive from an informational point of view, our reluctance to engage in meaningful conversation eventually becomes apparent to others.

What are we playing here, hide-and-seek?

NONVERBAL FENCES

All the barriers to communication we have discussed thus far have involved speaking and writing. Before ending this chapter, let's consider some nonverbal deterrents to effective communication.

Power positions. Have you ever noticed how employees who have been communicating freely with one another tend to tighten up when their boss arrives on the scene? The conversation becomes even more strained when a top official of the company drops by. Employees stop talking among themselves to focus on the official, and an artificial exchange takes place between the official and one or two outspoken employees.

Why do business leaders hold themselves apart from their employees this way? How many times have we heard people say that, if and when they are ever promoted to a management position, *they* will continue to think of themselves as one of the gang? When they strive to maintain old relationships, however, the newly appointed managers find that their subordinates (their former associates) will not let them remain "one of the gang." Moreover, these nonverbal fences exist not only between employees and their supervisors but also between all layers of management: between supervisors and middle managers, and between middle managers and top management.

Symbolic distance. Although the office manager's desk may be no farther than 15 feet from the people being supervised, the symbolic distance is much greater. Unlike Japanese businesses, where managers are typically placed among the workers they supervise, managers in U.S. companies are generally located behind barriers: a wall, a partition, even on separate floors of the building.

We like to think that these "fences" help us establish different levels of authority by indicating which employees are in pivotal positions and which are not. If we were to walk into a strange company, for example, we could probably determine who is important and who isn't by the presence or absence of partitions, private offices, carpeting, windows, separate dining rooms, special rest rooms, and dozens of other status symbols. Now who is on the right track here, the Japanese or the Americans? Do these "fences" serve a useful purpose? Do they interfere with flows of communications? Or both?

Physical distractions. Close your eyes and listen to the surrounding noise. Can you hear the blowing of an air-conditioning unit? The hum of fluorescent lights? The roar of passing traffic? The chattering of voices? The flipping of pages? The noise level in businesses is often more pronounced, with the added clacking of typewriters and the ringing of telephones. Beautiful females and handsome males offer a more pleasant type of distraction, and every office seems to have its own special clown, each of which represents a potential barrier to effective communications.

Yes, it's true! This chapter has presented you with a lot of problems and very few answers. But if you will take another look at the contents at the front of the book, you will see that the chapters to come deal with these sensitive areas of business communication.

DISCUSSION AND REVIEW QUESTIONS

1. What possible reason could any government employee have for using "federalese"?

2. What is your reaction to statements by lawyers that legal documents must be written in legal terminology if those documents are to "stand up in court"?

3. Do business people tend to skirt issues by talking around a subject? If you believe they do, can you provide any concrete examples?

4. What action has the State of New York taken to simplify legal documents?

5. Define the term *semantics,* and provide one or two examples of related problems in our everyday communications.

6. Why do we sometimes experience difficulty communicating with foreigners, even though they converse with us in English?

7. What can we do to overcome the communication problems that result from cultural differences?

8. If someone should accuse you of being too subjective, what does that person mean?

9. What is wrong with making our biases known to others; aren't we part of the "let it all hang out" generation?

10. How will the use of broad generalities lessen the effectiveness of our communications?

11. If a credibility gap exists between business managers and their employees, what can be done to resolve the problem?

12. What are some examples of overcommunication?

13. What may be the adverse effects of writing memos that are not actually required?

14. Why do some managers insist on receiving certain reports when they do not even read them?

15. Why do we sometimes find it necessary to overcommunicate?

16. Define the term *selective perception,* and provide an example from your personal life.

17. What does our self-image have to do with defensive communication?

18. What is defensive language? Can you provide some personal examples?

19. What barriers to effective listening were cited in this chapter? Can you think of any others?

20. Comment on the following statements:
    a. Sure, I'm being promoted to department manager, but you will find that success won't change old Jimbo.
    b. I recommend that we extend the office wall clear to the ceiling so that employees won't be able to overhear conversations between the manager and individual employees.
    c. How can anyone even suggest that your attractive new employee in the accounting department could be a communication barrier? Hell, he's the center of conversation.
    d. I talk my head off all day long, but no one seems to listen.
    e. Let's place the plant superintendent's office down on the factory floor right alongside the supervisors' offices.

PART TWO
MECHANICS, GRAMMAR, AND DIRECTION

Rather than hiding this section near the back, the customary practice in this sort of book, here it is right up front. Why? Because the author is convinced that people must learn the rules of writing before they can write.

But can't students just write naturally? The answer to this question is, "No, they cannot!" They must follow certain rules and guidelines if their business communications are to be acceptable, and these rules are constantly changing. The following statement by a key employee of a big corporation helps to illustrate this point:

The improper use of grammar, including punctuation and spelling, is one of the biggest headaches in today's business world. We have entry-level employees who have completed secondary school education, and some who have even completed work for an associate degree at a college or university, who have no idea how to put a sentence together.

It is highly important that prospective employees learn these skills before they apply for a job. Businesses today have neither the time nor the money to devote to training employees in remedial English. BFGoodrich has several training programs in business communications for its employees through the Company's Institute for Personnel Development.

It is my opinion, however, that every piece of communication that originates in any of the Company's many departments should be reviewed by each department manager before it is sent to the recipient. A department manager has overall responsibility for every communication initiated in his department. Every word, every comma, and the structure of a sentence as a whole are highly important in communicating proper information, especially if some action is being requested.

W. T. Duke
Director of Community Relations
The BFGoodrich Company

So if the rules are always changing, isn't it a waste of time for students to learn them before beginning work? No, it isn't. The rules change, but they don't change that quickly. If you master the materials in this section of the book, you can become aware of future changes as they occur through your regular reading of newspapers and magazines; and your reading of recent editions of books like this one every five years or so will also help you remain current.

Which words should be abbreviated, and which should be capitalized? Should you use the word or the figure when writing numbers? Where do you need commas, semicolons, and colons? What about quotation marks, apostrophes, and dashes? Which words are "in," and which ones should you avoid? What about the length of sentences and paragraphs? The following four chapters provide you with definitive answers to these types of questions, and Chapter 7 puts the icing on the cake by introducing some general tips for communicating successfully.

3

MASTERING A FEW MECHANICS

This chapter contains lots of detail, but the fact that you already know some of the rules will make the materials relatively easy for you to handle. You only need to master those elements with which you are unfamiliar.

Don't be so lazy, Chas.

ABBREVIATIONS: USE THEM SPARINGLY!

The human animal generally seeks the path of least resistance. Students often display this trait by abbreviating many words that should be written in their complete form. You may use the following abbreviations when you are confident that the reader will understand them:

Business terms (some with periods and some without)

CEO (chief executive officer)

C.O.D. (collect on delivery)

COBOL (Common Business-Oriented Language)

e.o.m. (end of month)

F.O.B. (free on board)

FORTRAN (FORmula TRANslation)

GNP (Gross National Product)

memo (memorandum)

No. (number, when followed by figure)

Inc. (incorporated)

Government agencies (do *not* follow the letters with periods)

AEC (Atomic Energy Commission)

CAB (Civil Aeronautics Board)

DOT (Department of Transportation)

EEOC (Equal Employment Opportunity Commission)

FAA (Federal Aviation Agency)

FCC (Federal Communication Commission)

FDIC (Federal Deposit Insurance Corporation)

FHA (Federal Housing Administration)

FPC (Federal Power Commission)

FRB (Federal Reserve Board)

FTC (Federal Trade Commission)

ICC (Interstate Commerce Commission)

OSHA (Occupational Safety and Health Administration)

SEC (Securities and Exchange Commission)

Names of states (in mailing addresses only)

Examples: IN (Indiana), SC (South Carolina), and CA (California). See page 146 for a complete listing.

Time expressions (you may use either small or capital letters)

Examples: 9:30 a.m. (9:30 A.M.), 2:45 p.m. (2:45 P.M.)

Do not use a.m. (A.M.) or p.m. (P.M.) unless preceded by figures.

(no)   I'll see you in the A.M.

(yes)   I'll see you tomorrow morning.

(yes)   I'll see you at 8:30 a.m.

Titles with names

Dr. Mary Beth Hughes (only one space following the period)

Mr. Ronald P. Schneider (only one space following each period)

Harry M. Pfitzer, D.B.A. (Doctor of Business Administration)

Ms. Diane Washington (regardless of marital status)

Sen. Hartwell (abbreviated when using last name only)

Company names

Solomon Bros., Inc. (when abbreviated in the company's letterhead)

Metric prefixes and units (no periods required)

k (kilo), h (hecto), da (deka), d (deci), c (centi), m (milli), m (meter), g (gram), l (liter), C (Celsius)

Although many abbreviations are used with business forms, you should *not* abbreviate the following words in letters, memos, or reports:

Days, months, and holidays

(no)   Employees will return from the Xmas holiday on Mon., Dec. 30.
(yes)   Employees will return from the Christmas holiday on Monday, December 30.

Geographic areas

(no)   L.A. is located on the W. Coast.
(yes)   Los Angeles is located on the West Coast.

Person's name

(no)   Let Geo. do it.
(yes)   Let George do it.

School subjects

(no)   I took college classes in acctg. and econ.
(yes)   I took college classes in accounting and economics.

Words in addresses

(no)   The shipping address is 1612 W. 27th Ave.
(yes)   The shipping address is 1612 West 27th Avenue.

Now try to determine what, if anything, is incorrect about the sentences in the following self-check.

SELF-CHECK: ABBREVIATIONS

Slide a piece of paper downward as you read, exposing the correct sentences and explanations only after you have studied the test sentences.

1   Congress recently raised the interest rates on F.H.A. loans.

Congress recently raised the interest rates on FHA loans.

Do not place periods after each letter in the abbreviation.

2   You are to begin work on Mon. at 8:30 AM.

You are to begin work on Monday at 8:30 A.M. (or a.m.)

Do not abbreviate days of the week.
Must place periods following *A* and *M*.
Notice that the period following *M* also ends the sentence.

3   Turn west when you reach 24th St.

Turn west when you reach 24th Street.

Do not abbreviate *street*.

4   We will hold the conference in San Jose, Calif. the week after Xmas.

We will hold the conference in San Jose, California, the week after Christmas.

Do not abbreviate *California* or *Christmas*.

5   Robt. Snyder sent a COD shipment to 2318 N. 22nd Ave.

Robert Snyder sent a C.O.D. shipment to 2318 North 22nd Avenue.

Do not abbreviate *Robert, North,* or *Avenue*.
Place periods after each letter in *C.O.D.*

CAPITALIZATION: YOU MUST HAVE A REASON!

People who are uncertain of which words to capitalize sometimes overcapitalize, beginning every important word with a capital letter. To write correctly, and to make our communications attractive, we must follow these rules:

Days, months, and holidays (first letter of each word)

Example: Independence Day falls on the first Tuesday in July.

Historical events (first letter of each word)

Example: We have had continual inflation ever since World War II.
Example: Nearly half the labor force was idled during the Great Depression of the 1930s.

Important documents (first letter of each significant word)*

Example: The Bill of Rights is an important part of the Constitution.

Directions (only when referring to specific regions)

Example: Many companies are moving from the Midwest to the South.
Example: The company is located at 1203 West 16th Street.

Otherwise, directions (*west, east, north, south*) are not capitalized.

Addresses (first letter)

Capitalize *street, boulevard, avenue,* and *drive* only when referring to a specific street, boulevard, avenue, or drive.

Example: Please deliver the order to 1710 North 103rd Street.
Example: They are located on one of the boulevards.
Example: They are located on Glendale Boulevard.

Family relationships (when substituted for a name)

Example: Will you please hand the check to Mother?

*Significant words include all words except articles (*a, an, the*), conjunctions (*and, but, or, nor, for*), and prepositions (*of, for, in, through, between, as, with*).

We capitalize *mother* because we could substitute the mother's name (let's say, Olga) for the word *mother* so that the sentence would read, "Will you please hand the check to Olga?"

Example: His father is president of the company.

To substitute *John* for *father* would read: "His John is president of the company," which doesn't work. Therefore, we do *not* capitalize *father*.

Stated another way, we do *not* capitalize words denoting family relationships when those words are preceded by possessive words such as *his, my, your, her, their, our, Jack's*.

Person's title and name (first letter only)

Example: Miss Rhonda E. Norton
Example: Mr. William R. Rogers
Example: Dr. José P. Ortega

Occupational positions (when following person's name; otherwise, optional)

Example: Mr. James Mitchell, Executive Vice-President
Example: Ms. Martha Jamison, Comptroller
Example: Martha Jamison is the new comptroller.

Titles of articles and publications (first letter of each significant word)
Example: An article titled "The Success and Failure of the Glasser Corporation" appeared in the June issue of *Business Week*.
Example: Every business major should read *Fundamentals of Modern Business*.

Language courses (first letter only if it is a proper noun)

Example: She is studying English, algebra, French, and psychology.

Direct quotations (first letter of first word)

Example: She then commented, "We expect to hire several college grads."

Complimentary closes (first letter of first word)

Example: Very truly yours
Example: Yours very truly
Example: Very sincerely

Words relating to numbers immediately following (first letter only)

Example: Mr. and Mrs. Baldwin will arrive on Flight 261.
Example: Those figures are in Section 4 of the report.
Example: Will you send two copies of your Invoice 26133?

SELF-CHECK: CAPITALIZATION

Slide a piece of paper downward as you read, exposing the correct sentences and explanations only after you have studied the test sentences.

1	Her Father is the President of the Corporation.
	Her father is president of the corporation.
	Do not capitalize *father* because it cannot be replaced by the person's name and because it is preceded by the possessive word *her*.
	No reason to capitalize *president,* because it does not follow a person's name.
	No reason to capitalize *corporation,* because a specific corporation is not referred to.
2	Many Businesses will be closed on monday, Labor day.
	Many businesses will be closed on Monday, Labor Day.
	No reason to capitalize *businesses.*
	Must capitalize days of the week and holidays (both words here).
3	The truck, which is owned by some company in the east, was traveling west on 65th avenue.
	The truck, which is owned by some company in the East, was traveling west on 65th Avenue.

Use *East, West, North,* and *South* (capitalized) only when preceded by *the,* denoting a specific and sizable geographic location.

Capitalize *avenue (street, drive, boulevard, road)* when it is a specific avenue.

4

Our professor of history spent a lot of time discussing the industrial revolution.

Our professor of history spent a lot of time discussing the Industrial Revolution.

You must capitalize historical events.

Do not capitalize *history,* because it is not a proper noun.

5

Ms. Springer, who is arriving on flight 211 at 3:20 p.m., will discuss her new book, *The Life and Death Of Socialism.*

Ms. Springer, who is arriving on Flight 211 at 3:20 p.m., will discuss her new book, *The Life and Death of Socialism.*

Capitalize *flight,* because it relates to the number immediately following.

Either *p.m.* or *P.M.* is correct.

Capitalize only the significant words in the names of publications, including the first word (*the,* in this instance).

Isn't it time you stopped guessing?

NUMBERS: WORDS OR FIGURES?

When you write letters, memos, telegrams, and most other types of business communications, you will generally be dealing with numbers. Follow these rules when deciding whether to spell out the number or give it in its numeral form:

Beginning a sentence: Use words

Example: Sixteen employees earned merit increases.
Example: Thirty percent of our employees have more than ten years
           seniority.

Ages of people: Use words

Example: This applicant is not yet twenty-one years of age.

Fractions standing alone: Use words

Example: The price of the stock declined by one quarter of a point.
Example: Nearly one half of our employees are union members.

Periods of time: Use words

Example: Our contract is for a thirty-second commercial.
Example: The commercial will be aired every sixty minutes.

Amounts of money: Use figures

Example: The net amount of the invoice is $450.25.
Example: Your check for $215 has now been processed. (not $215. or
           $215.00)
Example: Our balance-of-payments deficit was $27 billion.
Example: The Chairman of the Board at Dow Chemical Co. received
           compensation for one year of more than $1.6 million.
Example: Tomatoes are selling for $23.00 per case, compared to $22.50
           last month. (Zeros used for cents position in first figure be-
           cause second figure includes cents.)

Credit terms: Use figures

Example: Terms on the invoice are 2/10, n/30.
Example: The terms on our household items are 3/10 e.o.m.

Days and years: Use figures

Example: If you order today, payment will not be due until February 15.
Example: The transaction was finalized October 15, 1979.

Do not place the day before the month (15th of February or 15 October
1979).

Use ordinals with dates only when they are not preceded by month.

Example: We expect to receive the merchandise by the 24th.
Example: We expect to receive the merchandise by June 24.

Number of units: Use figures

Example: We ordered 16 No. 3610 circuit breakers.
Example: The truckload includes 1,310 cases of applesauce.

Percentages: Use figures (except at beginning of sentence)

Example: Our net income increased 15 percent over last year.
Example: Sixteen percent of our inventory was lost.

Do not use percent sign (%) except in tabulated materials.

Time of day: Use figures

Example: If we begin the meeting at 9:00 a.m., we should finish by 2:30 p.m.

Addresses: Use figures

Example: Please send the order to our warehouse at 1610 West 7th Avenue.

If you encounter a situation where none of these rules apply, or if you cannot recall the applicable rule, spell numbers of ten or lower and use figures for those that are greater than ten.

SELF-CHECK: NUMBERS

Slide a piece of paper downward as you read, exposing the correct sentences and explanations only after you have studied the test sentences.

1	500 people attended the convention.
	Five hundred people attended the convention.
	Do not begin a sentence with figures.

2	Joyce earned forty-five dollars for only 16 hours of work.
	Joyce earned $45 for only 16 hours of work.
	Use figures and dollar signs for quantities of money. Use figures for the hours worked because they are greater than ten.
3	We mailed our first notice to Apex Corporation on the 21st of March 1979.
	We mailed our first notice to Apex Corporation March 21, 1979.
	Place the day after the month. Do not use ordinals with dates unless month not shown.
4	Yes, we can give you the 7% discount on a purchase of sixteen units.
	Yes, we can give you the 7 percent discount on a purchase of 16 units.
	Use figures for percentages, except at beginning of sentence. Use percent sign only in tabulated materials. Use figures for number of units.
5	They requested delivery at 16001 West Twenty-Second Street by noon.
	They requested delivery at 16001 West 22nd Street by noon.
	Use figures for street numbers.
6	Our annual sales totaled three million dollars.
	Our annual sales totaled $3 million.
	Use dollar sign and figures for dollars in millions and billions, except at beginning of sentence.

<u>$$$ talk louder than words.</u>

SYMBOLS: WORDS OR SIGNS?

We may use the dollar sign freely in all types of business communications, but all other symbols (such as @, #, ¢, and &) may be used only in tables, invoices, and other tabulated materials.

<u>People who don't use dictionaries are gamblers.</u>

SPELLING:
PERSISTENCE AND A GOOD DICTIONARY

Grade school textbooks provide many rules for spelling, but few people can remember them all. We discard these rules at an early age because we find they are unreliable; there are too many exceptions to the rules.

Fortunately, we can spell most words by sounding them out, because they are spelled the way they are pronounced. We also spell many words, especially those that are spelled differently than they are pronounced, through sight—by taking a mental picture of the words.

Unfortunately, no one can spell all words. When we know we can't spell a word, or when we are in doubt, we check it in a recently published dictionary. Even people who are good spellers rely on dictionaries—at home, at school, and at work—to check the spelling of words as they use them and to expand their vocabularies by checking the meanings of newly encountered words.

As you progress through your college curriculum, many business terms will become a permanent part of your standard vocabulary. Correspondingly, you will routinely spell such words as *personnel, management, executive, corporation, demographics, laissez-faire, free rein, merchandise, mortgage, oligopoly,* and *subsidization.* You may save a lot of time, effort, and possible embarrassment, however, by studying the following list of words frequently misspelled in business communications. As an added precaution, you might want to mark this section with a paper clip and refer to the list when in doubt.

Words Commonly Misspelled in Business

absence	available	conspicuous	enthusiastic
accelerate	bargain	continuously	entirely
acceptable	beginning	controlling	environment
acceptance	belief	convenient	equipment
accessible	believe	convincing	equipped
accidentally	believing	courteous	equivalent
accommodate	beneficial	criticism	erroneous
accompanying	benefited	criticize	especially
accomplish	budget	deceive	exceed
accumulate	bulletin	deductible	excellent
accurate	bureau	defendant	existence
achievement	business	deferred	existent
acknowledgment	calendar	deficiency	expense
acknowledging	cancel	definite	experience
acquaint	cancellation	dependent	explanation
across	candidate	describe	facilities
advantageous	career	description	familiar
advisable	catalog	desirable	feasible
aggravate	category	despair	February
aggressive	certain	develop	finally
allege	changeable	difference	financially
allowance	chargeable	disappearance	forward
analysis	collectible	disappoint	freight
analyze	column	disastrous	generally
announce	commission	disbursement	government
apologize	committed	discipline	grammar
apparatus	committee	discussion	grateful
apparent	commodities	dissatisfaction	guarantee
appealing	comparatively	distribute	guidance
appearance	competent	divide	handling
appreciate	competition	efficiency	happiness
approach	conceivable	efficient	harass
appropriate	confidence	eighth	height
argument	confidentially	either	hurriedly
arrangement	consent	eligible	immediately
assistant	controlled	eliminate	immensely
association	conscience	embarrass	impossible
attendance	conscientious	encouraging	incidentally
attorney	conscious	endeavor	incredible
automatically	consistent	enforceable	independent

Words Commonly Misspelled in Business (Cont.)

indispensable	obstacle	procedure	success
inevitable	occasion	propaganda	suffered
influence	occupant	proportion	sufficient
install	occur	psychology	superintendent
intelligence	occurred	pursue	supersede
intelligent	occurrence	quality	supplies
intentionally	offered	quantity	suppress
interfere	omission	questionnaire	surely
interrupt	omitted	realize	surprise
irrelevant	operate	receipt	sympathize
judgment	opinion	receivables	temperature
knowledge	opportunity	receive	temporary
labeled	originally	recognize	tendency
laissez-faire	paid	recommend	thorough
legible	pamphlet	refer	through
legitimate	parallel	referred	totaled
leisure	particularly	reference	toward
license	perceive	repetition	transferring
lightning	permanent	representative	tremendous
likable	permissible	requirement	typical
lying	perseverance	research	unanimous
maintenance	personnel	resistance	undoubtedly
management	persuade	restaurant	unnecessary
manual	pertain	ridiculous	unusual
manufacturer	pertinent	sacrifice	useful
meant	physically	safety	usually
millionaire	pleasant	schedule	valuable
miniature	policies	secretary	various
minute	practical	seize	vegetable
miscellaneous	practically	separate	vice versa
mischievous	precede	severely	voluntary
monotonous	predictable	signature	Wednesday
moral	predominant	significant	weather
morale	prefer	similar	weight
mortgage	preference	simultaneous	whether
movable	preferred	sincerely	writing
necessary	prevalent	source	write
neither	privilege	strenuous	written
noticeable	probably	succeed	yield

You cannot take the time to look up all words in a dictionary, of course; and you won't have this list available at all times. After studying it, therefore, consider the words in the following self-check to see if you can identify which ones you should check in the dictionary (or list). Then, if you are dissatisfied with your performance, spend some additional time studying the list of words.

SELF-CHECK: SPELLING

Cover the column at the right side until you have identified the column or columns containing words that may be misspelled.

	A	B	C	D	Answers
1	changable	committee	apearance	finally	A, C
2	knowlege	receipt	source	competent	A
3	supplies	reccomend	judgement	obstacle	B, C
4	assistent	controlled	cincerly	safty	A, C, D
5	recieve	analyse	compitition	devide	A, B, C, D
6	approach	impossible	gratful	government	C
7	Wedesday	intelligent	writting	typical	A, C
8	yield	suprise	Febuary	freight	B, C
9	representative	quantity	questionaire	precedure	C, D
10	opinion	weight	unanomous	uneccesary	C, D
11	proportion	apealing	changable	supplies	B, C
12	recomend	opportunity	maintnance	schedule	A, C
13	association	continously	decieve	managment	B, C, D
14	opinion	writen	nether	morgage	B, C, D
15	comission	develope	thorough	appologize	A, B, D

QUIZ: MECHANICS AND GRAMMAR

What, if anything, is incorrect about the following sentences?

1. Female Employees must become more assertive if they are to acheve Managment positions in busness.

2. The Purchasing Mgr. ordered two hundred cases, but we recieved only 150.

3. Our new offices are located at 168 no. seventh st.

4. 300,000 or so new businesses are begun each year.

5. Of the three hundred thousand new businesses started this year, 180,000 will fail within five years, which is a failure rate of 60%.

6. The Advertising that we hear on the radio and see on TV are examples of Visual Communications.

7. Acceptance of the programme will be an important step towards the success of this corp.

8. I would like to develope a better schedule for servicing our customers on the west side of town.

9. Their invoice 26104 is for fifty dollars, which brings the total to $165.42.

10. Shall we send a check for $50.00 and pay the balance on wednesday, Dec. 15th?

11. We will continue our meeting next Thurs. in the P.M., if Marge and Geo. can be there.

12. The six percent interest that the bank pays on my savings account doesn't even come close to keeping pace with inflation.

13. After Stephen works forty-eight hours at the office each week, he takes Saturday courses in acconting, speach, and spanish at City College.

14. After reading an article entitled "Leading Economic Indicators Rise In December," the economist said, "our G.N.P. for the year has increased about seven percent."

15. Jack Prentiss, president of Wallett Industries, Inc., is just like his Mother, very achevement oriented.

4

PUNCTUATING
CORRECTLY

Have you ever heard anyone say anything nice about traffic signals? Probably not, because we tend to view them as a necessary evil—something that we must contend with if we are to avoid accidents and traffic citations. But imagine the hassle of driving through a large city without such devices. The trip would be time consuming and extremely hazardous.

Similarly, some people view commas, semicolons, and other forms of punctuation as useless and bothersome. But consider the difficulty we would experience without these essential writing aids, as illustrated in the following unpunctuated paragraph:

In March at the start of the current economic expansion the ratio was 82.5 using the 1967 average as a base of 100 the ratio rose almost without interruption until last April when it reached a high of 104.7 since then however it has been wobbling badly it fell to 104.4 in May dropped to 103 in June recovered slightly and then resumed the decline in December the last month available it was 101 nearly four points below the level of last spring.

Adding punctuation, we have a readable paragraph:

In March, at the start of the current economic expansion, the ratio was 82.5 (using the 1967 average as a base of 100). The ratio rose almost without interruption until last April, when it reached a high of 104.7. Since then, however, it has been wobbling badly. It fell to 104.4 in May, dropped to 103 in June, recovered slightly, and then resumed the decline. In December, the latest month available, it was 101, nearly four points below the level of last spring.

Placing punctuation in the wrong places is like placing traffic signals in the middle of city blocks rather than at intersections, causing readers to become just as confused as drivers would be. To make our written communications effective, therefore, we must learn the functions of all forms of punctuation and know when we should or should not use them.

The pause that enlightens.

COMMAS , , , , , , , , , ,

Except for the period, which will be discussed later in this chapter, the comma is a writer's and reader's best friend. Commas enable writers to separate or join words, phrases, clauses, and sentences; and they tell the reader when to pause or (through their absence) when to read full speed. Correspondingly, commas enable us to express ourselves on paper in much the same way that we express ourselves in person.

> *Set off dependent phrases and clauses at beginning of sentences.*

Clause: *Because he acted foolishly,* a reprimand seems advisable.
Phrase: *Under these circumstances,* a reprimand seems advisable.

Unlike a phrase, a dependent clause has a subject (*he*) and a verb (*acted*).

When we add a dependent phrase (or clause), such as "Under these circumstances," at the beginning of an already complete sentence "A reprimand seems advisable," we must set off the dependent phrase (or clause) from the rest of the sentence with a comma.

> *Connect sentences.*

Example: I like the work, but the pay is too low.

When we combine two complete sentences into one with the use of connecting words *and, but, or, nor,* or *for,* we must place a comma at the end of the first sentence.

> *Separate parts of a series.*

Example: Please return the first, third, and fourth copies.
Example: We must increase productivity, reduce costs, and minimize taxes.

Yes, the comma preceding the connecting word (*and,* in both of these examples) is needed.

Separate descriptive words.

Example: The program turned out to be a long, profitless undertaking.

In effect, we are using the comma to replace the word *and* in this sentence.

Introduce a direct quote.

Example: The department manager shouted, "I want to know just who you think is in charge here!"

Set off descriptive phrases.

Example: Miss Smith's memo, which contains 12 pages, outlines the program very effectively.
Example: Joe James, our acting superintendent, is a very valuable employee.

The phrases set off with commas were added to already complete sentences to tell the reader something about the length of the memo and exactly who Joe is. All such phrases must be set off from the rest of the sentence with commas.

Set off direct addresses.

Example: Okay, Joe, we will make the corrections.
Example: Leslie, your education and experience are very impressive.
Example: Your education and experience are very impressive, Leslie.

When we write as though we are talking with others, we set off their names with commas.

Set off added phrases which question what was just said.

Example: We are going to accept their offer, aren't we?

Set off added phrases which have the opposite meaning of what was just said.

Example: We are seeking applicants with talent, not just coursework.
Example: The boss is interested in results, not excuses.

Set off words such as "yes" and "no."

Example: Yes, we can deliver your order today.
Example: No, we are not interested in extending the contract.

Set off name of state when used with name of city.

Example: Your shipment passed through Kansas City, Missouri, on June 12.

No commas are required when only the city or the state is used.

Example: Your shipment passed through Missouri on June 12.

Set off the year when used with month and day.

Example: June 1, 1945, is the date the company was founded.
Example: June 1 is the due date.
Example: Your first payment will be due in March, 1980.

Use of a comma in the final example is optional.

Set off qualifying words.

Example: We can meet the deadline, perhaps, by working overtime.
Example: No one returned our phone calls, however.
Example: However, no one returned our phone calls.

Notice that *perhaps* and *however* are *not* being used as connecting words in these examples.

Specify quantities in thousands.

Example: More than 32,000 consumers responded to the survey.
Example: Our net income for the year was $3,216,011.32.

SELF-CHECK: COMMAS

Slide a piece of paper downward as you read, exposing the correct sentences and explanations only after you have studied the test sentences.

1	After receiving many inquiries the office manager decided to reply.
	After receiving many inquiries, the office manager decided to reply.
	Set off the dependent phrase with a comma.

2	We wanted to fill the order but we were out of stock.
	We wanted to fill the order, but we were out of stock.
	Use a comma when connecting two complete sentences with *and, but, or, nor,* or *for.*

3	They sell toys nationwide with the assistance of agents brokers and wholesalers.
	They sell toys nationwide with the assistance of agents, brokers, and wholesalers.
	Use commas to separate parts of a series.

4	Pam is an experienced dedicated employee isn't she?
	Pam is an experienced, dedicated employee, isn't she?
	Separate descriptive words with commas. When an added phrase questions what was just said, set it off with a comma.

5	Purchase orders received today and there are several should be included.
	Purchase orders received today, and there are several, should be included.
	Use commas to set off descriptive phrases and clauses.
6	We must begin production today not next month.
	We must begin production today, not next month.
	Use commas to set off phrases which have the opposite meaning of what was just said.
7	That package however was forwarded from Columbus Ohio last week.
	That package, however, was forwarded from Columbus, Ohio, last week.
	Set off qualifying words such as *however* (when not used as connecting words). Set off name of state when used with name of city.
8	Yes shipment was made October 4 1979 from New York City.
	Yes, shipment was made October 4, 1979, from New York City.
	Set off words such as *yes* and *no*. Set off the year when used with both month and day.

It's not a bird; it's not a plane; it's supercomma.

SEMICOLONS ; ; ; ; ; ; ; ; ; ;

We use semicolons in much the same way that we use commas, but semicolons are more powerful than commas; they are "supercommas."

Join sentences without connecting words.

With: Government spending was at a record high, *and* a tax increase soon followed.

Without: Government spending was at a record high; a tax increase soon followed.

So how do you know when to use a connecting word and when not to? The choice is yours. You must decide which way sounds better. For variety, you may use connecting words in some sentences and only semicolons in others. Two thoughts must be closely related, of course, to combine them into a single sentence.

Join sentences with words other than and, but, or, nor, *or* for.

Example: We like the style, but we question the price.
Example: We like the style; however, we question the price.

We must use the semicolon-comma combination with connecting words such as *however, therefore, consequently, moreover, nevertheless, whereas, otherwise,* and *for example.*

In the preceding example, the word *however* is read with the second part of the sentence (*however, we question the price*). If, instead, you wish the connecting word to be read with the first part of the sentence, you reverse the semicolon and comma.

Example: Employee productivity declined significantly last month. Jan has been doing better, however; we recommend an immediate increase in her salary.

In this sentence, the connecting word *however* relates more closely to the first part of the sentence. The option of reversing the semicolon-comma combination in this manner enables us to express our thoughts more accurately.

When using semicolons, place them after closing quotation marks.

Example: The supervisor said, "Let's apply a little psychology in our labor relations"; he soon resumed his autocratic ways, however.

We use a semicolon here to join two complete sentences without the use of a connecting word.

Replace commas with semicolons when commas are used elsewhere.

Example: We place a high value on fast express service by trucking companies, because we do not like to keep excessive amounts of merchandise on hand; but we are very careful to avoid exorbitant shipping rates.

When we have competing commas in a sentence, we use a semicolon (supercomma) with the connecting word. The semicolon helps readers spot the major break in the sentence, the place where two sentences are connected.

Separate parts of a series when commas are used within the parts.

Example: Absenteeism has been extensive: Joe missed six days; Jim, nine days; and Judy, seven days.

Instead of stating that Jim missed nine days and that Judy missed seven, we use commas to show that the word *missed* has been deleted. Having used commas in this manner, we must use semicolons to show readers where the main divisions are located.

The hybrid form of punctuation.

COLONS : : : : : : : : :

We sometimes treat colons like commas, but they are not commas; and we sometimes treat them a little like periods, but they are not periods. In this unique role, colons provide us with added flexibility in expressing our thoughts on paper.

Announce a following list or series.

Example: The workers are seeking three benefits: increased wages, shorter hours, and improved fringes.

We *wish* to use a colon here, because it introduces a following list. We *may* use a colon in this manner only when it is preceded by a complete sentence:

Example: The three benefits the workers seek are increased wages, shorter hours, and improved fringes.

A colon following the word *are* would not be preceded by a complete sentence; therefore, we continue into the following series without any introductory punctuation.

When a complete sentence follows the colon, we capitalize the first letter of the first word.

Example: One point is obvious: We must invest more money.

Announce a descriptive clause.

Example: This department is under the direction of just one person: James P. Culligan.

A colon has the effect of emphasizing whatever words follow it—the person's name, in this instance.

If we wanted to deemphasize the person's name, we would replace the colon with a comma.

Separate hours and minutes.

Example: The second shift of workers begins at 3:30 p.m.

Announce a direct quotation.

Example: Ms. Rochester then made the following statement: "Beginning next month, all overtime will be allocated strictly on the basis of seniority."

Notice that the colon is preceded by a complete sentence; otherwise, we would use a comma in its place.

SELF-CHECK: SEMICOLONS AND COLONS

Slide a piece of paper downward as you read, exposing the correct sentences and explanations only after you have studied the test questions.

1	Business was good this year next year should be even better.
	Business was good this year; next year should be even better.
	Semicolon used to connect two complete sentences.
2	At the price suppliers are charging we cannot make a profit on resale but we must meet the price of our competitors.
	At the price suppliers are charging, we cannot make a profit on resale; but we must meet the price of our competitors.
	Set off dependent clause with a comma. Use a semicolon to connect the two complete sentences because of the competing comma.
3	Stock prices are at a yearly low therefore we cannot afford to sell now.
	Stock prices are at a yearly low; therefore, we cannot afford to sell now.
	Use the semicolon-comma combination with connecting words such as *therefore*.
4	All had been big sellers breakfast cereals which totaled $3 million coffee $2 million and cat food $1 million.
	All had been big sellers: breakfast cereals, which totaled $3 million; coffee, $2 million; and cat food, $1 million.
	Use a colon to introduce a series preceded by a complete sentence. Use semicolons in a series that also contains commas.

5	The four elements of marketing are price product place and promotion.
	The four elements of marketing are price, product, place, and promotion.
	We cannot use a colon after the word *are* because it would not be preceded by a complete sentence.

6	They promised to deliver the merchandise by 530 pm.
	They promised to deliver the merchandise by 5:30 p.m.
	Use a colon to separate hours from minutes. Place periods after the *p* and the *m*, with no spacing in between.

But does it belong to someone?

APOSTROPHES ′′′′′′′′′′

We use apostrophes to relate possessions, characteristics, and behavior to specific individuals or groups.

Show possessive for words that can be either singular or plural.

Example: The wrecking firm moved the employee's car from the company parking lot.

Example: The wrecking firm removed several employees' cars from the company parking lot.

The reader knows that we are speaking of only one employee in the first example, because we have placed the apostrophe before the *s*.

We place the apostrophe after the *s* in the second example because we are speaking of more than one person.

Show possessive for words that are distinctively plural.

Example: We now produce 33 different types of children's toys.
Example: Will you please send us three gross of men's handkerchiefs?

Unlike the word *employees,* plural words like *children* and *men* do not end in *s.* Therefore, we add an *s* after the apostrophe.

Show possessive for proper names ending in s.

Example: Mr. Jones's report was very comprehensive.
Example: Ms. Harris' department had the greatest increase in productivity.

We added *'s* to the first sentence because *Jones* is a one-syllable word.

We added only an apostrophe to the second sentence, because *Harris* has more than one syllable.

Avoid assigning possessives to inanimate objects.

(no) The building's exterior is badly in need of paint.
(yes) The exterior of the building is badly in need of paint.

Show possessive for time.

Example: When may we expect to receive last month's reports?
Better: When may we expect to receive the reports for March?

Use possessive words preceding ing *words when the words refer to people.*

Example: Tom's arriving late slowed the entire assembly line.
Example: Our calling all employees by their first names has improved morale noticeably.

Other examples of possessive words are *their, your, his, her,* and *my.*

Use apostrophes for contractions of the words it *and* is.

Example: It's going to be a long bargaining session.
Example: The building is old; when will its roof need replacing?

The second example uses the possessive form of *it,* which does not require an apostrophe. Adding an unnecessary apostrophe to the possessive form *its* is one the commonest, and most damning, grammatical errors in English.

SELF-CHECK: APOSTROPHES

Slide a piece of paper downward as you read, exposing the correct sentences and explanations only after you have studied the test sentences.

1   Managers should consider the workers feelings (several workers)

Managers should consider the workers' feelings.

Place an apostrophe after the *s* to show that we are writing about the feelings of more than one worker.

2   We check each persons productivity once every hour.

We check each person's productivity once every hour.

Place an apostrophe before the *s* because writing about just one person.

3   Today is Jones day off, but tomorrow is Adams rest day.

Today is Jones's day off, but tomorrow is Adams' rest day.

We add *'s* to *Jones* (one syllable) to form the possessive and only an apostrophe to *Adams* (two syllables).

4   This computers speed is relatively slow.

The speed of this computer is relatively slow.

Do not assign possessive to inanimate objects.

5	The retailer raising the price resulted in fewer sales. (one retailer)
	The retailer's raising the price resulted in fewer sales.
	Use possessive form for words preceding *ing* words (*raising*) when the words refer to people (*retailer*).
6	Its going to extend its useful life.
	It's going to extend its useful life.
	Use apostrophe for contraction of *it* and *is,* but not for the possessive form *its.*

That's exactly what I said, dum-dum.

QUOTATION MARKS " " " " " " " "

We use quotation marks to enclose the exact words of other people. But quotation marks may be used for several additional purposes.

Enclose direct quotes of others.

Example: The sales manager stated emphatically, "This sales campaign is essential to survival of the company."

Always capitalize the first letter of the first word in a quote.

Always place periods before closing quotation marks.

Example: "Go ahead and make the refund," he said, "or we may lose the account."

In effect, we are setting off *he said,* which is not part of the quote, with commas.

Notice that we do not capitalize the first letter of the first word where the quote is continued.

Use only one set of quotation marks to enclose a multiple-sentence quote.

Example: The customer commented as follows: "The bill is correct. We agree. More time is what we need."

Use apostrophes in place of quotation marks to identify a quote within a quote.

Example: The speaker then stated, "The term 'social responsibility' has many meanings."

Discuss words and define terms.

Example: I disagree with your definition of the word "success."
Example: The term "negotiable instrument" may be defined as "a written obligation that can be transferred from one person to another."

Enclose slang expressions and nicknames.

Example: I view the entire proposal as a lot of "bunk."
Example: This letter is to introduce our new production manager, Winnie "Sledgehammer" Johnson.

Cast doubt on something.

Example: What does our marketing "team" have to report this month?

Questions whether the marketing people are functioning as a team.

Example: What does our "marketing" team have to report this period?

Suggests that the marketing people may be some kind of team other than a marketing team.

Enclose titles of articles.

Example: The information is from an article entitled "Eastern Airlines Stakes Its Rebound on a Bid To Buy European Craft."

Notice that only the significant words in the title are capitalized and that the closing period precedes the closing quotation marks.

SELF-CHECK: QUOTATION MARKS

Slide a piece of paper downward as you read, exposing the correct sentences and explanations only after you have studied the test sentences.

1 The personnel manager replied we should reward employees on the basis of merit not tenure.

The personnel manager replied, "We should reward employees on the basis of merit, not tenure."

Precede the quote with a comma, capitalize the first letter in the quote, and place a period before closing quotation marks.

2 We will ship the order she said as soon as we verify their credit standing.

"We will ship the order," she said, "as soon as we verify their credit standing."

Set off *she said,* placing the first comma before the closing quotation marks. Do not capitalize *as,* because it is only the first word in a continuation of the interrupted quote.

3 My definition of the word arbitrator is one having the power to decide.

My definition of the word "arbitrator" is "one having the power to decide."

When referring to a particular word, set it off with quotation marks. Also enclose definitions with quotation marks.

4 The credit manager said can you hold just one minute? John is on the other line. I'll be right back.

The credit manager said, "Can you hold just one minute? John is on the other line. I'll be right back."

	Place all three sentences within one set of quotation marks. Capitalize the first letter of the first word in the quote.
5	The magazine article was titled Why Johnny Can't Read—or Write.
	The magazine article was titled "Why Johnny Can't Read—or Write."
	Place titles of articles within quotation marks.

Togetherness can be communicative.

HYPHENS - - - - - - - - - -

Some words are spelled with hyphens. We also use hyphens to combine words that describe other words, to write numbers, and to divide words at the end of lines.

Spell some words with hyphens.

Example: Our company president is a self-educated person.
Example: She is the first woman to attain the position of vice-president within this corporation.

Most words beginning with *self* are hyphenated.

In recent years, most internal hyphenations of words after prefixes (such as *re-, pre-, sub-, co-, de-,* and others) have been dropped. For example, the word *cooperation* was once spelled *co-operation.*

Example: Top management has decided to deemphasize television exposure this year.

So how are you supposed to know which form to use? Consult a recently published dictionary when in doubt.

Join some descriptive words.

Example: George, this is certainly an up-to-date report.
Example: Such under-the-table practices are quite common.
Example: Joyce sent a three-page letter to them.

The hyphenated words describe the words immediately following.

Example: Will this be a two- or a three-page letter?

We use the word *page* only once, near the end of the sentence, to avoid needless repetition.

Do not hyphenate words ending in ly.

Example: The newly formulated plan appeared incomplete.

The word *newly* describes the word *formulated* (not the word *plan*); therefore, we do not connect the two words.

Hyphenate fractions only when they describe the word immediately following.

Example: Nearly two thirds of our employees voted for union representation.

Example: The union received a two-thirds majority of the votes cast.

The fraction in the first example does not describe the word immediately following (*of*); whereas the fraction in the second example does describe the word immediately following (*majority*).

Avoid misinterpretation.

Example: Many businesses are experiencing a small shipment problem.

Example: Many businesses are experiencing a small-shipment problem.

Example: Many businesses are experiencing a small shipment-problem.

In the first example, the reader cannot determine whether the problem concerns small shipments or whether a shipment problem is of small dimensions.

The second example specifies that a problem exists with respect to small shipments, and the third example refers to a shipment problem that is not very significant.

These are examples of the ways we may use hyphens to express our thoughts accurately.

Hyphenate spelled numbers greater than twenty.

Example: twenty-one, thirty-three, ninety-five

Divide words at the end of lines.

Example: eval·u·a·tion

We may split the word *evaluation* in any of three places, as shown in the dictionary. Rather than dividing this word between the first and second syllables or the second and third syllables, however, we should keep single-letter syllables with the first part of the word, carrying only the syllable *tion* to the following line.

Do not divide one-syllable words.

Example: through, serve, charge

Do not divide words with fewer than seven letters.

Example: letter, report, detail, active

Do not divide a word at the end of a page.

Include the entire word on the first page or carry the entire word to the following page.

Do not divide the names of people.

(no)   Ron-ald, Mr. Dickin-son.

Instead, carry the undivided name forward to the next line.

These words are important, dear.

DASHES − − − − − − − − −

On a typewriter, dashes are two hyphens—back to back—with no spaces on either side. We generally use them to emphasize a word or phrase that follows.

Example: Their product entry—the winning one—is still on display.
Example: The corporation maintained a secret account of over $10 million, most of which was distributed among politicians in hidden donations—to presidents, presidential candidates, congressmen, and lesser officials.

To have used a comma here in place of the dash would confuse the reader because of competing commas elsewhere in the sentence. Dashes enable us to include additions to sentences that would otherwise make the sentences too long.

It's Greek to me.

UNDERSCORE _____

We use the underscore on a typewriter to specify that words should be in italics, including foreign words and the names of publications. We also use the underscore to emphasize important words.

Identify words as foreign.

Example: A common business expression is <u>caveat emptor</u> (let the buyer beware).

If this sentence were in a book or magazine, the two Latin words would appear in italics as *caveat emptor.*

Identify names of publications.

Example: The timely article appeared in the February 22 issue of <u>Business Week.</u>

Example: The title of the book is <u>Business Math Basics.</u>

Notice that the underscore is continued between words.

Emphasize important words.

Example: We do <u>not</u> want a replacement for the damaged machine.

To make a long story short . . .

ELLIPSIS . . . .

We use the ellipsis to tell the reader that some words have been omitted from a quotation.

Example: Mr. Randolph made the statement, "*The Wall Street Journal* is the most widely read publication among business people . . . in addition to extensive financial information, the weekday newspaper carries summaries of important national and international news events."

The three dots, which are separated from one another by one space, indicate that words which the writer considers unimportant to the meaning of this sentence have been omitted from Mr. Randolph's original statement.

Example: Ms. Spriggs stated, "The Dow Jones Industrial Average is computed on the basis of the closing prices of the same stocks each day: 30 industrial stocks, 20 railroad stocks, and 15 public utility stocks. . . . "

When we use an ellipsis at the end of a quote, we add an extra dot to serve as a period.

	SELF-CHECK: HYPHENS, DASHES, AND UNDERSCORES
	Slide a piece of paper downward as you read, exposing the correct sentences and explanations only after you have studied the test sentences.
1	The airline has government authority to operate around the world flights.
	The airline has government authority to operate around-the-world flights.
	Connect the three words with hyphens to describe the word immediately following.
2	The assistant manager appears very self sufficient.
	The assistant manager appears very self-sufficient.
	Words beginning with *self* are usually hyphenated.
3	The provision was adopted by a two thirds majority of the members.
	The provision was adopted by a two-thirds majority of the members.
	Hyphenate fractions when they describe the word immediately following.

<table>
<tr><td>4</td><td>I suggest that you read The Decline of Unionism in the current issue of Business Week.</td></tr>
</table>

4	I suggest that you read The Decline of Unionism in the current issue of Business Week.
	I suggest that you read "The Decline of Unionism" in the current issue of Business Week.
	Place title within quotation marks, and underscore the name of the publication. Notice that no comma is required before the first quotation marks, because this is the title of an article, not a quote.
5	The highly priced Fiat is a prestige item.
	Correct as shown.
	Highly describes *priced,* not *Fiat;* therefore, no hyphen is required.
6	When the clerk has scanned all the products, the computer categorizes each item meat, produce, canned goods, and bakery products.
	When the clerk has scanned all the products, the computer categorizes each item—meat, produce, canned goods, and bakery products.
	We use a dash here, rather than a colon, because we are adding words of explanation to the sentence, rather than announcing the words that follow.

There's something else you should know, Harold.

PARENTHESES ((((( )))))

When we find that our communications are overladen with punctuation, we may switch to parentheses for clarification. The word *parenthesis* (with an *i*) is singular, and the word *parentheses* (with a long *e*) is plural. Parentheses are also handy for numbering the parts of a series or listing.

Use when there is too much competing punctuation.

(no)   As citizens were displaced in primary industries, agriculture, fishing, and mining, they found jobs in secondary industries, manufacturing. Then, as businesses automated their factories, displaced workers were absorbed into tertiary industries, service jobs.

(yes)   As citizens were displaced in primary industries (agriculture, fishing, and mining), they found jobs in secondary industries (manufacturing). Then, as businesses automated their factories, displaced workers were absorbed into tertiary industries (service jobs).

Set off parenthetical remarks.

Example: The auditors then studied the balance sheet (this is when the trouble began) before deciding to recheck their original computations.

Example: The auditors then studied the balance sheet before deciding to recheck their original computations. (This is when the trouble began.)

When an entire sentence is placed within parentheses, as is done here, it is capitalized and punctuated in the usual manner only when it stands outside surrounding sentences. Within a sentence, however, it should neither be capitalized nor ended with a period. Exceptions are short exclamations:

Example: As soon as they received the news (if only we had known in time!), they canceled the order.

Defining organizations and agencies with acronyms.

Example: The Organization of Petroleum-Exporting Countries (OPEC), composed of Arab oil-producing countries and Venezuela, joined forces in the early 1970s to establish common (uniform) prices for their petroleum. Having a monopoly on this form of energy, OPEC countries raised petroleum prices dramatically.

Once we have related the organization or agency to the identifying letters, using parentheses, we may use just the letters, without parentheses.

Note that a synonym for the word *common* is also included in parentheses.

Number the parts of a series or listing within a sentence.

Example: A charter is a written agreement between (1) the corporation being formed and the stockholders and (2) between the corporation and the state in which the charter is secured.

Enclose figures in legal and quasilegal documents.

Example: The contractual amount is three million dollars ($3,000,000).

Stop, look, and question.

PERIODS, EXCLAMATION MARKS, AND QUESTION MARKS . . . . . ! ! ! ! ! ? ? ? ? ?

We all know when to use periods, exclamation marks, and question marks, so let's discuss the spacing required with their use and their placement with quotation marks.

Use two spaces at the end of sentences.

Example: Here is an important direction! You are to fill all orders in the same sequence as they are received. Do you anticipate any problems in complying with this order? If so, please notify your immediate supervisor at once.

Space only once after periods in abbreviated titles.

Example: Who submitted the order, Dr. Messer or Mrs. Fulbright?

Do not space following periods in single-letter abbreviations.

Example: They authorized us to ship the order C.O.D.

Notice that the last period also ends the sentence.

Do not space following abbreviated time designations.

Example: You may expect our telephone call at exactly 12:10 p.m.

Place periods before closing quotation marks.

Example: She commented, "This is my final warning."

Place exclamation marks before closing quotation marks.

Example: The manager yelled, "Come on, let's get back to work!"

Analyze the situation for question marks.

Example: She then asked, "Which copy should I return to the buyer?"
Example: Did she ask, "Which copy should I return to the buyer"?

The quote in the first example contains the question, so we place the question mark within the quotation.

Because the entire second sentence is a question, we place the question mark after the closing quotation marks. Note that this custom applies only to question marks (and exclamation points); not periods, which always fall inside the final quotation marks.

As a matter of courtesy, we often state commands as questions, in which case we use periods instead of question marks.

Example: Since payment is now eight days past due, will you please send your check to us for the full amount of the bill.

Example: After completing your sales campaign in Portland, will you concentrate your efforts on our Boston market.

SELF-CHECK: PARENTHESES,
EXCLAMATION MARKS, AND QUESTION MARKS

Slide a piece of paper downward as you read, exposing the correct sentences and explanations only after you have studied the test sentences.

1 | Three government agencies regulate transport companies: Interstate Commerce Commission, Civil Aeronautics Board, and Federal Maritime Commission. (Number each part of the series.)

Three government agencies regulate transport companies: (1) Interstate Commerce Commission, (2) Civil Aeronautics Board, and (3) Federal Maritime Commission.

Place the last number after the conjunction *and.*

2 | The director asked whom do you recommend?

The director asked, "Whom do you recommend?"

Because the quote is the question, we place the question mark before the closing quotation marks.

3	Did the director ask whom do you recommend?
	Did the director ask, "Whom do you recommend"?
	Place the question mark after the closing quotation marks because the entire sentence is a question.
4	She then yelled into the phone we won't pay your bill until we receive a corrected invoice!
	She then yelled into the phone, "We won't pay your bill until we receive a corrected invoice!"
	Place the exclamation mark within the quote, where the yelling takes place, preceding the closing quotation marks.

QUIZ: PUNCTUATION

What punctuation, if any, should be added to each of the following sentences?

1. In a planned economy important economic decisions are made by the government.

2. Joan returned from Ecuador this morning and we were quite pleased with her initial report.

3. Fiscal policy involves two actions government taxation and government spending.

4. Gross national product GNP represents an attempt by the government to estimate the market value of all final goods and services produced in a one year period.

5. The consumer price index CPI the most widely used index is based on the prices of a wide assortment of consumer goods.

6. In trying to control inflation however the federal government is confronted with an almost impossible situation.

7. Atlantic and Pacific Stores A&P once the country's largest grocery chain recently closed one third of its 3500 stores.

8. If employees do not belong to a union they may become responsive to appeals from union organizers if they do belong to a union mistreatment may result in a reduction in productivity or in strikes.

9. The responsibility of managing a business especially a large corporation is tremendous.

10. How should the term well paid be defined.

11. Do you believe that business salaries and benefits from between $500000 and $1000000 per year are justified or would you recommend that the government place a limit on business incomes?

12. Two meetings were held in Cleveland Ohio during that period one on December 13 1979 and another on January 1 1980.

13. Your order was received friday at 430 pm therefore the package was not mailed until monday.

14. Sales were high in all three categories housewares $27000 appliances $34525 and furnishings $12221.

15. Her exact words were yes we will buy all 2000 cases.

16. The signature is hers there is no doubt about it.

17. The workers output for march does not compare well with their productivity for february.

18. Martha I believe that your employees would benefit from reading How Do Those Japanese Workers Do It in todays Wall Street Journal.

19. General Motors has subsidiaries auxiliary companies that they own and operate in Mexico Canada Australia New Zealand South America and western Europe.

20. Many firms both small and large have a need for short-term loans from time-to-time and banks are an important source of such funds.

5

CHOOSING
THE BEST WORDS

We all play several roles in life. To certain people, for example, you may be a friend, an enemy, a lover, a rival, or a spouse. To others, you may be a colleague, a competitor, a customer, an employee, a student, a taxpayer, a voter, or a combination of these roles. We all are sons or daughters of our parents, and some of us are also the parents of others.

Similar distinctions exist in business. As an employee, you will experience superior-subordinate relationships—sometimes as the superior, sometimes as the subordinate, and sometimes playing both roles simultaneously. You will also communicate with other employees within your particular company and with such diverse groups outside the company as consumers, retailers, wholesalers, shareholders, suppliers, and government representatives.

Much of our success in dealing with these people depends on our choice of words. We must choose words that other people will understand, but without talking down to them. If we are to capture and maintain their interest, we must use words that reflect our sincerity and objectivity; and, equally important, we must make certain that we are using words correctly.

So where do we begin? An important first step in sharpening your language skills is to read this chapter carefully and work with the self-checks until you comprehend the materials thoroughly. But that is only the beginning of the required effort. If you are to broaden your choice of words, you must constantly strive for improvement. Ask acquaintances to help you on a day-to-day basis, if they are qualified to do so. Read a daily paper regularly, one or two weekly magazines, and an occasional book. A lot of work, yes, but is there any skill more important in business, or in life generally, than communicating effectively? Certainly not!

We exhort investors to interpose
disintermediation with circumspection.

CHOOSE THE SIMPLER WORD

Are we trying to impress people with our high level of intelligence, or are we trying to communicate with them? Most of us want to impress others favorably, but we should not burden the reader (or listener) with complex words when more commonly used substitutes are at our command. The following list helps to illustrate this point:

Replace the complex word with	*a simpler one*
Government aid *alleviated* the impact of the flood.	lessened
What *alternatives* to we have?	choices
We do not *anticipate* any problems.	expect
When is the sales promotion to *commence*?	begin
Transistors are important *components*.	parts
Why don't we *consolidate* our efforts?	combine
See if they will *convert* the freight charges from collect to prepaid.	change
The high rate of returns *denotes* an increasing degree of customer dissatisfaction.	reflects *or* suggests
When can you *effect* delivery?	make
When did they *initiate* the program?	begin *or* start
This product represents our *initial* attempt to enter the market.	first
Be sure to *inquire* about their credit terms.	ask
What *precipitated* the decrease in profits?	caused
Will you please send us a *remittance* for $25.	check
We *utilized* their services twice last month.	used
The shipment was quite *voluminous*.	bulky
Will you please *expedite* delivery?	rush

But what about all those big words you worked so hard to master? The complex word is still appropriate when it (1) enables you to express your thoughts more precisely, (2) replaces several other words, or (3) avoids repetition. Before opting for the big word, however, be certain that you are not communicating at too high a level for the other person.

SELF-CHECK: CHOOSING THE SIMPLER WORD		
Cover the right column until you have chosen substitutes for the italicized words at left.		
1	They did not *apprise* us of their spring sale.	inform
2	We will *compensate* you well for the effort.	pay
3	When was the letter *forwarded?*	mailed *or* sent
4	Shall we *interrogate* our employees about it?	ask *or* question
5	I think that we should *terminate* the program.	end
6	Do you have *verification* of payment?	proof

Okay, so I don't think you're the greatest.

USE SINCERE WORDS

We should avoid expressions of certainty when we are only assuming what the reactions of others might be.

> Example: We are confident that you will rest well on your new waterbed.
> Example: Considering the age of your toaster, we know that you will be pleased with a $10 adjustment.

For all the writer knows, the reader of the first sentence may become seasick on the waterbed; and there is no way that the writer of the second sentence can anticipate the reader's response to the $10 adjustment.

Keeping in mind that broad assumptions such as these tend to irritate and offend, we should word our communications to suit others, not ourselves.

Expressions of surprise are usually nonproductive.

Example: We were very surprised to hear that you are unhappy with your new typewriter.

Example: We have never received a complaint quite like yours.

The first statement indirectly questions authenticity of the customer's complaint, implying that customer dissatisfaction with the product is practically unheard of. The second statement suggests that the customer is unique—even weird, maybe.

We should avoid statements that cast doubt on the integrity or normalcy of others, because the response will almost always be negative.

Qualify your statements to avoid broad generalities.

(no)   Everybody in Congress is opposed to the new energy bill.

(yes) Almost everybody in Congress is opposed to the new energy bill.

When, if ever, did all members of Congress agree on any substantive issue? Use words such as *seems, almost, appears, usually,* and *generally* to qualify your remarks when absolute certainty does not exist. We could improve the sentence further by providing precise numbers of Congressional members who oppose the bill.

SELF-CHECK: USING SINCERE WORDS

Improve each sentence before reading the suggested wording that follows.

1	Shipment was delayed three days by floods in the Midwest, of which you are no doubt aware.
	Shipment was delayed three days by floods in the Midwest.
2	We were shocked to learn of your dissatisfaction with your new calculator.
	If you will return the calculator or take it to any authorized agent, we will be happy to repair or replace it for you.

3	You still have not made payment on the earlier purchase.
	We have no record of your having paid for the earlier purchase.

Tell it like it is, Cindy Lou.

USE OBJECTIVE WORDS

Most business people emphasize the favorable attributes of their products and services, and they deemphasize any unfavorable characteristics. This is the name of the game, right? In doing so, however, they should minimize their use of *est* words (such as *best, greatest, cheapest, largest, fastest, newest*) unless they can support their claims with factual data. Although exaggerated business claims may be viewed as harmless "trade puffery," people soon respond to the overuse of such words with scepticism and mistrust.

We should also avoid the careless use of flowery words such as *tremendous, wonderful, fabulous, spectacular, superb,* and *super* because they tend to confuse. For example, the reader's interpretation of the following sentences may differ drastically from the intended messages:

Example: This mattress is our deluxe model.
Example: The new employee's performance has been superb.

The reader (or listener) of the first statement may think that the retailer is talking about a top-of-the-line mattress, only to discover later that the best mattress is labeled "*super* deluxe." Similarly, the word *superb* in the second sentence could have several meanings, depending on how freely the person making the statement uses such words. It's a matter of economics: Complimentary words are worth considerably more when they are scarce (used sparingly).

Another way to increase your objectivity is to use precise terms.

(no)   We plan to complete construction of the building soon.
(yes) We plan to complete construction of the building by June 13.

The word *soon* could mean next month to the builder but next week to the buyer.

(no)   John can type very fast.
(yes) John can type 65 words per minute.

Typing very fast might mean 65 words to one person but 80 or more to someone else. To be even more precise, we might indicate the length of test taken and the number of errors made.

SELF-CHECK: USING OBJECTIVE WORDS

Improve each sentence before reading the suggested wording that follows.

1	The purchase of this house would be the best investment you could make.
	The purchase of this house would be a wise investment.
2	Sales for 1979 were outstanding.
	Sales for 1979 increased 15 percent over the previous year.
3	This is our high-speed printer.
	This unit prints 10,000 lines per minute.

Things could be worse, Gerald.

EMPHASIZE THE POSITIVE

Rather than stating a thought in a negative way, why not emphasize the positive?

- (no) We cannot process your claim until you complete and return the enclosed form.
- (yes) We will adjust your account as soon as you complete and return the enclosed form.

Instead of telling customers what we cannot do, we tell them what we can do. Avoid negative words such as *cannot, mistake, failure, delay, fault, excuse, cheap, dispute, complaint, blame, reject, claim, sorry,* and *inconvenience.* Words that accuse, scold, or express anger cause people to react defensively to our communications; and we are trying to make friends in our business transactions, not adversaries.

If certain words irritate others, why not replace them with **euphemisms**? Euphemisms are relatively pleasant words and phrases, or, as one student described them, "sugar-coated words." Some people go too far with euphemisms. Rather than referring directly to the dreaded confines of solitary confinement, for example, administrators at one prison dubbed the small chambers as "meditation centers." During the Vietnam encounter, military leaders referred to our bombing attacks on the enemy as "protective reaction," a term that was more acceptable to the people back home. Similarly, directors of our Central Intelligence Agency referred to a group of their employees charged with assassinating certain foreign leaders as the "health adjustment committee."

I am not proposing that business people use euphemisms to deceive; but if we know that a word offends, why not replace it with a less abrasive substitute:

(no)   You had better have a good *alibi* this time.
(yes) You had better have a good *reason* this time.

(no)   Maybe they would be interested in our *cheaper* model.
(yes) Maybe they would be interested in our *less expensive* model.

(no)   We took action immediately upon receipt of your *complaint*.
(yes) We took action immediately upon receipt of your *inquiry*.

Select the "sugar-coated" word when you can do so without distorting the intended message.

SELF-CHECK: EMPHASIZING THE POSITIVE

Improve each sentence before reading the suggested wording that follows.

1	We are not arriving at the airport until 7:45 p.m.
	We will arrive at the airport at 7:45 p.m. on TWA Flight 333.
2	I gave her a serious lecturing.
	I discussed the problem with her.

> 3 | We disputed their claim that prices are lower this year.
> --
> We questioned their statement that prices are lower this year.

But it was good enough for Grandpa.

USE FRESH TERMINOLOGY

When young people in the 1960s approved of something a speaker said, they would yell, "Right on!" It was a clever and effective expression at first, but so many people began using the term that it became a **cliché** (a trite phrase). How would you react today, for instance, if you heard someone say "Right on!" Wouldn't you think of the person as rather corny?

Other examples of phrases that have recently become clichés are "Have a good day," "at this point in time," and "the bottom line." When you hear phrases (or words) repeated often, avoid using them.

Many of the following phrases, all of which should be avoided, were outdated even before the 1960s:

do not hesitate to contact me	same (regarding same)
is to acknowledge receipt of	thanking you in advance
as regards to	the writer *or* undersigned
as per your letter	the above captioned
at an early date	under separate cover
attached hereto *or* herewith	believe you me
attached please find	few and far between
by and large	in connection with
will you kindly	in receipt of
due to the fact that	of the above date
enclosed please find	last but not least
please be advised that	we remain *(at end of letter)*
we trust that	afford us the opportunity to
pursuant to our conversation	due to the fact that
regret to advise	in accordance with
said (the said invoice)	

But how can we remember all these trite phrases so that we can avoid using them? It's easy; simply write as you talk. We don't use such phrases when we are talking; so why should we resort to them when writing?

Some clichés may be classified as "golden oldies": *hit the nail right on the head, beating around the bush, a dime a dozen,* and many others. Avoid using these dated expressions, especially when their use might confuse the person with whom you are communicating.

SELF-CHECK: USING FRESH TERMINOLOGY

Improve each sentence before reading the suggested wording that follows.

1   We wrote to you on December 15 with reference to employment.

   We wrote to you on December 15 about (concerning, regarding) employment.

2   Please do not hesitate to contact us if we can be of further help to you.

   Please let us know if we can help you further.

3   We are today in receipt of the merchandise.

   We received the merchandise today.

Hello, Mrs . . . Miss . . . Ms. Jones.

DESEX YOUR COMMUNICATIONS

In the past, when we referred to a student, a worker, or a member of almost any group, we conveniently used the pronouns *he* and *him.* But with women now constituting nearly half the work force, it is inappropriate to continue this pattern. The most practical way to overcome this deficiency in our communications is to speak and write in the plural form. Rather than referring to an individual, we speak and write in terms of more than one person.

(no) *The auto worker* receives considerably more money than workers in most other industries because *he* belongs to a powerful union.

(yes) *Auto workers* receive considerably more money than workers in most other industries because *they* belong to a powerful union.

All auto workers are not males, as implied in the first statement; therefore, we avoid making a distinction between male and female workers by referring to auto workers as a group.

SELF-CHECK: DESEXING YOUR COMMUNICATIONS

Improve each sentence before reading the suggested wording that follows.

1	Businessmen who are in business for themselves work many hours each week.
	Most people who are in business for themselves work many hours each week.
2	If an investor believes that market prices are going to decline, he sells; if he believes prices are going to rise, he buys.
	If investors believe that market prices are going to decline, they sell; if they believe prices are going to rise, they buy.

And a big 10-4 to you, good buddy.

EMPLOY JARGON SELECTIVELY

The word **jargon,** in the modern sense, refers to terminology that is understood only by members of a particular group. Truckers carry on radio conversations that, until recently, only made sense to truckers. Musicians have a language that is exclusively their own, and the same can be said for mathematicians, geologists, psychologists, sociologists, accountants, and many other groups. When outsiders listen to members of these disciplines conversing with one another, it is similar to overhearing people speaking a foreign language.

The use of jargon isn't necessarily bad. It is more efficient for data processing employees to speak or write to one another of CRTs, CPUs, and IOCs, for example, than to take the extra time that would be required to use nontechnical language. We should always keep the receivers of our communications in mind, however, avoiding terminology that may be "foreign" to them.

Jargon is sometimes defined as slang, and we can usually improve our communications by replacing slang words with more precise ones:

(no) Our trucks are *eating* a lot of gasoline.
(yes) Our trucks are *using* a lot of gasoline.

(no) Their *necks* are *on the line* this time.
(yes) Their *careers (jobs, futures)* are *in jeopardy* this time.

Also avoid word fillers. When we cannot think of the correct word, we sometimes fill the air with such "nonwords" as *and such, and that sort of thing, and what not, etc.,* and the repetitive *ya know, ya know, ya know.* If you catch yourself using word fillers, slow your talking speed to allow time for a better choice of words.

Other words that may be categorized as slang are *get, got, real, really, feel,* and a variety of swear words. Improve your communications by replacing *get* with a more precise word:

(no) He is trying to *get* a spare part for the machine.
(yes) He is trying to *find* a spare part for the machine.

(no) Prices are *getting* very high.
(yes) Prices are *increasing* significantly.

You don't even have to replace *got* with another word; simply delete it from your sentence:

(no) You have *got* every product that we offer.
(yes) You have every product that we offer.

(no) Unions have *got* one important advantage, leverage.
(yes) Unions have one important advantage, leverage.

Improve your communications by replacing *real* and *really* with more acceptable words, or with no word at all:

(no) Her sales presentation was really impressive.
(yes) Her sales presentation was extremely impressive.

(no) That was really nice of them.
(yes) That was nice of them.

Avoid words that suggest we are relying more on emotion than on intellect:

(no)   We *feel* that we will be able to do a better job for you.
(yes) We *believe* that we will be able to do a better job for you.

(no)   We *feel* that Plan C will be best.
(yes) We *have determined* that Plan C will be best.

To avoid the possibility of offending, never use swear words in your business communications.

	SELF-CHECK: **EMPLOYING JARGON SELECTIVELY** *Improve each sentence before reading the suggested wording that follows.*
1	Extended unemployment can wipe out a worker's savings. -- Extended unemployment can deplete a worker's savings.
2	Many businesses have gotten hit by the recession. -- Many businesses have suffered from the recession.
3	That is one item they ain't got. -- That is one item they don't have.

Hey, big spender!

ECONOMIZE ON WORDS

To avoid cluttering our communications with useless words, we should not combine words that have identical meanings:

Instead of stating	*use only*
basic fundamentals	basics *or* fundamentals
but nevertheless	but *or* nevertheless
carbon copy	carbon *or* copy
component part	component *or* part
each and every	each *or* every
free gift	free *or* gift
if and when	if *or* when
rules and regulations	rules *or* regulations
sum total	sum *or* total
thought and consideration	thought *or* consideration
true facts	truth *or* facts

We may also streamline our communications by replacing wordy phrases with one or two words:

Instead of stating	*use only*
afford us an opportunity to	permit us to
we are in agreement	we agree
at the present time	presently *or* now
are in a position to	can
for the purpose of	for
How come?	Why?
give consideration to	consider
in the amount of $25	for $25
in the event that	if
in the neighborhood of	about
in order to	to
in order for	for
in view of the fact	because
subsequent to	after
with reference to	about *or* concerning

Finally, we should avoid the use of needless prepositions:

(no)   Joyce is sorting *out* the files.
(yes) Joyce is sorting the files.

(no)   Set it *down* on the counter, please.
(yes) Set it on the counter, please.

(no)   I wish that they would do a better job of cleaning *up* this office.
(yes) I wish that they would do a better job cleaning this office.

(no)   When are you going *down* to our plant in Puerto Rico?
(yes) When are you going to our plant in Puerto Rico?

(no)   The hardware store was the last place I worked *at.*
(yes) The hardware store was the last place I worked.

	SELF-CHECK: ECONOMIZING ON WORDS
	Improve each sentence before reading the suggested wording that follows.
1	We have asked them to recheck their figures again.
	We have asked them to recheck their figures.
2	We wrote a letter in order to establish a written record of our conversation.
	We wrote a letter to establish a record of our conversation.
3	We are flying over to Houston tomorrow.
	We are flying to Houston tomorrow.

It's "effect"! (Or is it "affect"?)

USE THE CORRECT WORD

One of the worst offenses we can make in our communications is to use a word incorrectly. Let's take a few minutes, therefore, to examine several sets of words that are commonly misused:

affect/effect

To *affect* means to influence; it is an action word that acts upon (influences) a word or words that follow.

Example: The mistake will *affect* (influence) her chance for promotion.

Effect is the result or outcome of something, and it is followed somewhere in the sentence by the word *on*.

Example: What effect (result) will the mistake have *on* your promotion?

We can also use *effect* as an action word meaning to *bring about* or *cause to happen.*

Example: We can *effect* delivery immediately.

between/among

Use *between* when discussing two people or things and *among* when discussing more than two:

Example: Divide the bonus *between* the two employees.
Example: Divide the bonus *among* all 15 employees.

ter/est

Use *ter* words when comparing two people or things and *est* words when comparing more than two.

Example: Jan is a *better* (faster) typist than Jim.
Example: Jan is the *best* (fastest) typist in the office.

number/amount fewer/less

Use *number* and *fewer* when discussing anything that can be counted, and use *amount* and *less* for anything that cannot be counted.

Example: A great *number* of *people* responded to the questionnaire.
Example: Roger has an enormous *amount* of *energy*.
Example: Our new catalog contains *fewer* product *offerings*.
Example: Consumers seem *less enthusiastic* about our new product offerings.

balance/remainder

Use *balance* in an accounting sense, when referring to money that is owed or left over, and use *remainder* for anything other than money that is left over.

Example: The San Jose Bottling Company owes a *balance* of $135.
Example: The *remainder* of the work can be left until morning.

eager/anxious

A person who is *eager* has pleasant expectations; someone who is *anxious* is suffering from a degree of anxiety or fear.

Example: Ted was *eager* to begin his three-week vacation.
Example: Doris was *anxiously* awaiting a reply from the Internal Revenue Service.

compliment/complement

Use *compliment* (with an *i*) to praise someone and *complement* to discuss things or people that go well together.

Example: The boss *complimented* Martha on a job well done.
Example: The new files *complement* the office decor.

continuous/continual

Anything that is *continuous* is without pause; something that is *continual* occurs regularly but with interruption.

Example: The roar of the machine was *continuous*.
Example: The ringing of the phone was a *continual* irritation.

farther/further

Farther (beginning with *far*) pertains to distance, and *further* concerns degree or anything other than distance.

Example: How much *farther* is it to the airport?
Example: Let's discuss the proposal *further*, shall we?

in/into

In deals with location, and *into* involves action.

Example: The files are *in* the bottom drawer.
Example: Jamie tossed the files *into* the bottom drawer.

principle/principal

Principle refers to a law or an assumption; *principal* can refer either to the head of a high school, to something that is most important, or to money.

Example: A general *principle* of business management is that each employee report to only one superior.
Example: Ms. Prescott is *principal* of West High School.
Example: Profit maximization is our *principal* (major) objective.
Example: The payments are $250, including *principal* and interest.

advise/advice

Advise is something that we do, and *advice* is something that we give or receive.

Example: Be sure to *advise* her of her rights.
Example: The personnel manager gave us some good *advice.*

accept/except

When we *accept,* we receive; when we *except,* we exclude.

Example: Did the new employee *accept* your advice?
Example: All employees *except* José are members of the union.

cite/sight/site

To *cite* means to present; whereas *sight* refers to vision and *site* to location.

Example: Employees *cited* Article 34 of the union contract as grounds for their action.
Example: They will check your *sight* to make certain that it is perfect.
Example: This land is the *site* for our new assembly plant.

capitol/capital

Capitol is the name for the main government building; *capital* refers to the main city of a state, province, or country, or to possessions of monetary value, including money.

Example: He will be at the *capitol* building all day tomorrow.

Example: Edmonton is the *capital* of Alberta.

Example: Business properties such as vehicles and machinery are called *capital* goods.

Example: She invested nearly all of her *capital* (money) in the common stock of IBM Corporation.

self/selves

These affixes help us form reflexive words. The decision of whether to use *me* or *myself*, for example, depends on the first part of the sentence.

Example: Will *you* tell them something about *me*?

Example: May *I* tell you something about *myself*?

To use a word with *self* or *selves*, we must be referring to the same person or persons mentioned elsewhere in the sentence. We use *me* in the first example, because *me* and *you* are not the same person. We use *myself* in the second example, on the other hand, because *myself* and *I* are the same person. Also consider the following examples:

(no)   *I* like *me*.

(yes) *I* like *myself*.

(no)   Why don't *you* take a closer look at *you*?

(yes) Why don't *you* take a closer look at *yourself*?

(no)   *They* (children) don't always do what is best for *them*.

(yes) *They* don't always do what is best for *themselves*.

I/me he/him she/her they/them we/us who/whom

We use *I, he, she, they, we,* and *who* as subjects for our sentences—as the person, place, or thing that is the center of discussion (usually at the beginning of the sentence).

Example: *I* will be there.

Example: Tom and *I* will be there.

Example: *We* plan to take immediate action.

Example: *They* have guaranteed delivery by 2:00 p.m.

Example: *Who* issues the contracts?

We also use these words with *is* and *were*.

Example: This *is she*. (when answering the telephone, perhaps)

Example: If it *were I* making the decisions, things would be different.

We use *me, him, her, them, us,* and *whom* in all other situations (usually at the end of the sentence or clause).

Example: Did you phone *him*?
Example: Hand the letter to *her*, please.
Example: The agreement was between *him* and *me.*

If *who* and *whom* still give you trouble, here is an easy rule to follow. If you can substitute either *he* or *she*, you should use *who*.

Example: *Who* is responsible for petty cash? (*She* is responsible.)

The sentence makes sense if we replace *who* with *he* or *she*, so we use *who.* If the word can be replaced with *her* or *him,* on the other hand, we use *whom.*

Example: You are waiting for *whom*? (You are waiting for *him.*)

If we replaced *whom* with *he* or *she,* the sentence wouldn't make sense, but *him* or *her* fits nicely; therefore, we use *whom.*

The distinction between *who* and *whom* is becoming less important each year, so when in doubt, use *who.* Similarly, when we are confronted with a choice between *whoever* and *whomever,* current practices dictate that we use *whoever.*

who/which/that

Who refers only to people, and *which* refers only to things or animals. *That* is more flexible, applying to persons, things, or animals.

Example: Rhonda is the employee *who* (that) received the award.
Example: Is this the machine *that* is broken?

datum/data

Datum is singular for *data,* but it is seldom used. Many business people erroneously use *data* as a singular word, but most writers of business magazines and textbooks use it correctly.

(no)   Is this the data you wanted?
(yes)   Are *these* the *data* you wanted?

(no)   This data is incomplete.
(yes)   *These data* are incomplete.

all ready/already

All ready describes a mutual state of readiness or preparedness; *already* means *prior to a specified time.*

Example: The members were *all ready* to begin the meeting.
Example: The purchasing manager had *already* placed the order.

all together/altogether

All together refers to a group as a whole, and *altogether* means completely.

Example: The machine parts were *all together* on the shop floor.
Example: The marketing manager developed an *altogether* different
           approach for introducing the new product.

SELF-CHECK: USING THE CORRECT WORD

Cover the words in the column at right until you have decided on the correct word.

1	How will the transfer (affect/effect) her future?	affect
2	Which approach would be (better/best), dividing the overtime (between/among) Janet and Rod or (between/among) all three employees?	better between among
3	A large (number/amount) of customers appear (anxious/eager) for our spring sale to begin.	number eager
4	Randy is (continuously/continually) (complimenting/complementing) employees on the quality of their work.	continually complimenting
5	There is one envelope for (you/yourself) and one for (me/myself).	you me
6	The argument is strictly between Jack and (I/me).	me

7	To (who/whom) did you say to hand the report?	whom
8	Yes, Mr. Prentiss, it was (they/them) who called.	they
9	He is the employee (that/which) we hired last week.	that
10	Will shipping our products from a plant that is (farther/further) away have a significant (affect/effect) on our costs?	farther effect

QUIZ: CHOOSING THE BEST WORDS

Improve the following sentences where needed.

1. We regret to inform you that we cannot ship your order until June 3 because of a shortage of raw materials; we trust that the delay will not inconvenience you too greatly.

2. We want to acknowledge receipt of your letter and to thank you for your business.

3. When will they be in position to implement the program?

4. We know that you will like our new Toasty-Woasty cereal because it is cheaper than other brands.

5. How come the government came down on them so hard?

6. Businessmen should pay more closer attention to ethics and stuff, you know.

7. If an applicant is to receive a credit card, he must entirely complete the application.

8. Which of these soft drinks do you like better: A, B, or C?

9. When you finish cleaning off the counter, will you recheck the cash register one more time?

10. To who do they want to sell it, to Scott or to he?

11. Do you feel that me being at the meeting will have a positive affect on the group?

12. We cannot understand your reasoning, but we are willing to discuss your complaint farther.

13. Although the mailman always delivers our mail on time, the manager complains about the postal service continuously.

14. With our own corporate jet, we can get to our plant in Florida much faster than when using a commercial airline.

15. We received your complaint, but we cannot process your claim until you fill out and return the enclosed form.

16. No, the adjustment will not affect your credit record.

17. The payments on your new home will be $365 per month, including principle, interest, and taxes.

18. You worry about yourself, and I'll be concerned about me.

19. Whom is in charge of the personnel department?

20. Is this the data you requested?

6

FORMING SENTENCES AND PARAGRAPHS

If we were to think of writing as a puzzle, which many people seem to do, we would find that we have already familiarized ourselves with important parts of the puzzle: mechanics, punctuation, and word choice. Now all we have to do is put the parts of the puzzle together to form interesting sentences and paragraphs.

Sentence fragments are immature.

SENTENCE STRUCTURE

Let's begin by making sure that we know a complete sentence when we see one. To be complete, a sentence must have a person, a thing, or an event (the subject of the sentence) involved in some kind of physical or mental activity (the predicate or action part of the sentence).

(no) Believed that stock prices were going to decline.

(yes) John believed that stock prices were going to decline.

The first example is a **sentence fragment** because it doesn't have a subject; it doesn't tell us who believed that stock prices were going to decline. The second example is a **complete sentence** because we have added *John* as a subject, as someone who performs the mental action that follows.

(no) The size and shape of the office and the amount of protection needed.

(yes) The size and shape of the office and the amount of protection needed are two important considerations.

The first example is a fragment because it is without a predicate. Adding the action phrase *are two important considerations* to the second example gives us a complete sentence.

Action phrases (predicates) must contain verbs (action words) such as *is, are, was, were, wrote, said, spoke, studied, am going to, have written,* and *will try to.* The subjects in the following examples are underscored once, and the predicates are underscored twice.

Example: Small investors pay higher brokerage fees than large ones do.

Example: Are you going to request a stock certificate?

Example: Investors do not need to pay cash for the total amount of their investments.

Example: The idea gained popularity very quickly.

Example: The most that investors can lose in the stock market is the amount that they originally pay for their stocks.

Example: Check the price of wheat when you talk with them.

We assume the subject of the final example to be *you,* even though it isn't shown. Why? Because we sometimes talk and write in this abbreviated manner.

When we add words like *although, because,* and *since* to the beginning of a complete sentence, the sentence sometimes becomes a fragment.

Complete: Most people who join informal work groups do so for increased security.

Fragment: *Since* most people who join informal work groups do so for increased security.

Both examples include a subject and a predicate, but the word *since* makes the second sentence incomplete. By itself, the statement doesn't make sense. So why do we add such words to our statements? We do so when we are going to combine them with other sentences.

Complete: Since most people who join informal work groups do so for increased security, management may dissuade employees from joining such groups by helping them feel more secure in their jobs.

Adding the word *since* changed the first part of the sentence into a dependent clause (a fragment if used alone), which we added to an independent clause (a complete sentence in itself). The resulting statement is a complex sentence.

Do you remember the three structural types of sentences? We may use either simple, complex, or compound sentences in our communications, or a combination of all three types. The preceding examples (except for the last one) are **simple sentences** because they contain only one subject and only one predicate. When we add a dependent clause or phrase (a fragment) to a simple sentence, we refer to the resulting combination as a **complex sentence**.

Fragment: In most small companies.

Simple: One manager handles all personnel problems.

Complex: In most small companies, one manager handles all personnel problems.

We bring the dependent phrase (fragment) and the simple sentence together to form one complex sentence. Could we have added the dependent clause to the end of the simple sentence rather than at the beginning? Certainly!

Example: One manager handles all personnel problems in most small companies.

The way you form a sentence depends on which way sounds most natural to you, and the choice generally depends on what you have said or written just before.

Notice that no comma is required when we place the dependent phrase at the end of the sentence, because it reads well without one.

A dependent phrase (fragment if used alone) is placed within the following simple sentence, rather than at the beginning or end of the sentence:

Example: The manager, breaking with tradition, permitted a new employee to make the bank deposit.

If you question the need for commas to set off the dependent phrase, try reading the sentence without pausing where the commas are now placed.

We form **compound sentences** by combining two complete sentences:

Complex: While applicants are talking, interviewers usually record the answers to important questions.

Simple: Applicants should use care when responding to questions.

Compound: While applicants are talking, interviewers usually record the answers to important questions; therefore, applicants should use care when responding to questions.

(If you do not know why we used a semicolon and a comma with the connecting word *therefore,* you should review these forms of punctuation on page 55.)

So what kinds of sentences do we use—simple, complex, or compound? We use all three types of sentences, while avoiding the overuse or underuse of any one pattern. The following paragraph helps to illustrate this important point:

> We received your order this morning. The credit manager approved your request. We are receiving a new supply of 24/8 oz. peaches tomorrow morning. We will ship your order as soon as the peaches are received. Consolidated Freightways will deliver the order to you in about four days.

Try reading the paragraph aloud. When we use too many simple sentences, we irritate our readers. We don't talk in this choppy fashion, so why should we write that way? Streamline your writing by combining some of your thoughts into complex and compound sentences. Doesn't the following paragraph read better than the previous one?

> The credit manager approved your request, which we received this morning; and we will ship your order tomorrow morning, immediately upon receipt of a new supply of 24/8 oz. peaches. You may expect delivery by Consolidated Freightways in about four days.

This is not to suggest that you avoid simple sentences entirely; they are just as important as complex and compound sentences. We use all three types of sentences so that we may write naturally, the same way we talk. We may even combine simple and complex sentences or two complex sentences into one, so long as we do not permit the sentence to become too long or too complicated.

SELF-CHECK: SENTENCE STRUCTURE

Before looking at the answers in the column on the right, determine whether the statements are fragments or simple, complex, or compound sentences.

1	If department managers judge an employee's performance to be inadequate, they should dismiss the employee.	complex
2	A much more effective practice, however, is to choose an employee within the department to show the new employee around.	simple

3	The business concepts of planning, organizing, leading, and controlling.	fragment
4	Employers should begin all training programs with an analysis of company needs.	simple
5	Some employees are paid hourly wages; others participate in incentive programs.	compound
6	Although she is usually responsible for arranging insurance coverage for employees.	fragment

Don't change mopeds in the middle of a stream.

SUBJECT-VERB AGREEMENT

We must keep our subjects and verbs in agreement, and we can easily do so by keeping our subjects firmly in mind.

Example: The production manager was at the meeting.

Example: The production manager and his assistant were at the meeting.

The production manager is the singular subject of the first example, which requires the singular verb *was. The production manager and his assistant* (joined with the word *and*) is the plural subject of the second example, which requires the plural verb *were.*

When we have the connecting words *or* or *nor* in the subject, rather than *and,* we pick a verb to agree with the part of the subject that follows the word *or* or *nor.*

Example: Either Mr. Brown or his employees are responsible for the overcharge.

Example: Neither the employees nor their supervisor is responsible for the overcharge.

In the first example, the plural verb *are* agrees with the plural part of the subject *his employees.* In the second example, the singular verb *is* agrees with *their supervisor.* You wouldn't say "His employees *is* responsible" or "Their supervisor *are* responsible."

When we place a dependent phrase or clause between the subject and the verb, we must be especially careful to choose the correct verb.

Example: Mr. Brown, not his employees, is responsible for the over-charge.

Example: The success of all the programs depends on teamwork.

The verb *is* in the first example relates to *Mr. Brown,* and the verb *depends* in the second example relates to *success,* not *programs,* even though the word *programs* is placed next to the verb.

Although we may be thinking of an entire group of people when we use the words *each, everyone,* and *everybody,* we must match them with singular verbs.

Example: Each employee is responsible for his or her own timecard.

Example: Everyone at the meeting was in agreement.

Example: Everybody at the meeting was pleased with her presentation.

The word *none* presents a special problem. We treat it as a singular word in formal communications and as a plural word in informal communications.

Formal: None (not one) of these problems is insurmountable.

Informal: None of these problems are insurmountable.

Which form should you use? We recommend the formal wording only when writing term papers for college courses; rely on the informal usage at all other times.

We must also pay special attention to our use of the word *number.* Treat the word as singular when it is preceded by *the* and make it plural when preceded by *a.*

Example: The number of employees who are qualified for the position is insignificant.

Example: A large number of employees are qualified for the position.

We must make certain that the action part of our sentences relates to the intended subject.

(no) Hundreds of thousands of jobs will become available each year because of the need to replace *those* who die or retire.

(yes) Hundreds of thousands of jobs will become available each year because of the need to replace *employees* who die or retire.

The first sentence suggests that the jobs will die or retire. We avoid confusion by replacing the word *those* with *employees.*

Also consider the following statement written by a student in a business communications class:

(no) I alerted the manager, and he was caught trying to leave the store without paying.

(yes) I alerted the manager, and he caught the person trying to leave the store without paying.

The first statement suggests that the manager was caught stealing, which was certainly not the intended message.

To avoid repeating words, we often use word substitutes. When doing so, we must make certain that the substitutes agree with the words they are modifying.

(no) If *a creditor* violates truth-in-lending laws, *they* are subject to a $10,000 fine.

(yes) If *a creditor* violates truth-in-lending laws, *he* or *she* is subject to a $10,000 fine.

(yes) If *creditors* violate truth-in-lending laws, *they* are subject to fines of $10,000.

By using a plural subject (*creditors*), a plural verb (*are*), and a plural substitute (*they*) in the final example, we can avoid a gender preference (*he, she*).

When we begin sentences with the words *there* and *it,* which should be done sparingly, we must know what they relate to before deciding which verb to use.

Example: *There is* (or *There's*) *a new employee* in the accounting department.

Example: *There are several items* on the agenda today.

We can use *There is* or *There's* in the first example because we are discussing only one of something (a person, in this instance). We must use

There are in the second example, rather than the widely misused *There's,* because we are discussing more than one of something.

Similarly, we must keep our tenses straight. Rather than discussing past, present, and future events interchangeably, we must decide which time frame we want to use and stick with it.

(no)   When employees *are* unionized, they usually *began* the grievance
        procedure with complaints to their union representatives.
(yes) When employees *are* unionized, they usually *begin* the grievance
        procedure with complaints to their union representatives.

The first example switches from the present (*are*) to the past (*began*). To keep the tenses parallel in the second example, we relate the present (*are*) to the present (*begin*).

Try to maintain this consistency within each of your paragraphs, changing tenses from one paragraph to another only when there is an obvious need to do so.

SELF-CHECK: SUBJECT-VERB AGREEMENT

Determine what, if anything, is wrong with each sentence before looking at the correct versions.

1	Everyone is asked to contribute their time to the cause.
	Everyone is asked to contribute *his* or *her* time to the cause.
2	Which one of the employees are responsible for the error?
	Which *one* of the employees *is* responsible for the error?
3	The chairman of the board and his assistant are planning the meeting.
	Correct as shown, using a plural verb with a plural subject.

4	A large number of adjustments is involved, but none of them is very complicated. (Assume that this communication is informal.)
	A large <u>number</u> of adjustments <u>are</u> involved, but <u>none</u> of them <u>are</u> very complicated.
5	While discussing the problem with my supervisor, the idea occurred to me.
	The idea occurred to me while I was discussing the problem with my supervisor.
	(First sentence suggests that the idea was discussing the problem with the supervisor.)
6	More females attain management positions in personnel departments than she does in any other area of business.
	More *females* attain management positions in personnel departments than *they* do in any other area of business.
7	There's several reasons for responding promptly to inquiries.
	There *are several reasons* for responding promptly to inquiries.
	or
	The *reasons* for responding promptly to inquiries *are* . . .

. . . five, fourth, 3rd, secondly, 1, blast-off!

PARALLEL CONSTRUCTION

We must keep other parts of sentences in agreement with one another as well as the subjects and verbs, to maintain parallelism in our speaking and our writing.

Avoid **double negatives;** rather than accompany negative words such as *aren't, isn't, won't,* and *cannot* with the negative words *none* or *nothing,* use the positive words *any* or *anything.*

(no)   We *aren't* going to send *none* of them to San Francisco.
(yes)   We *aren't* going to send *any* of them to San Francisco.

(no)   I *don't* have *nothing* to do with setting company policy.
(yes)   I *don't* have *anything* to do with setting company policy.

Similarly, be certain to accompany the word *hardly* with positive words.

(no)   We *can't hardly* wait until the new supplies are received.
(yes)   We *can hardly* wait until the new supplies are received.

Also avoid contradicting yourself by including a word that doesn't agree with what you have already said.

(no)   There is *absolutely no way* we can complete the order today *unless* we work overtime.
(yes)   The only way we can complete the order today is by working overtime.

Finally, we must maintain **parallelism** among the elements of a series.

(no)   The assistant personnel manager is responsible for hiring employees, training an employee, promotions, and to discipline employees.
(yes)   The assistant personnel manager is responsible for hiring, training, promoting, and disciplining employees.
(yes)   The assistant personnel manager's responsibility is to hire, train, promote, and discipline employees.

One element of the first example refers to *employees* (plural) while another refers to *an employee* (singular). Two elements begin with *ing* words, and one is an infinitive (*to discipline*).

We achieve parallelism in the second example by using *ing* in each element of the series and by using the word *employees* only once, at the end of the sentence; and we make the third example parallel by using infinitives (to hire, to train, etc.), but dropping the word *to* on all but the first element. Consider these additional examples of parallelism:

(no)   firstly, secondly, and third
(yes)   first, second, and third

(no)   (1), (2), finally . . .
(yes)   (1), (2), (3)

(no)   recruit applicants, test applicants, interviewing applicants
(yes) recruit, test, and interview applicants
(yes) recruiting, testing, and interviewing applicants

	SELF-CHECK: PARALLEL CONSTRUCTION *Determine what is wrong with each sentence, if anything, before looking at the correct version.*
1	I handled payroll records, accounts receivable assistant, checking invoices, and some typing. I handled payroll records, assisted with accounts receivable, checked invoices, and typed letters.
2	They delivered 24 cases of peaches, but we didn't want none until next week. They delivered 24 cases of peaches, but we didn't want any until next week.
3	I don't believe that Jody should be given a raise, and that's final. Jody shouldn't be given a raise, and that's final.
4	First, we must concentrate on increasing net sales. Secondly, we must search for ways to reduce costs and expenses. First, we must concentrate on increasing net sales. Second, we must search for ways to reduce costs and expenses.

Variety is the spice of writing.

INTERESTING SENTENCES

We can pump some life into our sentences by avoiding repetition, by using directive words, and by employing active construction. We often may eliminate repetition from sentences by simply deleting one or two words.

Example: We hope that you will *reapply* with our company *again* next summer.

Example: There are *at present* 300 million credit cards *now* in use.

Reapply and *again* are redundant, so one should be deleted; the same is true of *at present* and *now* in the second example.

Rather than repeating the names of places or things, vary your word choice.

(no)   *Auditors* didn't have to contend with computers in the past; now *auditors* must be familiar with the operational characteristics of computer systems.

(yes)   *Auditors* didn't have to contend with computers in the past; now *they* must be familiar with the operational characteristics of computer systems.

(no)   His behavior affects the *help* that he hires to *help* do the work.

(yes)   His behavior affects the *people* that he hires to *help* do the work.

(no)   Any way we do *it, it* will be costly.

(yes)   Any way we do *it, the process* will be costly.

And, therefore, similarly, accordingly, moreover, consequently, and *correspondingly* are examples of **directive words**. They inform the reader or listener of the direction of our thoughts—in this case, that our thoughts are continuing in the same direction as before. Directive words that inform others we are "shifting gears" by going in a different direction include *but, however, nevertheless,* and *whereas*.

Without: Jean Meadows related well to representatives of truck lines, rail carriers, and steamship companies. When she was chosen to replace the retiring traffic manager she did not perform as well as expected.

With: Jean Meadows related well to representatives of truck lines, rail carriers, and steamship companies. When she was chosen to replace the retiring traffic manager, *however,* she did not perform as well as expected.

Because we previously made a positive statement, the word *however* alerts the reader that we are switching to a negative result. Without the directive word, the reader would flounder.

Without: Many studies have illustrated that a manager's recognition of a job well done will motivate employees to work harder. We should observe and comment when employees perform well.

With: Many studies have illustrated that a manager's recognition of a job well done will motivate employees to work harder; *therefore,* we should observe and comment when employees perform well.

The directive word *therefore* provides continuity by guiding the reader (or listener) through a "because of *that,* then *this*" pattern of logic.

Although we may improve the flow of our thoughts with directive words, overusing them will make our communications sound artificial.

We may control the tone of our communications somewhat by placing directive words at different places within our sentences. The word *therefore* may be placed in any of three places in the following statement:

Example: *Therefore,* we should be hearing a lot more about wage and price controls.

Example: We should be hearing a lot more, *therefore,* about wage and price controls.

Example: We should be hearing a lot more about wage and price controls, *therefore.*

So where do we place directive words—at the beginning, middle, or end of our sentences? You must decide which arrangement sounds best. The first and third sentences sound natural, but the second sounds awkward. The positioning of directive words depends to a great extent on what has just been said or written.

Punctuation helps our readers, right? Of course, but punctuation also slows readers. Commas cause readers to pause, semicolons represent even longer pauses, and periods bring readers to an abrupt halt. When possible, therefore, we should form our sentences in ways that will minimize punctuation.

(no)   *For example,* students may work toward four-year degrees, but they will usually perform better if they concentrate on just one semester at a time.

(yes) Students may work toward four-year degrees, *for example,* but they will usually perform better if they concentrate on just one semester at a time.

We need a comma before the connecting word *but,* so we place *for example* at that point; we slow the reader only once instead of twice by breaking the sentence with punctuation only one place in the sentence instead of two.

By placing the dependent clause at the end of a sentence rather than at the beginning, we can usually avoid slowing the reader with a comma.

(no)   *To inform upper management of progress made,* accountants prepare charts and graphs every three months.

(yes) Accountants prepare charts and graphs every three months *to inform upper management of progress made.*

We may avoid slowing the reader with an unnecessary period by combining two sentences into one.

(no)   Some managers make business the center of their lives. They spend many hours at work each week.

(yes) Some managers make business the center of their lives, spending many hours at work each week.

We converted two simple sentences to one complex sentence.

All well-written books, magazines, and newspapers are written in **active voice**. All you have to do to make your writing active is to use people, places, and things as the subjects of your sentences.

Passive: The program was coordinated by Miss Bassett.
Active: Miss Bassett coordinated the program.

Passive: The idea of divestiture, the "breaking up" of giant oil companies, is now being considered by Congress.
Active: Congress is now considering the idea of divestiture, the "breaking up" of giant oil companies.

Writing in active voice makes our writing more interesting to read. When we happen to be discussing a topic that is unpleasant, however, we can soften our statements by using **passive voice**.

Active: Mike made three serious errors in this income statement.
Passive: This income statement contains three serious errors.

Passive voice makes the sentence less accusatory. Rather than using the person's name as the subject of this negative message, we remove *Mike* from the sentence entirely.

Make your sentences more interesting by telling the reader what the catch-all word *this* actually stands for.

(no)   This is expected to increase to $125 billion by 1985.
(yes)   *This amount* is expected to increase to $125 billion by 1985.

(no)   Everyone wants to be treated fairly; this is normal.
(yes)   Everyone wants to be treated fairly; *this reaction* is normal.

A final way to make your sentences more interesting is to minimize the use of *it* and *there* at the beginning of sentences.

(no)   It is suggested that we meet again on October 16.
(yes)   I suggest that we meet again on October 16.

(no)   There is an important reason for postponing the project, insufficient funds.
(yes)   The main reason for postponing the project is insufficient funds.

You may, however, be unable to avoid such lackluster beginnings in some sentences, especially when writing without the use of personal pronouns (I, we, you) in formal reports.

SELF-CHECK: INTERESTING SENTENCES

Check to see how you would improve each sentence before looking at the improved version.

1 | Since marketing employees make such an important contribution to profits, marketing employees should be paid more.

Since *marketing employees* make such an important contribution to profits, *they* should be paid more.

2	Employees must be able to respond to a wide range of questions. New employees participate in a two-week training session before actually beginning work.
	Each employee must be able to respond to a wide range of questions. *Correspondingly* (*Therefore, Accordingly, Consequently*), new employees participate in a two-week training session before actually beginning work. (Could also combine into one sentence.)
3	Mr. Davis, in an attempt to avoid a late charge, predated his check.
	In an attempt to avoid a late charge, Mr. Davis predated his check.
	or
	Mr. Davis predated his check, in an attempt to avoid paying a late charge.
4	The $3,000 sale was made by Sylvia Blair.
	Sylvia Blair made the $3,000 sale.
5	We must first identify the main selling points of our new product. This may help us convince customers to buy more.
	We must first identify the main selling points of our new product. This *information* may help us convince customers to buy more.
	or
	We must first identify the main selling points of our new product, to help us convince customers to buy more.
6	It's going to be a very profitable year.
	Profits will be very high this year.

Short is beautiful; pass it on.

PARAGRAPH STRUCTURE

You have been told to group related sentences into paragraphs, but this guideline doesn't mean that you must exhaust an idea before beginning a new paragraph. After writing two or three sentences, look for the slightest reason to end the paragraph and begin a new one: a new subject, a different time period, a change of mood, a new stage of development, a switch from a negative concept to a positive one (or vice versa). Why? Because paragraphs that are too long appear forbidding to the reader.

Notice that most newspaper and magazine articles begin with very short paragraphs, usually made up of only one sentence. This pattern exists because newspaper and magazine editors know that readers are more likely to read a particular article when the paragraphs are relatively short—especially the beginning paragraph.

So just how short or long should you make your paragraphs? A paragraph in a letter may range anywhere from a single line to as many as 12 or 14 lines. A paragraph in a business report, on the other hand, may range from as few as 4 or 5 lines to as many as 18 or 20, with anywhere from 8 to 12 lines as a desirable average. The practice of continuing a paragraph for an entire page or more is no longer acceptable.

QUIZ: SENTENCES AND PARAGRAPHS

1. Use any textbook, other than this one, to find and record the following kinds of sentences:
   a. Simple
   b. Complex
   c. Compound (two simple sentences combined)
   d. Compound (one simple sentence and one complex sentence combined)
   e. Compound (two complex sentences combined)

2. Determine which of the following statements are complex sentences or fragments. Then, using your own words, convert the fragments to complete sentences:
   a. In today's economy, alternative sources of power.
   b. Supplies of electricity produced from fuel oil, on the other hand.
   c. Must determine what kinds of buildings will be needed.

    d. The machines and equipment must be arranged according to a plan that will permit an efficient flow of raw materials and finished goods.

    e. Permit their employees to set their own hours, within certain limits.

    f. Are responsible for maintaining the quality of products.

    g. "Payola" is a more acceptable word than "bribes," perhaps, but the meanings are similar.

    h. Should base their product decisions on market research.

    i. There's a few more customers awaiting service.

3. Check the following sentences for parallel construction and make any needed corrections:

    a. If a business is to increase profits, their products must be widely advertised.

    b. Inflation and unemployment is two problems that seems impossible to resolve.

    c. Three other employees and I was at the convention.

    d. Mr. Green and his assistants were honored at the awards banquet.

    e. Neither Ms. Smith nor her assistants was present to accept the award.

    f. Every one of our customers have claimed a refund of the overcharge.

    g. Everybody, including all the new employees, were invited to the company party.

    h. The number of labels that you ordered were insufficient.

    i. When a person uses only their own money to begin a business, we refer to the business as a "sole proprietorship."

    j. More than 26 trained guards was assigned to the security force.

    k. When a teenager is earning the minimum wage, they received the same wage as many adults earn.

    l. When no competition exists, businesses charged monopolistic prices.

    m. The price that consumers see when they look at a sticker on the window of a new car was the manufacturer's suggested price.

    n. When retailers disappoint customers, they often will not do business with them again.

    o. We are confident that the new word-processing system will be a very big seller, we believe.

    p. I can't hardly realize that holiday sales are already underway.

    q. I instructed the owner's of the new custodial service to scrub the floors, polishing the woodwork, wash the desks, and to make certain that all doors are locked before leaving.

    r. Please make certain that we don't sell none of the new stock before the older stock has all been sold.

    s. When interviewing Ms. Jamison, the telephone rang twice.

4. Eliminate any repetitive elements that you can identify in the following sentences:
   a. Be sure to submit right away a reasonably low bid on the government contract by July 15.
   b. College graduates are in greater demand than people without degrees; therefore, college graduates are more likely to find employment.
   c. Ask the sales manager if he plans to repeat the sale again this spring.

5. Change the following sentences to active voice:
   a. Merchandise brokers are used by many companies.
   b. Computers and computer equipment are referred to as "hardware" by people in the computer industry.
   c. Details of the program were presented by Margaret Lance.

6. Change the following sentences to passive voice:
   a. Mike Jacob didn't double-check all items on the shipping list.
   b. You failed to show our purchase number on the invoice.
   c. Tina Juarez, the assistant personnel manager, rejected all three applicants.

7

GETTING READY
TO COMMUNICATE

Getting ready to communicate? But, you ask, isn't that what I have been doing for the last two or three chapters? Yes you have, and this chapter builds on that knowledge by showing you how to plan your messages and how to communicate naturally. Although this chapter is relatively brief, you may find it the most valuable section of the book. If you give the suggested methods of planning a try and follow the S★T★A★R guidelines, you will find that communicating well is a lot easier than you thought it was.

Full speed in the right direction

PLANNING THE COMMUNICATION

Whether you are playing chess, striving for a touchdown, driving to work, or taking an essay examination, you need a plan. The same statement is true of business communications; before you reach for the telephone or begin pounding the typewriter, take a minute to plan the best strategy.

Identify the objective. What do you want to accomplish with the communication? What is the desired response? If your ultimate goal is to land a job, the immediate objective may be to secure an interview. When refusing credit to a potential customer, one objective may be to retain the person's goodwill. In responding to a routine inquiry about a product, your underlying objective will be to make a sale. Identify the objective of your communication and keep it your primary focus throughout the communicative process.

Select the medium. Once you have established the objective (or multiple objectives) of your communication, you must choose the best medium for transmitting the message. The different levels of communication media are illustrated in Figure 7-1.

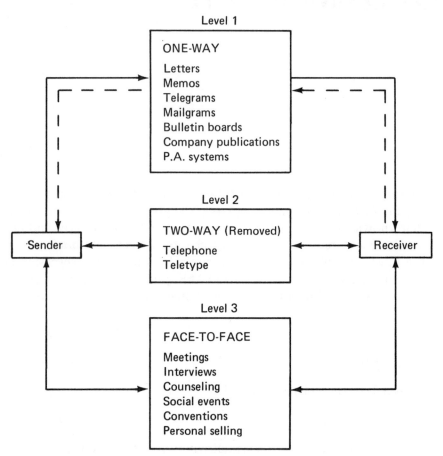

Figure 7-1 Levels of communication media (dotted line represents delayed feedback).

Level 1 communications are one way, and a response (dotted line) may take anywhere from several hours (telegrams) to several days or weeks (letters, memos, and mailgrams). Both Level 2 and Level 3 media provide you with immediate feedback (notice that the arrows point in both directions), and Level 3 media add the extra opportunity to observe the other person's actions and reactions.

Your choice of the most effective medium for transmitting a message depends to a great extent on the content of the message. What is the length of the message? How important is it? What are the cost considerations? Is the message routine or urgent? How soon do you need a response? Is a permanent record of the communication needed? Which medium is most likely to motivate the other person to respond in the desired manner?

An intelligent choice of media requires a thorough knowledge of the characteristics of each medium and the exercise of good judgment. Although it may appear less costly to write or phone a customer instead of traveling to his or her place of business, a personal demonstration of your product might secure the sale where the letter or phone call would not. Similarly, issuing a bulletin to a group of employees may appear to be the least costly method of communication, but group meetings would provide invaluable feedback not realized with a bulletin. The attributes of each of the three levels of communication are discussed at length in the following chapters, to help you decide which media are most effective in a wide variety of business situations.

Organize the message. A common mistake many students make is to begin writing answers to essay questions before developing a comprehensive plan of attack. Such students have difficulty concentrating on what they are writing because their minds must search for each element of the answer as they go along. Panic sets in when the ideas don't come in a steady flow, when they realize that they have omitted key points or, worse yet, when they must start over. How much easier and more effective it is to outline key points first! Then, rather than worrying about the order of ideas, they are free to concentrate on quality of expression.

Many business people fall into a similar trap. They start writing before deciding what they want to say or the order in which they are to say it. They are disorganized, and their communications show it. Rather than moving from one idea to the next in a logical sequence, they scatter their thoughts and their communications lack impact.

Whether you are answering a test question or communicating in business, you may keep your thoughts on track by taking the time to organize your ideas—before you start communicating. Identify the key points to be made, and then organize them from past to present, from the most important to the least important or vice versa, alphabetically or geographically. Use whichever approach you judge to be most appropriate for the situation at hand, and then do your writing in a comparatively relaxed and systematic manner.

Time the transmittal. Timing is an important consideration with most of our communications. Do we have time to wait for a response to our letter, or should we phone? If we are writing to someone in a distant city, we can expect to wait anywhere from eight to ten days for a reply—assuming that the other person answers promptly.

Timing is even more important when phoning. When people at one end of the country phone people at the other end, they must allow for a three-hour time differential. When it is 3:00 p.m. in Los Angeles, for example, the clocks in New York City read 6:00 p.m., meaning that most of the offices there are closed. Conversely, if a New Yorker places a 9:00 a.m. call to San Francisco, the offices in that Western city will not yet have opened.

We should use empathy where other people are concerned. Unless our communication is urgent, we should avoid phoning others the first thing in the morning—before they have had a chance to organize their activities for the day. It is also considered bad manners to phone someone just before closing time, especially on a Friday, unless the message is very important. Many people believe that a psychological advantage is to be gained by placing phone calls early in the afternoon, theorizing that people are more relaxed and receptive after having resolved most of their pressing problems during the morning hours and just after having eaten lunch.

<u>But I want to be a superstar.</u>

USING THE S★T★A★R APPROACH

Wouldn't it be great if we could follow some formula that would guarantee our success as business communicators? Although there is no such formula, we will communicate better by keeping four important guidelines in mind:

★**S**ERVICE

★**T**IME

★**A**UDIENCE

★**R**EASON

We may combine the first letters of these four words to form the word STAR, a convenient way of remembering the following guidelines.

Service. One company advertises that customer satisfaction is its most important product, and the managers of that company urge employees to adopt a service attitude in their business transactions. But is such indoctrination necessary? Don't employees realize that their companies would not exist without suppliers, wholesalers, retailers, and consumers?

Not always. When people work for a very large corporation, they sometimes think of the company as right at the center of everything important—that the rest of the world exists mainly for the corporation's benefit. Such an attitude should be avoided, of course, because it is erroneous and self-defeating.

Regardless of how important or unimportant your position within an organization, you will be more productive when you adopt a service attitude. When you approach business transactions with a "What can I do for you?" attitude, your communications will reflect a tone of consideration, courtesy, and helpfulness. Write and talk in terms of the other person's interest, rather than your own—relying more on the words *you* and *your* than on *I, my, we,* and *our.* Remember, employees have the responsibility of making friends for their companies and departments—not enemies.

Time. Whether you are speaking or writing, place yourself in a specific time frame. If you are discussing the past, try to imagine the action as it took place in the past. If you are discussing the present, place yourself in that situation. By identifying closely with the time frame you are discussing, you will avoid the tendency to switch tenses unnecessarily; you will be able to keep the verbs *is, are,* and *were* and their complements straight without having to give them much thought. Attention to these technicalities will be minimized, freeing you to write in a more natural style.

Audience. A similar approach works for picturing your audience, the people with whom you are communicating. Instead of writing to a government agency, a company, or a department, try to imagine the specific person (or persons) who will read your correspondence. Pretend that you are in a face-to-face situation with your readers—sitting across the desk from them or enjoying a friendly cup of coffee together. When we write to inanimate objects such as departments, divisions, and companies, our correspondence tends to be cold and impersonal. Keeping a specific audience in mind helps us overcome the disadvantage of communicating at a distance.

Reason. Finally, we should keep the main purpose of our communication in mind. If the purpose of our letter or phone call is to answer a specific question the other person has asked, we should concentrate on answering the question and avoid introducing extraneous materials.

But what if the person has more than one point to make in the communication? There is no rule against covering more than one subject in a letter or during a telephone conversation, so long as the subjects relate specifically to the person with whom you are communicating. But do not expect the receiver of your letter to pass it to someone in another department when finished with it. Instead, send separate letters.

Keep the meaning of the letters S★T★A★R in mind for assignments in school and in business. The S★T★A★R approach is helpful when you are planning your communications, during the time you are actually communicating, and in reviewing the effectiveness of your completed messages. Although this type of doublecheck does not guarantee that you will become a "star" communicator, the approach will encourage you to strive for improvement.

Won't you please stop playacting?

COMMUNICATING NATURALLY

In pretending that you are communicating directly with readers, write in the same way you would talk with them. What? Use the same words and phrases I'd use if I were talking to someone in person? Exactly! A natural approach, using everyday language, is the key to good writing. Instead of switching to an artificial vocabulary for your written communications in an effort to impress, write to people exactly as you would talk to them. The advantages are twofold: First, your communications will improve dramatically. Second, writing in a natural manner (your own style) is much easier than trying to imitate others.

A department manager included the following sentence in an interoffice memo: "In compliance with your directive of the 14th, all overtime work is being discontinued forthwith." Would he actually use such terms when speaking? Of course not! He would probably *say* something like this: "Beginning with today's afternoon shift, we are stopping all overtime work." So why doesn't he write like he talks? Clearly, this manager's effectiveness would increase significantly if he adopted a more natural approach to written communications.

Many students ask, "How do I begin the report?" and "What do I say in the letter?" Asked what it is they want to say, they are usually able to express it orally. To this my response is, "That's it; write it the same way you just said it." Follow this advice and you will be on your way to communicating "naturally."

Do it now!

COMMUNICATING PROMPTLY

The longer you postpone writing a letter, the more difficult it is to write. As a matter of practice, *do it now*. Always have a pen (typewriter), paper, carbon paper, envelopes, and stamps at hand—at home and at the office—so that you are prepared to write.

If you put off writing a letter that should be written, the thought of having left something undone remains with you; it will take just as long to write the letter next week as it would today—and probably longer. Get in the habit of communicating promptly, while the details are fresh in your mind.

Don't strive for perfection at the beginning. After you have planned the main parts of your communication, try to get some words on paper. For most people, getting started is the most difficult part of writing. Once you have written a rough draft of whatever it is you are writing, you can improve your word choice, sentence structure, and other details. Eventually you will be able to do it right the first time.

Sometimes striving for perfection of the final communication can even be counterproductive, because people who dwell too long on a single communication soon view writing as a tedious task. Do the best you can without being overly critical of the results. Sure, a few years from now your efforts today may seem primitive, but that's an indication that your writing has improved in the meantime. And that's progress.

DISCUSSION AND REVIEW QUESTIONS

1. What would be your primary and secondary objectives in writing letters?
   a. Refusing credit to an applicant.
   b. Telling a personnel manager who has offered you a job that you have accepted a position with another company.
   c. Reprimanding an employee who has violated company regulations.
   d. Telling a customer that you are refunding an overpayment.
   e. Informing a business customer that you can ship only part of an order.

2. What medium would you choose for transmitting the following messages?
    a. Place an order with a company in another city for a product, the price for which is expected to increase at any moment.
    b. Inform a customer that his order was shipped this morning via American Airlines.
    c. Instruct a manager at a branch office of your company that the procedure for completing the payroll is being changed next month.
    d. Announce to all clerical employees that the offices will be closed and employees released from their duties at 11:30 a.m. next Friday and every Friday thereafter.
    e. Announce to employees that the building is to be evacuated immediately.

3. About what time of the day would you place the following phone calls?
    a. It is now 9:30 a.m. and you realize that you will be unable to keep a 3:00 p.m. appointment with an important customer.
    b. It is now 8:00 a.m. in New York City, where you work, and you want to discuss several important items of business with a supplier on the West Coast.
    c. It is now 10:00 a.m. and you are planning a follow-up call to two important customers, hoping to persuade them to select your product instead of a competing one.
    d. You have sent two form letters to a business customer concerning payment of an invoice. Having received no reply, you have decided to phone to see what's wrong.

4. Cite at least three reasons for organizing your message before you begin communicating.

5. Briefly describe the S★T★A★R approach to communicating in business.

6. What are the potential benefits of adopting a service attitude in business transactions?

7. Should top managers of large corporations adopt a service attitude when dealing with the lower-level managers who report to them? Explain.

8. It is often a good practice to picture an audience of more than one person when you are writing. Why?

9. If you have two problems to discuss with the same company, one about accounts receivable and the other about accounts payable, why shouldn't you discuss both problems in the same letter?

10. Rather than communicating in the suggested "natural" manner, wouldn't it be to our advantage to write in a way that would cause the reader to think that we are even more knowledgeable and intelligent than we actually are?

11. It's easy to tell someone else to "Do it now!" when it comes to writing letters, memos, and other business communications; but is it realistic to believe that business people can take the time from their busy schedules to follow this advice?

12. Should we strive for perfection in our business communications? Explain.

13. Why should we avoid the overuse of such words as *I, my, we,* and *our* when communicating in business?

PART THREE
MEMOS, LETTERS, AND TELEGRAMS

You should find this section of the book of particular benefit because we are now ready to deal with the specifics of interoffice memos and business letters. We will also identify some of the expenses related to the use of memos and letters, along with some proven methods for reducing these expenses. Business leaders view memos, letters, and related costs as extremely important, as illustrated in the following comments by an officer of a leading bank:

Why is the appearance of letters so important? Every human wears an invisible label in large letters which reads "I'M IMPORTANT!" Sloppy, unattractive letters say just as loudly, "You're not important; you're not worth receiving a quality product." Sloppy, unattractive letters also reflect on the quality and calibre of the goods or services provided by the individual or company.

Costs are important also. We at First National reduce the cost of our communications by using preprinted forms and telephone calls where appropriate, and through the operation of a word-processing center. Word processing enables us to work smarter, not harder. Well-trained operators—not interrupted by phone calls, customers, taking manual dictation, or running errands for bosses—working with sophisticated but easily operated equipment, can produce from two to ten times as many documents as a secretary in a traditional position.

The focus is still on good writing, however. Whether the "word" goes out on paper or via some form of CRT terminal screen, clarity of expression remains important. Whatever the mode of transmittal, "garbage in" still equals "garbage out."

Mary C. Yarnell
Staff Officer
First National Bank of Arizona

Mode of transmittal? CRT terminal screen? Word processing? If these terms are foreign to you, they won't be for long, because Part 3 includes a chapter on electronic communications and another on word processing—two areas of increasing importance in business communications.

8

WRITING INTEROFFICE MEMOS

A new employee's first encounter with written communications usually involves memos. Why? Because memos are generally less critical to the welfare of the company than letters are. Employees send memos to one another, not to customers, suppliers, or other groups outside the company. Unlike a letter, therefore, a memo that is poorly written or conceived cannot damage the company's public image.

Just because memos are circulated within the company, however, doesn't mean that you should give them casual treatment. Your superiors, your peers, and your subordinates will judge your performance to a great extent on the quality of these written communications. In fact, well-written memos can very well represent a crucial step toward a successful career in business.

Better put it in writing, Ned.

PURPOSE OF MEMOS

But how do I decide whether to make a phone call or write a memo? To answer this question, let's consider the several purposes of a memo.

Convenience and economy. Wouldn't it be easier to telephone another employee than to write a memo? Yes, a phone call would be more convenient and less costly than a memo—if you and the other employee work in the same geographic area. If the communication involves a long-distance call, on the other hand, a memo may be more economical and therefore more practical. We also rely on memos for transmitting highly technical communications rather than overwhelming others with detailed telephone conversations.

Multiple recipients. Although we might use the telephone to convey a message to one or two people, this approach would be impractical when several recipients are involved. Rather than visiting or calling each member of a committee regarding the agenda of an upcoming meeting, for example, we would outline the agenda in a memo and send a copy to each committee member. Similarly, we wouldn't phone individual employees to announce a change in company policy. Instead, we would write a memo and post it on strategically positioned bulletin boards. Or, if the communication were very important, we would circulate a memo and have employees acknowledge their receipt and understanding of the message by placing their initials on the memo and returning it to us.

Confirmations. Even when employees do communicate with one another in person or by telephone, some conversations must be confirmed with written communications. If several managers agree on a change of procedure, for example, they don't just shake hands on the agreement. One of them must record the agreement with a written memo as a way of avoiding future misunderstandings and conflict. Then, if one of the managers or anyone else should later question the change, the confirming memo provides a permanent record of the original agreement. But isn't such a confirmation a type of "defensive" communication? Of course it is, but employees should protect themselves in this manner when important issues are involved.

Hey, man, this is too easy.

STANDARD MEMO FORMAT

Before reading further, take a minute or two to study the sample memo in Figure 8-1. Notice that in addition to the company name and the words "Interoffice Correspondence," the standard memo form carries several headings: DATE, TO, FROM, SUBJECT. These headings provide useful reminders to senders so that such detail is not overlooked, and they also make the message easier to understand. Instead of having to read the entire message to learn what it is about, for example, the receiver simply looks at the subject line.

Not only do we forego the formalities of salutations and complimentary closes, but memos are generally less formal in tone than letters. Memos should be relatively informal because they carry messages among members of the corporate group—not to outsiders.

A.D. SCHMIDT CORP.
INTEROFFICE CORRESPONDENCE

<u>DATE</u> January 27, 1979   <u>COPIES TO</u> Joyce Randolph
                                              Tom Yeager
___<u>TO</u> Jim Rucker   Rod Meecham

_<u>FROM</u> Jossie Smeltzer

<u>SUBJECT</u> Warehouse Selection, Rochester, New York

I have met with the managers of L&J Frozen Storage in Rochester, Jim,
and they appear eager to handle our new pet food line. Here are the main
provisions of their facility:

1. Their main building is located near the center of
    Rochester.

2. It is served by six major truck lines and two railroads
    (list attached).

3. They have ample space to accommodate our estimated monthly
    average of 4,500 cases.

4. Their monthly storage charge is 13 cents per case, including
    unloading--plus a 5-cents-per-case charge for individual
    deliveries at the warehouse.

5. They have membership in the NAPW.

These provisions appear more favorable than those offered by the City Center
facility, and, unlike City Center, L&J does <u>not</u> handle any competing brands
of pet food.

If you agree with my assessment of these two options, please let me know
right away, so that I may instruct Rod Meecham to make an in-person check
of the L&J building sometime next week. If not, we will try to find some
alternative.

ceh

Enclosure

Figure 8-1 Sample interoffice memo

Date line. Spell the month and show the date and year, without the use of abbreviations and without using hyphens or diagonals. Also avoid the date form used by the military.

(yes) February 2, 1979
(no)   2-2-79
(no)   2/2/79
(no)   2 February 1979 (military version)

Addressee line. Whether we show the addressee's title depends on the degree of formality within the organization. If everyone is on a first-name basis, you may omit titles.

TO: Bill Miller
TO: Janice Walker

If you are working in a more formal atmosphere, on the other hand, or if you wish to show special respect for the addressee, include the person's title and position.

TO: Mr. William F. Miller, Sales Manager
TO: Ms. Janice E. Walker, Assistant Traffic Manager

Sender line. The entry on the FROM line also depends on the degree of formality that exists within a company. If the atmosphere is relatively informal, you may use your first name or nickname and omit your middle initial.

FROM: Pat Ringo
FROM: Joe Patrick

Under more formal circumstances, or if the company is very large, list your full name and position.

FROM: Patricia Ringo, Traffic Coordinator
FROM: Joseph R. Patrick, Inventory Control Department

Note that we do not use a title with our own names. Others may refer to us as Mr. or Ms., but we do not use these titles of courtesy in connection with our own names.

We should sign or initial every business document we write, and most people place their inititals on memos immediately following their names—as shown on the sample memo in Figure 8-1. Some business people place their initials or full signature at the very end of the message instead, as a deterrent to anyone who might add some comment to the memo without the sender's knowledge or permission.

Subject line. You should pay special attention to the subject line for two reasons. First, it specifies the nature of the communication, so that readers may determine the importance of the message and whether or not it is urgent. Second, the subject line provides a guide for filing.

Who usually does the filing of letters and memos? Quite often it is the most recently hired and least experienced person in the office, and this person usually decides where to file memos on the basis of the subject line. Therefore, the file clerk would probably place the memo in Figure 8-1 somewhere in the W's or in a special folder marked "Warehousing."

Body of the memo. Although there is nothing wrong with double-spacing a memo, especially if it runs several pages, most business people use single spacing. Several pages? Yes, memos may take up only part of a page or they may be quite long. If your boss asks you to provide details of your trip to a company facility in another country, for example, you may have a difficult time confining the report to one or two pages.

You should allow at least 1 inch for your margins on both sides and at the bottom of the page. If your memo is longer than one page, use blank sheets (without the usual memo headings) for the following pages and allow at least 1 inch for the top margin. These additional pages should also reflect the name of the addressee, the current date, and the page number.

Example:

> Jim Rucker
> January 27, 1979
> Page 2

ICE lines. The letters **I, C,** and **E (ICE)** stand for

> I—identity of typist
> C—carbon copies
> E—enclosure

The letters "ceh" at the bottom of the memo in Figure 8-1 are the typist's initials. That's right, typists want to claim credit for their good work, and their bosses want to know who is responsible when something is typed wrong. If you type your own memos, you do not need to list initials in this manner.

Typists usually place at the bottom of the page (below their own initials) the names of employees who are to receive copies, but the memo form in Figure 8-1 designates a special place at the top of the page for this information.

Three people received copies of the memo. So how many copies did the typist make? Four copies were required: one for each of the three people listed at the top right corner of the page and a copy for the sender's file. We keep copies of *all* of our written communications.

In writing the memo to Jim Rucker, Ms. Smeltzer included some traffic information (a list) relating to the warehouse. In doing so, she alluded to the enclosure in the body of the memo (at the end of item 2 in the listing), and added the word "Enclosure" at the bottom of the memo. This notation serves as a reminder to the sender to include the traffic information when mailing the memo, and it alerts the recipient to check for the additional information.

Short form. Rather than placing brief messages on a long memo form, an unattractive and wasteful practice, most businesses also have a short form. The short memo is usually 5½ inches long, compared to 11 inches for the long form, and both the long and short forms are the standard 8½ inches wide. Figure 8-2 illustrates the type of message typically communicated on a short form.

CULINARY CANNING CO.
INTEROFFICE MEMORANDUM

DATE: November 12, 1979   SUBJECT: Labels for 303 W&S Cling Peaches

TO: Sidney Starr

FROM: Kim Peterson

San Francisco Printing Company is sending 24,000 labels to us today via UPS. Will you please phone me immediately upon their arrival, Sid?

Kim

Figure 8-2 Short form memo

So why didn't Kim telephone this information to Sid? Because the memo provides a detailed record. If Sid forgets to phone Kim when the labels arrive, Kim possesses written evidence (a copy of the memo) that she instructed him to do so, and the blame will be on Sid. Sid probably likes the arrangement also, because the memo provides him with a reminder to take the required action upon his receipt of the labels.

As with all written communications in business, we make an extra copy of memos for our files. With most memo forms, we must use carbon paper and blank pages to make copies, but carbonized forms are also available. Memos are often some color other than white to distinguish them from other documents circulated within the company.

Round-trip forms. Many companies use multicopy reply memos similar to the one shown in Figure 8-3, which is a product of Diamond International Corporation. You, the sender, enter the name of the addressee, the date, and your brief message in the top half of the form—making sure to sign your name. You then pull out the middle (yellow "originator" copy), which becomes your file copy. You mail the form, with the original (white) and bottom (pink) copy still attached to each other and with the carbons intact.

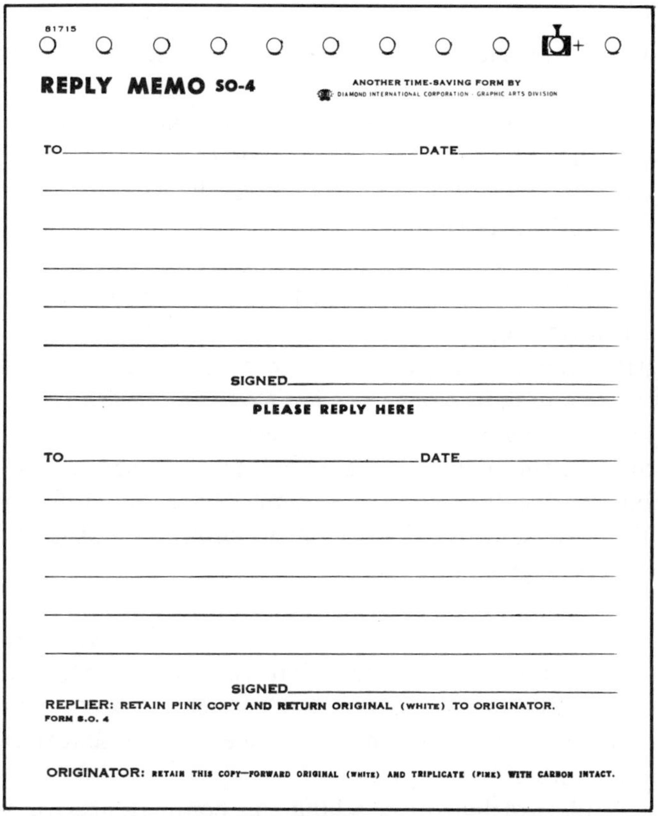
81715

REPLY MEMO SO-4

ANOTHER TIME-SAVING FORM BY
DIAMOND INTERNATIONAL CORPORATION · GRAPHIC ARTS DIVISION

TO________________ DATE________

SIGNED________________

PLEASE REPLY HERE

TO________________ DATE________

SIGNED________________

REPLIER: RETAIN PINK COPY AND RETURN ORIGINAL (WHITE) TO ORIGINATOR.
FORM S.O. 4

ORIGINATOR: RETAIN THIS COPY—FORWARD ORIGINAL (WHITE) AND TRIPLICATE (PINK) WITH CARBON INTACT.

Figure 8-3 Sample reply memo

The addressee places his reply, if one is called for, in the bottom portion of the memo—along with your name, the date, and his signature. He then removes and discards the carbons, retains the pink copy for his file, and returns the original to you. Upon your receipt of the reply, you do not need to retrieve your file copy to see what you said at the beginning. The entire communication is before you: your message and the addressee's reply. These forms are available in different sizes—long or short, narrow or wide—and you may order them with the name of your company printed at the top. They are not inexpensive, as you may have surmised, but they save time. And when you save time in business transactions, you usually save money.

Let's keep it on track.

SOME GUIDELINES

As mentioned at the beginning of this chapter, our superiors, peers, and subordinates tend to judge us by our written communications, and since we use memos to correspond with these groups, it makes sense to try to write impressive memos. Just how can we impress others with our memos? We can do so by going directly to the main point of our message, by providing complete information, and by spelling out the action we are seeking.

Get to the point. If you want to "shoot the breeze" with other employees, give them a ring on the telephone; or, better yet, spend your coffee or lunch break with them. Although we do want to maintain a friendly tone in our interoffice communications, we don't want to waste our time or that of the reader by including unnecessary verbiage.

Notice in the memo in Figure 8-1 that the sender didn't make any small talk about the weather, the state of the economy, or her love life. After establishing the purpose of the message in the subject line, she related every sentence to the subject—right on track.

Provide complete information. We should move directly to the point in our memos, but not to the extent that we omit important information. Include all pertinent data, and organize it in the clearest way possible. Again using the memo in Figure 8-1 as an example, notice that the sender aided the receiver by listing and numbering key points.

A useful guideline in checking the completeness of your information is to place yourself in the position of the receiver. Ask yourself if you could respond to the message on the basis of the information included. Remember, an incomplete message invariably results in additional communications.

Specify action. When your message requires action on the part of recipients, don't make them guess what you want them to do. Spell out the action; be specific. The sender of the memo in Figure 8-1 is seeking Jim Rucker's "go ahead" on arrangements with L&J Frozen Storage, and she asks for his response "right away." For the best effect, position requests for action at the end of your communications.

The short memo form in Figure 8-2 illustrates all of these features. The sender moves right to the point, provides essential information, and asks for specific action—no fuss, no muss. Aren't memos handy? You can say what you have to and let it go at that, with absolutely no frills. In striving for brevity, however, don't spare words like *please* and *thanks*. Although your company may not have a rule about courtesy toward fellow employees, coworkers, like most people, generally respond favorably to considerate treatment.

Look, Mom, no stamps.

INTEROFFICE MAIL

Much of the U.S. mail that arrives at the company mailroom consists of purchase orders for the firm's products (or services). Personnel in the mailroom must deliver these orders to the product distribution department. When people in the distribution department have secured credit approval from the credit department, organized the orders into shipments, and reserved the products with the inventory-control department, they send the papers to the traffic department. After selecting a transportation company, traffic personnel process the shipping papers and send them to employees in the shipping department. When personnel in the shipping department have shipped the products, they return signed copies of the shipping papers to the traffic department, and the traffic people distribute copies to several areas of the company, including product distribution, data processing, and records. Get the idea? People in business don't just correspond with suppliers and customers; most of their communications are within their own organization.

Rather than running all over the place exchanging documents, employees of the different departments mail their communications in interoffice envelopes. The two most commonly used envelopes are light brown and measure 4 by 9½ inches (letter sized) and 9½ by 13 inches (document sized). The front of the envelope usually reflects the company name, and the remaining space (front and back) is lined for addresses—as illustrated in Figure 8-4.

CULINARY CANNING	Cross out previous name and reuse envelope. Do not seal.
~~Sam Levine~~	~~Distribution~~
~~Martha Olivas~~	~~Credit~~
Roger Sparks	Warehouse

Figure 8-4 Portion of letter-sized interoffice envelope

In this way one envelope can be recycled anywhere from 60 to 90 times, depending on its size. The user simply marks out the last name on the envelope, writes in the name and location of the next addressee on the following line, inserts the message, tucks in (but doesn't seal) the flap, and places it in the outgoing mail. Mailroom personnel usually collect and distribute interoffice mail among all departments several times each working day.

Let's doublecheck it.

CHECKLIST: INTEROFFICE MEMOS

Is a memo the best medium for this message?

☐ Do we need a response?
☐ Can we wait for a mailed response?
☐ Would a telephone call eliminate the need for further correspondence?
☐ How many copies are needed, including one for your (the sender's) file?
☐ Which is more appropriate, the short or long form?
☐ Would a reply (round-trip) memo be more appropriate?

Did you complete the headings properly?

- ☐ Did you spell out the month and show the day and year?
- ☐ Is it advisable to show the addressee's title (Mr., Ms., Dr.) in this particular communication?
- ☐ Did you place your initials after your name or at the end of the message?
- ☐ Does the subject line provide an appropriate guideline for filing?

Is the body of the memo well organized and attractive?

- ☐ Are your ideas organized in some logical sequence?
- ☐ Did you list and number key points (if several)?
- ☐ Did you avoid unnecessary verbiage and get right to the point?
- ☐ If you used more than one page, did you include the addressee's name, the date, and the page number (on all but the first page)?
- ☐ Have you included all relevant information?
- ☐ Did you specify the desired action (if any)?
- ☐ Should you have included a deadline for the reader's response?
- ☐ Did you allow a margin of about 1 inch on both sides and at the bottom of the page?

Did you include all the necessary information at the bottom of the memo?

- ☐ Are the typist's initials shown (unless you typed it yourself)?
- ☐ Did you list the names of those (if any) who are to receive copies?
- ☐ Did you indicate that there are enclosures (if any)?

Did you check the communication for accuracy?

- ☐ Are dates, quantities, and other numbers accurate?
- ☐ Are all names spelled correctly?
- ☐ Are all words spelled correctly?

BUSINESS APPLICATIONS

After deciding whether to use a short- or long-form memo, respond to each of the following situations. Enter the usual memo headings on regular stationery.

1. As district sales manager in Los Angeles, you have just learned that Sylvia Blanchard has been appointed district sales manager in Chicago. Sylvia began work with the company only three years ago as one of your sales representatives in Los Angeles. Write a memo congratulating her on this promotion and offering any needed assistance with the new job.

2. As a supervisor in the company plant, you must respond to a worker's claim for two hours' overtime. Ross Miller claims that Paul Marshall, who has less seniority than he has, was called in yesterday between 8:00 and 10:00 p.m. to repair a broken water line. You had instructed your secretary to call Miller for the job, but two phone calls to his home were not answered—even though Miller claims that he was home all evening. Write a memo to Miller denying the claim, and without actually making copies, show on the original that copies are being sent to the plant superintendent and to the personnel manager.

3. As assistant sales manager for Moon Shuttle Toys, Inc., you have just read in *Business Week* magazine that the railroads are increasing their freight rates by 6 percent. Write a memo to the traffic manager to determine whether our prices are high enough to absorb these added transportation costs. More specifically, you would like to see the results of their (the traffic department's) most recent rate study.

4. In your position as credit manager, you are becoming more and more concerned that Jimbo's Appliance Stores have been taking the 2 percent cash discount for paying within 15 days of the invoice date, even though they are paying as long as 10 or 15 days after the discount periods. You know that your disallowance of the discounts may result in the loss of some of their business, and Jimbo's is one of the company's biggest accounts; but you also know that (1) the law prohibits you from giving preferential treatment to customers and (2) you want to collect the money when it is due. Write a memo to Herbert Smothers, the sales manager in your company, to see if he can suggest a solution to the problem.

5. As chairperson of the Employees' Committee on Internal Operations, you have in your possession a ten-page report on trends in fringe benefits. Since fringes are to be the main topic on the agenda for Thursday's committee meeting, distribute copies of the report—along with a memo informing all members (Jamie Brinks, Hal Newman, Jim Worthington, Jane Hildebrand, and Robert Gross) of the topic and suggesting that they read the report before coming to the meeting.

6. The personnel manager has asked you, his assistant, to prepare a memo in his name (as though he wrote it) concerning the employment of Harold Mason. The final decision in hiring Mason for the position Assistant Financial Manager hinged on his broad training and experience: Graduated from Indiana State University with a B.S. in Business Administration, spent five years in the finance department of Lear Manufacturing in El Paso, Texas, and worked three years as administrative assistant in the

finance department of Smeltzer Oil Co. Ltd. in Calgary, Alberta, Canada. Mason, who is married and has two young children, will begin work with this company (Wilmington International) next week. The memo introducing Mason as a new employee is to be posted on all company bulletin boards.

7. Although you have worked in the receiving department only two weeks, your boss asks you to send papers that relate to damaged merchandise to Ken Mosley in the claims department. Overnight Transport delivered an order from Industrial Supplies Company. During unloading, you noticed that one package showed signs of having been crushed at one corner, and when you shook the package you could hear some broken glass. You rejected the package and had the truck driver note the rejection on the freight bill, initialing the notation; and the driver took the damaged package. Send the noted freight bill and a copy of the receiving report to the claims department, along with a brief explanation of what happened.

8. In your position as payroll clerk, write a memo to Joseph Dirks, Plant Superintendent, questioning the timecard submitted for Ronald R. Roberts, a drill-press operator. Dirks is in charge of the entire plant, and he will probably pass your memo to an assistant for reply; nevertheless, company procedure dictates that you send all correspondence relating to plant operations directly to him. Roberts' timecard shows that he worked eight hours each day, Monday through Friday, and four hours on Saturday. You believe that the total time worked was 44 hours, but the total shown on the timecard is 46 hours.

9. You are the assistant manager of the accounts payable department but are acting as manager this month while Janet Spriggs, the regular manager, is on vacation. Before leaving, Mrs. Spriggs told you that she had been having trouble with Bill Wilson; despite her repeated warnings, he persists in "sluffing off." Mrs. Spriggs advised you to (1) keep an eye on Wilson, (2) discuss with him any shortcomings in his work, and (3) record the events in a memo to Paul Jamison in the personnel department. Although Wilson claimed to be far behind in his work, he arrived 20 minutes late on Monday, 15 minutes late on Tuesday, and 20 minutes late on Wednesday. Additionally, he took more than twice the allowed time for his coffee breaks and stretched the lunch period by 15 minutes each of the three days. When you discussed the problem with Wilson on Wednesday afternoon, he assumed a cooperative attitude; and he was on time and very productive the following Thursday and Friday. Although he also arrived on time the following Monday, comply with Mrs. Spriggs's instructions by writing a memo to Paul Jamison.

10. Working as a clerk in the distribution department, you have an idea that
    would eliminate the need for much of the letter writing now being done in
    that department. After every shipment has been forwarded, you and
    others in the department write formal letters to the consignees (the people
    who are to receive the shipments). As you view the situation, however,
    the prompt mailing of invoices would make these letters unnecessary,
    because all the essential information is included on the invoices. You also
    figure that the data-processing department could just as easily issue and
    mail invoices on the day following shipment as they could several days
    thereafter. Present your idea to the personnel department by writing a
    memo and placing it in the suggestion box.

9
ADOPTING A LETTER STYLE

The rules for writing business letters are undergoing rapid change for two reasons. Business people are becoming less formal in their communications, and they are finally acknowledging the fact that more and more women are participating in the world of business. What, more rules? Yes, there are certain conventions that you must follow if your letters are to be widely accepted in business, but isn't it easier to follow a few guidelines than to "play it by ear"?

Let's save some time, though, by breaking a few conventions. Rather than considering all the traditional letter forms, including some our grandparents felt right at home with, let's focus on what is happening in business today. To accomplish this objective, this chapter categorizes the features of 1,134 business letters—including hundreds of letters received by the author during the past three years and numerous letters received by his colleagues and students. These letters are from many different types of businesses and industries throughout the United States and Canada.

What you always wanted to know about letters.

PARTS OF A LETTER

You should familiarize yourself with all the parts of a letter before trying to combine the pieces into a final product. Consult the complete letter in Figure 9-1, however, as a guide when reading the following pointers.

300 North Avenue } Return address
Atlanta, GA 30313 }
October 4, 1979 } Date

Mr. Fredrick S. Perry
Ideal Mills, Inc.
30 West Monroe Street } Receiver's (inside) address)
Chicago, IL 60603

Dear Mr. Perry: } Salutation (*or* attention line *or* subject line)

Usually I am very pleased with Ideal utensils and pans, so I recently
purchased eight loaf pans to increase my supply. I normally buy only one
or two items to determine whether the product is satisfactory. In this
case, however, I felt that I could safely purchase all of the needed
items because of my previous satisfaction with your products.

I was very disappointed, therefore, when the pans proved unsatisfactory.
To bake any yeast-based dough, the temperature must be high (400-425
degrees) initially. With the new pans, however, this temperature caused
the surface dough that was in contact with the pan to become extremely
dark and tough. A similar situation occurred with cakes, even though
the temperatures were comparatively moderate.

I first spoke with the grocery store manager where I purchased the pans.
He referred me to your district manager, who, in turn, suggested that I
write directly to you. I am enclosing the cash register receipt and am
requesting a refund of $26.35.

Sincerely, } Complimentary close

E M McIntyre } Signature

E. M. McIntyre } Typed name

Enclosure } The receipt that was included

Figure 9-1 Sample letter (on personal stationery)

Sender's address. Always make certain that your own address is shown on
the letter. If you are writing on company stationery (letterhead), the name of
the business is printed at the top, and the return address and telephone number
are listed either at the top or at the bottom of the page. For personal letters,
as in Figure 9-1, you must place your return address above the date line.

Date line. Show the date of writing on all letters, spelling out the name of
the month and avoiding ordinals (*nd, rd, th*).

(no)   Nov. 26th, 1979
(yes) November 26, 1979

Receiver's address. If you are writing to a specific individual, show the person's complimentary title and name on the first line of the address.

Example: Mr. John H. Rowden
          Miss Pamela Rochester
          Mrs. Rhonda Wells
          Ms. Patricia R. Golden
          Dr. S. E. Campella

If you know the position of the person within the company, place it directly after the person's name or on the next line—depending on which arrangement is most attractive.

Example: Miss Rita Cloister, Manager
          The Sharpe Shoppe

Example: Mr. J. R. Remington
          Assistant Personnel Manager
          Smothers Manufacturing Co.

Example: Ms. Paula R. Scott, Assistant
          Director of Customer Services
          The General Instrument Corp.

The job title fits nicely on the top line of the first example and on the second line of the second example, but we used part of the first line and all of the second line for Ms. Scott's title in the third example. Each of these addresses is well balanced, with no very long lines and no extremely short ones. Notice that when we place all or part of a job title on the first line we separate it from the person's name with a comma. People are proud of their titles, so be sure to include them when known.

If you are writing to the person at a business address, place the name of the business on the second line. Use the next line for the street address, and the last line for the city, state, and zip code.

Showing the position   *Position not known*

Ms. Paula R. Scott, Assistant   Mr. Patrick R. Golden
Director of Customer Services   Rolodex Corporation
The General Instrument Corp.   P. O. Box 315
17000 St. Clair Avenue   St. Paul, MN 55101
Cleveland, Ohio 44110

Do not abbreviate directions, or the words *Street* or *Avenue*. The letters *P.* and *O.* in the address at the right are the abbreviation for *post office*. When you use a box number, place it between the company name and the last line (the city, state, and zip code).

Although some business people continue to spell out the names of states on letter (inside) addresses, they should use only the two-letter state codes for envelope (outside) addresses. These codes are listed in Figure 9-2.

Alabama . . . . AL	Illinois IL	Montana . . . . MT	Puerto Rico . . . . PR
Alaska . . . . AK	Indiana . . . . IN	Nebraska . . . . NE	Rhode Island . . . . . . RI
Arizona . . . . AZ	Iowa . . . . IA	Nevada . . . . NV	South Carolina . . . . . SC
Arkansas . . . . AR	Kansas . . . . KS	New Hampshire . . . . . NH	South Dakota . . . . . . SD
California . . . . CA	Kentucky . . . . KY	New Jersey . . . . NJ	Tennessee . . . . TN
Colorado . . . . CO	Louisiana . . . . LA	New Mexico . . . . . . NM	Texas . . . . TX
Connecticut . . . . . . CT	Maine . . . . ME	New York . . . . NY	Utah . . . . UT
Delaware . . . . DE	Maryland . . . . MD	North Carolina . . . . . NC	Vermont . . . . VT
Dist. of Col. . . . . . . DC	Massachusetts . . . . . . MA	North Dakota . . . . . . ND	Virginia . . . . VA
Florida . . . . FL	Michigan . . . . MI	Ohio . . . . OH	Virgin Islands VI
Georgia . . . . GA	Minnesota . . . . MN	Oklahoma . . . . OK	Washington . . . . WA
Guam . . . . GU	Mississippi . . . . MS	Oregon . . . . OR	West Virginia . . . . . . WV
Hawaii . . . . HI	Missouri . . . . MO	Pennsylvania . . . . . . PA	Wisconsin . . . . WI
Idaho . . . . ID			Wyoming . . . . WY

Figure 9-2 Two-letter state codes

Avoid the use of periods with the state codes, and leave two blank spaces between the state codes and the zip codes. If you are answering another business letter, the zip code will be shown in the company's letterhead (the printing on the stationery). If it is not, you must find the number. Most large companies subscribe to the *National Zip Code Directory*, but you also may secure this information by phoning the post office and telling them the name of the city and the street address. Zip codes for local addresses are shown on a map near the back of your telephone directory.

Salutation. When business people direct letters to specific individuals, they usually follow the address with a **salutation.** We wouldn't think of calling other business people "Dear" when talking with them, but most of us (84 percent, in the sample survey) continue to do so when we write letters. Several people (0.5 percent), however, have dropped the word "Dear" from their salutations. Use whichever of the recommended forms you wish from the following list, but avoid the more flowery and sexist saluations in the *Not recommended* column.

Recommended	*Not recommended*
Dear Mr. Greenspan:	Sir:
Mr. Greenspan:	Dear Sir:

Recommended	*Not recommended*
Dear Ms. Peters:	My Dear Sir:
Ms. Peters:	Gentlemen:
Dear Miss Randolph:	My Dear Mr. Powell
Ms. Randolph:	To Whom It May Concern:
	Dear Madam:

Similar rules apply to correspondence with government officials.

Examples	*Examples*
Mr. President:	Governor Green:
Dear Mr. President:	Dear Governor Green:
Senator Smith:	Mayor Harley:
Dear Senator Smith:	Dear Mayor Harley:

Follow the salutation with a colon in business letters and other types of formal correspondence, reverting to a comma only when writing to close friends and relatives.

Business letters	*Personal letters*
Dear Bill:	Dear Martha,
Hello, Sally:	Hi, Mom,

But what if we are writing just to a company, rather than to a person within a company? Until recently, we circumvented the problem by using the word *Gentlemen.* When we consider that women constitute almost half the work force, and that the large majority of them are employed in office jobs, this masculine term seems inappropriate.

So what can we use as a substitute? Although there is no pat answer to this question, several people have offered suggestions—some of which appear practical, others less so.

Possible substitutes	*Impractical suggestions*
Hi:	Ladies and Gentlemen:
Hello:	Greetings:
Good morning:	Gentlepersons:
Dear Friends:	Dear People:
Dear Customer:	

If you feel comfortable using *Hi, Hello,* or *Good morning,* then use them. After all, we do rely on these words to begin many of our conversations. Maybe you will find *Dear Friends* or *Dear Customer* to be appropriate in certain situations, but *Ladies and Gentlemen* seems more fitting for announcing a vaudeville act than a business message. The salutation *Greetings* sounds too much like bad news from the government, and *Gentlepersons* and *Dear People* are a little too "far out." Maybe you can come up with a better idea.

But why should we go through this formality when we are writing about routine business transactions with people we don't even know? If you feel this way, you may omit the salutation altogether. Quite a few business people are doing so, and when they omit the salutation they also dispense with the traditional complimentary close. Either use both or neither.

Subject line. The **subject line** provides us with a practical replacement for the salutation. Rather than referring to the person's name a second time with a salutation, simply state the main topic of the communication.

Example	*Example*
Mr. Jon Smithe, Office Manager	Miss Cindy W. Wells, Office Manager
St. Regis Plating Company, Inc.	PABCO Industries, Ltd.
10 Davis Drive	1616 Ypres Road
West Cambridge, NH 02138	Indianapolis, Indiana 46204
Subject: Our Invoice 49566	Subject: Your statement of 11/15/79

The entire subject line is underscored only in the first example, and the complete name of the state is used only in the second example. Since both are correct, these are choices you must make when adopting your own particular letter format.

Attention line. **Attention lines** sometimes offer a way around the salutation dilemma. When we have no way of directing our letters to specific people within businesses, it is haphazard to route a letter just to the company. Rather than addressing a letter to the St. Louis headquarters of General Dynamics Corporation, which employs tens of thousands of people, we may use an attention line in place of a salutation.

Example: General Dynamics Corporation
Pierre Laclede Center Building
St. Louis, Missouri 63105

Attention: Accounts Receivable Department

Example: General Dynamics Corporation
Pierre Laclede Center Building
St. Louis, MO 63105

Accounts Receivable Department

The word *Attention* is included in the first example (with or without the colon), but not in the second one; whereas the entire attention line is underscored only in the second example. As with the subject line, these are choices you must make.

Textbook authors and other people may instruct you to use attention lines when writing directly to individuals, and they may suggest that you use salutations with attention and subject lines. Don't believe them, because it just isn't done that way in modern business communications.

Modern	*Outdated*
Mr. Joe Marsh JRB Appliances, Inc. 2514 Seaway Lane Beaumont, TX 77704	JRB Appliances, Inc. 2514 Seaway Lane Beaumont, Texas 77704
Dear Mr. Marsh:	Attention Mr. Joe Marsh Gentlemen:

If the communication is for Mr. Marsh, why not address the letter directly to him?

Modern	*Outdated*
TLM Computer Systems, Inc. 1600 Broadway New York, NY 10019	TLM Computer Systems, Inc. 1600 Broadway New York, NY 10019
Attention Sales Department	Attention: Sales Department Gentlemen:

The attention line helps to minimize the clutter by providing us with an excellent replacement for this cumbersome and outdated salutation.

Body of letter. Single-space all business letters, and double-space (leave one blank line) between paragraphs. Do *not* indent the first line of each paragraph. The only purpose of indentions is to tell the reader when we are beginning new paragraphs, but we convey this message by double-spacing between paragraphs. Such indentions are time consuming for typists and give the letters a jagged appearance.

If at all practical to do so, confine the first paragraph in letters to two or three lines—usually just one sentence. The same advice applies to the ending paragraph. Try to hold the middle paragraphs to a maximum length of from 12 to 14 lines—depending, of course, on the nature of the topics discussed.

Complimentary close. If we use a salutation, we definitely include a complimentary close. The most widely used close, as evidenced by the sample survey, is just one word: *Sincerely* (58 percent of the sample letters). The most commonly used closes are listed as follows in descending order, with those used most frequently at the top and those used least frequently at the bottom; the column at right lists some interesting but infrequently used closes.

Popular closes	*Interesting closes*
Sincerely,	Hasta luego, (until later)
Very truly yours,	Hurriedly,
Sincerely yours,	Regards,
Cordially,	Thank you,
Best regards,	With warmest regards,
Yours truly,	Best wishes,
Yours very truly,	

Would we even consider ending a business conversation on the telephone by saying, "I'm yours very truly"? Of course not, which is the reason that most business people opt for the least offensive *Sincerely*. Why include such an ending at all? That is a question some people are beginning to ask themselves, as they break with tradition by omitting such trivia from their letters. If, on the other hand, you wish to show a high degree of respect for a business person or government official, use the word *Respectfully* as the complimentary close.

The *Dartnell Management Report* advises that some people tailor complimentary closes to express their true feelings. If Margaret Simes is unhappy with the person she is writing to, for example, she may end the letter "Angrily, Margaret Simes." Similarly, a firm in Sweden sells stationery with a choice of the sender's facial expressions printed near the signature line: a happy face, a look of concentration, an irritated expression, and one of open rage—enabling the sender to use the stationery with the picture that best fits the mood of the message.

Signature, name, and title. Type your name directly below the complimentary close, allowing anywhere from three to five blank lines between the two for your signature, and show your position within the company or the department where you work on the following line.

Example

Sincerely,

Susan L. Snodgrass
Susan L. Snodgrass
Marketing Department

Example

Very truly yours,

R. Dennis Meeks
R. Dennis Meeks, Manager
Product Distribution Department

Ms. Snodgrass lists her department, rather than a title; and Mr. Meeks lists part of his title on the same line as his name, separating the two with a comma, and carrying the remainder of the title to the following line. The form that you select depends on (1) whether or not you have a title and (2) the length of the title or department name. Some letters still reflect the company name on the second line following the complimentary close (all in upper case), but most business people now consider the practice to be redundant and unnecessary.

Modern

Very truly yours,

R. Dennis Meeks
R. Dennis Meeks, Manager
Product Distribution Department

Outdated

Very truly yours,
JRB APPLIANCES, INC.

Susan L. Snodgrass
Susan L. Snodgrass
Marketing Department

Why show the person's name twice, once in the signature and also typed? The typed name avoids the frustration that readers experience when they must rely on illegible signatures for identifying writers. Why, then, don't letter writers take enough time and effort to write their names more clearly? Some business people must sign their names dozens of times each day, which often makes speed seem more important than clarity; and others seek to make their signatures unique by making them fancy. What about your signature? Can you write it quickly? Does it have character?

ICE lines. **ICE** is an easy acronym to remember for the words **initials, copies,** and **enclosures.** When a letter is typed by someone other than the writer, the typist's initials should be placed at the left margin, two lines below the name and title (or department) of the writer. Some typists persist in showing the initials of the writer in addition to their own, but most people now consider this practice redundant and unnecessary.

Modern	*Outdated*
bt	SLS:bt
ems	RDM/ems

If you wish to send copies of a letter to others in addition to sending the original to the addressee, list the name or names of the people below the typist's initials—leaving one blank line in between.

Example	*Example*
bt	ems
cc: Ms. Margaret Carlson	cc: Mr. William Bell
	Miss Jennifer S. James

When you include documents with letters, such as a price list or an invoice, place the word "Enclosure" or its abbreviation below the typist's initials. Also specify the number of documents enclosed, if there are more than one; and it is sometimes advisable to identify the enclosures.

Example	*Example*
Enc.	Enclosures: Current price list
Enclosure	Certified invoice
Enclosures (2)	

Postscripts. If you forget to mention something important, can you just tack on a P.S.? No, the letter should be retyped. When business people use postscripts in today's letters, they usually do so for emphasis. They begin one double-space (that is, leaving one blank line) after the last line of the letter, often omitting the letters *P.S.*

Example: P.S. Don't overlook our Summer Sale that begins this Thursday. It will be a long time before you see another one quite like it.

Example: Don't overlook our Summer Sale that begins this Thursday. It will be a long time before you see another one quite like it.

The identifying P.S. is included only in the first example, and the message is underscored in the second example for added emphasis. Which form do you prefer?

Appearance conveys a very forceful message.

PLACEMENT ON PAGE

Now that you are familiar with all the possible parts of business letters, the challenge becomes one of bringing them together attractively. The first consideration, of course, is the quality of the paper and the typewriter ribbon. Make certain that the paper is of good quality (not the erasable kind), that the type is clean, and that the ribbon is sufficiently dark. Then you may decide on a letter style.

Modified or full block. Examples of the two most popular letter styles are shown in Figures 9-3 and 9-4. Approximately 50 percent of the survey letters were modified block, 41 percent were full block, and the remaining 9 percent were an unacceptable mixture of the two forms. If you use modified block, place the date, the complimentary close, the signature, and the writer's name and title at the right side of the page. If you use full block instead, begin all writing at the left margin.

So which form should you use? Again, the choice is yours. Although the modified block requires more work (the typist must strike the tab key four extra times for each letter), many people believe that this form appears better balanced and therefore more attractive. Notice that the first lines of the paragraphs are *not* indented. Indenting single-spaced paragraphs takes extra time and serves no useful purpose.

Consider the letterhead. All companies have their individualized letterhead, and you should place letters on the page in a way that will complement this information. In Figure 9-3, for example, the left margin is aligned with the beginning (left side) of the letterhead, and the date is aligned with the telephone number in the letterhead. Notice also that the complimentary close is in line with the date.

But isn't all this a little picky? Yes, but it only involves setting the margin and tab stops—something the typist must do anyway—and the resulting letters are much more attractive than when elements of a letter are placed on the page helter-skelter. Remember, if you use full block (Figure 9-4), you need only be concerned with setting margin stops—not tab stops.

⇨ QUALITY FOODS CORP.

772 BONITA STREET   SAN PEDRO, CA 90053   (213) 916-1211

October 31, 1979

J. C. Spencer Wholesaling Co.
210 South Michigan Avenue
Chicago, IL 60604

SUBJECT: Unearned discounts

Our credit terms are 2/10, n/30, as specified in our sales-order
confirmations and as printed on our invoice forms. When paying our
Invoice No. 13205 of August 31, 1979, therefore, the cash discount
of $73.12 should not have been deducted. The discount period ended
September 10, but your check did not arrive in our office until
October 15.

A similar situation exists with respect to our Invoice No. 14229 dated
September 10. Although payment was not received until September 30,
ten days past the discount period, you deducted the 2-percent discount
of $63.15.

We are prohibited by federal law from offering preferential treatment
to individual customers; therefore, we are enclosing copies of these
two invoices and asking that you respect our established terms of
sale by sending us payment of the two unearned discounts in the amount
of $136.27.

James M. Cummings, Manager
Accounts Receivable Department

pvm

Enclosures

Figure 9-3   Modified block format

SPRINGER AUTOMOTIVE
FULL SERVICE AUTO SUPPLIES AND ACCESSORIES

June 15, 1979

Mr. Charles L. Richards
United Petro Company, Inc.
1621 West 48th Street
Pittsburgh, PA 15219

Dear Mr. Richards:

We are interested in purchasing 500 cases of 6/12 oz. Sure Stop brake
fluid, as advertised in your special bulletin of June 10 at $15.90 per
case. Our offer to make the purchase is contingent upon the product
meeting our established specifications, and we will require a minimum
of 10 sample cans.

Do you anticipate any specials on your antifreeze coolant? We are
projecting sales of 3,000 cases of 6/1 gal. premium fluid, and plan
to make a purchase decision no later than July 15.

Sincerely,

Clara M Cooke

Clara M. Cooke
Purchasing Agent

rle

cc: Mr. William Fields
     District Sales Manager

16103 NORTH 17th WAY   MINNEAPOLIS, MN 55401   (612) 914-2222

Figure 9-4   Full block format

Set the margin stops. Although placement of the margin stops on your typewriter depends to a great extent on the design of the letterhead you are using, the usual left-hand margin is 1½ inches. If you are using **elite** (small) type, space in 18 spaces from the left edge of the paper. If you are using **pica** (large) type, allow 15 spaces. Leave a margin at the right of the page of from 1 to 1½ inches. This spacing is appropriate for letters, memos, and reports.

If you don't know whether your typewriter is elite or pica, type the following sentence and compare it with the examples:

Elite: `Type this sentence to check the size of your type.`

Pica: `Type this sentence to check the size of`
`your type.`

Balance the letter vertically. You wouldn't want your letters to appear scrunched at the top or bottom of the page, so you must plan your vertical spacing before you start writing. Vary your spacing (blank lines) to accommodate the length of your letter, as illustrated in Figures 9-5 and 9-6. Notice that the typist leaves many more blank lines for the four-line letter than for the longer one.

Multipage letters. Most companies stock a special form for use as additional pages to letters that are longer than one page. If such a form is not available, use blank stationery of the same quality as the letterhead paper. Leave at least a 1-inch margin (six blank lines) at the bottom of the previous page, and show the addressee's name at the top of the new page—along with the date and page number—beginning about 1 inch (six blank lines) from the top edge of the paper.

Example:

Charles L. Richards
June 15, 1979
Page 2

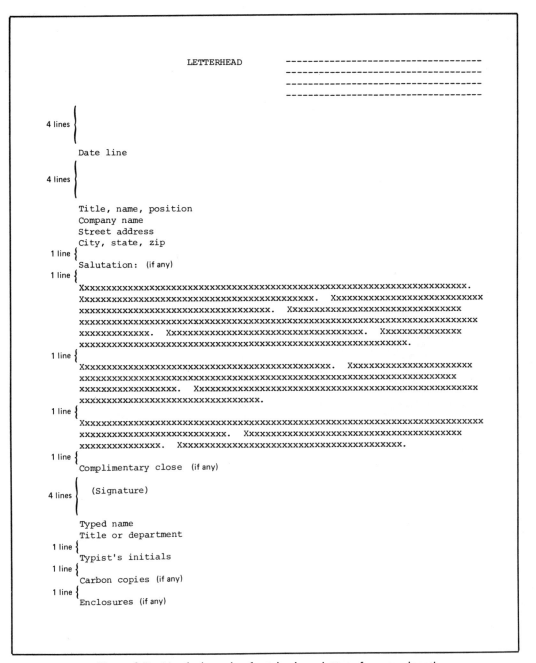

Figure 9-5   Vertical spacing for a business letter of average length

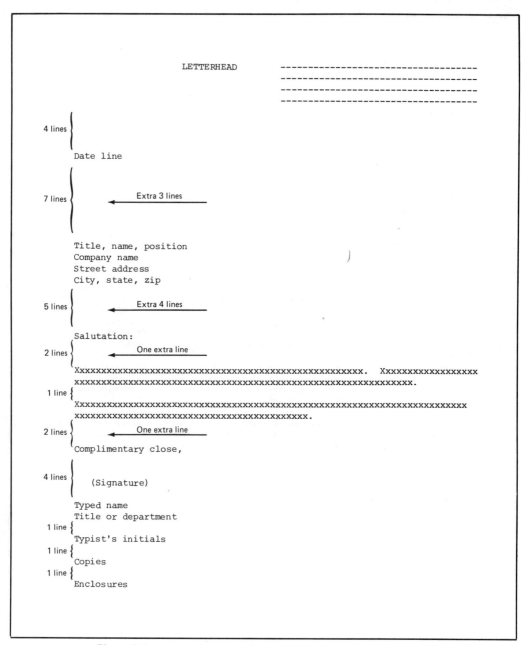

Figure 9-6   Vertical spacing for a relatively short business letter

Don't blow it now, Janice.

PREPARATION OF ENVELOPES

Preparing the envelope is just as important as preparing the letter, because the letter is of no value if it doesn't reach the proper address within a reasonable time. Although you only need to place the receiver's address on most envelopes because the name of your company is already printed in the upper left corner, there is a right way and a wrong way to do this; and you must know how to handle attention lines and mailing instructions.

Return address. Business envelopes have the sender's return address, including the company name, printed at the top left of the envelope. If you are writing a personal letter using a blank envelope, you must enter this information yourself.

Example:

Elizabeth M. McElviney
300 North Avenue
Atlanta, GA   30313

Receiver's address. The standard business envelope measures 9½ inches across and 4¼ inches vertically.* Begin the receiver's address 4 inches from the left edge (48 spaces elite and 40 spaces pica) and 2 inches (about 12 blank lines) from the top edge of the envelope. Although many people continue to type addresses on envelopes in the same form as inside addresses (page 145), the Postal Service is requesting that we use the form shown in Figure 9-7, which involves the following guidelines:

1. Capitalize all letters.
2. Eliminate all punctuation.
3. Single-space all lines.
4. Leave two blank spaces between the state abbreviation and zip code.
5. Leave blank space to the right of and below the address (below the dotted line in Figure 9-7).
6. For letters being mailed to multiunit buildings, type the room or suite number at the end of the street address (on the same line).

*Be sure to check with the Postal Service before buying odd-shaped envelopes, because they now return to the senders all pieces of mail smaller than 3½ by 5 inches. Odd-shaped letters larger than that but weighing one ounce or less are accepted, but a surcharge of seven cents is assessed on each such mailing.

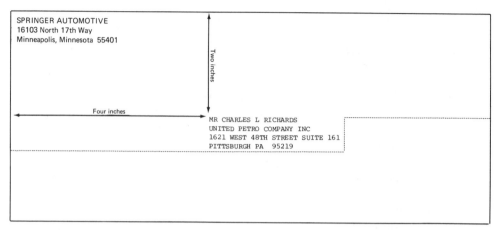

Figure 9-7 Spacing for standard-sized business envelope. The dashed line indicates that nothing should be written or typed below or to the right of the receiver's address.

This format is easier to use once you become accustomed to the change, and it enables the post office to automate sorting processes more fully.

Attention lines. When we are writing to specific individuals within companies, we address our letters to them. When we don't know a specific individual, we resort to attention lines. Place attention lines on envelopes immediately following the name of the company.

Example: J. C. Spender Wholesaling Co.
Attention Accounts Payable ◄─────────
210 South Michigan Avenue
Chicago, IL 60604

Mailing Instructions. If you want the U.S. Post Office to give a letter special handling, place the instructions in the upper right corner of the envelope, allowing room for postage (about nine lines from the top edge of the envelope).

Example:

Postage

REGISTERED MAIL

Inserting the letter. Let's not make a big deal out of folding and inserting letters, as people used to do. Simply fold the page into thirds as illustrated in Figure 9-8.

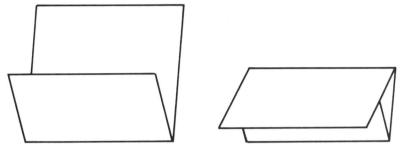

Figure 9-8   Folding a business letter

Whether the letter is placed into the envelope one way or another has no importance. Virtually no one pays any attention to such trivia, and employees other than the reader generally open the mail.

Learn a little, save a lot

MAILING THE LETTER

Comedians on radio and television poke a lot of fun at the U.S. Postal Service, and business people often blame many of their own mistakes and delays on this government service. In actuality, more than 99.9 percent of the mail is delivered on time and in good condition. To benefit fully, however, you must be aware of the different levels of service and the various postal systems available for processing mail.

Postal services. Business letters, except for mass mailings of advertisements, are sent first class. The first ounce costs whatever the price of a regular postage stamp might be at the time you are reading this book, with each additional ounce costing slightly less than the first one.

Do not waste money by sending letters within the United States via air mail, because the post office now moves all first-class mail to distant places by air. If you are mailing publications, newspapers, or bulk mail, be sure to check with the post office beforehand for information about second-, third-, and fourth-class rates and regulations.

The post office offers several types of special handling. When you send a letter **special delivery,** a mail carrier at the destination post office makes a special trip to deliver the letter. If your letter or other documents are of special value, **registered mail** guarantees separate handling, and the postal employees must personally sign for the envelope at each exchange point. If you seal the envelope with any kind of supportive tape, make certain that it is *not* cellophane or masking tape. Sealed areas all around the envelope must be suitable for stamping with an inked stamper by postal employees.

Certified mail also provides an official record of the mailing, and at a much lower cost than for registered mail, but your envelope is not handled separately from regular mail. For an additional charge, you may request a return receipt for both registered and certified mail, and the postal department will return a card to you showing the date of delivery and the signature of the addressee.

You may use **express mail** within the continental United States for anything from a letter to a 70-pound package. If you deliver your item to one of the designated post offices (ask the post office for a list) before 5.00 p.m., delivery to the addressee's home or business sometime the next day is guaranteed. The cost of this service is high, but the post office refunds the full price to the sender if delivery is made later than promised.

If any of your mailings is destined for other countries, ask the post office for specific information concerning rules and rates. You may also check any almanac for a limited amount of postal information, including data relating to international mail service.

Also be sure to check with postal employees when dealing in large volumes of mail. They will advise you of the benefits of presorting your mail and presenting it to them in mailing trays or mail sacks. Such handling is necessary in some instances to secure lower mailing rates, and presorted mail is sent on its way faster than mail that must be sorted at the post office. You may even discover that your business is entitled to special pickups of mail by postal employees.

Postage equipment. No matter how small or large the mailing operation, private companies offer many devices to speed the process. Even a business that mails no more than ten letters a day may benefit from the purchase of a hand-cranked postage meter. At the other extreme, large businesses may buy electrically powered meters (see Figure 9-9) that automatically feed, seal, postmark, meter-stamp, count, and stack up to 200 pieces of mail per minute. No, postage meters do *not* actually manufacture stamps. To buy $1,000 worth of postage, for example, you take the sealed meter box to the local post office. They take your $1,000, set the meter to reflect an additional $1,000 postage, and reseal the box.

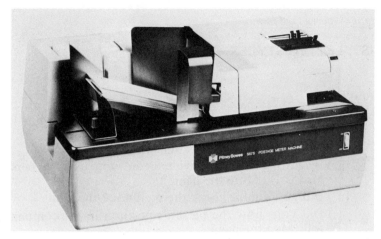

Figure 9-9   Pitney Bowes Model 5675 postage meter
mailing machine (Photo courtesy Pitney Bowes)

Metered mail, like that illustrated in Figure 9-10, has a more businesslike appearance, since practically all businesses now use postage meters. Also notice in Figure 9-10 that you may include an advertisement with your metered mail.

Figure 9-10   Sample of metered mail (Courtesy Pitney Bowes)

Postage meters provide closer control over postage because all mailings are re-corded; and, since the post office doesn't have to cancel stamps on metered mail, it moves through the post office and on its way faster than stamped mail.

Businesses that have a high volume of mail each day may also find it economically feasible to buy machines that fold letters and place them into envelopes automatically. Machines that open incoming mail are also available.

Wonder what I've overlooked this time.

CHECKLIST: LETTER STYLES

Top of letter

- ☐ If not using company letterhead, did you include your return address above the date line?
- ☐ Did you avoid abbreviations in the date line?
- ☐ If writing to an individual, did you use the person's title (Mr., Ms., Dr.) before the name?
- ☐ Did you double-check the spelling of the name?
- ☐ Did you show the person's position in the company, immediately following the name?
- ☐ If you are writing to a business employee, did you follow the person's name with the company name?
- ☐ Did you show either a post office box or a street address, but not both?
- ☐ If you used the two-letter state code, did you avoid the use of periods after each letter?
- ☐ Did you include a zip code? The correct zip code?
- ☐ Did you include an acceptable salutation (see recommended list on pages 146 and 147), an attention line, or a subject line—but not more than one of these?

Body of letter

- ☐ Did you single-space the body of the letter?
- ☐ Did you begin each line at the left margin, rather than indenting the first line in each paragraph?
- ☐ Are the first and last paragraphs relatively short?
- ☐ Did you confine the middle paragraphs to from 12 to 14 lines?

Bottom of letter

- ☐ Did you use a popular close (see lists on page 150)?
- ☐ If you omitted the salutation, did you also omit a complimentary close, and vice versa?
- ☐ Did you allow enough space to accommodate your signature?
- ☐ Did you follow the space for your signature with your typed name?
- ☐ Did you follow your typed name with your title or the name of your department?

Bottom of page

☐ If someone other than you typed the letter, are the typist's initials shown?

☐ If you are including other documents with your letter, did you show the word *Enclosure* and identify the number or types of documents enclosed?

☐ If you are sending copies of the letter to people other than the addressee, did you show their names and titles at the bottom?

☐ Do you have a comment to emphasize that would make the desired impact in a postscript?

Placement on page

☐ If you used modified block, did you align the complimentary close with the date line?

☐ If you used full block, do all lines begin at the left margin?

☐ Does the placement of your letter complement the letterhead?

☐ Did you leave approximately 1½ inches at the left and 1 inch at the right and bottom?

☐ If your letter is more than one page in length, did you show the addressee's name, the date, and the page number at the top of the additional pages—leaving a 1-inch margin at the top?

Envelope preparation

☐ If you are not using a business envelope, did you include your return address in the upper left corner—including your zip code?

☐ Did you place the receiver's address about 4 inches from the left and 2 inches from the top?

☐ Did you include the complete address: receiver's title (Mr., Miss, Mrs., Ms., Dr.) and name; the company name; the street address (with no abbreviations); and the city, two-letter state code, and zip code?

☐ If not writing to an individual, did you include an attention line following the company name?

☐ Did you place any special mailing instructions below the stamp area?

☐ Did you fold the paper in thirds before putting it into the envelope?

☐ Did you use the correct amount of postage?

BUSINESS APPLICATIONS

1. Using modified block, write a letter to a local department store, using the actual address (including the zip code), questioning a $25 charge—a charge that appears on this month's statement but about which you have no recollection or record. Indicate in the letter that you are enclosing your check for the balance of the bill, $145.15, which does not include the $25 in question.

2. Assume that you wrote a letter two weeks ago to PARFAB Diet Foods Company, 993 West Grand Blvd., Detroit, Michigan 48202, complaining about a can of their peaches you had purchased. The can was only half full, and the contents were much too sweet. Diane Collins in the Customer Relations Department wrote a letter to you dated June 12 saying that they are sending you a package of three complimentary cans of good-quality peaches. She also expressed appreciation for your calling the problem to their attention and asked that you use an enclosed envelope to return the can lid with the can code or simply relate the can code to them. Using full block, write a letter thanking them for this action and telling them that the can code is AX3214BB. Assume also that today's date is June 15 of the current year.

3. Write a letter to Juan R. Salvadore at 200 North Atlantic Boulevard, Monterey Park, California 91754, thanking him for his recent order for 250 units of Model 2156 pencil sharpeners. You are out of stock of the item at this time, but expect to receive a new shipment on September 16. Today's date is September 10 of the current year. Salvadore is the owner of Office Supplies Company, Inc. Assume that your letter will be typed by someone with the initials J.E.C. on company letterhead, and that you work in the Product Distribution Department. Indicate on the letter that a copy is being sent to William Buckner, a sales representative with your company.

4. Write a letter to Macon Printing Company, 755 Mulberry St., Macon, Georgia 31201, ordering 30,000 labels for B&H 6 oz. Tomato Sauce. Instruct them to send the invoice (bill) for the labels to you but to ship the labels via Greyhound Express to the Great American Food Company, 244 Lexington Avenue, Winston-Salem, North Carolina. The labels are desperately needed at the Winston-Salem plant, and an employee there will pick up the labels at the Greyhound station when they arrive there. Use a subject line.

5. Turning sideways a regular 8½ inch by 11 inch page, draw lines to represent standard-sized business envelopes (9½ by 4¼). Using both sides of the single piece of paper, enter the mailing addresses for each of the preceding four applications. For Applications 3 and 4, you may assume that the company name and address are printed on the envelopes.

6. As a clerk in the Inventory Control Department of a manufacturing company, write a letter to Molly Sharpe at Lightning Storage and Delivery Co., Inc., 511 College Ave., Rochester, New York 14607. Their Warehouse Receipt A-26155 shows that 488 cases of No. 121 screws were received into storage from rail car SP 611232. Since 500 cases of screws were included in the shipment, ask them what happened to the other 12 cases. If they were missing from the shipment or damaged en route, they should have sent claim papers with the warehouse receipt. Use a salutation and complimentary close, and assume that you are writing on letterhead. Send a copy of the letter to Jim Rickets, the claim agent in your company.

7. Assume that you are the assistant traffic manager at Moore Electric Co., which is located at 1206 Oakton Street, Morton Grove, Illinois 60053. Write a letter to your business communications instructor using the letter format you consider most attractive. Describe your reasons for having chosen either full or modified block, and discuss the importance of writing business letters that are attractive to the reader. Using a blank, business-sized envelope, enter the return address as though it were printed on the envelope, complete the envelope, and submit the letter to your instructor inside the unsealed envelope.

8. Write a letter to Holmes Manufacturing Co., 5200 Bellevue Ave., Detroit, Michigan. The zip code there is 48207. As the claim agent for your company, you have received their Credit Memo 42617 for $48.25. You must credit their account for this amount, but before you can do so you must have a copy of the motor carrier's inspection report and a noted copy of the freight bill.

9. After receiving the inspection report and freight bill mentioned in Application 8, you file a claim with North Eastern Truck Lines at 1321 West Street, Brooklyn, New York (zip 11222). In a form letter dated November 11, 1979, the trucking company advises that the claim cannot be processed until they receive a certified copy of your invoice to Holmes Manufacturing. The number of the invoice is 49929, and it was originally

issued on August 13, 1979. A notation at the top of North Eastern's form letter asks that you refer to their File 26R14 when replying. Assume that you are sending a certified copy of the invoice to them, and prepare a letter to send with it.

10. George J. Foxhoven, who is a sales representative for Ace Trucking Company at 499 Riverview Drive, Totowa, New Jersey 07512, has been giving your company special service during the rush season this past two months. He put in many hours of overtime each evening helping coordinate the flow of empty cartons and finished products. Write a letter of appreciation to George's boss at the trucking company, Stanley W. Whittier, District Sales Manager. The name of your company is Yu Importers, Inc., where you have the title Distribution Manager. (*Hint:* Keep it brief.)

10

MINIMIZING
LETTER WRITING

Before writing a letter, ask yourself these two questions: Is this letter necessary? Is there a better way to communicate the message? You should have a good reason for writing a letter, because letters cost money, sometimes a lot of money. You should also consider the practicality of using substitutes for letters.

Is this trip really necessary?

REASONS FOR WRITING LETTERS

Business managers devote much time budgeting company funds for such expenses as wages, rent, electricity, telephone, and postage. Every expenditure is subject to careful analysis. Before spending money that has been budgeted for written communications, we should exercise similar constraint by making certain that a letter is the best medium for our message.

Doesn't interrupt. A letter doesn't interrupt the receiver the way a phone call does. Unless a person has a secretary to screen incoming calls, a ringing telephone usually intrudes on the receiver's work processes, thought patterns, and conversations; everything is stopped to answer the telephone.

Okay, so maybe you prefer to capture the other person's attention immediately with a phone call. But if the interruption happens to catch the person at an inconvenient moment, you may have blown the chance of conveying your message successfully. Conversely, the receiver of your letter may lay it aside until time permits reading it at a more leisurely pace—at a time when the person might be more receptive to your message.

Provides a reminder. When a phone call is ended, that's it; it's all over; and, as the old saying goes, "out of sight, out of mind." Sure, the other person *might* make a note of your comments while talking with you on the phone, and the person *might* give you the desired response. A letter, on the other hand, enables you to present your complete thoughts in a logical sequence—to tell the whole story without fear of interruption by the recipient. Also, unlike a telephone conversation, the letter remains in the other person's possession as a reminder of your request for action.

After a publisher's sales representative had discussed a new textbook with the author of this book, she followed the in-person conversation with a letter. She didn't tell him anything in the letter that they hadn't already discussed at length, but the letter enabled her to highlight the main features of the book and it served as a reminder that the book was available for immediate adoption.

Establishes a record. After discussing complex business transactions with others, in person or over the telephone, we usually follow up with a letter of confirmation. We want to "put it in writing." Unlike the fleeting telephone conversation, the letter provides the receiver and the sender (file copy) with a permanent record of the exchange. There is a proliferation of letter writing in business today, despite increasing reliance on telephones, largely because of the need to record business transactions.

But wouldn't a recorded telephone conversation serve the same purpose? Maybe, but how would you decide in advance which calls to record? Recording all calls would be expensive, and it would be much more difficult to locate a particular conversation on a tape than to retrieve a letter from a filing cabinet.

We must also consider the legal implications of recording telephone conversations. First, federal law requires that the person doing the recording notify the other person that their conversation is being recorded. Second, the person doing the recording must purchase and use an audible beep pump, an electronic device that emits a tone over the telephone line every few seconds to remind whoever is talking that their words are being recorded.

Sometimes saves money. Does it cost less to write a letter than to pay for a telephone call? The answer to that question depends on the distance involved and the length of the telephone conversation, as compared with the cost of a letter. When employees routinely use the telephone for long-distance calls, the bill at the end of the month can be staggering. Correspondingly, many business leaders frequently admonish their employees to rely less on the telephone and more on letters.

REASONS FOR <u>NOT</u> WRITING LETTERS

Sometimes a letter is just not the appropriate vehicle for a particular communication. The time element is the most important consideration, but the cost of letter writing is also a major factor when deciding whether to write letters or use the telephone.

Can't wait for the mail. If you want to buy 50,000 bushels of wheat at the current market price, you had better *not* submit your bid in a letter, because the price of wheat may change several tmes before you consummate the deal. Similarly, if you know that your competitor is about to close an important sale, the transaction may be finalized before you can get a letter to the customer. We rely on the telephone for urgent messages such as these, often confirming our conversations with follow-up letters.

Receiver might not answer. Letters often leave us hanging. Even under the most favorable of circumstances, we cannot expect an answer for a week to ten days; and the wait may be extended several more days if the other person doesn't respond promptly. When a reply is not forthcoming, our imaginations come into play: Maybe the other person is on vacation. Maybe the letter was lost in the mails. Maybe the person isn't interested in what we had to say. Maybe this and maybe that.

A telephone call is more definite. Not only do we hear the person's verbal response to our questions, we may detect the degree of enthusiasm and interest (or the lack of it) by listening closely to voice tone and methods of expression. If the other person is away from the office, we receive information about his or her return. By using the telephone, therefore, we often avoid days or weeks of delay and uncertainty.

Cost may be too high. What does one business letter cost? $1.00? $2.50? $5.00? Estimates range from as low as a few cents to as high as $25.00 per letter, but the cost varies widely with the situation. To illustrate, let's consider some of the costs involved in letter writing.

Dictation is usually the most costly element in letter writing, because the person who composes the letter is the highest-paid employee involved in the process. But consider the disparity here. When the president of International Harvester spends 15 minutes dictating a letter, the cost is about $140, because he is paid more than 1 million dollars each year. For a middle manager receiving a more modest salary of $50,000, the cost of 15 minutes of dictation is $6.51.

Secretarial time is usually the second highest cost, and this cost depends on the secretary's income, the amount of time devoted to letter writing, and the number of letters typed. If two secretaries each earn $50 per day and both spend half their time typing letters, the secretary who turns out 10 letters per day costs the company $2.50 per letter, compared to $1.25 per letter for the secretary who types 20 letters. We must also consider equipment and supplies required by the secretary: a typewriter (initial investment of from $600 to $1,000), ribbons, correction tape, dictation equipment, stationery, carbon paper, and a host of other items.

But what about space requirements? The person who dictates the letter and the person who types it occupy many cubic feet of space, space which must be built, maintained, and air conditioned. There are also mailing and filing costs to consider. When we assign a portion of these overall costs to each letter, we can see that a cost estimate of even $25 per letter might be on the low side.

Some business people say that it is more realistic to consider **incremental costs.** Instead of worrying about the total cost of writing each letter, we view the services of the dictator and secretary, the building, the typewriter, and air conditioning as bought and paid for. Since they are already in place, we consider only the additional costs involved in writing additional letters: the cost of stationery, typewriter ribbons, and postage. Using the incremental approach, the cost of each additional letter may be 50 cents or less.

Legal record needed. We may need a legal record of our communication, a document that will "hold up in court." But does the carbon copy of a letter meet this criterion? Isn't it possible for the writer to fabricate a letter by writing it after the fact, entering an earlier date, placing a copy in the files, and throwing away the original? Of course it is possible, except for mail that is either registered or certified, and it is for this reason that business people have difficulty convincing judges and juries that letters have actually been sent when adversaries testify under oath that the letters were never received.

So if a letter won't suffice, how can we establish a legal record? We may do so by sending a Western Union telegram. The several levels of Western Union service, services that are extremely important in contemporary business, are discussed at length in the following chapter.

Eureka!

SUBSTITUTES FOR LETTER WRITING

We can overcome some of the disadvantages of letter writing by using substitutes. We may use carbonized memos, form letters, canned letters, and postcards.

Carbonized memo forms. In the distribution department of a medium-sized food processing company, several clerks dictated letters each time an order was shipped from their warehouse to a customer, and stenographers typed the letters on company letterhead. When management consultants learned that these letters were being addressed to brokers—that is, people who were effectively working for the company—they quickly put a stop to the time-consuming and costly practice.

Instead, they instructed the clerks to write their messages on carbonized memo forms similar to the one illustrated in Figure 8-3. And rather than dictating their memos for reproduction by stenographers, the clerks were directed to write or type their own messages on these forms. The formalities of salutations and complimentary closes were no longer necessary, and, unlike letter writing, the clerks could cross out any errors on the memos and just keep writing. The memo forms were an excellent substitute for letters.

Form letters. Form letters serve a very useful purpose in business communications. They are impersonal, but many of our business transactions with other companies are routine and impersonal. When we find ourselves writing the same type of letter many times, therefore, we should compose a form letter and have it duplicated. Such a letter is illustrated in Figure 10-1. Rather than dictating a letter every time they notice an error on a vendor's invoice, the people in this company simply type in the date and inside address at the top, and check or fill in the appropriate blanks below, making certain to keep a copy for their own file. Form letters ease the letter-writing burden for the sender, and the receivers of form letters soon accept the procedure as a natural and very acceptable part of their business transactions.

ROHRE

ROHRE ASSOCIATES INC.   215 California Street
San Francisco, California 94111

Invoice No. _____dated_____

For_____

When processing the above document, we find the following exceptions:

_____Incorrect pricing

Cases	Item Description	Priced at	Should be
_____	_____	_____	_____
_____	_____	_____	_____
_____	_____	_____	_____
_____	_____	_____	_____

_____Label allowance not shown.

_____Swell allowance not shown.

_____Marine insurance charged in error.

_____Incorrect terms. Should be_____.

_____Corrected invoice requested. Mail two copies to ROHRE--SF.

_____Check requested. In favor of member buyer. Mail to ROHRE--SF.

                                    ROHRE ASSOCIATES, INC.

Figure 10-1   Sample form letter

People who receive form letters like the one in Figure 10-1 immediately recognize them as such. But modern technology enables us to personalize form letters to a significant degree. With the use of word-processing equipment, as discussed in Chapter 12, we can enter the person's name in the address and at strategic places in the body of the letter—along with information that relates specifically to the reader—making the communication appear to have been written specifically for the individual reader.

Canned letters. If you are saying to yourself that form letters are too impersonal in some situations, you are absolutely correct. But we still should avoid writing the same types of letters over and over. If there is a feature about your company's product or service that requires frequent explanations to customers, for instance, write the best letter that you can in responding to the customer. Then use the same letter as a guide when responding to similar demands in the future.

Some companies carry this idea to the extreme, developing entire books of canned letters (letters prepared in advance). For example, a credit manager might instruct an assistant to write a Form 213 letter to a particular customer, using paragraphs A, B, and D. If we use such a system, we should do so with extreme caution, to make certain that our letters make sense. Although canned letters are usually grammatically correct, they are sometimes a little off target, leaving the recipient confused and perplexed.

Postcards. Many people use postcards to reduce the volume of letter writing. Paul Dean, a newspaper columnist, uses the postcard illustrated in Figure 10-2 to replace as many as 50 letters a day. He says that the cards force him to write tightly by restricting his replies to a maximum of two paragraphs (short ones, obviously), while at the same time enabling him to acknowledge information and to answer inquiries in a personal way. Consider the time and money he conserves as opposed to writing formal letters, and he saves a few cents postage every time he mails a card in place of a letter.

Dear Maggie Eitzen:

Terrific.

Thanks for following through.

Sincerely,

THE LOS ANGELES TIMES

Figure 10-2 Postcard substitute for letters (Courtesy Paul Dean, columnist for *The Los Angeles Times*)

Postcards can also be used for lengthier messages. After writing to a publisher concerning an adjustment in the subscription price for their magazine, the author received a card with the following message:

> We have received your recent communication concerning your subscription.
>
> Please be assured the matter will be handled promptly. If additional information is needed or a detailed reply is required, we will write again.
>
> Thank you for your interest.

About ten days later a follow-up card arrived:

> Your communication regarding your subscription will have our immediate attention. There may be a short delay before the correction becomes effective, but you have our assurance that adjustment will be made with the earliest possible issue.
>
> If you do not hear from us again, you can be certain your wishes are being followed.

The cards were preprinted, with only the author's address having to be typed. Were they effective? The author believes so. They corresponded promptly upon receipt of his letter; they told him what he wanted to hear (that they were complying with his wishes); and they did it in the most efficient and least expensive way. Many businesses computerize messages such as these, further lowering the cost of each communication.

Businesses sometimes use cartoon cards effectively. Cards (and envelopes) similar to those depicted in Figure 10-3 are available in quantities of at least 100 in black and white or color, and the vendor prints the company name and address on each card for an extra charge. Cartoon messages are less costly than letter writing, certainly; and in many situations they can be much more effective than letters. What would your reaction be to this type of communication?

  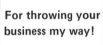 

Figure 10-3   Cartoon cards as substitutes for letters (Courtesy Harrison Publishing Co., Asheville, N.C.)

Memo forms, form letters, canned letters, and postcards are not the only substitutes for conventional letter writing. We can also send teletype messages throughout the United States and to foreign countries, and we can use regular business telephones to transmit pictures of business documents to distant offices. The various types of electronic communications are discussed in Chapter 11, and modern techniques for lowering the cost of letter writing are presented in Chapter 12.

DISCUSSION AND REVIEW QUESTIONS

1. In what ways is letter writing sometimes more appropriate than using the telephone?

2. Although a telephone call may capture the other person's attention immediately, it may not have the desired effect. Explain.

3. How does a letter establish a permanent record?

4. Do letters represent official records of business transactions?

5. What is the least amount of time you must wait in the continental United States for a reply to a letter that you are mailing today (Tuesday), assuming that the other person answers promptly?

6. Under what conditions is a telephone call more practical than writing a letter?

7. Which costs more, a letter or a phone call? Explain your answer.

8. Why may the writing of a letter in one office cost less than 1 dollar, while the cost of a similar letter written in another company may cost more than 100 dollars?

9. What are some of the costs that must be considered in computing the full cost of writing each letter?

10. How can the costs of letters typed by different typists vary so drastically if the typists are earning the same hourly wage?

11. When we consider only the incremental cost of letter writing, what major costs do we ignore? Do you believe that such a view is practical?

12. What are some workable substitutes for letter writing?

13. How does a canned letter differ from a form letter?

14. If carbonized memo forms cost more than regular company stationery (which they do), how can their use result in lower communication costs?

15. Are form letters too impersonal to be used in business communications? Explain your answer.

16. How do business people generally react to form letters they receive from employees of other companies?

17. How can form letters be more useful than regular letters to both the sender and the receiver?

18. Can you think of a situation in which your business communications instructor might benefit from some type of form communication to students?

19. What are the potential benefits and hazards of using canned letters?

20. In what types of situations would cards be inappropriate?

21. Respond to the following statements:
    a. Since she is so busy all the time, maybe the best way to get her attention is to call her on the telephone.
    b. Should I make a copy of this memo for our files?
    c. Since the people in our office don't have enough work to keep them busy, the cost of writing a few more letters each day is practically zilch.
    d. As a matter of precaution, let's record all important incoming and outgoing phone calls.
    e. I like to write letters, so who needs substitutes?

11

COMMUNICATING ELECTRONICALLY

Electronic devices have long provided several alternatives to letter writing; the telephone has been in existence many years, and the telegraph has been around even longer. Businesses began using teletype machines extensively in the 1950s, and centralized data banks were introduced in the 1960s. This chapter provides an overview of the complex and efficient communication networks that have resulted from these developments.

Aren't they the Pony Express people?

WESTERN UNION TELEGRAMS

If you were to ask the next several people you meet about the status of Western Union, they would probably connect the name with the era of a wild and woolly West. People tend to link Western Union with early railroading, when telegrams were handled at nearly every railroad station. Well, we have news for those people; Western Union did begin service in the mid-1800s and did displace the Pony Express service, but the company has since evolved into a modern corporation that does business in excess of $200 million annually.

Business orientation. Western Union still offers service to individuals. You can phone a toll-free number (see your telephone directory) to send a telegram, for example, and the charge will be placed on your next telephone bill. You may also send up to $300 to another person through Western Union

—if you have a Master Card and if the person to whom you are sending the money has access to a Western Union office.

But who wants to send a telegram, when they can can phone someone for a comparable charge? Most individuals send money (checks or money orders, not cash) in the mail rather than wiring it. Second-day mail delivery is commonplace, and, you will recall from Chapter 9, express mail guarantees next-day delivery.

As more and more people replaced telegraph services with telephone and mail service, the managers of Western Union directed more of their services toward the business community. Telegrams have been replaced as the mainstay of their business by teletypewriter services, leased systems, commercial money orders, mailgrams and datagrams—all of which are discussed in this chapter.

Straight telegrams. Exactly what is a **telegram**? A telegram is a message, usually a brief one, that is sent over Western Union wires with teletypewriters. To send a birthday greeting to someone right now, for instance, you call the toll-free number and give the destination address, message, and your name to an operator who, as you talk, types the information on a memory keyboard. Viewing the typed message on a cathode-ray tube, which is like a television screen, the operator corrects any errors without having to retype the entire message. When the message appears perfect, and after reading it back to you as a double check, the operator simply presses a button to send the message on its way to the designated Western Union office.

Messenger delivery is available in large cities for an extra charge, but messages to suburban areas and small cities and towns are phoned from the nearest Western Union office. Confirmation copies of phoned telegrams are mailed upon request.

Western Union charges a flat rate for the first 15 words, the rate depending on the distance, plus an extra charge for each additional word. To minimize costs, therefore, the sender must condense the message. Consider the following communication:

Original message

I'll be arriving at the Los Angeles International airport on Wednesday at 9:15 a.m. on American Airlines Flight 316. Please arrange for me to see Mr. Cantrell at Alpha Beta Company sometime in the morning, so that I can catch a return flight at 2:30 p.m. See you then, Margaret.

Condensed version for telegram

Arriving LAX Wednesday 10:15 American 316. Must see Cantrell Alpha Beta before noon same day.

The essential elements of the original message appear in the condensed version, and the word count is reduced from 49 to 15, meaning that the sender will pay the minimum charge for a telegram to Los Angeles.

Up to five combined letters, numbers, and symbols such as LAX (airline abbreviation for Los Angeles International airport) are counted as one word, as long as there is no spacing between the letters, numbers, or symbols. Correspondingly, if the sender specified 9:15 a.m., as in the original message, Western Union would count it as two words, even if the space between the numbers and the letters were removed.

Overnight telegrams. Day letter service is no longer available, and night letters are now called **overnight telegrams**. Rates for overnight telegrams are significantly lower than for straight telegrams, and you may include up to 100 words before extra-word charges are assessed. An overnight telegram sent today will be delivered tomorrow morning.

Look, a talking typewriter.

TWO-WAY TELETYPES

Two-way communications between customers represent the greatest volume of Western Union's business. Practically all medium-sized and large companies rent or own **Telex** or **TWX** units.

Telex service. Businesses may rent or buy Telex (and TWX) units from Western Union, the company that originated the service, or from any of several competing vendors. When a unit is connected to Western Union's Telex network, the business that is subscribing to the service may communicate directly with any of 75,000 other subscribing companies in the United States, Canada, Mexico, and Alaska—and with any of 250,000 companies on other continents.

A Telex unit is essentially a typewriter. The keyboard differs from a typewriter keyboard only slightly in having no separate row of numbers. Instead, the top row of letters (Q, W, E, R, etc.) becomes numbers after you depress a **numeric** key, and the top row converts from numbers to letters after you press a **letter** key. Anyone who can type can quickly learn to operate a Telex.

Upon dialing another company (just as they would make a telephone call), and after employees at the other company have acknowledged their presence on the line, users may either communicate directly on teletypewriter keyboards or by running previously prepared tapes. It is common, for example, for employees of two companies to carry on a discussion with each other using the teletypewriter keyboards, and each has a printed copy as a record of the two-way communication.

But when specific messages or detailed information is to be transmitted, operators usually record the communications on five-place paper tape as they are typing. Operators check the printed copies for accuracy, and after making any necessary corrections in the tapes, they direct dial the other companies and run the tapes at a speed of 66 words per minute. An automatic identification feature of the equipment ensures that the correct terminal has been reached, and Telex equipment provides an automatic acknowledgment of each message successfully transmitted. In this way messages can be sent to unattended teletypewriters in other offices, even at night when those offices are not open for regular business.

Telex service provides two-way communications and permanent records of the communications. The main advantage of the service compared to other communication media, however, is the price. A Telex message costs anywhere from one fifth to one half the price of a telephone call; and if the other company doesn't answer your Telex call because the line is busy or out of order, you simply send the message to Western Union Teleprinter Computer Services, and a Western Union computer forwards the message when a connection can be made.

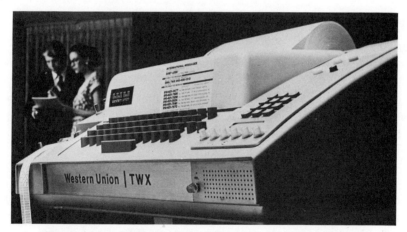

Figure 11-1   A Western Union TWX teletypewriter (Courtesy The Western Union Telegraph Company)

TWX service. Bell System developed the TWX network and later sold it to Western Union—a system of 50,000 teletypewriters throughout the United States and Canada that, like Telex, connects with 250,000 machines overseas. TWX machines (see Figure 11-1) are similar to Telex units except that they have four rows of keys—almost identical to typewriters. They transmit messages at a faster 100 words per minute; and they utilize seven-place paper tape on both incoming and outgoing messages that is compatible with most computer systems. The TWX system also allows for conference calls, where people in several locations use teletypewriter keyboards to communicate with one another at the same time.

Compatible systems. So which service is better, Telex or TWX? The choice depends in a large part on the type of industry involved. Businesses in some industries depend on Telex, and businesses in other industries use TWX. Western Union issues directories for each service, listing all subscribing companies in both alphabetical and Yellow Page format. Telex provides lower-cost service for some companies, depending on the particular price zone that applies to their location. Businesses that send relatively long messages, on the other hand, may reduce communication costs by using the faster TWX service (100 wpm versus 66 wpm).

Subscribing to one service does not preclude access to the other system, however. By using a Western Union Service called Infomaster, you may use a Telex to reach any TWX subscriber, and a TWX subscriber can reach you through the same service. There is no need to subscribe to both services.

Hey, this must be important.

ONE-WAY GRAMS

You may also use Telex and TWX machines to send telegrams—a service that we have already discussed—as well as mailgrams, datagrams, and cablegrams. Telex and TWX rates are significantly lower, in fact, than if you phoned Western Union for either of these services.

Mailgrams. **Mailgram** service is provided through the joint efforts of Western Union and the United States Postal Service. Western Union directs mailgrams to teletypewriters at major post offices located nearest the destination addresses. Messages are removed from the teletypewriters and stuffed into window envelopes automatically and sent by mail carrier on the next scheduled delivery. Mailgrams are slower than telephone calls or telegrams but faster than mailed letters; and they provide a legal record of communications.

The Western Union insignia and the official emblem of the U.S. Postal Service are printed at the top of the mailgram form and envelopes, along with the word "Mailgram" in large letters, conveying a sense of importance and urgency; and the receiver must open the envelope and observe the contents to determine its source. Mailgrams are considerably less costly than long-distance telephone calls or telegrams; and if the same message is sent to more than one address, the cost of each mailgram declines by more than one half the single-message rate.

Mailgrams provide an ideal medium for priority communications, and you may speed the transmission process by storing frequently used messages or parts of messages in a Western Union computer. You can provide a list of addresses later, or the addresses may also be stored at Western Union. Then, upon your command, the Western Union computer matches the addresses with the stored message, adds personal data to the message if desired, and transmits the resulting mailgrams electronically to the appropriate post offices.

Datagrams. But let's say that you are in another city and want to send some important information to your home office. Assume further that it is after 5:00 p.m. at the home office and no one is there to answer the telephone. Under such conditions, you may turn to Western Union's 24-hour **datagram** service.

If your company has added datagrams to its Telex or TWX service and has provided you with a Western Union datagram card, you may call a toll-free number (see telephone directory) and give the information to a Western Union operator. The operator uses a magnetic keyboard and cathode-ray tube to record the information as you dictate, and transmits the datagram directly to your company's teletypewriter. The message will be at your home office when employees begin work the following morning, and its transmittal will have cost less than a long-distance telephone call.

Cablegrams. For communications to locations overseas, businesses may send **cablegrams.** The name is becoming misnomer, however, since most international communications are now transmitted via satellites, not over cables. In fact, Western Union now operates Westar, its own satellite; and more than 9,000 miles of terrestrial microwave is integrated with the satellite system.

What is this, a monopoly?

OTHER WESTERN UNION SERVICES

As mentioned earlier in this chapter, individuals may send up to $300 by using a Western Union charge card money order. Similarly, when a business has established a commercial money order account with Western Union, employees may send money to one another—24 hours a day, seven days a week.

Businesses that have Telex or TWX machines may subscribe to a News Alert service, whereby Western Union transmits major United Press International bulletins directly to business offices. Telex and TWX customers may also dial Western Union for specific stock reports, or they may have reports of their choice sent automatically and at specific times of the day or week.

Our computer is a demigod.

DATA BANKS

Many businesses rely on computers to such a great extent for their communications that they would be hard pressed to function without them. When you reserve a seat on an airplane, for example, the reservation clerk doesn't have to telephone or teletype a reservation center; the computer is the reservation center. The computer keeps track of the number of seats available, reducing the count each time another one is reserved.

Similarly, we no longer write letters to reserve motel rooms weeks in advance of a motor trip. We simply call a toll-free number and a reservation clerk queries a computer in the same way that airline clerks do, but for rooms rather than airplane seats. If no accommodations are available, the computer reveals the nearest locations where vacancies do exist—and lists the prevailing prices. How did motel companies handle all this detail before the invention of computers? A few people made reservations by mail, but the large majority of travelers just pointed their vehicles toward their destinations and hoped that motel space would be available when needed.

Data banks are not used just for reservation purposes, of course. Many companies store all pertinent information in centralized computers, where employees may draw on and add to the information bank in the performance of their duties; and business people depend on computers for the generation of virtually all business reports.

Let's dial a picture.

ELECTRONIC MAIL

So far, we have discussed the electronic transmittal of words, words that operators must key into teletypewriters or computers. But what if we want to send a **facsimile**–not a retyped version, but an exact copy of the original document? If we have a facsimile machine like the one shown in Figure 11-2, the process is simple.

Figure 11-2   Facsimile machine in use (Courtesy Qwip Systems, a Division of Exxon Enterprises, Inc.)

Facsimile machines are used for transmitting exact copies of such documents as letters, contracts, legal briefs, newspaper clippings, photographs, sketches, and drawings. Upon reaching the destination office by telephone, employees at each end place their telephone receivers into couples (cradle-like devices) and the sending operator begins feeding materials into the facsimile machine. Since documents are transmitted at a rate of 4 minutes per page, the sender must pay for a 4-minute phone call for each page sent, plus a modest monthly rental for the machine.

Facsimile machines are relatively slow, therefore, and copies must be made on a special type of paper measuring no more than 8½ by 11 inches. Despite these drawbacks, this method of communication represents a significant step toward the eventual displacement of most regular mail service. The U.S. Postal Service is already experimenting with electronic mail service–using satellites for transmittal, along with coding devices that prevent unauthorized persons from reading intercepted communications.

They are sorting and sending messages from one post office to another electronically, with mail carriers delivering the communications to homes and businesses. Eventually–say, in ten to fifteen years–postal employees will route all regular mail directly into our homes and businesses electronically–with no need for trucks, trains, buses, or airplanes to haul the mail and no need for carriers to deliver it; and the service will be instantaneous, reliable, and relatively economical.

DISCUSSION AND REVIEW QUESTIONS

1. What types of electronic services are offered by Western Union?

2. Do individuals or businesses constitute the nucleus of Western Union's business? Explain why.

3. What is a telegram, specifically, and in what ways does a straight telegram differ from an overnight telegram?

4. Describe the process that takes place when individuals call Western Union to send telegrams.

5. How does the delivery of a telegram addressed to an individual differ from one directed to a large business?

6. In what ways does Telex service differ from TWX service?

7. Do teletypewriters provide one-way or two-way communications? Explain.

8. Which system enables two-way communications with each business having a printed record of the exchanges, Telex or TWX?

9. Describe the process that takes place when one company uses a Telex or TWX to send a message to another company that has only a TWX machine.

10. What is the advantage of using paper tape to transmit Telex and TWX messages?

11. Why is TWX paper tape more useful to some businesses than Telex tape?

12. What are the main advantages of Telex and TWX service, compared to telephone communications?

13. Which of the two systems is better for a company that routinely sends lengthy messages?

14. Describe Western Union's mailgram service, and relate the speed of delivery to telephone and mail service.

15. When communicating with Telex or TWX paper tape, is it necessary to condense messages as we do with straight telegrams?

16. You have just telephoned a company in another city to order (your Purchase Order No. 16217) 500 cases of Product Code 3312A at $8.35 per case, 750 cases of Product Code 3312C for $9.10 and 1,000 cases of Product Code 4134 at $12.50 per case. The merchandise is to be shipped to your Pittsburgh, Pennsylvania warehouse (they know the address) via Consolidated Freightways tomorrow, and freight charges are to be

"F.O.B. delivered" (shipper pays the freight). Assume that today's date is July 5 of the current year, and prepare a suitable communication to confirm the telephone order with a straight telegram.

17. Respond to the following comments:
    a. Most cablegrams are not actually transmitted over cables.
    b. Hey, Jim, I'm stuck in Minneapolis without any money. I still have two more days of business here, but I lost my cash and my credit cards. What do I do now?
    c. I don't want you to read the figures to me over the phone. What I need instead is an exact copy of your income statement for last month; and I need it today.
    d. My job as a mail carrier is very secure because the country will always need mail carriers.

12

WORD-PROCESSING METHODS

Electronic computers are changing the way we live. Checkout clerks at grocery stores are turning their main duties over to computers. Computers keep track of airplanes, buses, trucks, and railcars; and they are used to operate fully automated assembly lines in modern factories. Many small businesses rely on computers to some extent, and computers are essential to the operation of most large businesses.

Computer technology is equally applicable to the modern office. Magnetic keyboards, visual display screens, optical scanning devices, "intelligent" copiers, and other types of electronic equipment are being used to convert traditional offices into highly productive word-processing centers.

That's right, Dad, now I have my own secretary.

TRADITIONAL METHODS

Until recently, the manager-secretary combination was the general pattern in business offices. The business manager (almost always a male) dictated letters directly to a secretary (invariably a female). The secretary typed the letters, the boss signed them, and the secretary prepared them for mailing. Being assigned one's own secretary was a very important step in an employee's progress up the organization ladder and, as such, was a highly prized status symbol.

Conventional typewriters. But even the best of typists can't hit all the right keys all of the time. If she made an error near the beginning of a letter, out it came (rip, tear) and into the wastebasket. If she made errors later in the letter, after she had already typed a paragraph or so, she would make corrections with either a rubber eraser, correction fluid, or correction tape. She had to correct the carbon copy also, and if she happened to be making several copies the task became even more tedious. After passing the point of no return, that place in the letter where she vowed not to start over, no matter what, the secretary generally typed very cautiously, with speed (or lack of it) depending on the number of copies that would have to be corrected if she struck a wrong key. Also, the secretary often had to redo letters that had been perfectly typed, to make deletions and additions requested by the dictator.

Filing cabinets. Secretaries kept one copy of every communication, and it became the unenviable duty of some office employee to file these copies in alphabetically arranged folders located in four-drawer file cabinets. Most offices had whole rows of file cabinets to provide enough space to store copies for at least one year.

At the end of the year, office employees would transfer these files to storage areas—usually older steel files or files made of less expensive cardboard. The older files would then be stored away from the main office, causing employees wanting access to them to leave their offices and undertake extensive search routines. Eventually, someone would destroy the file copies after the required period of retention.

Glaring deficiencies. The inefficiencies of the traditional office are obvious. Someone else had to answer the secretary's phone when she was in the boss's office taking dictation. She wasted many minutes each session awaiting the next barrage of words to come pouring forth. And if he decided to accept an important phone call during this time, the secretary just sat there waiting, and waiting, and waiting.

Some managers attempted to overcome these inefficiencies by switching to dictation machines. Rather than dictating letters and other documents directly to secretaries, they spoke their thoughts into recording devices. Before typing final copies, however, secretaries often typed rough drafts of recorded messages—a very time-consuming process.

When typists made several attempts at writing letters before producing mailable versions, they not only wasted expensive letterhead, carbons, and ribbons, they also wasted a lot of time. Only those typists who were exceptionally fast and accurate, in fact, could turn out more than 20 letters or so during a regular workday.

Traditional filing systems were especially wasteful. The prompt filing of incoming mail and copies of outgoing mail was a continual problem, and locating a particular document among the thousands of pages represented a formidable challenge—often resulting in conflict and accusation among office employees. Companies had to maintain storage areas ranging from small storerooms to large warehouses, moreover, just to house old records.

<u>Wow, this place looks just like NASA.</u>

WORD-PROCESSING CENTERS

Although employees at many small businesses continue to rely on traditional office procedures, many firms are equipping their offices with **word-processing (WP) equipment.** They generally place the equipment in centralized areas and refer to the operations as **word-processing centers.**

Source documents. Rather than having secretaries come to them for dictation, the people doing the writing are responsible for getting the messages to their WP centers. Depending on the system, employees may write messages in longhand, dictate them to a recording device in their offices, or use their telephone to dictate directly to recording devices located in word-processing centers.

Figure 12-1 Word-processing operator using display system. The keyboarded data appear on the CRT screen and, once the operator has made any necessary corrections, the printer in the background types the document. (Courtesy Xerox Corporation)

Magnetic keyboards. Operators in WP centers use standard typewriter keyboards to type messages onto magnetic disks, and, if the units have a CRT (cathode-ray tube) like the one pictured in Figure 12-1, messages appear on screens as they type. Operators may type fast without fear of mistakes, because mistakes can be easily corrected. When operators are aware of mistakes as they type, they need only backspace and type over incorrect words, and the correct words appear on the screen—no apparent strikeovers, no manual erasures.

Operators do not strike the carriage return key as they reach the end of lines, because most WP machines end lines and begin new ones automatically. And operators do not need to worry about format, because WP machines handle the spacing. When writers desire the modified block format, for instance, WP machines arrange the correct spacing automatically. (We call word processors "machines" even though they operate electronically.)

When operators have finished keying the information, they check the screens for errors. If they find misspelled words, they just type over them. If they notice that words have been omitted, they enter them. If they want to add words, they add them. But, you may ask, won't additions make the lines too long and deletions make them too short? No, they won't, because most WP machines automatically adjust the length of altered lines and all following lines to keep the right margins straight.

Business forms. Frequently used forms may be stored magnetically and called forth to CRT screens for typing purposes. With WP machines making all tabulations automatically, operators just enter the data. After checking the screened documents for accuracy, operators instruct printers to type the information onto preprinted carbonized forms. With some models, operators simply type the data on continuous lines rather than in specific areas of the forms, and WP machines automatically place the words and numbers in the correct format during printing operations.

Repetitive materials. Operators do not need to type the same address or the same message repeatedly. They store such information on magnetic disks instead, and call it forward when needed. In the same manner, operators may send the same message to several (even thousands) of addressees without having to retype it even once; and they personalize each message by including the names of addressees and other relevant data.

Statistical data. When operators enter statistical data with totals into some WP models, the units automatically run continuous totals as the figures are entered. When the entries are complete, operators may check the machine totals with the totals shown on the source documents. When the totals disagree, operators check their own entries for accuracy before returning the original document to its source for checking. Some WP units also enable operators to compare statistics for the current period (day, week, month, year) with stored figures for earlier periods, with the WP unit automatically printing the percentage increase or decrease.

High-speed printers. Having made any necessary corrections in the screened image of documents, and after having placed paper in a separate unit (a printer), operators instruct the WP machines (by pressing a certain key) to type the documents. Many printers type in both directions, as the typing element moves from left to right and as it returns to the left, at speeds of from 300 to 3,000 words per minute. Some printers have round typing elements (**spheres**), and others have faster spiderlike devices (**daisy wheels**), both of which will make from six to ten carbon copies.

Easy revisions. Employees in WP centers return typed documents to the originators. When originators are satisfied with the product, they add their signatures and place them in outbaskets for mailing. If they decide instead to make changes, they simply note the changes on the printed documents and return them to their WP centers.

Since the documents are stored magnetically on recordlike disks until operators are certain that the documents have been approved, any alterations can be done without having to rekey entire documents. When writers notice that a word has been misspelled, for example, operators may instruct their WP units to correct the word in the text and to search the entire text to see if the same word has been misspelled elsewhere. Corrections of any additional misspelled words are then automatic.

When writers decide to underscore certain words or phrases, operators may instruct their WP units to search out the particular words or phrases and underscore them. But what if writers decide to rearrange the paragraphs? No problem—WP machines quickly rearrange the ordering of paragraphs without the necessity of retyping. Additionally, operators may instruct WP machines to type communications in either one or two columns and to **right-justify** all lines (make right margins perfectly even).

High-speed copiers. Xerox Corporation was the first to mass market **copy machines**, with IBM and other large companies eventually following. The recently developed copier-duplicator pictured in Figure 12-2 makes 4,500 copies per hour, or 1-1/4 copies every second. The unit copies on one or both sides of the paper, and collates (sorts) the resulting pages.

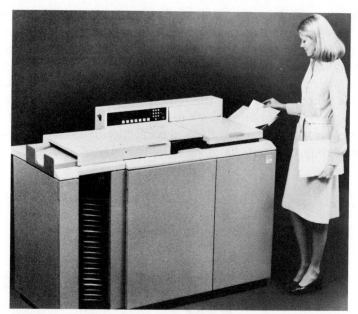

Figure 12-2   IBM Series III Copier/Duplicator, Model 20
(Courtesy International Business Machines Corporation)

New developments in copiers may represent the next major breakthrough in word-processing technology. Using an ink-jet printing device, the copier pictured in Figure 12-3 accepts magnetic data and ink-sprays it on paper at the rate of 900 words per minute. This copier also prints addresses on envelopes and matches the envelopes with appropriate copies of the letters as they are produced. It should not be very long, therefore, before word-processing operators will simply press a button to convert screened images directly to printed documents—without the rat-a-tat-tat of conventional printers. Ideally, the photo mechanism that produces the final documents will fold and insert them into envelopes, attach the correct postage, and sort them for mailing.

Micrographics. **Micrographics** provide a neat answer to the filing problems outlined earlier in the chapter. Instead of stuffing filing cabinets and boxes with new and old records, some that will be used again and many that will not, more and more companies record their files on microfilm. The present state of the art enables them to film letters, reports, pictures, tables, graphs, and many other types of documents, in either black and white or color.

Businesses can now record thousands of documents on very small areas of film, and, with the assistance of minicomputers, can retrieve specific documents instantaneously and automatically. Existing equipment also makes it possible for employees to update filmed documents. If the company charged too high a price on the sale of a particular item, for example, the employee making the refund can observe the related invoice on a screen. And, if the company's micrographic equipment is sufficiently modern and sophisticated, the employee may use a keyboard to update the filmed invoice—noting on the film the amount refunded, the reason, and the date. Existing equipment also makes it possible for employees to reproduce on paper any of the microfilmed documents—instantaneously. Can anyone doubt that we are well on our way toward development of the much-heralded "paperless office"?

Figure 12-3 Ink-jet printer that operates at speeds of up to 900 words per minute. It automatically addresses envelopes and matches them with letters being printed. (Courtesy International Business Machines Corporation)

Cost factor. How much does all of this equipment cost? If you were to buy a keyboarded CRT (cathode-ray tube) and high-speed printer today, at the time this book is being written, you would pay anywhere from $10,000 to $20,000. By the time you read the book, however, prices may be significantly lower. Just as the prices of hand calculators entered a rapid decline, so too will the prices of WP equipment decline—as a greater number of companies expand production and compete more fiercely for this relatively new market.

But who can afford to pay $10,000 or more for a typewriter, even if it is a supertypewriter? A more appropriate question might be, "Who can afford *not* to buy one?" Assuming that the new typing system enables two people to do the work that previously kept three people occupied (a reasonable estimate), the savings will pay for the equipment in about one year. Moreover, the units will continue saving money for many years thereafter; the only part of the system that suffers any wear is the printer, and it has only a dozen or so moving parts.

One of the most frequently voiced complaints about word-processing centers is that the turnaround time is too long. Employees complain that by the time communications are prepared and returned for signing, they have forgotten the details involved. **Optical scanning readers (OCRs)** help to over-come this problem. Rather than having typists use expensive WP units to type original documents, which for even a medium-sized company might require two or three expensive units, companies may buy fewer word processors and use them only for editing previously typed materials. With an OCR, every Selectric typewriter in an office may be used as an input mechanism.

Secretaries type letters, reports, and other documents as usual on rela-tively inexpensive typewriters. Documents typed correctly the first time don't need editing on word processors. When a major alteration is required, one that would involve extensive retyping, the secretary goes to a nearby WP area and runs the document through an OCR unit, displaying the document on a CRT screen. The secretary then uses the WP keyboard to make the necessary altera-tions—using the expensive WP equipment only to circumvent the chore of retyping lengthy or difficult materals.

It'll never work.

PLAN OF ACTION

The implementation of a word-processing system is not an easy task. When people have spent years preparing for and using traditional office methods, they tend to resist new ideas or procedures that materially alter the status quo. Recognizing this potential problem, management should plan the WP system carefully and undertake programs designed to gain employee acceptance and cooperation.

Outline the system. Word-processing systems should be tailored to the particular company, to accommodate varying conditions. One company might need five keyboarded-CRT units and just one printer for example, while another company might need three CRTs, two printers, and an OCR. The managers of one company may want to link the WP equipment with a computer, while others may not.

The most difficult choice in the planning stages, of course, is the selection of a particular make of WP equipment. Representatives of those employees who will use the service and those people who are going to operate the equipment should be identified as early as possible, so that they can help with the selection process.

To avoid the costly mistake of buying or leasing the wrong equipment, management should consider a wide variety of models, seeking demonstrations and feasibility studies from vendors and visiting word-processing centers that are already operational. They should keep in mind, however, that a system which works well for one company might be inappropriate for another.

An important issue is whether or not the word-processing center should be centralized. Centralization enables a company to gain maximum utilization from relatively few units but necessitates frequent mail service between the center and the offices it serves. Decentralization, on the other hand, places WP units near the offices (the same floor, at least) so that secretaries may use the equipment themselves in conjunction with their regular typewriters.

Potential obsolescence is a major concern with selecting word processors. Purchasers should be certain that the equipment is programmable, so that the memory units will receive new programs as they are developed by vendors. The state of the art is changing so rapidly that it would be impractical to change equipment each time a new feature is introduced to the market. Changing vendors, moreover, is complicated by the fact that their units are not compatible. To take advantage of a recent development by another vendor usually requires a complete change of equipment.

Sell the concept. So how do we overcome the built-in resistance to word processing mentioned earlier? The best way to gain acceptance, cooperation, and even enthusiasm from employees is to involve them in the planning stages of the system. Create dissatisfaction with traditional methods by identifying all existing problems and inefficiencies, and challenge employees to help the company maintain pace with the changing times.

Don't overestimate the willingness of business managers to adopt the new system. Case studies show that top managers often display formidable resistance to procedural change. Maybe they have dictated letters to the same secretary for many years. Maybe they had unpleasant experiences with cumbersome dictation equipment during an earlier period. Even more likely, maybe they fear the loss of an important status symbol—their secretaries.

Since managers generally respond to arguments based on sound economic concepts, they should be presented with the projected savings (in $$$ and

¢¢¢) with the new system. They also might be more receptive when they realize that their secretaries will have more time to assist them with administrative duties. Selling management on the merits of word-processing systems is important, because their support is essential to successful implementation.

Secretaries have even more to lose than their bosses do. Far from being enthusiastic about the new word-processing equipment, they generally imagine the obsolescence of long-nurtured typing and shorthand skills. But dictation and typing usually constitute only a portion of secretarial duties. Other responsibilities remain, such as handling telephones, making appointments, arranging itineraries, and preparing agenda for meetings. With the right attitude, and freedom from dictation and typing chores, secretaries may often assume a greater portion of the workload from their principals.

When word processors are introduced at some companies, secretaries receive the new title "administrative secretary"; and, to offset removal of dictation and typing duties, they are assigned to more than one principal. Greater responsibility? Yes! More interesting work? Certainly! Better opportunity for promotion? Definitely!

Once a vendor has been chosen, ask the sales representatives to conduct several demonstrations. Show the people who will be using the system how it will benefit them and the company, and make certain that those who will actually be operating the system have an opportunity to try it out. When word processors are demonstrated properly, most observers are amazed at their potential.

Set realistic goals. Don't promise more than the sytem can deliver. Don't promise employees that their documents will be prepared and returned (turnaround time) within two hours when it will be closer to four. Don't promise error-free documents, because people will still make mistakes—even when using word processors. If top management demands cost projections at the beginning of the program, don't be overly optimistic. Expected savings generally aren't realized until the second or third year of operation, after employees learn how to use the system properly; and many of the benefits are in quality of production rather than cost reductions.

Introduce in stages. Managers of some companies have taken a "big bang" approach to implementation, removing all typewriters and requiring all employees to rely totally on word-processing centers. In all reported incidents, this approach has been traumatic for the people who operate the centers. They were bombarded with a barrage of source documents the operators had never seen before. The resulting delays in production produced a great deal of criticism and the need for new rounds of pep talks.

A more successful approach is to introduce new WP services in stages.

Instead of serving all comers, begin handling the correspondence for just one department. The first stage enables dictators to become acquainted with the new procedures, the operators to become comfortable with the equipment, and the person coordinating the system to learn just what can be accomplished in a given time period. As each stage is perfected, include additional departments until the entire company is being served efficiently.

Maintain control. The quickest way to turn people off on a word-processing center is to lose some of their materials. Therefore, the WP supervisor or a special controller should be responsible for controlling the flow of paper to, from, and within the center. Records should be kept (called **logging**) of all materials entering the center, whether by messenger (a magnetic tape, a handwritten original, or a typed document returned for revision) or through a centrally located dictation mechanism. The center should be able to account for the receipt and delivery of all documents and the current status of those being processed.

WP operators take dictation either from cassette tapes received in the company mail or from centralized tape units. Following dictation into the centralized units, or even while materials are being dictated, operators transcribe directly to word processors. The tape drives show the amount of dictation remaining on any one tape, and transfer devices enable WP supervisors to equalize the typing load among the operators.

Machine X-12, take a letter, please.

DICTATION GUIDELINES

If a word-processing center is to prove economical, employees must be persuaded to dictate their communications into some type of magnetic device. And, for optimal results, the people doing the dictating must follow prescribed guidelines.

Try dictation. Many people are reluctant to dictate their correspondence. They feel pressured when a secretary is waiting to record a steady stream of words, and some people are under the impression that they cannot organize their ideas well when talking to a dictation machine. So what do they do? Many authors write their communications in longhand before dictating or handing them to secretaries for typing. Such a practice should be discouraged, because those employees who hold positions important enough to involve much writing are usually being paid too much money to spend their time pushing pencils. For maximum efficiency, they must be persuaded to dictate their communication—preferably to a recording device rather than a secretary.

When dictating to secretaries, most people accumulate materials until they have several items to dictate at once. This approach forces dictators to rethink the situation surrounding each letter while dictating, and improper preparation just prior to dictating wastes the time of secretaries unnecessarily.

Machine dictation methods are much more convenient. If you wish to respond to a letter you have just read while the response is fresh on your mind, you simply reach for a hand-held microphone, press a "Record" button with your thumb, and start talking. If you are interrupted during machine dictation, you may press a button for an instant replay of the last few words dictated. If you make a mistake in your dictation, press another button to alert the typist to watch for a correction. The machine does not represent any type of pressure on dictators because it does not start squirming or looking askance no matter how long it takes them to formulate their ideas.

Individual dictation units are portable, fitting nicely on desk tops. Pocket-sized units are also available. Whether desk-top or pocket-sized, these dictation machines utilize reusable cassette tapes that are easily handled—in interoffice mail and through U.S. mail. Some centralized systems also use regular telephones as part of their dictation systems. By picking up a push-button telephone at the office or at home, employees may dictate directly to word-processing centers—day or night, 24 hours a day.

But what if employees make mistakes while dictating letters from home? After dialing the WP center, they press the 1 key on their telephones to start a magnetic tape. They press the 2 for corrections, the 3 for replay, and so on. Employees may dictate rush communications to special tapes for priority service, and they may close dictating sessions by either pressing the 4 key or hanging up the receiver. Pretty convenient? Yes, and very economical when the volume of written correspondence is sufficiently large.

Provide complete information. Employees who dictate directly to secretaries typically hand the files to secretaries at the end of dictating sessions. This procedure enables the secretaries to look at correspondence from other companies to copy the addresses, to proofread the spelling of names, and to check any unfamiliar terms that may have been used during dictation.

When dictation is to a tape in a word-processing center or to a cassette tape that is to be mailed to the center, the WP operator does not have the advantage of these files. Therefore, the dictator must provide complete information: the name of the addressee, the company name, the address (even the zip code), and the spelling of names and terms in the text of the communication.

Communicate thoroughly. Don't mumble when you dictate, especially during machine dictation. Secretaries taking shorthand can ask dictators to repeat something they miss, but magnetic tapes cannot. If any part of your communication is unclear to the transcribing operator, completion of the document is delayed. Begin by specifying the kind of communication it is—a long or short letter, a memo, a personal note. Also indicate the number of copies required, if more than the usual file copy. Then, when dictating the communication, clearly pronounce and spell all words that might be confused; for example, the italicized words in the following paragraph should be spelled during dictation:

> We received a bid from *Matheson* Electronics, but we question their credit standing. Before making a final decision on the contract, however, we will check their *Dun & Bradstreet* and the financial reports that accompanied their bid. In the meantime, will you please check with Robert W. *Smyth* at International Bankers to determine the status of the mortgage loan that is shown on the Matheson balance sheet. Smyth is the chief credit officer of International's *Royston* Branch at 1612 West *Orlin* Way in Belmont, California, and the zip code is 94002.

The dictator would rightfully expect the typist to be able to spell such words as *electronics* and *international,* and would spell the name *Belmont* only if it were a distant city. Some knowledge of surrounding geographic areas is assumed, and an acquaintance with commonly used business terms (such as *balance sheet*) is expected.

Edit the output. It is tempting sometimes to leave the signing of correspondence to others, especially when the turnaround time is several hours. But to do so is risky. If at all possible, check completed communications for accuracy and appearance and sign them yourself. If you cannot be available to edit correspondence, assign the task to someone who is familiar with the transactions being discussed and who can spot an error when one exists. When employees sign letters dictated by someone else, they should sign the dictator's name and follow the signature with their own initials. Keep in mind that *all* your correspondence is a reflection on both you and your company.

DISCUSSION AND REVIEW QUESTIONS

1. Why are some business managers reluctant to use word-processing centers?

2. Why do many secretaries resist the introduction of WP systems?

3. What's wrong with traditional office methods, where certain employees dictate letters directly to secretaries?

4. If typists can type just as fast or faster on late-model typewriters as they can on word-processing machines, can they turn out just as much work with the use of typewriters? Explain your answer.

5. What are the various source documents with which WP operators must work?

6. Why can people type on WP machines with less concern for typing errors than when using conventional typewriters?

7. Why are revisions of letters and other documents so easy with WP equipment?

8. What are micrographics, and why are such systems needed?

9. What is the application of optical scanning readers (OCRs)?

10. How can OCRs be used to reduce the turnaround time experienced with many WP centers?

11. How can secretaries use selectric typewriters as input devices for WP equipment?

12. Why is the careful selection of WP equipment so important?

13. What is wrong with removing all regular typewriters from a company and introducing a WP center all at once?

14. What is the role of administrative secretaries, once a WP center is fully operational?

15. How may employees use word-processing centers from their homes?

16. Some people don't like to dictate to secretaries, and some even avoid the use of dictation equipment. Why?

17. Why should employees who do a lot of writing be persuaded to use dictation equipment rather than writing their communications in longhand?

18. Why must the people who dictate to magnetic devices for transcription in WP centers provide more complete information than when dictating directly to secretaries?

19. What is the procedure for signing someone else's mail?

20. Why is it wise to sign your own mail whenever possible?

21. Respond to the following comments:
    a. Many companies are using WP machines to automate their offices.
    b. I hate to use our WP center because it takes so long to get a letter back and into the mail.
    c. We don't need any WP equipment in a small company like this one.
    d. Is that typist ever going to flip when she learns that I want to reverse the order of the first and third paragraphs in this legal document!
    e. If we are going to buy a new WP system, maybe we had better do it now before prices increase.
    f. I understand that First National Bank has one of the best WP centers in the state. We are not in the bank business, but we want a system just like it.

PART FOUR
PSYCHOLOGICAL TECHNIQUES

When you plan a communciation, first determine if it falls within a specific category. Is it a routine communication? Are you conveying good news or bad news? Are you asking for money? Are you trying to sell someone a product, a service, or an idea? When a communication falls within an identifiable category, you may realize superior results by following established guidelines. The following statement by an official of a leading airline illustrates the practicality of this approach to business communications.

The Consumer Relations Department of American Airlines responds to about 7,000 written communications each month. We think that it is important to reply promptly, and we have time standards within which the writer should hear from us—five to seven working days is the norm.

A great number of the letters we receive fall into predictable subject classifications such as fares, food, schedules, and compliments; and these are readily answered using model letters with a personalized style that has been well received in the past.

There are occasions when it is not possible to grant a passenger's request; when this happens, great care is taken to explain our position clearly—the reasons might be tariff restrictions, safety factors, lack of ticket or baggage stubs. When we are relaying good news, on the other hand, such as a monetary adjustment for a missed meal or damaged bag, we tell the passenger the good news right at the start of the letter and then apologize for the mishap.

In letters requesting past-due payments, we take the view that 99 percent of our travelers are honest but may temporarily be short of cash, may have been traveling and not at home to pay their bills, or may have forgotten. Our objective is to secure payment and maintain the customers' goodwill, so that they will remain users of our services.

Charles H. Startup
Director, Consumer Relations
American Airlines, Inc.

If you routinely begin and complete your communications without difficulty, if you are consistently sensitive to the feelings of others, and if you have a natural talent for persuasion, your reliance on prescribed formulas may be limited. If you do not possess these innate abilities, on the other hand, you will find the following chapters extremely helpful.

13
RESPONDING TO ROUTINE CORRESPONDENCE

Not all business correspondence relates to problem areas. Many people write to businesses to inquire about products, services, and prices; and businesses frequently receive letters of commendation from their customers. These **routine communications** are relatively easy to respond to, but we do not treat them casually. Prompt and courteous responses will almost certainly increase our business; whereas delayed and inappropriate responses tend to jeopardize future sales opportunities.

First, a moment of contemplation.

FORMULATE A MENTAL OUTLINE

Plan your communications, even when responding to routine inquiries. Having decided on the essential points of your communications, use the schematic in Figure 13-1 as a pattern for routine business communications.

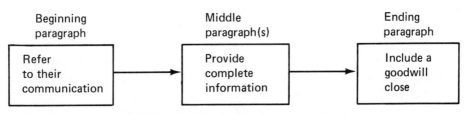

Figure 13-1   Outline for routine communications

Which of our thousands of letters are you referring to?

REFER TO THEIR COMMUNICATION

Businesses do not operate in isolation from one another. Most businesses depend on other companies for raw materials, supplies, and services. Conversely, many businesses sell their finished goods to other businesses. Each business is a customer of other businesses, and each business has other businesses as customers. The exchange of written and oral communications between two companies becomes extensive when they conduct transactions with each other on a regular basis. Rather than forcing the receivers of our many letters to match replies with copies of related letters they mailed to us to begin with, therefore, we start our correspondence with references to their specific communications.

Example: In response to your letter of January 23 . . .

Example: Here is the information that you requested in your letter of March 4.

Making reference to correspondence received is also a convenient way to begin our replies to individual customers and potential customers.

Example: Thank you for your letter of the 23rd, in which you . . .

Example: Your letter has been referred to Ms. Walker in our Customer Relations Department.

The initial correspondence is not always a letter, of course; many business letters are written in response to telephone and in-person conversations. We refer to these encounters at the beginning of our letters or conversations just as we do when responding to written communications.

Example: After our talk during lunch on Friday, Martha, we decided to . . .

Example: Your phone call this morning enabled us to . . .

When beginning a letter, a memo, or a conversation, ask yourself if there was a preceding communication (letter, memo, phone call, or face-to-face encounter) that should be referred to before starting the main part of your message. Provide other people with direction, rather than forcing them to undertake extensive search routines to learn what you are talking about.

We're not clairvoyants, you know.

PROVIDE COMPLETE INFORMATION

You will usually satisfy the other person and avoid additional communications by providing complete information the first time. If a business customer requests price information relating to the purchase of 1,000 cases of your product, for example, be certain to specify whether the price does or does not include shipping costs. Failure to provide such vital information invariably results in additional communications.

When consumers request information about the availability of certain products, include extra information. After discussing availability, provide information on model choices, color options, delivery dates, and terms of payment. Make your communications complete by trying to answer those questions that might arise in the minds of customers as they contemplate purchases. We may consider our communications to be 100 percent successful only when they do not require further exchanges for reasons of clarification.

We can often minimize the detail in our letters by including bulletins and brochures. Instead of describing the various models of a product, for instance, we can allude to an accompanying brochure. Instead of detailing our terms of sale, we can mention an enclosed bulletin.

Example: We are enclosing a brochure that describes the operation more completely.

Example: This product is available in several models and colors, as illustrated in the accompanying pamphlet.

What about copies of newspaper and magazine ads and other promotional materials? When writing to new customers, we may include promotional materials they would not have received during our regular mailings. As a matter of practice, however, we do *not* routinely include such materials with all correspondence. To do so would require that all employees who write letters be provided with advertising materials on a regular basis. Enclosure of the materials with their regular communications would result in duplicate mailings and additional postage charges. Rather than sending promotional materials to the relatively few customers with whom we correspond individually, therefore, we rely on mass mailings of advertisements to *all* customers.

When several items are involved, we often send them separately—the letter in one envelope, promotional materials in a separate one. We mention in our letter that the materials are being mailed separately, but we avoid the worn expression "under separate cover."

Example: You will also be receiving an operator's manual.
Example: We are mailing these materials separately.
Example: We will send a corrected invoice right away.

Remember, we still love you.

INCLUDE GOODWILL CLOSE

We have begun our letter by referring to the other person's communication to us in a brief first paragraph. We then added one or two medium-length paragraphs to provide the necessary detail. Now what?

Just as we avoid being terse when closing our telephone and in-person conversations, we avoid abruptness when ending our letters. Instead of just walking away from others at the end of conversations, we usually say something like "See you later," "Take care now," or "It's been nice talking with you." We ease out of our written communications in much the same way.

Example: Thank you very much for providing us with this information.
Example: We hope that you will be pleased with your new stereo.
Example: Let us know if there is any other way that we may help you.

We refer to such closing statements as **goodwill closes,** because they tend to please people and cause them to think well of our companies.

These are too easy.

EXAMPLES OF ROUTINE CORRESPONDENCE

Now let's put the pieces together to form some complete communications. We have just received Purchase Order 36130 from a new customer, and we are shipping all the requested items, except one, from our Los Angeles plant on May 8 via Yellow Freight Lines. The remaining item, 500 cases of Product A-612, is being shipped from our New Jersey warehouse on May 7 via Brown Motor Freight. Following the schematic in Figure 13-1, we write the following message.

Refer to their communication	Thank you for your initial order with our company, Purchase Order No. 36130.
Provide complete information	The 500 cases of Product A-612 will be shipped from our New Jersey warehouse on May 7 via Brown Motor Freight, and all other items will be shipped from our Los Angeles plant on May 8 via Yellow Freight Lines.
Add a goodwill close	We appreciate your business and will do our best to serve you well.

An investor has written directly to our company, Seymour Electronics, requesting a copy of our annual report for 1979. The letter is dated November 10, 1979, but our annual report for 1979 will not be available until February 5, 1980. Therefore, we must write a letter explaining that (1) we are sending a copy of last year's annual report at this time, and (2) we will send a copy of the new annual report as soon as it is published.

Refer to their communication	In response to your letter of November 10, we are enclosing a copy of our annual report for 1978.
Provide complete information	We will also send a copy of our 1979 annual report to you immediately upon its publication in early February. Please complete and return the enclosed card if you would like to receive copies of all future financial reports.
Add a goodwill close	Thank you for your interest in Seymour Electronics

Before selling to our company on credit terms, a new supplier has written a letter (dated October 3) requesting copies of our most recent income statement and balance sheet. Their request also includes a financial form that is to be completed and returned with the two financial statements. Our letter of transmittal (written on October 15) should follow the same pattern as the preceding communications.

Refer to their communication	We are returning the completed financial form that accompanied your letter of October 3.
Provide complete information	Enclosed also are copies of our most recent income statement and balance sheet, both dated December 31, 1979, and copies of our pro forma statements for the coming year. Both 1979 statements have been audited and approved by Smith, Finker, and Ralston Associates.
Add a goodwill close	Please let us know if additional information is required.

Working in the consumer relations section of an airline company, we have just received a very complimentary letter from a businessman concerning the services of Liza Herman, one of our Customer Service Agents. It seems that Liza's skill in the Portuguese language helped him locate a former business associate during a stopover in Portugal. Let's contribute further to the goodwill of this customer by responding promptly to his letter.

Refer to their communication	We were very pleased to receive your kind words about Liza Herman, and we know that Liza will also be pleased when she reads your letter.
Provide complete information	Although our language is the most common language throughout the world, many millions of people don't understand one word of English. It is for this reason that we recruit people who are skilled in several languages to work as Customer Service Agents on our international flights.
Add a goodwill close	Thank you for taking the time to tell us that you found this aspect of our service to be of special value.

The formula approach works very well, doesn't it? Once you recognize a particular communication as "routine," you write the prescribed segments for routine communications and presto, the letter is complete and highly readable. You may use the following guidelines when writing routine letters—but use them only as guidelines, not as substitutes for your own words. Also keep in mind the S★T★A★R approach (page 120), along with everything you have learned about mechanics (Part 2) and grammar format (Part 3).

Oops, I forgot to . . .

CHECKLIST:
ROUTINE CORRESPONDENCE

Beginning paragraph. Refer to their communication in one of the following ways:

- ☐ Acknowledge receipt of their written communication.
- ☐ Thank them for the communication.
- ☐ Express your enjoyment of a previous conversation.
- ☐ Casually refer to their communication when outlining their requests.
- ☐ Tell them that their communication is being referred to another person for reply.
- ☐ Express appreciation for their business, when their communication includes an order for products or services.

Middle paragraph(s). Provide complete information:

- ☐ Answer their specific questions.
- ☐ Include any extra detail that might prove helpful.
- ☐ Reinforce your statements and minimize verbiage by enclosing related brochures and pamphlets.
- ☐ Include promotional materials when appropriate, especially when corresponding with a new customer.
- ☐ Mention in the text of your letter materials that are enclosed or mailed separately.

Ending paragraph. Add a goodwill close in one of the following ways:

- ☐ Thank them for their interest.
- ☐ Thank them for taking the time to communicate with you.
- ☐ Express an optimistic look toward the future.
- ☐ Offer additional information or assistance.
- ☐ Thank them for directing their business your way.
- ☐ Mention their continued enjoyment of your product or service.
- ☐ Express your desire to respond to their future needs.

Remember. These are just guidelines. Strive to use your own words and ideas when following the suggested format.

BUSINESS APPLICATIONS *(Assume that you are using company letterhead.)*

1. As a sales representative for Harris-Schneck & Associates, Inc., write a letter to Mrs. Joan Bennett at 6840 North 16th Street, Apartment 27 in Syracuse, New York 13201. You are sending her a payment book for the purchase of furniture last month from Schultz Bros. Her first payment will be due on February 20, and subsequent payments will be due on the 20th of each month thereafter. Mrs. Bennett phoned you yesterday, February 2 (current year), asking when the first payment would be due.

2. In your position as assistant distribution manager of Ponds Corporation, you have just received an order from John Walyk at Nebraska Distributors, Inc. for 15 cartons of assorted toiletries and cosmetics. Their address is 1201 West 16th Street, Lincoln, Nebraska 86501. You have the product available, but the "ship to" section of their Purchase Order 95106 is blank. Write a letter asking them where you are to ship the merchandise and whether they prefer any particular trucking company. Use the current date.

3. You work for Metzger Insurance Agency, with no special title of your own, and you are sending an auto insurance policy to Miguel M. Sanchez at 6345 Orange Avenue, Lakewood, California 90614. Ask Mr. Sanchez to review the policy on his 1976 Dodge Dart to make certain that the coverage is exactly as he wishes it. Enclose a stamped return envelope and ask him to provide you with the number and expiration date of his driver's license, his birthdate, and his social security number. You need this information to update your files.

4. Referring to the situation in No. 3, assume that you receive an identical letter from Metzger Insurance Agency and that you find all aspects of the

policy to be correct. Send your response on regular stationery (not letter-head) to Rosalind Peters at the agency, 16201 Ocean Boulevard, Long Beach, California 90801.

5. As a sales representative in the New Products Division of S-Mark, Inc., you are reading a letter from Roberta Powell, an apparel buyer for Rannet Clothiers, Inc., 66 Exchange Street, Rochester, New York 14614. She is requesting price information on a new pantsuit that your company ad-vertised in the latest issue of *Women's World*. Although you introduced the pantsuit to the market just 30 days ago, orders for it have been coming in at an astounding rate. Tell this buyer that the pantsuit lists for $75.50 and that shipment can be made approximately 20 days after receipt of an order. Enclose a brochure that shows the different color combinations that are available.

6. As a clerk in the accounting department of a large food-packing company, write a letter to Garfinckel, Smith and Miller, Inc., at 250 Westchester Avenue, White Plains, New York 10604. In submitting their Credit Memo B-1218 of March 16 (current year) for $18.36, they did not include proof that advertisements were placed in the local newspapers as claimed. You cannot process the credit memo until this information is received. Date your letter March 25. (Proof of advertising normally consists of copies of the respective ads that have been clipped from local newspapers.)

7. In your position as assistant manager of the accounts payable department, you have just processed for payment Invoice No. 161278 from Whitmer Laboratories, Inc. Although you routinely instruct all vendors to submit invoices in duplicate and to show your purchase order number, Whitmer sent only the original invoice and did not show the purchase order num-ber. Write a letter advising them that you are paying this invoice but that the payment of future invoices will be subject to delay unless properly submitted. The address of Whitmer Laboratories is 8580 Stemmons Freeway, Dallas, Texas 75247.

8. You are an administrative assistant to the sales manager at Gardner-Atlas Company, and a memo you just received from the distribution depart-ment advises that Glasrock Systems, Inc., 1625 East 47th Avenue in Woodcliff Lake, New Jersey (zip is 07675) sent an order for 75 cases of woodcraft kits—their Purchase Order 21218. Write a letter advising the people at Glasrock that you are shipping the kits on January 12 (current year) via Red Ball Express, but that they should submit all future orders to the broker for their area, Heffernan and Schmidt, Inc., 250 North South Street, White Plains, New York 10625. Indicate in your letter that a copy is being sent to the broker.

9. Write a memo to members of the sales staff thanking them for their help with the recent sales campaign. On January 1 you established a sales goal of $2 million for the first quarter, but at the end of March sales exceeded $2.5 million. You attribute much of this success to the hard work and dedication of your staff and their skillful use of the broadcast and print media. Say something in the memo that will motivate them to keep sales at a high level during the ensuing three-month period.

10. In her letter of November 10 (current year), Loretta Holly of 17122 West Terrace Way, Nashville, Tennessee 37202 complained of dark veins in the Red Sockeye Salmon that she purchased at a local grocery store. She enclosed the can lid with her letter, from which you discerned that she had purchased a 1-pound can of your Seaside label—a choice product. Sockeye salmon is the best kind of salmon; it is relatively scarce and quite expensive. Despite the high quality of the product, the appearance often suffers from the presence of dark veins. The veins do not detract from the taste of the product, only the appearance; and there is no way of eliminating them. Compose a letter to this customer designed to dispel her concern about the veins and to keep her purchasing this brand of salmon regularly.

11. Working as a claims agent for Runard Steamship Lines, you received a letter from Robert E. Blake, 1600 S.W. Fifth Avenue, Portland, Oregon 97205. Having debarked from the *S.S. Aquarius* at your dock on April 15 (current year), he and his wife were short one piece of luggage—a light brown overnight case. Write a letter dated April 25 explaining that such a case was unclaimed from that vessel. You did not know the owner, because the luggage carried no identification. You will send the case to him promptly via Parcel Post.

12. As a clerk in the public relations department of Pacific Corporation, you are replying to a letter from Billy Jean Craig, who is on the staff of *The Utopian,* a weekly paper issued to students at Apollo High School, 6047 West 47th Avenue, Glendale, Arizona 85302. Billy Jean noticed a magazine advertisement by Pacific Corporation that included a picture of workers planting new trees where others had just been removed, and requests that you send a black-and-white glossy print to her for reproduction in the school paper. Write a letter to accompany the photograph.

13. On May 3 (current year) you received an airline ticket and statement ($197.95) from Worldwide Travel Agency, which is located at 1212 West Market Street, Akron, Ohio 44316. The ticket number is B-1619, a round-trip fare from Akron to San Francisco. Since Stewart Simms will

not be able to use the ticket because of a change in plans, write a letter to return with the ticket and the statement. You are a staff assistant to Stewart Simms, and today's date is May 5.

14. As an employee in the customer relations department, respond to a complaint from Mrs. Leslie W. Foster at 9715 East 42nd Street, Elmwood Park, Maryland 21233. Mrs. Foster is incensed at having found ground glass in a can of your Starburst tuna. In a letter to this customer, explain that what she observed is not glass but struvite, a harmless substance that appears in about one of every million cans of tuna. Unlike glass, struvite dissolves in water (and in saliva) and poses absolutely no threat to the health of consumers. As an added measure of goodwill, send Mrs. Foster a three-can courtesy package of your choice product.

15. You work in the Guest Relations Bureau of Seaside Amusement Park in Honolulu, Hawaii 96813, and you are reading a letter from Mike Jacobsen of 85111 West Topanga Boulevard in Buena Vista, Arkansas 72210. Jacobsen and seven business associates visited the amusement park during a convention in Hawaii, and he expressed their complete satisfaction with Rita Yu, the tour guide. All members of the group were impressed by her knowledge of the facility and the courtesies she extended to them. Respond to this letter with a goodwill letter of your own, a letter so well conceived and written that it will serve as a guide for all future letters of this type.

14

DELIVERING GOOD NEWS

Businesses receive many requests from suppliers, wholesalers, retailers, consumers, government agencies, and the general public—requests for products, price adjustments, exchanges, refunds, employment, credit, and many types of information. When business people respond to these requests in the affirmative, giving others what they are seeking, we refer to their replies as **good news communications.** Although most people respond favorably to the receipt of messages bearing good news, regardless of the word choice or organization used, the following pages present several guidelines for deriving the greatest amount of goodwill from such communications.

You may be cool, but you still need a plan.

EMPHASIZE THE POSITIVE

Good news messages are relatively easy to communicate, but a good plan makes the task even easier. The schematic in Figure 14-1 provides some guidelines for emphasizing the positive aspects of good news communications.

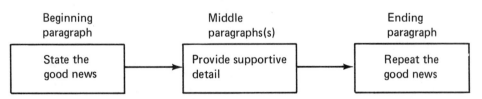

Figure 14-1   Outline for good news communications

Psychologists contend that most people remember the opening and closing remarks of letters and conversations more vividly than what is written or said in between these remarks. We may put this theory into practice when we are conveying good news.

First, the good news.

BEGIN WITH THE GOOD NEWS

A main consideration with many messages is whether to use **deductive** or **inductive** reasoning. With the deductive approach, we begin the communication with the main point of the message. With the inductive approach, we preface the main part of our message with a related explanation. When conveying good news, the more effective approach is clear; we follow the deductive method by placing the good news right up front. Consider the following opening remarks:

Example: We have just received approval for the issuance of full coverage on your 1979 Corvette.

Example: Although the warranty on the heating unit for your waterbed ended more than 60 days ago, we have decided to replace it free of charge.

Example: Closing costs on your new home totaled $946.50, or $45.50 less than originally estimated.

When the situation allows us to give people what they have asked for or what will please them, we don't keep them guessing about our answer. Instead, we remove the pressures of uncertainty by stating our positive response at the beginning of the communication.

Isn't it pleasant doing business with us?

PROVIDE SUPPORTIVE DETAIL

As the diagram in Figure 14-1 shows, the pattern for conveying good news begins and ends the communication by mentioning the good news. But to do this tactfully, we must separate both references to the good news with a middle paragraph or two.

A middle paragraph or two? About what? The content of the middle part of the communication depends on the situation. If you are providing automobile insurance, replacing a defective product, or refunding money, as in the preceding examples of opening remarks, you may provide some detail regarding the transactions.

Example: Your own vehicle is insured against loss, except for the first $100, up to but not exceeding $6,000. Bodily injury liability insurance of $50,000 for each person is included, with a maximum payment of $100,000 for each accident. Property damage liability (damage that may be inflicted on the property of others) is covered up to $10,000 for each accident, and related medical payments will be paid to a maximum of $2,000.

Example: The L-1214 heating unit is guaranteed for one year, but we construct them to last much longer than that; and the overall performance of this particular model has resulted in an outstanding record of reliability. When a control unit malfunctions as yours has, therefore, we would rather replace it than to have customers assume critical views of our fine products.

Example: Interest on the mortgage balance of $38,400 from July 13 to August 20 amounted to $256.00, instead of $296.00—a difference of $40.00; and the prorated taxes from July 13 to the purchase date were $61.50, instead of $67.00—an additional difference in your favor of $5.50.

The second example includes two attempts to resell the company's products, specifying that the heating units are made to last a long time and mentioning the company's "fine products." A certain amount of resell in good news letters can be very effective; we may alleviate any doubts that our customers may be having by restating the positive qualities of the products. The following sentences are additional examples of ways that we may resell our products in the middle sections of good news letters.

Example: You made a wise decision to buy your new home when you did, because we have had several people express interest in the property since you bought it.

Example: Despite this initial inconvenience, your new refrigerator will provide you with many years of satisfactory service. In fact, *Consumer Guide* recently judged this particular model to be the best designed and most energy-efficient refrigerator on the market.

Customers often experience what salespeople refer to as "after-purchase blues," especially when something goes wrong with the products they have just bought. When we correspond with them about repair, replacement, or some other type of adjustment, therefore, we should attempt to resell the items—to reassure customers that they have made wise purchase decisions in selecting our products.

Don't jeopardize the goodwill objective of good news communications by mentioning self-sacrifice. By telling customers about the trouble involved in accomplishing what they request, you may cause them to feel indebted to you, which in turn may make them reluctant to conduct further business transactions with your company—reasoning that if anything should go wrong with another of your products or services they would be embarrassed to bother you with a second request for assistance. Just convey the good news, and forget about any personal inconvenience you may have encountered.

One more time, once.

REPEAT THE GOOD NEWS

As a way of generating as much goodwill as possible from good news messages, we again refer to the good news in our closing paragraphs. To illustrate, let's close the letters that we have written in the previous sections: (1) extending insurance coverage, (2) exchanging the waterbed heating unit, and (3) refunding an overcharge on the purchase of a home.

> Example: We are pleased to be able to provide this coverage, and the policy will be mailed directly to you from our home office within the next week to ten days. Please check it carefully and let us know if you have any questions.

> Example: You may take the enclosed card to any authorized dealer in your area, along with the used heating unit, for free replacement of the unit or for full credit toward the purchase of any other heating unit.

> Example: Our check for $45.50 is enclosed.

We opened these three communications with mention of the good news, provided some detail, and closed with a second reference to the good news. This pattern allows us to write well-balanced letters that leave readers with positive thoughts about our products and our company.

Put it all together and what do you have?

EXAMPLES OF GOOD NEWS COMMUNICATIONS

So we have a beginning, a middle, and an ending, just as with routine communications; we have changed only the content of those segments. To illustrate further, let's consider several business situations that call for good news communications. Having just received a letter from a customer concerning a mistake that we made in one of our billings, we find that the customer is correct and a refund is in order.

State the good news	We agree with the figures cited in your letter of March 29, and we will refund the amount requested.
Provide supportive detail	Procedural errors such as this one, which resulted from a misplaced price tag, occasionally slip through--in spite of very stringent control measures. Thank you for setting us straight, and you may be sure that we will do everything within our power to see that all future billings are 100 percent accurate.
Repeat the good news	You will receive our check for $22.50 within the next few days.

As an assistant to the personnel manager, let's inform a person of acceptance for employment, having selected him from among several other applicants; and, as before, let's mention the good news at both ends of the communication.

State the good news	We are pleased to offer you the position of Assistant Production Manager at our Westgate Plant.

Provide supportive detail	Your background is ideal for the job, and your availability for work on July 1 is timed perfectly for this particular assignment. Ralph Snyder, to whom you will report directly, was especially impressed by your knowledge of assembly-line operations; excellent reports from your previous employers were also important in our decision to hire you from among several applicants for this position. Will you stop at my office for an hour or two before leaving for Westgate, to complete some tax and insurance forms? Please bring a copy of your birth certificate and any health or life insurance policies presently in effect.
Repeat the good news	Once again, Jeff, we are very happy to welcome you as a member of our Westgate production team.

In responding to a customer's letter requesting that we apply a quantity discount to previous purchases of our products, we find that the discount does apply to three purchases. We use the first paragraph to acknowledge our findings, the middle paragraph to explain our reasoning, and the final paragraph to reiterate the good news—the news that we are granting what the customer has requested.

State the good news	Having checked the information in your letter of June 19, we find that you are entitled to the quantity discount of 5 percent on each of your last three purchases.
Provide supportive detail	Our computer did not identify these orders as being eligible for the discount because each was for fewer than 500 units. But since the cumulative total of the three orders exceeds the required 500 units, all received before the close of our May sales program, you are entitled to the requested discounts of $16.01, $26.35, and $32.50.
Repeat the good news	We are allowing the discount, therefore, and crediting your account in these amounts.

An educator has requested black-and-white glossy prints of our Model X-1212 and L-1010 duplicating machines for use in a textbook that she is writing. We are sending the requested pictures, but we have only a color print of the L-1010 machine. The color print is suitable for reproduction in black and white, however.

State the good news	Here are the materials that you requested.
Provide supportive detail	The Model X-1212 duplicator is designed for relatively small business operations; the L-1010 is intended primarily for large volumes of information. The picture of Model X-1212 is in color, but our technicians assure us that the color contrasts are sufficiently distinct for satisfactory reproduction in black and white.
Repeat the good news	We hope that these materials prove useful to you, and we wish you the best of success with your project.

Good news letters are easy to write, compared to many other types of communications, and this three-step formula makes writing them even easier. Use your own words and phrases when writing or conversing, however, rather than trying to adapt the words of other people to fit your communications.

Let's check all the angles.

CHECKLIST: GOOD NEWS COMMUNICATIONS

Beginning paragraph. Begin with the good news, referring to their communications when appropriate, in one of the following ways:

- ☐ Acknowledge that they are correct.
- ☐ Inform them that their request has been approved.
- ☐ Advise that you are giving them what they want, such as
  - a refund
  - a discount
  - a replacement
  - an appointment
  - a job
  - materials and information
  - an adjustment
  - credit

Middle paragraph(s). Provide supportive detail, avoiding mention of self-sacrifice.

☐ Outline data related to the transaction, such as:
  • computational errors made
  • technicalities overlooked
  • wrong prices charged

☐ Reassure customers that they made wise purchase decisions by
  • calling attention to the favorable attributes of products.
  • citing public and professional recognition of products.
  • comparing with competing products.
  • presenting testimony of satisfied customers.
  • mentioning scarcity (limited supply) when applicable.
  • outlining warranty provisions.

Closing paragraph. Repeat the good news, adding goodwill comments where appropriate.

☐ Indicate that you are pleased to have taken the action.
☐ Provide instructions for any action that they must take.
☐ Tell them how and when the adjustments will be made.
☐ Include positive statements about future expectations.
☐ Express hope that materials will be helpful.
☐ Offer further assistance and best wishes.

Remember. These statements are not all-inclusive; they are only suggestions for ways that you may open, detail, and close good news communications. The exact words and phrases you use depend on your normal manner of speaking, since you will use your own words and phrases, and the particular business situation with which you are confronted.

Apply the S★T★A★R approach (page 120) to all business communications.

BUSINESS APPLICATIONS *(Assume that you are using company letterhead.)*

1. Working in the office of Mountain Pines Luxury Resort, respond to a request from Laura Peterson for a room with two double beds from December 5 through 11. Ms. Peterson lives at 2505 Elm Street in Dallas, Texas 75221, and the reservation is for three adults. You are reserving a room near the pool in a completely new section of the building, and the rate for three adults is $65 per day or $420 per week. Send two pamphlets with your letter: one that includes pictures of the interior and exterior of the

new section of the building and one that outlines activities available to guests. Her letter was dated November 1 and today's date is November 5 (current year).

2. In your position as assistant manager of Continental Finance Company, you have just received a phone call from Richard W. Simpson, 1616 Halstead Avenue, Rye, New York 10580. He and his family are planning an extensive motor trip through Canada, and he has requested a letter from Continental Finance authorizing him to take his 1979 Chevrolet across the border into a foreign country. Having checked the record and found that Mr. Simpson still owes approximately $1,500 to Continental Finance, but that he has been prompt with his payments during the past 23 months, you have agreed to provide him with the requested letter of authorization. Address and mail the letter directly to Mr. Simpson, and include an insurance booklet entitled *Traveling in Mexico and Canada.* Today's date is May 25 of the current year.

3. As a sales representative for National Underwriters Insurance Company, you have just received an automobile insurance policy from your main office in New York for Miss Rona Davenport, 2601 Huntington Avenue, Waterbury, Connecticut 06708. Forward the policy to Miss Davenport, informing her that the premium for the policy is $16.75 less than you originally quoted and that you are adjusting the finance agreement accordingly. Include with your letter several return envelopes for her use when making payments. Payments will be $31.86 every three months, with the first one coming due December 20. Today's date is September 15 of the current year.

4. As an employee in the Customer Relations Division of TransAmerica Airlines Corporation, you are reading a complaint letter from John R. Ralston, whose office is located at 1212 Eighth Avenue, San Diego, California 92112 (P. O. Box 1780). Mr. Ralston, who claims to be a regular customer of TransAmerica, missed a meal on Flight 211 on November 23 (today's date is December 15 of the current year). He explains that the flight attendants ran out of meals just before serving him. He has included a copy of his ticket and has requested a refund for the value of the meal. Complaints such as this one are not uncommon; even though extra meals are ordered for each flight, the number of last-minute sales often exceeds the number of extra meals ordered. Write a letter of explanation to accompany a $7.50 check that you are sending to Mr. Ralston.

5. As an administrative assistant in the sales department of Colorado Canning Company, you have received a letter dated August 5 (current year) from

Janice C. Jacobs, Purchasing Agent for Ryder Food Corporation, 235 South La Salle Street, Chicago, Illinois 60603. She is interested in contracting for 5,000 cartons of 48/8 oz. (48 eight-ounce cans in each carton) of tomato sauce and wants you to send six sample cans of the sauce. Write a letter to inform her that you are sending the six sample cans as requested, via United Parcel Service, plus an additional six samples from a batch of tomato sauce that was produced in Mexico. The price on the domestic product is $15.35 per carton, and the price on the Mexican product is $9.45 per carton, with the seller paying the shipping charges. Date your letter August 9 (current year), and show that a copy is being sent to Lydia E. Canally, Colorado Canning's sales representative in Chicago.

6. In your position as assistant manager at Register's Carpet Line, you are reading a letter from Roland Banister, who lives at 5419 East Euclid Lane, Glendale, Arizona 85302. He is questioning the sales tax that he paid on new carpeting that your company installed in his home last month. The price of the carpeting was $2,450 and the sales tax was $122.50. Mr. Banister learned from the installers, however, that the price of $2,450 included $350 labor, on which no sales tax should have been charged. Write a letter to this customer, explaining the assessment of a 5 percent sales tax on the $350 labor was an oversight and that you are enclosing a refund check in the amount of $17.50. Mr. Banister's letter is dated June 16 (current year), and today's date is June 21.

7. Working as a rate clerk for the Midwest Railway Company, you have received a claim from CG&I Steel Corporation, P. O. Box 977, Cincinnati, Ohio 45201. The claim is for a $165.25 refund of an overcharge on Freight Bill 26735. Having checked the rate and the math calculations on your copy of the freight bill, you find that they are entitled to the refund. Before you can issue a refund check, however, you must secure the original freight bill. Write a letter to Diane McCoy, Assistant Traffic Manager at CG&I, informing her of your findings and asking her to send the original freight bill to you. Her letter was dated October 4 (current year), and today's date is October 10.

8. You work in the Consumer Relations Department of Eagle Department Stores, Inc., a company which guarantees complete customer satisfaction in connection with all purchases. The company has sent a mechanic to the residence of Mrs. Margaret Filcher on three occasions to replace the condenser on a Cool Spot frostfree refrigerator that she bought at your Westside store 13 months ago. She has now written to you complaining of excessive noise from the electric motor that cools the refrigerator, and

asks that you take back the unit and refund her money. Although the refrigerator is no longer under the one-year warranty, you have decided to comply with Mrs. Filcher's wishes. You have arranged for a company truck to pick up the refrigerator next Wednesday morning, July 14 (today's date is July 6 of the current year), after which a refund check will be mailed. Write a letter to Mrs. Filcher, informing her of your decision to refund the full price of the refrigerator and inviting her to inspect the newer models that are presently displayed on your showroom floor.

9. You work in the sales department of A. J. Hunt Company, and have received a letter of inquiry dated August 1 (current year) form Marlin S. Whittier, who is vice-president of Gruehauf Corporation, Suite 16-A, First National Bank Tower, Atlanta, Georgia 30303. Mr. Whittier advises that he is thinking of buying a high-speed drilling rig from a competing company for $120,000 and is wondering if Gruehauf has a similar unit at a lower price. Inform Mr. Whittier that your company does manufacture such a unit that lists at $113,000, F.O.B. factory, Include with your letter two brochures that describe the dimensions and operational statistics of the Model M-317, a unit that you believe will meet his needs, and inform him that Robert Blakely, your sales representative in Jacksonville, will soon be in touch to provide additional information. Indicate on your letter that a copy is being sent to Robert Blakely, and date the letter August 4 (current year).

10. As a clerk in the Customer Relations Department of Combined Food Enterprises, Inc., you have received a letter dated February 20 from Regina Towers, 21211 West 16th Street, Rochester, New York 14614. She complains about a 16-ounce can of beef that is "puffy." You realize that Ms. Towers is speaking of a can that has "swelled," and you know that the contents of such cans may be poisonous. Explain to her that "swells," as they are referred to by people in the food industry, are not an uncommon occurrence with canned foodstuffs. Suggest that she carefully place the can in a plastic bag, so that the contents will not damage anything if the can should leak, and return it at once to her grocer. Combined Food Enterprises authorizes all grocers to refund the money on such returns, promptly and without question. Date your letter February 26 of the current year.

11. Functioning as a clerk for John J. Grubb Company, a company that builds single-family dwellings, you have received an official-sounding letter from Robert F. Gomez. He signed a contract last week for construction of a four-bedroom house on lot B-1612. Having since noticed that the telephone company is placing a large steel box on that lot, he is requesting that his home be built on an adjoining lot to the North. Since the city has not yet issued a building permit, you can make the change without cost to your company. Write a letter conveying the good news to Mr. Gomez. Also advise him that construction will begin in about three weeks on lot B-1614, the date previously scheduled. Mr. Gomez's letter is dated July 7 (current year), and today's date is July 12.

12. Working in the Inventory Control Department of a leading manufacturer, you have received a letter from Redmon's Dry and Cold Storage requesting payment of $65.25. Their letter, written by Joyce Pratten, is dated May 5, and today's date is May 8 of the current year. You have no record of ever having paid the invoice; therefore, you can make payment on the basis of a copy that was received with the letter. Inform Ms. Pratten of the situation and of the action that you are taking.

15

SOFTENING BAD NEWS

Businesses cannot always give people what they want; they must sometimes say "no." We refer to such messages as **bad news communications,** and we try to convey the bad news in the most acceptable way possible.

Even the boss would have to think a while about this one.

PLAN YOUR APPROACH

The primary objective in communicating bad news messages is the same as for routine and good news messages; we want to maintain or enhance the goodwill of those with whom we are communicating. We want them to think positive thoughts about our products and our services. But how, you may ask, can we deny people what they want and still retain their goodwill? We may do so by following the inductive approach outlined in Figure 15-1.

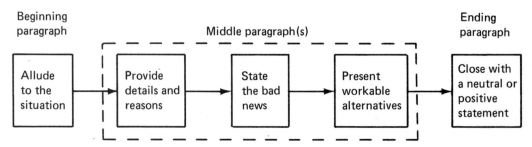

Figure 15-1 Outline for bad news communications (dotted lines indicate that the middle parts are sometimes combined into one or two paragraphs)

In the first paragraph, we briefly mention the situation that has served as the catalyst for our letter. We provide details, state the bad news, and present alternative courses of action in the middle section, which may consist of one or more paragraphs. We then close our letter with a short paragraph—a neutral statement or a positive comment about the future.

First, a little wheel-spinning

ALLUDE TO THE SITUATION

Bad news messages require the inductive pattern. Rather than going straight to the main point of the communication, as with good news messages, we assume an indirect approach. To illustrate, let's write negative responses to the three situations that were presented at the beginning of Chapter 14. We will decline the request for insurance on the 1979 Corvette; we will refuse to replace the waterbed heater; and, rather than refunding an overcharge of closing costs on the new home, we will ask the buyer to pay an undercharge.

Example: When you applied for insurance coverage on your 1979 Corvette, we told you that we would submit the application to our home office for consideration, but that coverage would not begin until approval was received.

Example: The heating unit that you returned has been checked in our laboratory.

Example: The estimated closing costs on the property at 6210 North Euclid Avenue, which we originally estimated at around $790, can now be compared with actual costs.

When writing beginning paragraphs to bad news letters, we avoid statements which might lead the reader to believe that good news is to follow. To preface bad news with statements of thanks or agreement would only make the impact of the bad news more pronounced when encountered by the reader. Instead, we begin with a statement of fact—a neutral statement concerning the situation.

Add a little padding.

PROVIDE DETAILS AND REASONS

After alluding to the situation, we still are not ready to break the bad news. We must first explain some of the factors that influenced our decision.

Example: You informed us at the time of your application that you had been cited for one moving violation and one chargeable accident. We find, however, that you have had three moving violations; although the state counts for licensing purposes only those moving violations during the past year, our company takes into consideration all such violations during the past three years.

Example: The pad and connecting cord in all of our heating units are sealed to provide complete safety to the sleeper in the event of a leaking mattress, which makes it impossible for our technicians to repair the heater or identify the exact cause of malfunction. They are fairly certain in this instance, however, that one or more of the wires within the pad have been broken, which (again as a safety feature) stops the flow of electricity through the pad. Broken wires may result from improper positioning during installation or from mistreatment of the pad once it is in place—such as children or adults standing on the waterbed or gouging it harshly with their knees or elbows.

Example: Interest on the mortgage balance of $38,400 from July 13 to August 20 totaled $316.50 instead of $296.00—a difference of $20.50; and the prorated taxes from July 13 to the purchase date were $73.00, instead of $67.00—an additional difference of $6.00.

Rather than hitting readers right between the eyes with bad news, we have prepared them for it. If we word our message correctly, readers will anticipate the bad news part of the message as the logical course of action. Who could blame an insurance company for refusing coverage to a high-risk driver? How could anyone expect a company to replace a heating pad that is no longer under warranty, especially if there is a possibility that it received improper treatment? And who would argue about having to make an extra payment for closing costs that are based on factual evidence?

And then the velvet sledgehammer.

STATE THE BAD NEWS

We then present the bad news—not in separate paragraphs where the bad news would be emphasized, but by adding a sentence or two to the preceding paragraphs, where the bad news will be deemphasized.

Example: Consequently, we cannot provide the requested coverage at this time.

Example: We must limit our warranty to one year, therefore, even though these units often last for many, many years; and since your heater is no longer under warranty, we cannot assume responsibility for its replacement.

Example: So that we may finalize the closing, will you please send us a check for $26.50?

In the first example, we are leaving the door open for future business by adding the words "at this time." Maybe the applicant will represent an acceptable risk sometime in the future. We "buried" the bad news in the second example by placing it at the end of a long sentence. But in both instances (first and second examples), we made sure that we conveyed the bad news, even resorting to use of the word *cannot*. Don't be so subtle in communicating bad news that you fail to make your point. Don't leave the reader wondering whether the subject is still open for discussion. Our meaning in the third example is abundantly clear; we are asking for more money.

But here's what you might do.

PRESENT WORKABLE ALTERNATIVES

The receipt of bad news often leaves readers in the lurch; for example, the insurance applicant is left without coverage, and the waterbed owner is without a functional heating unit. If we have assumed a service attitude toward our business communications, we must help people solve their problems; we must suggest alternative courses of action.

Example: We hope that you will come to us for your insurance needs sometime in the future—after you have established an acceptable driving record. In the meantime, we suggest you apply to a company that specializes in high-risk coverage such as Miles Insurance Group or TransGlobal Insurance Company.

Example: You may recall that the M-13 heater is the lowest priced of the three models that we offer. Our T-120 heater carries United Laboratories certification, and our T-150 (a solid-state unit) carries a five-year warranty.

When we cannot satisfy the needs of customers, as with the first example, let's refer them to companies that can. When one of our products does not meet the precise needs of customers, as in the second example, let's suggest alternative products that we offer. Isn't this the type of treatment that most of us expect from business people? In the absence of such treatment, customers often experience a feeling of being stuck with inferior products or services from companies that have no concern for their welfare; and they seldom patronize or speak well of those companies again.

Things are still going to work out, aren't they?

CLOSE WITH A NEUTRAL OR POSITIVE STATEMENT

We opened our bad news letters by mentioning something about the topic of discussion. Then, in a middle paragraph or two, we provided an explanation of our position, stated the bad news, and suggested alternative action that might be taken. Now, let's end the letter with a neutral or positive statement.

Example: Thank you for thinking of us concerning your insurance needs.

Example: Any of our four authorized dealers in your city will be happy to provide additional information and assist you with selection of the best unit for your particular uses.

Example: We thank you very much for the consideration that you have shown us during these transactions, and we hope that you experience many years of happiness in your new home.

Don't close your letter by asking them to contact you when and if you can help them in some other way. Since you didn't help them much to begin with, it is insulting to offer "additional help." Also avoid the common urge to include an apology in the final paragraph. If we have done all that is possible for the person, and if our decision is based on sound logic, there is no need to apologize. An apology unnecessarily reminds readers of the bad news and, when placed at the end of the letter, tends to leave them with unpleasant thoughts about our products and our company.

Even difficult messages can be made easy.

EXAMPLES OF BAD-NEWS COMMUNICATIONS

To illustrate further this suggested approach to communicating bad news messages, let's take four situations that were used in Chapter 14 as examples of good news messages. Rather than agreeing with the figures cited by the customer in the first situation, however, let's assume that she has erroneously shown a $42.50 silk blouse at the sale price of $20.00.

Allude to the situation	We have checked the prices shown in your letter of March 29 with our master price list.
Provide details, reasons, and then the bad news	Your figures are correct, with one exception; you list a silk blouse at $20.00 when the actual price is $42.50. Another customer might have placed this blouse among the sales items, or perhaps one of our salespeople inadvertently hung the blouse on the wrong sales rack. In either event, the correct price of the blouse is $42.50, and the total amount of your purchases during February is $135.15, as billed.
Present a workable alternative	We realize that you may not have purchased the blouse if you had known its true price and that you may wish to return it. If the item has not been worn and if it is returned promptly, therefore, we will gladly credit your account for the full purchase price.
Close with a neutral or positive statement	Please let us know if you have any further questions, Mrs. Smith, because we do value your patronage.

In our second example, we have decided *not* to hire Jeff Rogers for the position of Assistant Production Manager at our Westgate plant. This decision comes after Rogers has invested considerable time in completing an application, taking tests, and being interviewed.

Allude to the situation	As we mentioned during our first meeting, several people applied for the same position that you were seeking.
Provide details, reasons, and then the bad news	Your background in manufacturing operations is impressive and your references favorable, but other applicants had experience that was more directly related to our Westgate operation.

	Realizing the importance of the selection decision to all applicants, and in consideration of the interests that they expressed, the final decision was a group effort of four officers of the company. We wish that we could report that you were the successful candidate, Jeff, but such is not the case.
Present alternatives	Your application will be kept on file, of course, because of the possibility of future openings. You also might consider applying with Jonathan Industries, Inc., a New York based firm that is presently constructing new facilities in Colorado and Utah.
Close with a neutral or positive statement	We want you to know that we very much appreciate the time and effort that you afforded us during this selection process, and we wish you success in your search for a managerial position in production.

As our third example of a bad news communication, we will deny a customer's request that quantity discounts be allowed for three earlier purchases of our products. We offered a quantity discount of 5 percent only on individual orders of 500 or more units, but each of this customer's three orders were for less than that amount.

Allude to the situation	The discounts that you have requested in your letter of June 19 related to three individual orders.
Provide details, reasons, and then the bad news	If you will review our bulletin of May 1 (copy enclosed), you will see that the 5 percent discount applied to individual shipments of 500 or more units. We were able to offer this discount because of savings we experience with larger shipments. The cost of the paperwork and physical processing of one large order is about one third that of three smaller orders. Since your three orders were for 150, 250, and 200 units, even though the combined total exceeded the 500-unit minimum, they do not qualify for the quantity discount.

Present alternatives	Will it be possible for you to combine your smaller orders into one large order during future sales promotions such as this one? Maybe you and one or two other retailers will be able to submit your individual orders to us as one shipment, requesting that the trucker make split deliveries to your individual stores.
Close with a neutral or positive statement	Many of our customers operate relatively small retail outlets; therefore, we are always eager to help them benefit from all provisions of our sales promotions.

As a final example of a bad news communication, let's refuse an educator's request for pictures. We find that we are not the legal owners of the requested pictures, but we do have two other photos which might be appropriate.

Allude to the situation	We appreciate your offer to include in your upcoming publication a picture of one of our large steamshovels, because we value this type of publicity.
Provide reasons, the bad news, and alternatives	The pictures you have requested are the legal property of a professional photographer that we employ for all our publications; therefore, we cannot provide copies or authorization for their use. You may write to Professional Photographers at 1612 West 16th Street, Chicago, Illinois 60607, concerning use of the photos, but the fee involved for each print would be at least $50. As a possible alternative, we are enclosing black-and-white photographs of two of our series 210 models. If you use either of these two pictures, please make the credit line read "Courtesy FMQ Corporation."
Close with a neutral or positive statement	Thank you for your interest in our products, and good luck with your publication.

Check, doublecheck, and recheck

CHECKLIST: BAD NEWS COMMUNICATIONS

Beginning paragraph. Allude to the situation that gave rise to the communication in one of the following ways:

- ☐ Refer to their communication to you.
- ☐ Mention what they have requested.
- ☐ Advise that the communication has been given to you for reply or that you are handing it to someone else—if such is the case.
- ☐ Outline any action that has been taken, such as inspecting a product, calculating figures, and checking records.
- ☐ Inform them that you have been seeking authorization.
- ☐ Make a neutral comment about the situation at hand.
- ☐ Express appreciation.

    Do not make misleading statements that create false hope.
    Do not reveal the bad news before reasons have been given.

Middle paragraph(s). Provide details and reasons in one of the following ways:

- ☐ Tell them that their goods are no longer under warranty.
- ☐ Explain why it is necessary to limit such warranties.
- ☐ Suggest possible reasons for product failure, sometimes implying that part or all of the blame might rest with the user.
- ☐ Explain that the limitations you are imposing are the same for all customers.
- ☐ Provide facts and figures when available.
- ☐ Compare your products with competing products, when yours compare favorably.
- ☐ Compare their personal qualifications with the qualifications of competing applicants or employees, in decisions involving employment or promotion.
- ☐ Refer to official documents that contradict their claims.
- ☐ Tell them that their requests are unreasonable and explain why.

State the bad news by:

- ☐ Using positive language where possible.
- ☐ Being certain to make your point, using the words *cannot* and *deny* when essential to full understanding.
- ☐ Asking for money due your company.
- ☐ Deemphasizing it in long sentences and long paragraphs.

Present workable alternatives by:

      ☐ Suggesting substitute products.
      ☐ Referring them to another company.
      ☐ Suggesting corrective action that they might take.

Ending paragraph. Close with a neutral or positive statement by:

      ☐ Thanking them for taking the time to communicate with you.
      ☐ Thanking them for their help, if they have assisted you in any way.
      ☐ Expressing appreciation for their interest.
      ☐ Asking if they have any questions.
      ☐ Telling them that you appreciate their business.
      ☐ Mentioning the possibility of future relationships.
      ☐ Wishing them luck in their future endeavors.

      Do not repeat the bad news.
      Do not apologize.

Remember. Apply the S★T★A★R approach (page 120) to all types of business communications.

BUSINESS APPLICATIONS

1. As an employee in the finance department of The Read Corporation, write a letter to United Way in your city (check your telephone directory for the address and zip code). Refuse their request of June 3 for donations, explaining that the directors of your company prefer to support individual charities. Today's date is June 5 of the current year.

2. Working as a loan officer at First Federal Banking Services, write a letter to Joan M. Ralston, 1616 West Second Street, Dayton, Ohio 45402, declining her request for a credit card. Ms. Ralston is 18 years of age and has no credit history. Explain to her that to qualify for the issuance of a credit card she must establish a credit record for herself. One way to establish a credit record is to open a charge account at one or more stores, charge some purchases periodically, and make the payments on time. Maintaining one or more charge accounts for six months or so should qualify her for the credit card requested in her application dated October 1. Today's date is October 5 of the current year.

3. As assistant to the manager of a branch office of Conway Insurance Group, write a letter to Roland W. Marshall at 250 East 16th Street, Ventura, Califorina 93001. Explain to him that the annual insurance premium on his residence has been increased from $125 to $155. The increase affects all Conway customers, not just him; and savings may be realized by paying in two- or three-year multiples. By paying $286.75 for two years, he can save $23.25. By paying $418.50 for three years, he can save $46.50. The higher premium includes adjustments for increases in the value of his property during the past year (inflation). Date your letter December 20 (current year).

4. As a loan officer at Cleveland State Trust Company, write a letter dated March 3 (current year) to Russel R. Longer, President of Nortex, Inc., 32666 Euclid Avenue, Cleveland, Ohio 44117. Mr. Longer applied with your bank for a $20,000 business loan. In checking the Nortex financial statements, you find the company to be seriously overextended with debt. Although you view the earnings potential of the company to be promising, you consider the requested loan too risky for the bank to undertake. Recognizing Mr. Longer to be a man of means, however, you would be willing to loan $20,000 to Nortex for six months if he would personally endorse the loan. Nortex has had personal checking and savings accounts with the bank for seven years now.

5. Mr. and Mrs. James J. Falk have written to Tampa West, a resort hotel in Palm Springs, California, where you handle all requests for reservations. The Falks, who live at 1212 North 11th Place in Richmond, Indiana 47374, have requested their favorite luxury suite for January 6 through January 15. The suite will not be available until January 10, but you have several large rooms available in a new wing that adjoins the golf course. Reserve one of the rooms in the new wing from Janaury 6 through January 9, and the luxury suite from January 10 through the 15th; and write to the Falks to see if they will accept this arrangement. Today's date is November 12 (current year) and their letter is dated November 8.

6. As an employee in the product distribution department of Tempron Industries, Inc., you have received Purchase Order 66128 from Miller Exploration & Development Corp., 1667 Montano Road NW, Albuquerque, New Mexico 87107. The purchase order, which is dated August 10 (current year) and signed by Wanda Miller, calls for the immediate shipment of ten 2416X Tempron bits. These bits are used in high-speed drills by companies that mine uranium. Tempron will produce some 2416X bits next month, but has none of the bits in stock presently. Tempron stocks a more durable, diamond-headed Model 2420X that sells for $245.50, or just $75 more than the 2416X bits. Today's date is August 15.

7. Suburban Electric Company at 3632 North Avondale Avenue, Chicago, Illinois 60631, has deducted a cash discount of $63.16 when making payment to Valley Electric Manufacturers, Inc. Suburban is paying Valley's Invoice No. 66612, dated February 3 (current year) on February 20, seven days past the discount period. As assistant to the manager of accounts receivable at Valley Electric, write a letter (dated February 23) to the accounts payable department at Suburban, telling them that your credit terms provide for a discount of 2 percent only when payment is made within ten days from the date of the invoice. Deny the discount of $63.16 and ask for their payment in that amount.

8. Julie Wilson was one of eight applicants for a position in the accounting department at Tokheim Packing Company. Although she earned high grades in school and made a favorable impression on the interviewer, you have decided to hire another applicant who has extensive on-the-job experience that relates to the position being filled. As the assistant employment manager at Tokheim, inform Julie by letter that she did not get the job. She was interviewed on July 8 (current year), and today's date is July 15.

9. Mrs. Patricia Gomez, 1100 Maple Street, Rochester, New York 14611, has written (letter dated November 10) to Arrow Chemicals Corporation, where you work in the Customer Accounts department, asking for a refund of $36.50 for a Whirl-Away pastry gun that she purchased during January. Today's date is November 15 of the current year. She claims that the pastry gun doesn't perform in the way that she was led to believe. When she saw the product demonstrated at a local department store, nothing was said about having to dismantle and clean the gun before each refill—making it, in Mrs. Gomez's words, "an impossible undertaking." In your letter to this customer, inform her that the operating instructions for the Whirl-Away pastry gun are printed on the top of each carton—in large, bold print. Inform her also that the product is used by many commercial bakeries, where they have found it to be efficient and durable. Refuse her request for a refund.

10. You work in the public relations department of Univar Corporation, and Miss Janet Shapiro, a teacher at Elsworth Elementary School, has written a letter to you requesting a plant tour for 32 sixth-grade students. Your company specializes in the production of automobile bumpers, which involves the use of very heavy machinery. As a matter of company policy, tours are discouraged for everyone except officials from automotive companies. In fact, a tour through the factory involves extensive precautions against injury from boiling liquids and metal shavings. Write a letter to

Miss Shapiro declining her request. The school address is 1600 South 27th Avenue, Seattle, Washington 98104. Her letter is dated August 1, and today's date is August 5 (current year).

11. As a clerk in the government offices, State of Arkansas, you must answer a letter dated September 15 (current year), from Frank A. Simmons, 1512 West 64th Street, Harrison, Arkansas 72601. Mr. Simmons has filed a claim for workmen's compensation in the amount of $550. He was involved in an automobile accident six weeks ago on the way home from work, and hasn't worked since that time. Write a letter to Mr. Simmons, dated September 28, informing him that he does not qualify for workmen's compensation because his accident did not occur at his place of work. As an alternative, suggest that he file a claim with his insurance company.

12. Bill Miller, who works in your company as assistant traffic manager, has asked for a two-year leave of absence to attend a local community college full time. As administrative assistant to the personnel manager, write a memo (dated June 15, current year) in answer to his memo of June 1. Inform him that a leave of absence is impossible at this time; no replacement is available to fill his job, and his services will be vital when the department manager is on vacation during September. Suggest instead that Bill attend college part time, and include a copy of a recent bulletin that outlines provisions for reimbursement of employees for tuition and textbooks.

16

USING
PERSUASION

American businesses spend billions of dollars each year trying to persuade people to buy their products and services, and most of their advertising appeals follow the pattern discussed in this chapter. The techniques of persuasion are not confined to sales messages; we may follow the same pattern, for example, when trying to sell an idea to colleagues and when trying to land a job. This is not to say that the composition of all persuasive messages is an easy task; as you have probably observed, much of today's advertising is clever, original, and a product of the combined talents of professional writers, artists, and photographers.

And now, a few hundred words from our sponsor.

ORGANIZING SALES MESSAGES

Before beginning their sales messages, most writers of advertisements identify key selling points and thoroughly analyze the product or service to be advertised—including all related aspects of a company's operation. Having taken this critical first step, they plan their communications according to the guidelines in Figure 16-1. After designing the first paragraph to capture the interest of readers, advertisers attempt to maintain interest by relating the product or service to the needs and wants of readers. The middle part of the message is devoted to maintaining reader interest by making product claims and presenting supportive evidence. Advertisers use the final paragraphs to invite readers, listeners, or viewers to take the desired buying action.

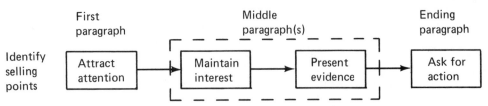

Figure 16-1 Outline for persuasive messages (dotted line indicates that the two middle steps are sometimes combined into a single paragraph)

Advertisers do not always follow this format, of course; they sometimes rely on pictures of their products, using very little, if any, verbiage. When advertisers must rely on words to convey persuasive messages, however, they usually follow the steps outlined in Figure 16-1.

Did you say, "P, P, P, and P"?

IDENTIFYING KEY SALES POINTS

A lot of planning goes into advertisements, and most advertisers take a systematic approach to the preparation of newspaper, magazine, billboard, radio, and television advertisements. Before even beginning work on advertising messages, they study the **four P's of marketing**: product, price, place, and promotion.

Beginning with the company's **product** (or service), they identify unique attributes of the product. Is it faster or more attractive than competing products? Is it more durable? Is the packaging distinctive? They compare **price**. When the price of the company's product is lower than that of competitors, price usually becomes a key selling point. When the price isn't competitive, advertisers usually avoid mentioning the subject. Advertisers also consider the availability of products, which they refer to as **place**. Is the product available at many stores? What types of stores?

The final consideration is **promotion**. Having identified the key selling points of a product—through analysis of product, price, and place—advertisers must decide on a method for communicating these points to consumers. Promotion includes personal selling, advertising, publicity, and all the appeals they may use to motivate consumers to sample their products.

<u>Look what I have!</u>

ATTRACTING ATTENTION

Persuading people to do what we want them to do isn't always easy. As a defense mechanism, people screen out most of the sales messages that they are confronted with each day. If an advertisement is to penetrate this protective screen, its opening statement must strike consumers as relevant to their personal interests.

Some advertisers gain this effect by promoting their products as **new and improved**.

Example: Your *** dealer has something new and exciting for you on his showroom floor.

Example: The new *** reduces tar intake without sacrificing flavor.

Urgency appeals are good attention getters.

Example: Wednesday and Thursday are RED HOT value days at your **** stores.

Example: End-of-month clearance of ****! While they last!

Advertisers of such products and services as auto tires and insurance often attract attention by using **fright appeals**.

Example: Don't compromise the safety of your family by . . .

Example: How would your family cope if something happened to you today?

When the price of a product or service is the main selling point, advertisers may use **thrift appeal** to good advantage.

Example: Would you like to save money on your next purchase of ****?

Example: Prices will never be lower than they are right now at ****.

Advertisers often use **bandwagon appeal** to impress consumers that they should move with the crowd and be popular by using certain products.

Example: Everybody's doing it, doing it, doing it. Doing what? Switching to Diet-Free ****, naturally.

Example: What? You're still using ****? Haven't you heard about ****?

Companies occasionally use **snob appeal** by implying that their products are intended for a specific segment of the market.

Example: **** cigarettes are *not* for just everyone.

Example: The new **** is designed for discriminating people, people who value a touch of elegance in their lives.

The most effective means of overcoming consumer resistance to advertisements is **sex appeal,** which usually involves the use of pictures. We might expect to see pictures of attractive men and women in ads that promote health spas and certain diet foods and beverages, but advertisers often use sex appeal to attract attention to products that have absolutely no relation to the human anatomy. A scantily clad woman sitting on the hood of a new car is not relevant to the appearance or operational features of the car, nor is a macho male sitting on a large Arabian horse related to the flavor of a particular brand of cigarette. But the presence of "beautiful people" in advertisements does attract a lot of attention to the products and services being promoted.

But this luxury is a necessity.

MAINTAINING INTEREST

Medical doctors are concerned with the ability of the human body to keep all bodily functions in balance, a condition they call **homeostasis.** Regardless of prevailing temperatures, our bodies make the adjustments necessary to maintain an almost constant 98.4 degrees. Similarly, psychologists speak of a mental imbalance called **cognitive dissonance,** theorizing that when people are discontent they take action to restore a mental balance. Advertisers strive to create cognitive dissonance among consumers by causing an imbalance that can be corrected only through the purchase of their products or services. Haven't you sometimes experienced discontent after being introduced to a particular product, wanting it so badly that you couldn't be perfectly happy until buying it?

Advertisers begin to create cognitive dissonance during the early stages of their advertisements by making enticing claims about their products and services.

Example: The new **** will outperform any car in its class.

Example: **** can help you lose 20 pounds in four weeks.

Example: The **** fleximatic will give you razor-close shaves, time after time.

Business people are seldom modest when it comes to praising the favorable attributes of their products and services. Consumers have come to expect a certain amount of trade puffery in advertsing, in fact, especially when the product or service advertised has outstanding features.

I ought to know, because I look just like a doctor.

PRESENTING EVIDENCE

Advertisers add to the cognitive dissonance of those consumers who get hooked on their advertisements by presenting evidence to support their product claims. One effective way to convince people that a product or service is worthy is to have a **famous person** make favorable comments about it.

Example: Bumper-to-bumper driving on a freeway can be hard on a car's engine, but I minimize engine wear and improve perform-ance by using the same oil in my family car that I use on the race track, **** motor oil.

Example: Hi, I'm ****. Shooting a weekly TV series keeps all of us hopping here on the set, often making it necessary for us to eat on the run. **** crackers help me minimize calorie intake while maintaining a high level of energy, and they are *very* tasty.

The Federal Trade Commission, the agency that regulates advertisers, is trying to increase the authenticity of such testimonials by requiring those people to use the products or services before endorsing them.

Advertisers have found that they can convince many consumers of the accuracy of their product claims by having **experts** (or apparent experts) voice favorable opinions about their products or services.

Example: As a biochemist, I appreciate the high nutritional value that is present in ****, and I serve it to my family every day.

Example: Medical doctors recommend **** twice as often as any other pain killer.

Some advertisers resort to **name calling** by directly comparing their prod-ucts with competing brands. They no longer refer to an anonymous Brand X, and they don't bleep out the brand name of the competing product.

Example: In a comparison with Sealy, Simmons, and five other leading brands, *Consumer Reports* judged the King Koil Spinal Guard mattress to be the most durable.

The most convincing way to support advertising claims, perhaps, is with **statistics.**

Example: The **** (foreign car) has an automatic transmission that reduces the engine RPMs by 31 percent in overdrive and delivers smooth, quiet, powerful performance. These features are enhanced by a 2.6 liter, 6 cylinder overhead cam engine—a combination that is unique to the new ****.

Example: With the ****, a typist can format page sizes up to 254 characters wide and 99 lines long. The low-cost diskettes (4 inches by 4 inches) store up to 70,000 characters each, to satisfy the demands of most typing jobs.

The objective of these various appeals, you will recall, is to convince consumers that our initial claims are credible, to convince them that our products and services are more appropriate for their needs and wants than competing products might be.

On your mark, get set, POW!

ASKING FOR ACTION

Having established cognitive dissonance by creating a nagging desire for the product or service being promoted, advertisers usually end their persuasive messages with appeals for action. They show consumers how mental comfort can be restored by purchasing the advertised items.

Example: Put yourself in the picture when you buy or lease a new **** at your **** dealer today.

Example: Why don't you begin your subscription to **** right now by calling (800) 866-4711, a toll-free number?

Advertisers sometimes follow a request for action by adding a statement such as "You'll be glad you did" and "Wouldn't you really rather own a ****?" But most advertising specialists contend that a greater impact is achieved when the persuasive message ends with a call for action—with no additional comments tacked on.

So this is how those large corporations do it.

SAMPLE SALES MESSAGES

Let's apply this four-step approach to persuasive communcations by com-
posing a sales message for a certain brand of moped (motorized bicycle).

Attract attention	More than 100 miles per gallon?
Maintain interest	No, we're not kidding. And when you swing your Ronda Moped into a filling station and say "fill 'er up," you'll be talking about pennies--not dollars.
Present evidence	The Ronda's two-stroke engine will speed you along at 30 mph for 125 miles on each gallon of regular gasoline. Farther if you decide to pedal part of the way. The Ronda Moped is great for your trips to school, the store, the beach, almost anywhere. No clutch-ing. No shifting. No parking problems. Just smooth, fun-filled riding.
Ask for action	See for yourself. Drop in at any Ronda dealer-ship first chance for a free trial ride.

Notice that product and place are emphasized, and that price is not mentioned.
Notice also that long senetences in advertisements are *out* and short sentences
and sentence fragments are *in*.

The length of the advertising message depends on the medium. If this were
to be a radio or television commercial, for example, we would plan the message
to fit the allotted time. Whatever the medium, though, we should avoid the
temptation to say all there is to say about a product. When too many words
are crammed into a limited space, people are inclined to block out the entire
message.

As a second example of persuasive messages, let's consider a home refrigerator. Athough competitive, the price of the Alaskan refrigerator is not a main selling point. The unit has all the usual features, plus a new snap-out ice maker.

Attract attention	No more yelling at Junior. No more wasted energy.
Maintain interest	Not with Alaskan's new snap-out ice cubes. The Alaskan refrigerator has tempered glass shelves, patterned steel doors, cold water tap, humidrawer control, 10-day meat keeper, egg bin, slide-out freezer drawers--all the standard features.
Present evidence	But the Alaskan also has snap-out ice cubes. No more standing there with the freezer door wide open. Just press a button and out snaps a cube. The family-size bin holds up to 300 cubes. Use one cube at a time or remove the entire bin. A super convenience. And practical too.
Ask for action	See the new Alaskan refrigerator in an exciting array of rich colors. Today. At most appliance stores.

Now, let's consider a service—a weight-loss clinic which includes the usual exercise programs. The service is directed at both men and women, and a special price is being offered through June 1. As in the preceding examples, our attention-getting opener is brief, and we lure consumers into the verbal picture we are drawing with frequent use of the word *you*.

Attract attention	Last chance to lose 20 pounds before going swimming.
Maintain interest	You will look great this summer in almost any of the new bathing suits if you let Slim-N-Trim help you trim off that excess weight.

Present evidence	Under the individually programmed guidance of our professional staff of doctors and nurses, along with a sensible diet, you will see those unattractive layers of fat fade away--quickly, safely, beautifully. Both men and women may enjoy our 3-week introductory program for only $5.* Includes participation in aerobic exercise classes and full use of our jogging track, exercise equipment, whirlpool, and sauna.
Ask for action	Stay in the swim of things. Call 934-2611 for an appointment with one of our weight counselors. And bring along a chubby friend. *Offer expires June 1.

Persuasive techniques are not confined to sales messages. We also use memos, letters, and conversations as tools of persuasion. If we were trying to persuade the managers of the company where we work to take a certain type of action, for example, we could follow the same persuasive format.

Attract attention	We recommend that a second shift of workers be added beginning October 1, and that construction of the proposed factory by temporarily postponed.
Maintain interest	Although we will have to pay a penalty rate for approximately 125 hours of overtime worked each day, the cost will be more than offset by the greater utilization of existing facilities. Postponement of construction will reduce the risk of loss in the event of a recession, and we probably will not have to pay as high a rate of interest on funds borrowed at a later date.

Present evidence	We have ample capacity at our existing plants, by adding a second shift of workers, to satisfy the projected demand for our products until about December, 1982.
	Several workers are prepared to assume supervisory positions, and we can hire additional supervisors from outside the company. Any shortages of managerial personnel will be filled by having our supervisors work anywhere from 10 to 20 hours overtime each week. The supply of unskilled labor is ample, but it will be necessary for us to assign from 10 to 20 hours of overtime to certain skilled employees. (Expanded report attached)
	Interest rates on building funds have never been higher than at present--from 11 percent to 12½ percent per annum. By postponing new construction for at least two years, therefore, we should be able to secure a borrowing rate that is low enough to offset the continuing effects of inflation.
Ask for action	If you agree with these recommendations, will you please authorize the addition of a second shift and postponement of construction.

We know that the addressee will read this interoffice memo; therefore, we do not have to give much thought to attracting attention. But we are trying to persuade this person to approve our recommendations, and a persuasive approach will go a long way toward helping us achieve what we want.

Did we touch all bases?

CHECKLIST: PERSUASIVE COMMUNICATIONS

Identify key sales points.

Product

☐ Is the product superior? Unique? New? Improved?
☐ Does the packaging have identifying characteristics?
☐ Is the product or service guaranteed?

Price

☐ Is the product or service competitively priced?
☐ Is the prevailing price limited to a specific time period?
☐ Is this a sales item?
☐ Does the price include delivery? Installation? Servicing?
☐ Should price be deemphasized or avoided entirely?
☐ Should the item be promoted as worth a relatively high price?

Place

☐ Where can the product or service be purchased?
☐ Is the product or service presently available?
☐ Is the point of purchase more convenient than those of competitors?

Promotion

☐ Are there any promotional gimmicks that may be used? A chance to win something? A free gift for taking prompt buying action? A cash rebate?

Attract attention by:

- [ ] Calling attention to the "new and improved" status of the product or service.
- [ ] Stressing the importance of taking prompt buying action.
- [ ] Outlining possible adverse consequences of not owning the item.
- [ ] Showing consumers how they can save money by buying the product or service.
- [ ] Informing consumers that many other people are already benefiting from use of the product or service.
- [ ] Implying that the item is intended for only certain types of people—a select group.
- [ ] Suggesting that use of the product or service tends to make the user more attractive to the opposite sex.

Maintain interest by:

- [ ] Making enticing (but supportable) claims about the product (service), price, or place.

Present evidence by:

- [ ] Using the endorsement of a famous person.
- [ ] Conveying the opinion of an expert.
- [ ] Comparing with competing brands.
- [ ] Presenting supportive data.

Ask for action by urging consumers to

- [ ] Request additional information.
- [ ] Take immediate buying action.
- [ ] Make similar comparisons for themselves.
- [ ] "Come in" for a demonstration.
- [ ] Sample the product or service.

BUSINESS APPLICATIONS

1. Write a newspaper advertisement for an electric range that has two 8-inch elements (burners) and two 6-inch elements. This unit, which normally retails for $599.95, is on sale at $559.50 from August 1 through 15. The range has the following features:

> Automatic, self-cleaning oven
> Porcelain-enameled lift-up cooktop
> Fluorescent worklight
> Lock, oven, and surface unit indicators
> Tempered glass backguard
> Bake window with oven light
> Clock with one-hour timer
> Sure-Temp oven control

The range is available in white, yellow, and gold at all Super Discount Appliance stores throughout the area. (The ad will include a picture of the range.)

2. Compose a newspaper ad for Central Business College at 1612 West 5th Street in your city—a centrally located address. The college provides instruction in typing, shorthand, legal transcription, medical transcription, computer programming, and general business subjects. Today's date is May 15, and the next 10-week classes begin June 2. When students have completed the individual programs in which they enroll, the college staff provides free placement service. Most classes meet three hours each week, and the tuition is $27.50 per hour.

3. Turn to the description of express mail on page 162, and write a full-page magazine ad for the U.S. Postal Service. Devote about two thirds of the ad to an attention-getting message in large, bold type. Use the remainder of the page for the rest of your persuasive message.

4. The Harbinger automobile, a new British import, gets 33 mph on the highway and 23 mpg in the city (EPA estimates). It has a 2.8 liter V-6 engine, power front disk brakes, rack-and-pinion steering, and four-speed floor-mounted transmission (all standard equipment). These two-door automobiles have room for four people, and they come in a variety of interior and exterior color combinations. The Harbinger, a very popular car in Europe, is a new entry to the U.S. market, and its delivery price is lower than that of the Volkswagen Rabbit. Prepare a magazine ad to accompany pictures of the car's interior and exterior.

5. Consider the four P's of marketing in connection with your college or university. Having identified as many selling points about your school as possible, decide on the best advertising approach for selling the seniors in nearby high schools on the merits of the school.

6. Prepare an advertising message for the medium selected in Application 5. If you decided on radio announcements (a free public service message, maybe), write an announcement. If you decided on a newspaper ad, write an ad, and so on.

7. Prepare a magazine advertisement for Super Lite charcoal starter (lighter fluid). Super Lite is a superior product that sells for a relatively high price, but it lights easily, quickly prepares the briquettes for use, and leaves no odor or soot.

8. As a clerk in the inventory control department of a large corporation, write a memo to Mr. Gregory W. Phillips, Assistant Director of Personnel. Try to persuade him to authorize your participation in a six-week training program that involves two weeks of training at the main plant, two weeks at the warehouse, and two weeks in several departments at the main office. You have been in your present position almost two years, during which time you have continued your formal education. You would like to participate in the training program sometime during the summer months, if possible, so that it will not interfere with your school program. Moreover, you believe that the training program will help you perform better in your present job and will provide insight that may prove helpful in the more responsible positions that you hope to hold someday.

9. Rental rates at Save-Way Auto Rentals are not as low as some companies for compact cars, but Save-Way rates for full-sized cars are 45 percent lower than those charged by their major competitors. They provide a fully equipped, air-conditioned Chevrolet Monte Carlo or similar car for $28.50 per day, including free gasoline for up to 100 miles of travel. And that price includes full insurance coverage. Compose a newspaper ad, to be accompanied by a picture of an attractive woman driving a large automobile, and invite readers to fill out an accompanying coupon for information about Special Accounts for businesses. Save-Way has agencies in all major cities throughout the continental United States.

10. Create a newspaper ad for the Pizazz Pizzeria, a very popular eating place for young people in the community. Their Thin-N-Crisp and Thick-N-Chewy pizzas are on sale until January 5, and the ad will be placed in the local newspaper from January 1 through 5. Large pizzas sell for $6.00 each, medium for $4.00, and small for $2.50. With each pizza purchased, customers will receive a free pizza the next size smaller. If they buy one large pizza, for example, they receive a medium pizza free; if they buy a medium pizza, they receive a small one free. To receive the free pizzas, however, customers must present a copy of the advertisement at time of purchase.

17

ASKING
FOR MONEY

Many businesses sell their products and services on credit, and the people in their accounts receivable departments are responsible for collecting these debts. But asking customers to pay their bills can be a touchy undertaking; business people want to collect money that is due their companies, but they do not want to lose valuable customers during the collection process.

What about people who don't pay their bills on time? Businesses that sell directly to consumers may charge their customers interest on unpaid balances; if no payments are forthcoming, they may discontinue further credit sales. But consider the dilemma of business people who sell their products and services to other businesses. What can be done when the late-paying customer is a giant corporation? If sellers become too demanding in their collection efforts, large corporations may cease doing business with them; and thoughts of canceling the credit of a large business customer is almost unthinkable.

But don't large corporations generally pay their bills on time? Most do, but many do not. With high interest rates (the cost of borrowing money), many companies retain money as long as they can—urging people who owe money to them to pay promptly, while delaying payments that they owe to other companies. As you can see, therefore, the writing of credit letters requires good judgment and an effective plan of action.

First, Dr. Jekyll, then Mr. Hyde.

THE GAME PLAN

We usually begin the collection process with a friendly reminder, gradually strengthening our approach to the point where we issue a final warning. We start out as "nice guys" and systematically strengthen our appeals. This four-step procedure is outlined in Figure 17-1.

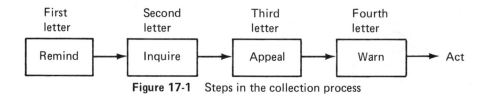

Figure 17-1 Steps in the collection process

Why, you might ask, can't we just telephone slow-paying customers? Since both the men and the women of most households now work, many telephone calls to residences during the daytime would go unanswered. Also, according to recently enacted consumer credit laws, telephone calls after normal business hours may be viewed as undue harassment of debtors.

It would be even more impractical to phone businesses regularly for information about past-due bills. People in the accounts payable departments of businesses cannot readily determine the status of the many bills they process for payment each day; and the cost of phone calls and the expenditure of employee time for making the calls would be prohibitive.

An additonal drawback to the use of telephones for collection purposes is that telephones leave us without written records. The file copies of collection letters, on the other hand, can be used as evidence that we are treating all customers equally. The law requires that we be consistent in our treatment of customers—not pressing some customers for the prompt payment of bills while overlooking slow payment by others.

Did you forget to remember?

ROUTINE REMINDER

We don't want to wait many days after bills have become due before sending a reminder. If we should let many of our customers pay late as a matter of practice, we would soon have thousands of additional dollars outstanding—money that is rightfully ours, money that we should be investing to increase our income. Within a day or so after bills become delinquent, therefore, we should send reminder letters, mailgrams, or telegrams.

Except for those customers who habitually pay late, we give our customers the benefit of the doubt. Maybe they have overlooked the bill. Maybe they have been on vacation. It is even possible that they have already paid the bills that we are writing about. We neither scold nor accuse; we simply remind customers that their payments are past due. Consider the examples in Figure 17-2 (to a consumer) and Figure 17-3 (to a business customer).

Did you forget about us?

The first of two $200 payments came due four days ago, but we still haven't received payment.

If you have not already done so, Ms. Smith, will you please send a check to us today?

Figure 17-2   Reminder (to a consumer)

Subject: Invoice No. 16422, August 12, 1979

Our records show that we have not received payment of the subject invoice, which, under the prevailing terms of sale, became delinquent September 12.

Will you please check to make certain that this invoice has been received and processed for payment?

Thank you.

Figure 17-3   Reminder (to a business customer)

Both letters outline the situation and provide friendly reminders. Some companies substitute humorous cards for reminder letters, as illustrated in Figure 17-4.

Figure 17-4   Cartoon cards as substitutes for reminder credit letters (Courtesy Harrison Publishing Co., Asheville, N.C.)

These cards are not inexpensive, even when purchased in large quantities, but you will recall from Chapter 10 that the cost of producing business letters is sometimes much higher.

You broke your writing arm, perhaps?

LETTER OF INQUIRY

When customers do not respond to our reminders within a reasonable time, we follow up with a letter of inquiry. We assume a "What's wrong?" and "How can we help you?" attitude. The examples in Figures 17-5 and 17-6 are continuations of the preceding situations.

Why haven't you responded to our letter of June 10?

The first payment of $200 is now 20 days past due, and the second payment of $200 becomes due just 10 days from today.

If unavoidable circumstances have prevented you from paying at the agreed times, please come in and talk the situation over with us. You will find us to be reasonable, understanding, and cooperative; and we will do our best to arrange some terms that you can manage.

If nonpayment has merely been an oversight, on the other hand, will you please send a check to us at this time for the $400 balance.

Figure 17-5   Inquiry (to a consumer)

Subject: Invoice No. 16422, August 12, 1979

This letter is our second inquiry concerning the subject invoice, the payment of which is now 25 days past due.

Did you receive the invoice? Have you processed it
for payment? Has a check been issued?

We are attaching a copy of the invoice, with the
thought that the original might have been lost in
the mails or otherwise misplaced.

May we have your payment of $1,212.50 right away,
please?

Figure 17-6   Inquiry (to a business customer)

Yes, we are pressing them a little. As already indicated, some people habitually use money that rightfully belongs to their creditors by paying their bills as late as possible. It is advisable to sound a note of urgency in these second letters, therefore, to convince customers that we expect to be paid on time.

We must be careful not to overstate our position during this second step in the collection process. Maybe there has been a tragedy within the consumer's family. Maybe the invoice actually was misplaced or lost. Or, as often happens, maybe the customer's check was misplaced or misapplied by employees in our own company.

Okay, now, let's get with it!

APPEAL FOR ACTION

If and when our second communication is ignored, we make an urgent appeal for action. We want our money, and we want it now. We do so by appealing to the customer's sense of fair play. We also appeal to the customer's honor, pride, and self-interest. The sample letters in Figures 17-7 and 17-8 illustrate this approach.

When you purchased your new dining room furniture on
April 15, you agreed to pay the balance of $400 in
two monthly payments, $200 on June 1 and $200 on
July 1.

We extended these interest-free terms to you as a
matter of courtesy, Ms. Smith, on the basis of your
credit standing within the community and your
agreement to make payments on the designated dates.

Won't you honor that agreement and protect your
credit reputation by making payment at this time?
You may clear the account by paying $400 before
July 15; otherwise, we shall begin assessing interest
charges from that date at the rate of 1½ percent
per month.

Figure 17-7   Appeal for action (to a consumer)

Subject: Invoice No. 16422, August 12, 1979

Although we recently reminded you that the subject
invoice for $1,212.50 was seriously past due, our
records show that as of October 20 the invoice remains
unpaid.

We value your patronage, but we must receive payment
within the next few days if we are to continue serving
you on a credit basis. Will you please send a check
to us today? If extenuating circumstances prevent
your making payment at this time, please sign and
return the enclosed interest-bearing note--along with
a letter of explanation.

Please help us continue our mutually beneficial
business relationship by taking immediate action to
correct this unfair and unfortunate situation.

Figure 17-8   Appeal for action (to a business customer)

We communicated our messages loud and clear, but we left the door open for
corrective action. If customers act promptly on our suggestions, we may be
able to salvage the business relationship. And, as most salespeople will attest,
attracting and keeping customers are essential functions in any business.

This is our last warning, Mr. Fink!

AN ULTIMATUM

By the time we reach the fourth step in the collection process, we have waited for our money for a significant period and have undergone the expense of writing and mailing three communications. We must now issue an ultimatum, as illustrated in Figures 17-9 and 17-10.

Since our three previous letters have gone unanswered, Ms. Smith, we must demand your immediate payment of $400 plus $6 interest, a total of $406.

Payment by August 15 is your last opportunity to settle this account without jeopardizing your credit rating. We plan to file a breach-of-contract report at that time with Central Credit Agencies.

Also, if payment is not received by August 15, we will take immediate action to repossess the dining room furniture.

What are we to do, Ms. Smith? Our course of action depends entirely on you.

Figure 17-9   An ultimatum (to a consumer)

Subject: Invoice No. 16422, August 12, 1979

Because of your failure to respond to our previous inquiries concerning payment of the subject invoice, we must suspend any further credit sales to your company.

Moreover, if payment in full (including interest at the rate of 12% annually from September 12 to the date of payment) is not received by November 30, we will be forced to assign the account to a collection agency.

Why don't you restore your credit standing with us and avoid future unpleasantries by making payment at this time?

Figure 17-10   An ultimatum (to a business customer)

We have issued ultimatums, certainly; but we have still allowed these customers to take positive action. We may be reluctant to sell to them on the same credit terms as before, but we probably haven't lost them forever as customers. By maintaining a firm but helpful attitude throughout the collection process, we may avoid adverse reactions from customers who would be offended by unduly harsh communications.

There is nothing sacred about this four-step approach to the collection process. The number of messages sent and their timing depends entirely on the situation. We may send telegrams to customers when a large amount of money is involved and write letters for all other delinquent accounts. We might write individual letters regarding large debts and send form letters for smaller ones.

Because it is impossible to present sample credit letters for every possible situation, the letters presented in this chapter are used only to illustrate one approach to the collection process—not as a guide for all collection communications. The tone and style of effective collection messages depend on several variables: the type of company you work for, its credit policy, industry patterns, and the customer's payment record.

Have we bugged them properly?

CHECKLIST: COLLECTION COMMUNICATIONS

Routine reminder

- ☐ Act promptly to let customers know that we expect them to pay on time.
- ☐ Assume that the customer has merely overlooked payment.
- ☐ Maintain a friendly tone, frequently using the words *please* and *thank you.*
- ☐ Consider the use of cartoon cards.

Letter of inquiry

- ☐ Try to determine what is preventing payment.
- ☐ Maintain a helpful attitude.
- ☐ Consider the practicality of asking for payment in full at this time.
- ☐ Keep it friendly—no accusations, no insinuations.
- ☐ Enclose a copy of the invoice (bill) if practical.
- ☐ Use a tone of urgency, but continue giving the customer the benefit of any doubts you may have.
- ☐ Consider the possibility of extenuating circumstances.

Appeal for action

- [ ] Ask for immediate action.
- [ ] Appeal to the customer's sense of fair play.
- [ ] Refer to protection of the customer's honor.
- [ ] Appeal to the customer's self-interest, honor, and pride.
- [ ] Suggest that the customer protect his credit standing by paying now.
- [ ] Hedge your remarks with such qualifiers as "Our records show that . . ." to avoid potentially embarrassing statements.
- [ ] Consider the imposition of penalty charges.
- [ ] Mention the possibility that credit sales may be discontinued.
- [ ] Provide alternative courses of action when possible.
- [ ] Maintain a positive attitude about future business relationships—if the customer pays now.
- [ ] Try to maintain the customer's goodwill.

Final warning

- [ ] Issue an ultimatum: discontinuation of credit sales, issuance of damaging credit statements, repossession of products, use of collection agency.
- [ ] Maintain a businesslike approach.
- [ ] Leave the door open for positive action by the customer for restoration of a viable seller-buyer relationship.

Remember

- [ ] Don't copy the letters in this chapter for use in class assignments or actual business transactions. Credit letters must be designed specifically for each business situation, and these sample letters are intended only as illustrations of the four-step collection process.

    Finally, don't overlook the potential benefits of using the S★T★A★R approach (page 120) when writing collection messages.

BUSINESS APPLICATIONS

1. Janice Blakey's credit account with your store (Betty's Boutique) is No. 14-2615-2. Her unpaid balance is $246.15, on which a minimum payment of $15.00 was due ten days ago—August 1 of the current year. Send a reminder letter to her at 7943 West Vickery Blvd., Fort Worth, Texas 76107.

2. Continuing with Application 1, it is now September 10, and Ms. Blakey has missed her second minimum payment of $15. Follow up on your earlier communication to her.

3. Mr. Claude Augustine of 16112 Precision Drive, Indianapolis, Indiana 46236, has not responded to several earlier attempts to collect for carpet-cleaning services rendered in the amount of $275. Your company, Brenco Carpet Services, cleaned the carpets throughout his residence on May 15. Today's date is August 23 (current year), and your previous letters were dated June 15, July 5, and August 1. In what we hope will be your final communication to Mr. Augustine, present him with an ultimatum.

4. As an employee in the credit department of CMT Instruments, Inc., you have just had a clerk in the distribution department ask for credit approval to ship $890 of products to Seymour Electronics, Inc., at 2316 North 15th Avenue, San Francisco, California 94005—their Purchase Order 16422. Seymour has a credit limit of $1,500 with CMT, but they still owe for two previous orders: CMT Invoice 23441 for $750 and Invoice 24337 for $600—dated February 15 and March 5, respectively. The terms of all CMT sales require payment within 30 days from the date of the invoice, with no discounts. Decide which department you should write to at Seymour, and date your letter April 4 (current year).

5. Anaheim Water Company, where you work, has provided bottled drinking water for nearly five years to Mrs. Janet Peterson at 24111 West La Palma Avenue, Anaheim, California 92801. As an employee at Anaheim Water, you have always billed Mrs. Peterson on a monthly basis. You mail an invoice to her about the 5th of each month for the previous month's service, and payment is due immediately upon her receipt of the invoices. Although you sent a reminder to her about payment for service during May (your Invoice 2613 of June 6), payment has not been received; nor has payment been received for service during June (your Invoice 2775 of July 5). Write an appropriate collection letter to her and date it July 25 (current year).

6. Thirty days have passed since you wrote the second letter to Mrs. Peterson (Application 5), but no answer has been received. Write a letter to her demanding payment, and place her on a cash basis for any future deliveries.

7. As an employee in the accounts receivable department of Arizona Cartage Company, you must try to collect a $12.50 balance-due bill from Best Products Company, 1123 14th Street, Chandler, Arizona 85224. Your company billed them for a 5,000-pound shipment at $1.50 per cwt. (per hundred pounds), or $75.00, but the people at Best Products say

they had understood before making the shipment that the rate would be $1.25, or $62.50. Write a letter to this customer, informing them that you are required by federal law to charge the published rate of $1.50, and ask that they pay the additional $10.50. This company is a relatively new customer of Arizona Cartage.

8. As an employee for a small maintenance company that provides janitorial services for Westside businesses, you are concerned that you have not received payment from Brinkman Industries for a $250 invoice (your company's Invoice 16128 dated June 3). You have since mailed a bill to Brinkman for services provided during June (Invoice 19998, July 2). As outlined in a contract with all customers, bills are payable within 10 days following their receipt of an invoice—in full, with no partial payments and no discounts. Since Brinkman is a relatively new account, and because considerable time has elapsed since you mailed the first invoice, skip the reminder stage of the collection process and begin with a letter of inquiry. Today's date is July 28 of the current year, and Brinkman's address is 11801 West La Brea Avenue, Los Angeles, California 90038.

9. Continuing with the situation presented in Application 8, Margeret Whitmer, an accountant at Brinkman Industries, called you on August 1, expressing dismay that the two invoices had not yet been paid and promising to mail a check to you that same day. It is now August 10, and no check has been forthcoming. Write a letter, appealing for immediate action and threatening to discontinue janitorial services.

10. Continuing with the situation in Applications 8 and 9, it has now been ten days since writing your last letter and there has been no response. Discontinue your service to Brinkman, effective five days from today, and threaten to turn the account over to a collection agency. But see if you can accomplish this communicative objective without completely eliminating the possibility of conducting future business transactions with Brinkman.

PART FIVE

ORAL, GRAPHIC, AND NONVERBAL COMMUNICATIONS

Business communications do not consist entirely of written communications, of course; oral, graphic, and nonverbal communications are equally important. Business people converse routinely on the telephone; they communicate face to face during individual exchanges, group meetings, and public appearances.

Graphic aids are an especially important adjunct to both written and oral communications, as the following comments by an insurance company executive confirm:

> Graphics are an important aid to communications, particularly in conveying abstract concepts. A graphic presentation should illustrate a concept in a way that people can relate to it physically, because people can best understand a concept if they can see, feel, and touch it. For example, a concept like "customary and reasonable fees" is used in Medicare and some group-health insurance contracts. In dealing with Medicare beneficiaries, we found that understanding of this concept can best be achieved through the use of graphics. First, the concept of "customary fees" is illustrated with a drawing of a physician surrounded by five bills—four for $10 and one for $12. The physician's "customary fee" is obviously $10. Second, the concept of "reasonable fees" is illustrated with a drawing of four physicians—three with a bill for $10 and one with a bill for $12. The "reasonable fee" is obviously $10. But we are just beginning to scratch the surface in using graphics to illustrate the abstract concepts in our benefit plans.

> I checked with our manager of Advertising & Public Information, concerning use of graphic materials by our sales people, who says that graphics play an important role in sales because they create interest and hold attention. The nature of life insurance sales is such that agents are kept "on stage" for periods often running an hour or longer. Therefore, agents need good graphic props. Most good agents develop their own point-of-sale materials to fit their personal styles of selling. Some agents prepare slide-tape or video-tape presentations, while others use simple scrapbooks. Agents

working in highly sophisticated markets need sophisticated graphics, but agents working in less sophisticated markets may intentionally want their graphics to have a homemade look. Graphics play an essential role in life-insurance selling, and most agents are skilled in their use.

> John R. Hundley
> Second Vice President, Personnel
> GENERAL AMERICAN LIFE Insurance Company

This insurance company executive also informed me that his company stresses the importance of letter writing, telephone use, effective listening, and nonverbal communication. Correspondingly, this part of the book deals systematically with these subject areas.

18

COMMUNICATING
BY TELEPHONE

The telephone is the most widely used communicative device in business, yet very few schools provide any instruction at all in the proper use of this invaluable instrument. Similarly, most business managers assume that new employees, no matter how inexperienced in the ways of business, will automatically be able to use telephones efficiently.

Such assumptions are erroneous and costly. Despite the thousands of hours that teenagers may log on telephones conversing with one another, their use of telephones during the first weeks on a job can be traumatic. To succeed in actual business settings, new employees must familiarize themselves with the intricacies of handling various types of telephone calls—incoming and outgoing, local and long distance, within and outside the company. Space does not permit a comprehensive description of the many types of telephone equipment presently available, some of which are very sophisticated, but the guidelines presented on the following pages may help you become a more efficient and effective user of telephones.

Will you hold the line a moment, please?

BEFORE YOU MAKE THE CALL

We have devoted considerable space to planning our written communications. Telephone conversations are no different in this respect; the various approaches that we discussed for routine, good news, bad news, collection, and persuasive messages apply equally to telephone communications. Before making a phone call, moreover, we should develop a plan of action. We should also consider the all-important time element.

Plan the communication. We often hear people anguish over having forgotten to discuss this or ask that—right after they have ended their telephone conversations. Avoid the expense and embarrassment of having to make follow-up calls by planning your phone conversations. Before you reach for the phone, determine the topics that you want to cover and list them in the most logical order of presentation.

A good plan saves money, because it helps you to minimize long-distance charges and to avoid wasting your time by keeping the conversation directed toward established objectives. Additionally, a planned conversation tends to make the other person view you as a well-organized individual who is in control of the situation. A good plan will even help you recognize when the telephone is not the best medium for the message. If several points must be discussed, and especially if the topics relate to more than one person at the other end of the line, a letter or two might be more effective and more economical than a phone call.

Consider the time element. In formulating your plan, give some thought to the time element. Try to avoid extended conversations with your stockbroker between 10:00 a.m. and 4:00 p.m. (Eastern standard time), for example, because that is the period that the New York Stock Exchange is open—the busiest time of day for stockbrokers. If you are calling people at their homes, don't place the calls before 9:00 a.m. (later on weekends and holidays), for fear of awakening them. Similarly, do not call anyone at home after 9:30 p.m. unless an emergency situation exists. And, as stated in an earlier chapter, avoid calling people at their offices at the very start of the business day; give them time to organize their business transactions for the day before calling. In his book *How To Hit the Telephone Jackpot,* Hubert K. Simon recommends specific times for calling accountants, bankers, builders, business executives, dentists, and other categories of business and professional people. In brief, be considerate of others as you use telephones to interrupt their activities, and especially when intruding on their personal lives.

Telephone rates sometimes govern the timing of our calls. When transacting business within the United States and Canada, we have four time zones to consider; and, as the map in Figure 18-1 illustrates, a three-hour difference exists between locations on the East Coast and the West Coast. For the Alaska-Hawaii time zone (not shown on the map), there is a two-hour difference in relation to Pacific standard time. When it is 9:00 a.m. in California, for example, it is only 7:00 a.m. in Alaska and Hawaii.

Long-distance transactions are further complicated by **daylight saving time (DLS),** because some parts of one state (Indiana) observe DLS the entire year and because two states (Arizona and Hawaii) never change to DLS time.

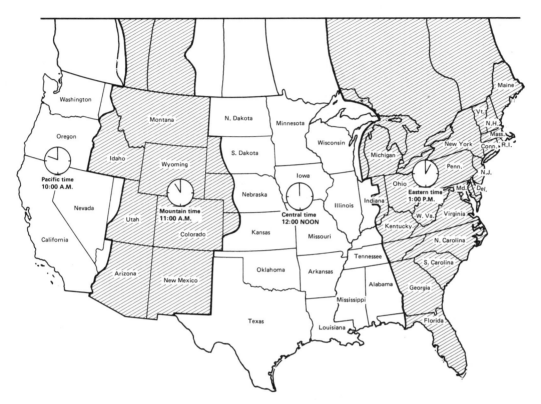

Figure 18-1　Time zones in the United States and Canada

People in all other states set their watches and clocks ahead one hour during summer months, beginning the last Sunday of April and ending the last Sunday in October.

When comparing the zone map in Figure 18-1 with telephone rate periods in Figure 18-2, we can time our calls to minimize costs. We may take advantage of the lower evening rates (about 37 percent lower than day rates) by phoning after 5:00 p.m. By placing calls after regular working hours (8:00 a.m. to 5:00 p.m.), for example, people in the East and Midwest pay the lower rates and are still able to catch people in their offices in Western cities. People in the West, on the other hand, may take advantage of the still lower night rates by coming into their offices a little early; all calls that begin before 8:00 a.m. are billed at the night rate, no matter how long the conversation. A call from San Francisco to New York City at 7:59 a.m. Pacific time, for example, will reach the person in New York City at 10:59 a.m. Eastern time, and will be billed at the significantly lower night rate. Many businesses utilize lower rates by transmitting sales orders and contacting delinquent accounts in eastern cities before 8:00 a.m. (night rates) and to points west after 5:00 p.m. (evening rates).

LOWEST RATES
DIAL-DIRECT ONE-MINUTE RATES

Dial-direct calls are those interstate calls (excluding Alaska and Hawaii) completed from a residence or business phone without operator assistance.

Dial-direct rates also apply on calls placed with an operator from a residence or business phone where dial-direct facilities are not available.

On dial-direct calls *you pay only for the minutes you talk.* The initial rate period is *one minute* any time of day or night.

Additional savings apply if you dial direct during the "discount" time periods indicated on the chart below.

8 A.M.	MONDAY TUESDAY WEDNESDAY THURSDAY FRIDAY SATURDAY SUNDAY
WEEKDAY 5 P.M.	**FULL RATE** Minimum charge: 1 minute
EVENING 11 P.M.	**35% DISCOUNT** from Full Rate. Minimum charge: 1 minute. **35%**
NIGHT & WEEKEND 8 A.M.	**60 % DISCOUNT** from Full Rate. Minimum charge: 1 minute.

Figure 18-2   Telephone rate periods

Dialing for dollars.

WHEN MAKING THE CALL

Important questions arise concerning the actual placement of phone calls. Are you going to dial the number yourself or rely on someone else to do it for you? When making long-distance calls, are you going to call person-to-person or station-to-station?

Dial it yourself. If you rely on a secretary or switchboard operator to place calls for you, the resulting inefficiencies more than offset any time you may save. While the other person is looking up and dialing a number for you, you may become involved with an incoming call. Imagine how frustrating it is to the person on the other end of the line to receive a phone call from someone only to find that the person (the caller) is talking with someone else on another line. Many companies avoid such hassles by having most employees place their own calls.

Record important numbers. The telephone companies seem determined to force us to look up our own numbers rather than permitting us to rely habitually on directory assistance; they now assess a charge for each inquiry after the first five inquiries each month (not including assistance for long-distance numbers), and the service is becoming progressively slower. You may save time and money, therefore, by regularly using a telephone directory. Upon locating the desired number in a directory, make it easy to refer back to the number by circling it.

But what about long-distance numbers? Switchboard operators in large companies often have copies of directories for all major cities. When such directories are not available, you may use the universal information number by dialing 1 (in those areas where it is required), the area code of the distant city (if outside your code area), and the number 555-1212. When it is probable that you will have a future need for the number, avoid the inconvenience of referring again to the universal number or a directory by recording the number with other frequently used numbers. Also, telephones are now available that enable you to record 30 or so of your most frequently called numbers so that you only need to press one button to call one of the numbers.

Rely on station-to-station service. When you are placing a long-distance call and do not know whether the other person will be available, what do you do? A person-to-person call generally isn't the best approach to such a situation. Studies show that **station-to-station** calls, even though they often result in follow-up calls to reach the other person, are more economical in the long run, because person-to-person calls are the most costly type of telephone service. When a station-to-station call fails to reach the intended person, it is some-times appropriate to leave word for the person to return the call, which relieves you of paying for the subsequent, and sometimes lengthy, conversation that eventually takes place.

If, after several attempts, you have not found the other person at his or her office, you may resort to person-to-person service. Dial 0 and tell the operator that you wish to talk to the specific person at such-and-such a number (include the area code). If the other person happens to be in the vicinity of the telephone but not immediately available, you may ask the long-distance operator to hold the line open for a maximum of one minute—hoping that the person will respond to your call within that time. If not, you will have to hang up and try again later. There is no charge for this service until the other person comes on the line.

Avoid operator-assisted calls. **Person-to-person calls** are expensive because they involve the assistance of operators. Credit card calls, collect calls, and calls billed to other numbers also require operator assistance; and they are relatively expensive. Although the telephone companies have made it possible for us to direct dial credit card and collect calls through what is called **zero-plus-dialing**, an operator must still come on the line to handle details, and the phone companies apply operator-assisted rates to such calls.

So how can you avoid the involvement of operators in such calls? You cannot do without operator assistance with collect calls, but you can minimize the use of credit cards. If you are making long-distance calls from your home during weekends, for example, to take advantage of the relatively low weekend rates (see Figure 18-2), direct dial the numbers rather than charging them to your employer with a credit card. Then, when the charges appear on your monthly phone bill, add them to your monthly expense account. If you don't have an expense account, submit a copy of the long-distance charges to your company for reimbursement. Management should be grateful that you have helped minimize the company's telephone bill.

Consider conference calls. Sometimes the quickest way to effect a meeting of several minds is to place a **conference call**. Dial 0 and ask for the conference operator. This person does the planning and the dialing to have all persons on the same line at the prescribed time, and the phone company doesn't begin charging for the service until all the intended people are on the line. The cost of conference calls can be high, depending on the distances and number of people involved, but consider the number of letters, miles of travel, and individual calls that can be eliminated by one conference call.

Just be your usual self: helpful, efficient, lovable.

DURING THE CONVERSATION

Your telephone behavior is important because you are a company representative. In the eyes of the public, you *are* the company. You may enhance your own image and that of the company, therefore, by following certain guidelines for good telephone usage and by treating every phone call with equal care.

Identify yourself. Most people, especially business people, don't have time to play guessing games, so the first thing you should do when someone answers your call is identify yourself.

Example: This is Armco Motors; is Mr. Ritzell available please?

Example: This is Manuel Ortega; may I please speak with Miss Lewis?

When you want some information but don't know whom to speak with, help the answering person by stating your business.

Example: This is Jim Snodgrass at Rainbow Electric; I would like to know when we may expect delivery of our order.

Example: This is Paula Chin at the Internal Revenue Service. May I speak to whoever is responsible for the issuance of W-2 forms, please?

Avoid using a title when identifying yourself, because many people consider it poor form to do so.

(no)   Public Relations, Mr. Phillips

(yes) Public Relations, Bob Phillips

(no)   Personnel, Dr. Randolph

(yes) Personnel, Marian Randolph

Speak clearly. Before talking on the phone, remove particles from your mouth such as pencils, gum, cigarettes, and candy. Enunciate clearly, so that the other person doesn't have to keep asking you to repeat yourself. New employees often become excited when talking with customers, especially on long-distance calls, causing them to talk too loud and too fast. You should be conscious of the cost of telephone calls, certainly, but the most effective way to communicate is to speak at a moderate pace in a natural voice.

Personalize the conversation. Most of us like to hear own own names as well as read them in print. Personalize your telephone conversations by catering to this need; refer to the other person by name throughout the conversation—without overdoing it, of course. Most employees also have an affection for their companies, so talk in terms of what is desirable for their company, rather than your own; and occasionally include the name of their company in your conversation.

Listen attentively. We often become so engrossed in what we want to say that we fail to listen closely to what the other person is saying. When we fall into this trap, two-way conversation breaks down and meaningful discussion becomes impossible. Listen closely to the other person and make notes of all important points discussed.

Closing the conversation. You don't want to talk on the telephone any longer than necessary, because needless conversation costs your company time and money—especially if your company is picking up the tab for a long-distance call. If you initiated the call, it is your responsibility to close it; in most situations, in fact, it is considered bad manners if the person receiving the call takes the initiative to end the conversation. Bring the call to a close firmly but gently by sending verbal signals that you are ready to end the conversation.

Example: Well, Betty, that covers everything I have to say.
Example: Is there anything else we should discuss at this time?
Example: Okay, Mario, I'll hang up now and let you get back to work.
Example: I have to run now, Jim; I'm already late for our department meeting.

Thanking the other person also provides an effective close.

Example: Thanks for taking the time to explain the situation, Ross.
Example: I appreciate this order, Jan, and so will the sales manager.

Such comments as "I'll be seeing you," "thank you," "goodbye," and "bye bye," are often the final words uttered before hanging up the phone. Care should be taken to avoid slamming the phone when you hang up, because the other person may still be on the line. Replace the receiver gently.

This is she; is this he?

WHEN RECEIVING CALLS

Incoming calls require special handling, and most companies strive for uniformity in the way employees respond. Without becoming involved in excessive detail, let's consider some useful guidelines.

Identify your company. Most large- and medium-sized companies employ switchboard operators to receive and direct incoming calls. And each company seems to have its special way of answering the telephone. At Honeywell, Inc., for example, switchboard operators are instructed to answer each incoming call with just one word, "Honeywell." Switchboard operators at The Greyhound Corporation say, "Good morning (afternoon), The Greyhound Corporation." Operators at Safeway Stores, Inc., reverse this response by saying, "Safeway, good morning (afternoon)." And the operators at Sperry Univac answer each incoming call with "Sperry Univac, may I help you?" Brevity of the initial response is important because of the thousands of times these words must be repeated each working day.

Identify yourself. When the switchboard operator routes a call to your phone, you should answer by identifying yourself. Company policy sometimes dictates that employees simply state their names, while other companies require employees to precede their names with the name of their departments.

Example: Product Distribution, Mel Tyler speaking.
Example: Purchasing, Dixie Lee.
Example: Warehouse, this is Louis.

As stated earlier in this chapter, do not use a title (Mr., Ms. Miss, Mrs., Dr.) when identifying yourself.

In some situations, calls from outside the company come directly to the telephones of individual employees, making it necessary for them to identify the company and themselves.

Example: American Airlines, Wayne Jenkins.
Example: TWA reservations, Pam Burns.

Most company managements discourage use of the word "hello" when answering telephones, dubbing it a waste of time.

Identify the caller. When callers do not identify themselves right away, we must ask them to do so. Don't continue talking, assuming that you recognize the caller's voice. Imagine how embarrassing it can be to think you are shooting the breeze with a colleague, only to find that a company executive or an important customer is on the other end of the line. Avoid such embarrassments by asking, "Who is this, please?" If taking the call for someone else, ask, "May I say who is calling, please?"

Take your own calls. When incoming calls are routed through switchboards and secretaries before reaching the people being called, three people become involved with each call; and callers sometimes feel abused by the time they reach the persons they are calling. Telephone procedure can be greatly simplified by having employees accept all incoming calls directly. Correspondingly, even key employees at some companies have individual phones (lines and numbers) which they answer themselves. Their phones are answered by other employees only when they are not present to accept calls themselves.

Be prepared. Don't go through a search routine when answering the telephone; have pencil and paper handy. You should also have a supply of call slips for recording calls for other employees. If someone asks for Nancy Stein and Nancy isn't available, record the caller's name, the name of the company or organization the caller represents, the caller's telephone number, and the time; and indicate whether Nancy is to return the call.

Be tactful. Use tact in explaining a person's absence from the office, avoiding such comments as, "Nancy hasn't arrived in the office yet (at 9:30 a.m.)," "Nancy has left for the day (at 3:30 p.m.)," and "Nancy is at coffee." More businesslike responses would be: Ms. Stein is not available just now, may I take a message?" and "Ms. Stein will be out of town all this week; would you care to speak with Mr. Gonzales?"

Press the right button. As mentioned earlier, telephone companies and other suppliers now offer many different types of telephone equipment, but the arrangement depicted in Figure 18-3 is characteristic of most business telephone systems. Keys similar to those pictured are located just below the dial or pushbuttons, and each telephone within the department would have an identical arrangement. Employees in the accounting department might have this arrangement of keys, for example, while employees in the distribution department would have a somewhat different arrangement.

HOLD	263-5914	263-5915	161	162	163	COM

Lighted Flashing   Lighted

Figure 18-3 Keys on a typical business telephone

The keys marked 263-5914 and 263-5915 are outside lines, lines for talking with people outside the company. The keys marked 161, 162, and 163 are company lines, to be used for talking with other employees within the company. The button at the far left is the **hold** key, and the button at the far right is the **intercom** key.

We place callers on hold when we leave the line for any reason, such as (1) announcing their presence on the line to another employee, (2) complying with their request to wait until the person they are calling is available to speak with them, and (3) locating information they have requested. We use the intercom line to talk with other employees who share our departmental telephone system, usually to inform them of incoming calls without having to shout back and forth across the office.

The constant light at the 263-5914 key in Figure 18-3 indicates that the line is in use. If we were to press that key on our telephone and pick up the receiver, we would interrupt a conversation. (Some telephone systems are designed to prevent accidental interruptions.) When the 263-5914 line is busy (as it is now) and someone dials the number, the call is automatically switched to the 263-5915 line and that key will begin flashing (as it is in this situation). We can answer the incoming call by pressing the 263-5915 key, picking up the receiver, and identifying ourselves.

If the caller on 263-5915 wishes to speak to Jean Simpson, whose desk is some distance from ours and who is already talking on 162 (her company line, which is lighted), we can say, "Ms. Simpson is on another line; do you wish to hold or may she return the call?" If the caller wishes to return the call, we record all pertinent information on a call slip. If the caller wishes instead to wait, we tell the caller that we are placing him or her on hold and then press the hold key (all the way down to avoid disconnecting the person who wants to wait). If Jean Simpson is still talking on the other line after 60 seconds or so has elapsed, we again press the 263-5915 key and let the caller know that Ms. Simpson is still talking on another line. Rather than placing callers on hold and forgetting about them, we regularly inform them of our efforts to connect with whomever they are calling—occasionally offering them the option of leaving a message rather than waiting.

Assuming the caller is still on hold and that the light on key 162 (Jean's company line) turns off, we press the intercom key at the far right, pick up the receiver, and dial Jean's intercom number (let's say it is 15), which makes a sound at her phone that is different from the usual ring. Jean responds by pressing the intercom key on her phone, picking up the receiver, and identifying herself; and we tell her that she has a call on 5915. Jean then takes the call by pressing the 263-5915 key on her telephone and identifying herself to the caller.

Transfer calls properly. Sometimes people call us when they should talk with someone else within the company. If the call has not come through a switchboard, the caller must hang up and redial. If the call has come through the company switchboard, on the other hand, we tell the caller who it is they should be talking to and that we are going to transfer the call. We then depress and release (once or twice) the button or holder that the receiver rests on when the telephone is not in use, to signal the operator. When the operator comes on the line, we request that the call be transferred to the correct number or person.

Respond promptly. Don't keep other people waiting unnecessarily. Answer the phone promptly—on the first or second ring, if possible. If the phone rings while you are talking on another line, ask the person you are talking to if you may place him or her on hold to answer another call. After pressing the hold key, press the flashing key, tell the caller that you are busy on another line, and ask if you may place him (the second caller) on hold for a moment. Then press the hold key before returning to the line that you were talking on before the interruption. But don't forget about the person you placed on hold. If you believe that your conversation will be lengthy, ask the second caller if you may return the call.

When you are going to be away from your office, be certain that someone will answer your phone and let them know the approximate time of your return. Make a practice of returning at the time specified and always return telephone calls promptly. If your work requires you to be out of the office regularly, you may benefit from a pocket-sized signaling device. When an important call is received, office personnel can signal you to go to the nearest phone and call the office.

DISCUSSION AND REVIEW QUESTIONS

1. What is the value of planning what you are going to talk about on the telephone? Why not just play it by ear as you go along?

2. How can a well-planned telephone call save money for your company?

3. In what way is the time element important when calling such people as stockbrokers, business executives, and people at home?

4. In what way can knowledge of the various time zones across the country help you minimize the monthly telephone bill?

5. Using the zone map in Figure 18-1, determine the difference in time between Oregon and Illinois.

6. When it is 6:00 p.m. during the summer months in New York City, what time is it in Arizona? (*Hint:* Arizona and Hawaii do not change to daylight saving time.)

7. Among the rate periods listed in Figure 18-2, which rates are the highest (excluding person-to-person rates)? Which are the lowest?

8. How can you find telephone numbers of people and businesses in distant cities so that you may place station-to-station calls?

9. If you must talk to a specific person who works in a company in another state, should you make a person-to-person call? Explain.

10. Why are the rates for collect calls and calls charged to credit cards higher than for station-to-station calls?

11. If you were staying at a motel in another city, how could you call your home office without using a credit card or calling collect? What would be the purpose of this action?

12. When the person you are calling answers the phone, what is the first thing you should say?

13. How can you personalize telephone conversations?

14. Who should bring a telephone conversation to a close?

15. What is the first thing you should say when answering a telephone call coming through a company switchboard?

16. What is the first thing you should say when receiving a call directly from someone outside the company?

17. What should you do when callers fail to identify themselves at the beginning of telephone conversations?

18. What are the benefits of having business managers take their own calls rather than having someone screen all incoming calls? Can you think of any business situations where screening would be desirable?

19. Providing that you have an array of keys on your telephone similar to those in Figure 18-3, what can you do if another phone begins ringing while you are talking on another line?

20. Why should you use care to make certain that the correct key on the telephone is depressed—before picking up the receiver?

21. What is the meaning of a flashing light on the key of a telephone? A steady light? No light?

22. How may we be certain that a person waiting on the telephone for information that we are checking does not overhear what we are saying to other employees?

23. Respond to the following comments:
    a. Ask the switchboard operator to place the call for you.
    b. Get the number from directory assistance.
    c. Data Processing, Mr. Chin speaking.
    d. Mr. Abts isn't in yet; I don't know what's keeping him.
    e. Ms. Kelly isn't at her desk just now, and I don't know anything about credit memos.
    f. Mr. Sherman is out in the warehouse somewhere, and there is no way that we can contact him until he returns to his office.

19

COMMUNICATING FACE TO FACE

Face-to-face communications are just as important as written and telephone communications, and maybe more so. Well-written memos and letters and the skillful use of telephones are essential to success in business, but the critical factor in shaping your future in business is often the impression you make on other people during personal exchanges.

The opportunities for face-to-face communications in business are virtually unlimited. In addition to established manager-manager, manager-employee, and employee-employee relationships, which require countless in-person exchanges, most companies rely heavily on committee meetings and employee counseling. Management must also consider the external environment, with related public speeches and media appearances.

Please, not another meeting.

COMMITTEE MEETINGS

Practically all large organizations—businesses, governments, schools, and churches—use committees for one purpose or another. A committee consists of several people brought together to perform a specific function. In a business setting, for example, small groups of employees may be charged with tasks ranging in importance from new-product development to organizing the employees' annual golf tournament. Among its dozens of committees, the U.S. Senate has a Finance Committee, Public Works Committee, and Veterans' Affairs Committee. Schools have committees for such areas of education as curriculum, commencement, and scholarships; and churches often have building, membership, and finance committees.

Committee meetings are a point of contention in most organizations. Many people view them as boring, fruitless, unending endeavors, while others consider them interesting, essential, and effective. Both views are correct, essentially; some meetings are ineffective and some are very effective—depending on the type of people who are members of a particular committee, the scope and powers of the committee, and the skills of the committee chairperson.

Conflicting appraisals. Compared to an on-the-spot decision or recommendation by a knowledgeable individual, committees are slow and expensive. All members must be informed of relevant details, and sufficient time must be allowed for thorough analysis and discussion of all major points. Committee decisions are often compromised because of group social pressures, as some members capitulate to the views of dominant or influential committee members. Committee meetings can also diffuse responsibility, resulting in individual nonresponsibility for group decisions, recommendations, and directives.

Why, then, are committees so widely used in business? As businesses have become progressively larger and more complex, no one person is able to understand all aspects of company operations well enough to make informed, comprehensive decisions. Consequently, experts from affected areas of the business are brought together to make group analyses and decisions. Several individuals work in unison to pool their knowledge, experience, and judgment to derive the best possible approach to a particular situation or problem. A side benefit of the committee approach to business management is that committee members and the employees they represent tend to be receptive to the solutions and recommendations they have influenced, often viewing the outcomes as more equitable than solutions and directives handed down by individual decision makers.

Group composition. The total committee, as with almost anything else, cannot be any better than the sum of its parts. If a committee is to be effective, therefore, management should exercise care in selecting its members. Most important, the committee must be made up of people with the necessary skills and background to fulfill the assignment. If the assignment is to perform a feasibility study for construction of a new warehouse, for example, committee membership should include employees who are knowledgeable in such areas as real estate, product distribution, traffic, inventory control, and finance.

The people who organize committees should use care when mixing different levels of employees. If a member of top management is appointed to a committee along with members of middle and lower management, employees at the lower level are apt to be inhibited by the presence of the higher-ranking manager. Correspondingly, committee members will be inclined to let the higher-level person dominate the discussion, and they will generally place greater emphasis on his or her comments.

The number of people that make up the committee is also important. Groups of fewer than five people often lack a sufficient input of ideas and expertise. When groups are composed of more than eight people, at the other extreme, less vocal members are sometimes too inhibited to contribute to the fullest extent. Ideal-sized committees, therefore, consist of from five to eight members.

Objectives and powers. To maximize employee productivity, managers must clearly assign tasks so that employees know exactly what is expected of them. Managers must also delegate a sufficient degree of authority if their employees are to assume responsibility for accomplishing assigned tasks. A committee is like an employee in this respect. If the committee is to be productive, management must outline exactly what is expected of it; and they must delegate enough authority to the committee to make it functional.

If the president of a company organizes a committee to analyze the current wage-and-salary structure, for example, he or she should make specific demands of the committee. Is the committee to analyze the wages of rank-and-file employees only, or are managerial salaries also to be examined? Is the study to be confined to the wage-and-salary structure of just this company or compared with those of similar companies? Is the committee to make recommendations or final decisions? Is the committee to be charged with introducing revised rate structures, or will others be responsible for implementation?

Once the task has been clearly defined and assigned, management must empower the committee to take whatever action is necessary to complete the assignment. If managerial salaries are to be analyzed, for instance, committee members must be given access to all related data; and if decisions of the committee are to be final, management should avoid second-guessing or otherwise frustrating those decisions.

Discussion leader. No matter how well a committee is organized and instructed, its success or failure rests to a significant degree with the discussion leader. Rather than calling a discussion leader chairman, as in the past, we now refer to the leader as **chairperson** or, more simply, **chair**.

Before each meeting, the chairperson should prepare and distribute agendas, listing in some detail the subjects to be discussed and the times for beginning and ending the meetings. Subjects should be organized strategically, so that the most important items will not be among those that may be postponed until a subsequent meeting. Sometimes it is advisable to plan topics of high interest for discussion during the last part of meetings, at a time when group interest tends to be at a low point.

Rather than having committee members read important materials during the meeting, the chairperson should distribute materials well in advance of meetings so that members may absorb the materials individually—before the meeting. The chairperson should also make certain that those people who are scheduled to make presentations during the meeting are well prepared for the occasion.

Chairpersons should begin meetings promptly. When meetings are delayed to await late arrivals, other members will soon assume the bad habit of arriving late. Meetings begun on time, on the other hand, suggest a note of urgency that motivates members to arrive at the scheduled time.

The chairperson should act as a coordinator during meetings rather than as a boss or dictator, and should be thoroughly versed in the proper procedure for conducting meetings, such as presented in *Robert's Rules of Order*. He or she should strive to create a permissive atmosphere where even the most timid individuals feel free to ask questions and contribute ideas without fear of embarrassment. The chairperson may motivate such individuals by directing specific questions their way and by rewarding them with supportive comments such as, "That's an important consideration, Anne," and "Let me make a note of that idea, William."

Conversely, the chairperson must tactfully counter the overzealousness of certain committee members. When people attempt to dominate a discussion, the chair must take the spotlight away from them by occasionally overlooking their offers to contribute and with such statements as "Just a minute, please; we haven't given Raymond a chance to voice his opinion," and "Will you please hold your comments for a moment, Mildred, while we summarize what has already been said?" Correspondingly, chairpersons should constrain their own urges to monopolize discussions.

The chairperson is responsible for keeping committee members moving in the right direction so that they will accomplish the assigned task in the allotted time. When people go off on tangents, therefore, the chairperson must guide them back on course; and the chair can often accomplish this objective by looking anxiously at whoever is talking or appealing to the person directly with comments such as "Your suggestion might be applicable if . . . " and "In this situation we are trying to. . . . "

The chairperson should not try to circumvent disagreement, because the discussion of opposing ideas often results in superior solutions. What the chair should do, however, is encourage members to deal with issues rather than personalities and to work toward the best solutions rather than engaging in win-or-lose contests.

The experienced chairperson will recognize when discussion of a subject has reached the saturation point, that moment when further discussion becomes counterproductive, and will attempt to end discussion. The chair will also recognize when agreement has been reached, end further discussion, and consider the next agenda item. In brief, an effective chairperson keeps meetings moving along—giving everyone an opportunity to contribute, avoiding irrelevant discussion, and striving to adjourn meetings on time.

How long should committee meetings last? There is no firm rule, but most meetings last anywhere from 1 to 1½ hours. Meetings of longer duration should be avoided or liberally interspersed with rest periods. After a meeting has ended, the chairperson remains responsible for the preparation and distribution of minutes (the record) of the meeting, a task that is usually assigned to a secretary or committee member. The chair must also make certain that committee members follow through with any actions recommended by the committee.

I'll bet this guy's a shrink.

INTERVIEWING AND COUNSELING

Businesses use interviews to select new employees, to evaluate employee performance, and to discipline some employees. Counseling is similar to interviewing but generally deals with the emotional problems of employees. Businesses, usually through their personnel departments, conduct millions of such interviews each year, which makes it important for us to consider some of the factors involved in planning, conducting, and summarizing employee interviews.

Planning interviews. Successful interviews are usually the result of good planning, and the first step in planning an interview is to establish the objective. Is the interview intended to help select the best of several applicants for a particular position? To assess an employee's job performance? To alter an employee's behavior? Having identified the objective of an interview, we can develop and organize our questions.

Questions may be directive or nondirective. Directive questions, as the term suggests, enable us to guide interviewees in the desired direction so that we may develop a composite picture of the person. The following questions are directive:

Example: How many words per minute do you type?
Example: Which area of business do you consider the most important: finance, production, or marketing?

Directive questions call for specific answers (sometimes a simple "yes" or "no") that allow us to compare the responses of different interviewees.

The following questions are nondirective:

Example: In what ways do you believe that computers contribute to the well-being of the average citizen?

Example: What are your views on this country's economic and political influence throughout the world?

Example: Do you believe that big businesses are good citizens?

Nondirective questions are designed to motivate interviewees to express a wide range of thoughts rather than specific answers, with the hope of gaining additional insight into the person's thinking.

Interviewers use both directive and nondirective questions, sometimes beginning with questions that require specific answers and finishing with open-ended questions, sometimes taking the opposite approach—depending on their objective and the situation at hand. Regardless of the approach, the key to good interviewing is to word questions in a way that produces effective two-way communication between the interviewer and the interviewee.

Conducting interviews. Interviewers can best motivate interviewees to communicate freely by putting them at ease—by being friendly, demonstrating a willingness to listen, emphasizing the positive, and being receptive to the other person's ideas and views. Interviewers should also acquaint interviewees with the objective of the interview—such as considering the interviewee's preparation for a particular job, assessing past performance, and discussing both sides of a disagreement. Knowing what interviewers are trying to accomplish enables interviewees to move in the same direction as the interviewers—toward the stated goal or objective.

As interviewees answer questions or make relevant comments, interviewers should make notes. Recorded responses and impressions enable interviewers to review key points. Without such records, interviewing can be much like house hunting; after looking at six or seven houses, most people have difficulty remembering what the first ones looked like. And interviewers should expect a certain amount of nervousness and defensiveness on the part of interviewees; it is natural for people to be self-conscious and cautious when they are being closely examined by people who may influence their incomes and careers.

Summarizing key points. At the end of interviews, interviewers must sort the relevant from the nonrelevant. During performance appraisals, the interviewer often conducts a summary with the employee, agreeing on key points that have been made and discussing any variances in interpretation. A similar approach is often useful in employee counseling, with interviewers discussing their findings (root cause of a personality conflict, existence of an alcoholic or drug problem, basis of marital discord, impending retirement anxieties) with employees, so that they may agree on any action that may be needed.

The task of judging people, their aspirations, and their problems on the basis of interviews alone is a very difficult one, and interviewer bias often complicates the task. We sometimes are unable to relate positively to certain people, for example, often explaining such reactions as "the chemistry was wrong" or "there was a conflict of personalities." Interviewers often identify, favor, and empathize with people who in some way remind them of themselves—same race, similar education, similar appearance, similar backgrounds, or from the same area of the country. Trained interviewers try to maintain a high degree of objectivity throughout the interviewing process by recognizing and overcoming their personal biases.

All week and not one "Knock, knock."

A FUNCTIONAL OPEN-DOOR POLICY

As mentioned in Chapter 2, when managers announce that their office doors are always open to all employees, such invitations often go unheeded by employees. The only functional type of open-door policy, therefore, is one that provides for specific face-to-face exchanges between managers and subordinates. Managements may effect such exchanges with the use of employee boards, social events, and daily contacts.

Employee boards. Many businesses have **junior** or **employee boards** that are made up of middle managers. These managers meet regularly with a high-ranking vice president to air their views on a wide range of company activities. Some companies go a step further, bringing workers into management phases of operations by appointing several workers to **advisory boards.** Management chooses the workers who are to serve on these boards, sometimes on a random basis, for periods ranging from one month to a year. All members are instructed to bring written questions to each meeting, and members of top management try to resolve during each meeting all such issues. Imagine the pride that these rank-and-file employees feel, knowing that they are being recognized in this way; and consider the security that their fellow workers experience, realizing that their representatives are providing them with a direct line of communication to top management.

Social events. Company dinners, picnics, sports outings, and other social events bring managers and their subordinates together in an atmosphere of informality. But the results of these efforts can be productive only when the two factions actually fraternize.

Social events do not accomplish the communication objective when people do not circulate freely. When company managers stay to themselves and employees congregete in their usual work groups, it is business as usual. Management must make a concerted effort, therefore, to encourage managers and their subordinates to relate to one another. The president of the company should be matched at the golf tournament with employees at different levels of influence in the company rather than with people that he sees regularly at the office; and the personnel manager's family should seat itself alongside a supervisor's family at the company picnic rather than next to some other executive's family. This type of communication is what company-sponsored social events are all about, if the events are to contribute to good employee relations.

Daily contacts. Committee meetings, interviews, and social events are relatively formal affairs, events that are organized by management. But sometimes informal exchanges can be much more effective. One company president delivers memos in person that he has written to top and middle managers rather than using the company mail, as a way of "getting to know the people who work for me a little better." The president of a large airline routinely arrives at the company cafeteria at 7:00 each workday morning to eat breakfast with different employees, employees who work at all levels of the company; and he encourages other company executives to follow his example. Similarly, many top managers make it a daily practice to walk through company facilities, offering employees an opportunity to make suggestions and air grievances. Not only do these managers learn what employees are thinking, they also convey to employees that company leaders recognize them as individuals and value their contributions to the company.

At last, I'm in show biz.

PUBLIC SPEAKING

Most of us at one time or another are asked to make some comments before groups of people, and business people are frequent targets of such requests.

How should you respond to such a request? How can you best prepare? What are some tips for delivering the speech? The next few paragraphs are designed to answer these and other questions related to public speaking.

Thorough preparation. Preparation is essential to successful speeches. Begin by determining *why* you have been approached; specifically, what is it they want you to talk about? Ask the planning committee to provide a profile of the audience: average age, common interests, educational backgrounds, occupations, and experience. Armed with this information, you can decide whether to accept or reject the invitation. Accept speaking engagements only if you are sufficiently familiar with the subject area to deliver a message that will be interesting, different, and timely. If your message has sufficient impact, news of it will not only spread by word of mouth, but also by the news media—a plus factor for both you and your company.

Most experienced speakers warn against the acceptance of last-minute invitations because hastily planned speeches often fall flat. Once having agreed to speak, decide on a major theme that has audience appeal—and stick with it. If you are to talk about the need for reducing capital gains taxes, learn as much as you can about the subject and avoid the temptation to talk about other types of taxes. If you are to speak about the high rate of teenage unemployment, do not go off on tangents about problems in international trade or monetary policy.

After you have researched the topic thoroughly, outline your thoughts on paper in the most logical order of presentation and begin writing your speech. Use words and terms that you normally use when talking and plan your opening remarks to capture audience attention.

Example: Do you realize that the military in this country spends more than $350 million each day—including Saturdays, Sundays, and holidays? And that they are asking for much, much more?

Example: Family income in the United States will increase 18.1 percent during the next five years, in today's dollars. Do you know what that increase will mean to the housing industry?

Maintain interest with the generous use of examples and case histories—especially those based on your own experiences. Consider using graphics to help tell your story. Pictures, charts, and lists should be kept simple, but not to the point of being childish, and they should be of professional quality. Use graphic aids, however, only when they are more effective than words in explaining complex situations and issues—not as substitutes for a well-prepared speech.

Highlight key points in your speech by underlining or circling them, or by placing key words on a series of note cards, being sure to note when a specific picture or chart is to be displayed. And then practice, practice, practice.

Present your speech to a mirror several times, then record and listen to your words. When you have polished the presentation to your satisfaction, condensing or expanding it to the desired number of minutes, try it out on your spouse, family, and friends.

Conduct a dress rehearsal during the final stages of preparation, just as professional entertainers do, by practicing in the type of clothes you plan to wear during the main event; and practice your speech in surroundings that resemble the actual setting as closely as possible. All this preparation will help to reduce anxiety during presentation of the speech by establishing a feeling within yourself that you have traveled this road before.

What about humor? Some authorities insist that speakers begin every presentation with a joke, and they suggest that speeches be interspersed with bits of humor. Other authorities warn speakers, especially novices, to avoid telling jokes and the related risk of laying a great big egg in front of an unforgiving audience. Most experts agree, however, that even experienced speakers should use jokes only when directly related to some major point of the talk. Speakers are sometimes startled when people laugh at statements that weren't intended to be funny. If this happens to you, make the most of the situation by laughing along with the audience.

As a final preparation for your speech, visit the room where you are to speak. If you are to speak at a luncheon, drop by the restaurant a day or so beforehand and ask to see where the meal is to be served. Check the microphone, if it is already in place, to make certain that you can adjust it properly. If you are to use slides, decide on the best place for the screen and check to see if electric outlets and extension cords are available. Having surveyed the area, you will be able to picture yourself in the actual setting as you practice your speech.

Effective delivery. As the time for your presentation draws nearer, the shakes may become more pronounced, but you should realize that even experienced speakers commonly suffer from severe nervousness—especially as they are being introduced. You can minimize this uncomfortable condition somewhat by realizing that butterflies bother most people, not just you, and by realizing that you are well prepared for the occasion. Physical activity is sometimes helpful: pressing your toes against the soles of your shoes, pressing your fingers firmly together under the table, bouncing your legs up and down on your toes (also under the table—and only if it has a tablecloth!), using care to maintain a pleasant facial expression while all this activity is going on.

Butterflies usually do not fly away until you are well into your speech, when you begin to realize in the back of your mind that everything is going well. But everything goes well only when you get off to a good start. Take plenty of time after you have been introduced, therefore, to make sure that the microphone is positioned correctly and that your notes are placed just right. Pause a moment to collect your thoughts before you begin talking, because the first statement generally sets the tone for the entire presentation. Correspondingly, your opening statement should be rehearsed to the point of perfection—correct emphasis, good voice inflection, proper volume. If you wish your words to sound warm and intimate, stand close to the microphone (3 to 4 inches) and talk in a relatively low voice. Stand farther away (8 to 10 inches) to project an impersonal tone.

Do not read any part of your speech, unless it is a quotation of a statement by an important person; use your notes only as a memory jog. Give the impression that your are looking at your audience, not the carpet or ceiling, by focusing your eyes on one person for five seconds or so, then another, and another. This approach will help you talk naturally, as though you were conversing with just one person; and it will help you relax.

But what should you do with your arms and hands? Nothing! Don't fold your arms across your chest, and don't clasp your hands behind your back. Stand there firmly and let your hands and arms take care of themselves, just as they do when you are engaging in everyday conversation. Once you begin to relax, your gestures will occur naturally to help you emphasize key points.

Keep the audience awake and interested by varying the tone of your voice from time to time, and by altering your pace. Remain sensitive to the audience, pausing when they laugh and during applause, speeding your pace during times when they are quiet and attentive. Most important, keep it brief. Some speakers become so enamored of their own voices and the favorable impressions they seem to be making that they continue talking, and talking, and talking. As the old saying goes, "Be enthusiastic, be sincere, be brief, and be seated." Remember also that your closing statement is almost as important as the opening one, so plan it well, rehearse it diligently, and deliver it with vigor.

Fielding questions. Many speeches are followed with question-and-answer sessions, and you should do well if you are knowledgeable in your subject area. Look directly at individuals as they are asking questions, but look at others when you are answering, to discourage questioners from interrupting your answers and attempting to debate with you. Don't let the questions continue for a long time, especially if your speech or the program has been lengthy. Bring the session to an end by offering to take just one or two more questions and sticking to it.

Radio and television appearances. Radio and television shows provide an effective forum for business people, and most of the guidelines offered for speech making apply equally to appearances on the broadcast media. If you are to be interviewed, prepare answers to probable questions rather than writing a speech. Enlist the services of your family and friends to conduct mock interviews, beginning with prepared questions and progressing to questions that are unplanned.

Phone the station and talk with the producer of the show a few days before your appearance to discuss the objective of your appearance and the types of visual displays that you are planning to use. Producers will sometimes accept a list of questions that you would like to be asked, but don't be surprised when the host rephrases the questions during the program. The professionals have found that when people respond to their own questions, they tend to give canned answers, almost as if they were reading them—just the opposite response from what the producers and talk-show hosts are seeking. Wear clothes that you consider comfortable and appropriate for the situation, realizing that shows taped during the day are sometimes aired at night. Avoid white and checked garments, and (for women) use a minimal amount of makeup.

Arrive at the station at least 30 minutes early, to avoid the excitement that develops when you are running late. You can use part of this time to familiarize yourself with the studio, and the host will probably visit with you for a few minutes before the show. When the lights come on and the cameras focus on you, avoid the natural urge to look directly at the cameras. Focus your entire attention on the interviewer instead, and continue your normal mannerisms and gestures—just as though you were conversing with someone in your own living room.

It's easy to give advice, admittedly, but sometimes difficult to perform. The only certain path to successful public speaking is through experience. So accept every offer to speak that comes your way: before groups at work, at school, at church, and various other organizations. Practice does make perfect.

But I prefer the sound of my own voice.

LISTENING GUIDELINES

Communication occurs when someone talks and someone listens. If you are not doing your share of listening, you are not actually communicating. Consider the following guidelines to effective listening.

Judge what is being said. Listen to the speaker's words rather than concentrating on what you may or may not like about the person. Even if you are unimpressed with the speaker's credentials, you will almost always learn something of value by listening closely. If you have placed yourself in the position of having to listen to someone (a speech, a meeting, a conversation), make the most of the time you are investing by actually listening.

Maintain an open mind. You may be opposed to minimum-wage legislation, price supports, or whatever it is the speaker is advocating, but don't let your convictions clog your ears. Listen closely to see what you can learn. You might even find that you have been on the wrong side of an issue all along.

Hold your fire. Enthusiastic listening is fine, but keep it in check. Listeners sometimes become so overstimulated when a speaker challenges their cherished beliefs that they stop listening and begin contriving ways to strike back. Keep cool and keep listening, so that you don't miss the points that follow. If you give the speaker half a chance, you may find that there are some issues on which you agree.

Listen actively. Resolving to listen more closely is a positive step, but active listening requires a greater dedication. Listen closely and show the speaker through your responses that you are interested. Take notes if the situation permits, listing key points as they are made; but don't become so engrossed in recording facts that you miss the speaker's main ideas. Make up your mind to listen actively beginning with the next person you meet, and you may be surprised how much smarter you will become—smarter in what you actually learn through effective listening and smarter in the way you are viewed by those who communicate with you.

DISCUSSION AND REVIEW QUESTIONS

1. When should businesses use committees rather than assigning tasks to individual employees?

2. Why do so many modern businesses rely heavily on committees?

3. If you were selecting members for a particular committee, what are some guidelines you would follow in making your selection?

4. Should management give committee members definite instructions, or should the committee be urged to decide what is to be done and how to do it? Explain.

5. Why are employees usually more receptive to directives by committees than to individual pronouncements?

6. What is the appropriate title for a person who leads discussion within committees? Can you think of a more appropriate title?

7. What can a chairperson do to motivate reticent committee members to participate?

8. Should the chairperson encourage or discourage disagreement among committee members? Explain.

9. If you were a business manager, how would you go about planning an interview with a person who is seeking a job with your company? With an employee who is not performing in the desired manner? With an employee who is being considered for promotion?

10. In the situation described in Question 9, would you plan to ask directive or nondirective questions? Explain.

11. When interviewing employees, how would you help them feel at ease?

12. Why are some social events organized by businesses almost useless so far as the improvement of employee relations is concerned? What actions can management take to improve the results of such efforts?

13. Can you think of conditions which would make it impractical for a company president to mingle with rank-and-file employees?

14. As an employee for a local business, how should you respond initially to a request that you address a group of business people?

15. How can a speaker capture the attention of an audience at the outset of a speech?

16. How can the person who is asking questions following a speech be discouraged from interrupting and attempting to debate the speaker's answer?

17. How can a person become an active listener?

18. How would you respond to the following comments?
    a. If you want to postpone progress indefinitely, just appoint a committee to study the problem.
    b. As chairperson of this committee, I have prepared a few handouts that I wish you would take a few minutes to read before we begin the discussion.

c. Let's wait a few minutes before beginning the meeting to see if Connie and Mike show up.

d. Why is it that no matter how long or short the agenda, we never seem to get out of these meetings on time?

e. I can't understand why I didn't receive a merit increase in salary; from everything that was said during the interview, I thought the boss was pleased with my work.

f. I don't know why they asked me to speak; I certainly don't know much about the subject.

g. Be sure to tell a lot of jokes during your speech next week because audiences like to be amused.

20

MAKING USE OF GRAPHIC ILLUSTRATIONS

When business people begin writing or talking in numbers, they soon lose the interest of their audiences—unless they accompany their remarks with graphic illustrations. It is important, therefore, for you to learn to construct and use various types of tables and graphs.

Now that makes ¢¢¢

TABLES

People in business commonly use **tables** to place numerical data in columns and rows, where readers can see more readily the relationships and meaning of numbers. Rather than trying to convey product sales information in paragraph form, for example, we may construct the following table:

Table 20.1   Annual Sales of Products A, B, and C
for Years 1971 through 1978

Year	Product A	Product B	Product C
1971	$40,000	$25,000	$ 5,000
1972	45,000	27,500	7,500
1973	37,500	25,000	10,000
1974	40,000	28,000	15,000
1975	32,000	22,500	15,000
1976	35,000	29,000	17,000
1977	30,000	23,000	18,000
1978	28,500	24,750	21,750

Tables must be properly labeled so that they tell the reader exactly what the data represent. Table 20-1 tells the reader that the data are for sales of three separate products for an eight-year period and that (1) sales of Product A have declined to a significant degree, (2) sales of Product B have fluctuated from year to year but with no significant increase or decrease for the eight-year period, and (3) sales of Product C have increased continuously.

Do the little lines ever run off the paper?

LINE GRAPHS

We may present a still clearer picture of the sales data given in Table 20-1 with a **line graph**. Although line graphs may consist of as many as four sections (**quadrants**), most line graphs in business contain only one quadrant, with the bottom line as the **horizontal axis** and the side line as the **vertical axis**.

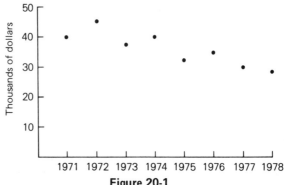

Let's begin a line graph by plotting the sales data from Table 20-1 for Product A. Normally, time is shown on the horizontal axis and dollar amounts on the vertical axis; to avoid the use of lengthy numbers, we often list money in thousands, millions, or billions of dollars. To plot the sales for Product A in 1971, we place a dot directly above the year 1971 at the 40 ($40,000) level. We place dots above each of the years in the same manner, as shown in Figure 20-1, and we connect the dots with a continuous line, as shown in Figure 20-2.

Figure 20-1

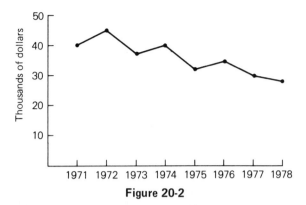

Figure 20-2

We then complete the graph by plotting the sales for Products B and C and by adding a description (labeling) of the information contained in the graph. The complete graph in Figure 20-3 presents readers with a vivid illustration of sales trends for these three products.

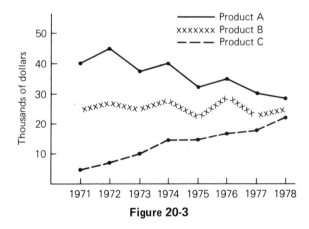

Figure 20-3

Notice in Figure 20-3 that Product A is represented by a continuous line, Product B by a series of small crosses, and Product C by dashes so that the reader can distinguish one product from another. Such distinctions are especially important when the lines cross one another, as these three product lines seem destined to do. We may also distinguish one line from the other on graphs by using a different-colored pen or pencil for each line.

I know what a bar is, but what's a graph?

BAR GRAPHS

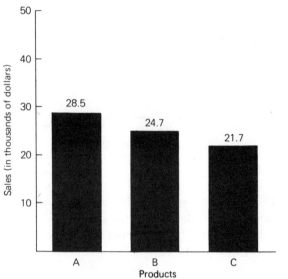

Figure 20-4
Product sales for 1978

We sometimes use **bar graphs** for the presentation of business data. Although a single bar graph cannot be used to illustrate sales data given in Table 20-1 for the three products for each of the eight years, we can plot the sales on a bar graph for a single time period—either a one-year period or the total of two or more years. Figure 20-4 shows a vertical bar graph for 1978 sales, and Figure 20-5 presents the same data in a horizontal bar graph.

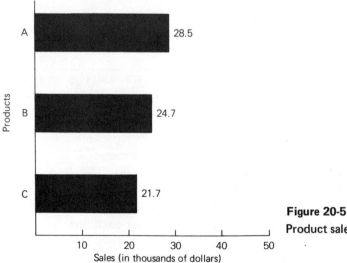

Figure 20-5
Product sales for 1978

But circles always leave me right where I started

CIRCLE GRAPHS

Circle graphs, sometimes called **pie graphs,** provide us with another method of presenting business data. Again using the data given in Table 20-1 for 1978 sales (one time period only), we follow six steps to construct a circle graph.

Step 1: Compute the total amount of whatever it is that you are plotting. Since we are concerned with sales for 1978, we total the sales for the three products: 28,500 + 24,750 + 21,750 = $75,000.

Step 2: Calculate the percentage that each segment is of the total by dividing each segment by the total.
$$28,500 \div 75,000 = 0.38$$
$$24,750 \div 75,000 = 0.33$$
$$21,750 \div 75,000 = \underline{0.29}$$
$$1.00$$

Step 3: Multiply the percentages by 360 (the number of degrees in a circle).
$$0.38 \times 360 = 136.8$$
$$0.33 \times 360 = 118.8$$
$$0.29 \times 360 = \underline{104.4}$$
$$360.0$$
(Sum of degrees should always be 360 degrees)

Step 4: Draw a circle with a compass (Figure 20-6), marking the place where the steel point is placed on the paper.
The size of the circle depends on your needs, and the same steps are taken for a very small circle as for a very large one.

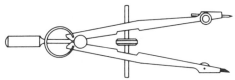

Figure 20-6   Compass

Step 5: Use a protractor (Figure 20-7) to mark the degrees.
Place the center of the flat part of the protractor at the center of the circle, as shown in the accompanying drawing, and draw a straight line from the center to the right edge of the circle. Follow the scale from the lower right of the protractor to the 136.8 (137 is close enough) and draw a straight line from that point to the center of the circle. Then place the flat part of the

protractor on the newly drawn line, with the center mark placed at the center of the circle, and mark 119 degrees for Product B. The area of the circle remaining is the 29% for Product C.

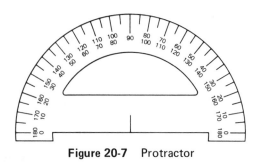

Figure 20-7   Protractor

Step 6:   Label the graph.

The completed circle graph of Figure 20-8 is shown after the segments and the graph itself have been properly labeled.

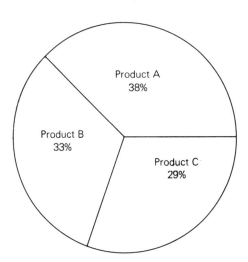

Figure 20-8   Product sales for 1978
(percentage of total sales)

Seeing is believing.

VISUAL AIDS

The table and graphs we have just discussed are suitable for inclusion in school and business reports as supplements to your verbal descriptions and explanations. They may also be modified for presentation on chalk boards, charts, overhead projectors, and movie projectors. But remember one important point: Visual aids must be kept relatively simple. If you burden the audience with too much detail, you will lose their interest.

Chalk boards. If your data are not extensive and if the room is not large, you may print large enough on a chalk board so that everyone will be able to read your table or graph. Place your information on the board before your presentation, if at all possible, because too much time taken for this purpose during a presentation will lessen the impact of your materials.

Having placed tables or graphs on a board ahead of time, cover them in some way until you are ready to use the data so that the audience will listen to what you are saying rather than reading what you have written. Direct your voice toward the audience rather than the board; and if you must turn your head away from the audience to write or explain something on the board, be sure to raise your voice so that everyone can still hear what you are saying.

The speaker pictured here is facing his audience directly while referring to a simple illustration on the chalkboard; notice the overhead projector and screen at the right (Courtesy Raytheon Company)

And what about that squeaking chalk? If you will take a few minutes beforehand to practice writing on a chalkboard, you will find that you can prevent this nerve-shattering noise by applying less pressure on the chalk. A practice session will also give you a good idea of the spacing and timing required for illustrations that you plan to develop during the presentation.

Charts. You may decide to use charts, rather than a chalkboard, because charts can be prepared ahead of time and kept out of sight of the audience until you are ready to discuss them; and they can be used more than once. The most common-sized chart measures about 30 by 40 inches, large enough to permit everyone in the audience to read the illustration. Charts that cannot be read at the back of the room are absolutely useless to those people who happen to be sitting there, so make your drawings and letters sufficiently large and use bold colors. Dark colors can be seen from quite a distance; light colors such as pink and yellow cannot.

Face your audience when discussing a chart, permitting yourself an occasional glance at the chart; avoid standing between the chart and the people you are addressing. Some speakers avoid blocking the audience's view by using a long stick to point at the parts of the charts they are discussing.

A corporate planning director using a zoning map to help make an important point during a presentation (Courtesy Samaritan Health Service)

Rooms regularly used for lecturing generally have some device for displaying charts. Check beforehand to determine whether charts may be hung from overhanging clips, tacked to a bulletin board, or taped to a wall. Many speakers use flip charts mounted on stands; when they finish with one chart, they flip it up and over to expose the chart that follows. When you use flip charts, it is a good idea to index them in some way so that you can refer to a specific chart without going through a lengthy search routine as your audience watches.

Overhead projectors. **Transparencies** for display with overhead projectors may be made from most documents by simply running each document (along with a blank transparency) through a multilith machine. If any part of a document is in color, however, the transparency must be made from a photocopy of the document. You may use felt-tip pens to add color to your transparencies.

Most overhead projectors may be operated from the front of the room, allowing the speaker to confront the audience directly while handling and discussing tranparencies. If the projector is the type that must be placed at the back of the room, try to arrange for someone else to project the transparencies on signals given by you from the front of the room.

Transparencies are generally superior to materials displayed on chalkboards or flip charts because the materials can be magnified on the screen to a significant degree, depending on your positioning of the projector in relation to the screen. They are also easy to handle and to store. The main disadvantage of transparencies is that they must be displayed in dark or semidark rooms, which often interfere with the rapport the speaker has established with the audience; so restrict your use of them. Do not torture your audience by continually turning the lights off and on as you discuss various transparencies; once you have closed or dimmed the lights, leave them that way until you have finished showing transparencies.

You may direct the audience's attention to different parts of an illustration by pointing with a long instrument to images on the screen or by using a pen or pencil to point to different parts of the transparencies. Some speakers use their pens and pencils as arrows, laying them right on the transparencies pointed toward the appropriate part of the illustration. As with most visual illustrations used in group presentations, transparencies should not have a cluttered appearance. Although the idea that you are illustrating may be complex, the illustration should be relatively simple.

A final note: Don't wait until the moment of your presentation to experiment with the overhead projector; set up the screen and test your transparencies beforehand so that the actual presentation will run smoothly. Don't unplug an overhead projector until the cooling fan has stopped running, because doing so will probably ruin the bulb. Learn how to replace a burnt-out bulb, and always have a replacement available.

Movie projectors. Many businesses have their own film libraries, and many lend their films to groups outside their companies. If you expect to talk before groups regularly, therefore, you should take a few minutes to learn to operate a movie projector. Always preview a movie before showing it to a group, to help you introduce the film properly and to note key points for discussion following the film. A preview is also necessary to make certain that the film supports the main points of your presentation. Even projectors with automatic feeders sometimes malfunction, so avoid any last-minute panic by mounting the film well in advance of your presentation.

BUSINESS APPLICATIONS

1. During 1975, Smith Bros. Construction, Inc., employed 74 people who earned wages totaling $1,320,000; during 1976, 89 employees earned $1,505,000; in 1977, 93 employees earned $1,613,000; in 1978, 105 employees earned $1,715,000. Construct and label a table containing this information.

2. Construct and label a line graph showing that Smith Bros. Construction, Inc., employed 74 people in 1975, 89 in 1976, 93 in 1977, and 105 in 1978.

3. Construct and label a vertical bar graph showing earnings by Smith Bros. Construction, Inc., of $1,500,021 in 1974; $1,950,332 in 1975; $2,130,450 in 1976; $3,212,616 in 1977; and $4,100,225 in 1978. (Show in millions of dollars, rounding to the tenths position, so that $1,500,021 becomes $1.5 million.)

4. At Smith Bros. Construction, Inc., an employee's earnings average $12,200, from which $1,800 is withheld for taxes and $960 is withheld for medical and pension plans. Construct a circle graph showing the percentage of wages that goes to (1) the employee as take-home pay, (2) taxes, and (3) the medical and pension plans. (Show all computations for the six steps involved.)

5. Using the data given in Table 20-2, construct and label the graphs described in a, b, and c following.

Table 20-2   Company Sales by Division
(1971-1978)

Year	Western division	Eastern division	Southern division
1971	$ 60,000	$165,000	$25,000
1972	70,000	167,000	33,000
1973	72,000	179,000	47,000
1974	77,000	171,000	58,000
1975	88,000	164,000	63,000
1976	99,000	154,000	68,000
1977	120,000	144,000	78,000
1978	122,500	140,000	87,500

a. Line graph showing each of the three divisions—in thousands of dollars.
b. Vertical bar chart showing sales (in thousands of dollars) for each of the three divisions in 1978.
c. Circle graph showing the percentage of sales for each division in 1978. (Show all computations for each of the required steps.)

21
COMMUNICATING NONVERBALLY

Most of us are fascinated by the possibility of being able to read other people's minds; just imagine the advantage we would have if we knew the innermost thoughts of our superiors, subordinates, colleagues, customers, competitors, friends, lovers, and enemies! Although the study of nonverbal communication doesn't come close to fulfilling this desire, careful analysis of the behavior of others can provide us with useful clues about their perceptions and attitudes.

What makes nonverbal communication so important is that a large part of our communications are unspoken; some authorities on the subject claim that as much as 50 percent of the impressions people convey result from non-verbal exchanges. In fact, our most important impressions of one another, the ones that are formed during the first four or five minutes of conversation, are based more on our subjective interpretation of nonverbal behavior than on our objective interpretation of spoken words.

More important, perhaps, when nonverbal signals conflict with verbal signals we tend to place a greater reliance on the nonverbal. How many times, for example, have you reflected on earlier conversations with such thoughts as, "They told me that they were satisfied with my performance, but I had the feeling they weren't entirely pleased"?

Many business people are demonstrating an interest in nonverbal communications by urging employees to read books and attend formal classes on the subject. If there is even a remote possibility that knowledge of nonverbal communications will help a salesperson interpret the thoughts of buyers more accurately, what salesperson could afford to be without that knowledge? If an understanding of nonverbal communications might provide management negotiators with some insight into the thoughts of union negotiators, and vice versa, what negotiator could afford to be without that understanding?

Because of the tremendous interest in the subject—and because of its potential impact—let's consider several forms of nonverbal communication. The knowledge gained should not only improve our understanding of human behavior but should also help us convey the desired image with our own nonverbal signals.

Will the real you please stand up?

PERSONAL APPEARANCE

Most of us adapt our attire to the current fashions, to greater and lesser degrees; some people follow fashions slavishly, others casually. The important principle to remember when dressing for business occasions is to keep your style simple and relatively conservative. You are generally expected to keep up with fashions, but you should modify your approach; the height of hemlines, the width of pant legs, and the width and tones of ties change frequently; so adopt a modified version of these garments.

Whether you are dressing for business purposes or for personal occasions, there are two good reasons for taking the conservative approach. First, if you follow fashion trends too closely, your clothes will be out of style with each new season. Accordingly, extreme styles draw attention to clothes, which will be more readily noticed when they are out of date. Second, a conservative approach in your choice of clothing will save you money because simple, modified styles can be phased out over a much longer period. Remember, you want the main event to be yourself and your performance, not the clothes you are wearing.

Regardless of fashion trends throughout the years, some businesses require that employees wear uniforms—not informal dress-alike clothes, but actual uniforms. Uniforms broadcast to the world that the wearer is an airline employee, a security guard, a bus driver, a host at Disneyland, or a member of one of hundreds of organizations throughout the country. To the observer, uniforms denote authority. To the wearer, uniforms represent a sense of belonging, and, if qualifying for the position is difficult, a strong sense of accomplishment and pride. In brief, uniforms convey forceful messages.

When the choice of wearing apparel is left to your discretion, you should dress for the role in business that you wish to play. If you are presently a middle manager and want top managers to view you as a serious candidate for higher positions, you should begin dressing the part. Dressing the part is simple; just emulate the person you want to follow or members of the group that you want to join. If you are seeking a job or already working at a place where people dress casually, then dress casually; if they dress conservatively, you should do likewise. Realize also that your shoes, your desk, your car, and your home are part of the overall impression you broadcast to others.

What about women who want to climb the corporate ladder but have no one to copy? Many books have been written on this subject, and the general consensus is that career women should wear feminine attire and hairstyles rather than imitating men, but their choice of clothes and grooming should be on the conservative side. The overall image projected should be one of a competent employee rather than a sex object.

Experts on dressing for success advise people in business to avoid fancy garments and gaudy colors. They contend that the color pink is too feminine, even for career women in business, and that gold, gray, and green are unflattering to the skin. Black and blue, on the other hand, are considered authoritative colors, with a pinstripe suit (for men and women) in either of these two colors being the most authoritative type of business dress. They advise against loud ties and scarves, and regard bow ties as more appropriate for circus clowns than for business people.

But doesn't following the leader and dressing conservatively represent a pretty dull approach to life? Maybe so, but we should keep in mind that we are talking about conditions as they are, not as we wish they were. Maybe people will someday be sophisticated enough to judge the person rather than the packaging, but we are still far removed from that idealistic state. If you doubt this statement, observe the improved responses you receive when you play the expected role in your dress, as opposed to when you do not; a real difference exists, and it is formidable.

Oh no! I forgot my breath deodorant!

PERSONAL HYGIENE

Good grooming consists of more than appearance; it also involves cleanliness. People with freshly manicured mails, unstained teeth, and clean hair are almost certain to surpass people who lack these attributes; but many otherwise intelligent people fail to receive this message. Another instructor referred a female student to the author recently for help with a resumé. In visiting with the student, however, the author found that her resumé was appropriate and her qualifications exemplary; her only apparent problem was hygienic. She was in dire need of a bath and a wide assortment of brushes, and this lack of attention to her body was frustrating her job-searching efforts.

Most of us, with the obvious exception of people who write television commercials, avoid mentioning body odor. The widespread use of man-made fibers, however, makes discussion of the subject even more pertinent. Extra care and protection should be taken with wearing polyester, nylon, or acrylic fabrics, as these synthetic materials develop offensive odors much more quickly than natural fibers do. And, of course, daily baths, frequent shampoos, and the use of antiperspirants are essential parts of good hygiene.

Close, maybe, but not too close.

PHYSICAL DISTANCE

Americans are demanding when it comes to having space. Most of us prefer living in large houses and riding in large cars. Correspondingly, we strive to avoid crowded living conditions and public transportation. These space preferences carry over into our conversations. Unlike most foreigners, who allow only 6 to 10 inches of space between their bodies and faces as they converse, Americans require anywhere from 3 to 10 feet.

We carry invisible **space bubbles** with us wherever we go, and the space requirements (bubbles) of some people are greater than those of others. Space bubbles of high-ranking business executives are usually large, as they barricade themselves from the masses with enormous desks and mammoth offices. Conversely, the space bubbles of rank-and-file employees are smaller, with relatively crowded working conditions and more intimate interrelationships.

When others violate our imaginary bubbles, we feel uncomfortable and usually reposition ourselves to maintain a comfortable distance. When people allow us an unusually large amount of space, on the other hand, we begin questioning their motives: Are they being "standoffish"? Have we offended them in some way? Unless there are desks or other physical objects to separate people, the best distance to maintain when talking with someone is about 3 feet—close enough to be able to talk normally, but far enough to avoid violating the other person's space bubble.

Americans commonly achieve bodily contact during public encounters, despite our penchant for plenty of elbow room; and the customary form of contact is the traditional handshake. Most of us (men and women) shake hands upon meeting people for the first time; and, unlike most foreigners who freely hug one another upon renewing acquaintances, we Americans usually confine our enthusiasm during such encounters to vigorous handshakes.

But there is a right way and a wrong way to shake hands. To be considered effective, a handshake should be firm—but not to the point of sending people to their knees in pain. Most important, we should avoid the so-called "dead fish" handshake. If you are not confident that you have an appropriate handshake, you should practice with someone who knows an effective handshake from an ineffective one, because a handshake should be "just right." If our handshake is too firm, it causes pain; and if it isn't firm enough, it connotes disinterest. If we hold the other person's hand too long, it makes the person uncomfortable; dropping the person's hand too abruptly has the same result. Maybe we would have been much better off if we had copied the American Indian custom of simply raising our right hands and saying "How." Think about it.

I believed everything I saw.

FACIAL EXPRESSIONS

We talk almost as much with our facial expressions as we do with words; and almost everyone within our society attaches the same meaning to each type of expression. When people raise their eyebrows or wrinkle their noses, for instance, we assume that they are skeptical of what is being said; and practically everyone interprets frowns as signs of discontent and smiles as signs of contentment.

But some expressions can have multiple meanings, depending on the circumstances involved. When one person winks at another during a social gathering, the wink would probably be viewed as expressing a romantic interest. A wink by one person to another during a business meeting, on the other hand, would probably suggest that whatever is being said isn't worth listening to. Crying can be an expression of happiness or despair, laughing can be an act of appreciation or ridicule, and a yawn can be a sign of weariness or boredom—depending entirely on the circumstances involved.

Our eyes are great communicative tools, and we learn to time our glances to fit different situations. If we focus our eyes on someone for even a few seconds too long, the other person often responds with a look of indignation, as if to tell us that we are intruding on his or her privacy. The acceptable "looking time" in a theater or restaurant is only a few seconds, and it is almost zero in crowded areas such as elevators and subways. The allowable "looking

time" during business conversations is relatively long, as we strive to demonstrate our honesty and dependability by looking one another "straight in the
eye."

I don't understand a word she says,
but I love the way she says it.

VOICE INFLECTIONS

Successful communication often results not so much from what we say, but
from the way we say it. Because deep tones tend to reflect confidence, we
should avoid the inclination to raise our voices to a high pitch during moments
of excitement. Similarly, we can exude confidence by talking smoothly at a
moderate speed rather than blurting out our thoughts in erratic stops and
starts. We can avoid a hypnotic monotone by frequently varying the volume
of our voices, and we can improve communication still further by clearly
enunciating each word.

Are you still listening, Roland? . . . Roland?

MOMENTS OF SILENCE

Sometimes silence speaks louder than words. When others let us talk without
interruption for extensive periods, their silence can result from a high level
of interest in what we are saying or it can indicate just the opposite—a lack
of interest. We must look for other nonverbal clues to help interpret their
behavior accurately.

Some people use silence as a tactic for motivating others to talk. Realizing
that most of us cannot tolerate a void in conversations, they sometimes withhold comment—hoping that through our continuous talking they will learn
something of interest. The only way to counter such a strategy is to refrain
from saying anything more than we had planned to say. If the silence persists,
we should insist on a two-way conversation by simply asking the other person
if he or she has anything further to discuss. Don't just keep talking.

Wow! Just look at those body messages.

BODY LANGUAGE

Whether we are aware of it or not, we all communicate with our bodies. When relaxed, at least, most of us use hand and arm gestures to emphasize key points. Crossed arms and crossed legs are considered formidable signs of rejection— a rejection of what has been said or a rejection of what the person expects others to say or do. An unfolding of the arms or legs or the loosening of a sweater, jacket, or tie, on the other hand, denotes a receptive attitude.

Postures convey messages also. Persons who tilt their heads to the side and lean slightly forward in their seats are probably interested in what we are saying; whereas those who hold their heads back and slouch in their seats may be conveying disinterest or even disrespect.

We also broadcast messages by the way we walk. We tend to view people with slovenly walks as—you guessed it—slovenly. Junior executives often walk at a rapid pace from place to place as a way of demonstrating their determination to "get the job done." Key officers of companies, on the other hand, usually move at a more relaxed pace as a way of demonstrating a high degree of confidence and control. Has your boss ever continued walking as you were talking? To do so is a sign of dominance by the person being addressed and a sign of submissiveness by the person who is walking alongside in order to continue a conversation. Leaning far back in a seat and placing one's feet on a desk while talking with others is also a sign of high dominance. Conversely, the person who sits erect during such an exchange is conveying a high degree of submissiveness.

When body language conflicts with verbal messages, most people rely on the former. You may be pleased with what another person is saying, for example, but if you notice that the person has both hands clenched tightly into fists, you will probably discount what is being said and conclude that the speaker harbors hostile feelings toward you or whatever is being discussed. When people place the fingers of one hand against those on the other hand to form a pyramid, the action is often interpreted as a sign of confidence; the higher the hands are held, the greater that confidence is supposed to be. Thumping fingers on a table or desk and tapping feet on the floor are widely recognized signs of impatience.

Oh, it's nothing, really.

PERSONAL POSSESSIONS

We can learn a lot about people by observing what they value most in personal possessions. What kind of automobile does the person drive? Is it practical, luxurious, or both? Is it a gas guzzler, or is it fuel efficient? Is it clean or dirty? Believe it or not, many people continue to judge others to a significant degree by the cars they drive. The home is an even more important barometer in our attempts to gauge the relative importance or acceptability of people. Is the structure and area functional or extravagant? Is it cluttered or well kept? Is it paid for or mortgaged to the hilt?

Cars and homes are sometimes status symbols, but they must take a back seat to the many types of status symbols in business. A partition that separates an employee's desk from those of other employees suggests that the occupant is in some way superior to those coworkers without partitions. A private office communicates the same message, but with much greater emphasis. Carpeting is another important status symbol. A large electronics firm has strips of carpet extending from the private offices of certain managers into an otherwise carpet-less hall. The carpet strips serve no purpose other than to let people passing in the hall know that the occupants of those offices are important enough to have their offices carpeted. Other status symbols in business are important-sounding titles, office windows, drapes, wooden desks, leather chairs, oil paintings, couches, private secretaries, expense accounts, company cars, and reserved parking spaces. A list of all business status symbols would be almost endless, and they all serve to convey a particular message—a message that is usually of measurable importance to the sender and the receiver.

Hey, is that all there is to it?

A WORD OF CAUTION

Sometimes a little knowledge about a subject is worse than no knowledge at all. So don't place too much reliance on interpretations based on what you have read in this chapter. The study of nonverbal communications is in its infancy, and relatively few of the generalizations cited here are based on scientific analysis. Treat the subject as interesting instead, and begin cataloging your own observations of people.

DISCUSSION AND REVIEW QUESTIONS

1. When nonverbal signals conflict with what a person is saying, which do we tend to rely on?

2. Are you dressed in a conforming way today, compared to those around you? Why?

3. Why do some businesses direct employees to wear uniforms? What are the benefits to the company? To the public? To the employee?

4. How should a businesswoman dress if she aspires to a high position within the company? How should a man dress in that same situation?

5. In what ways do Americans demonstrate "warmer" or "colder" personalities than most foreigners do when it comes to greeting one another?

6. Who requires the most space, Americans or foreigners? High-level employees or lower-level employees? Men or women?

7. What are our usual reactions when people stand too close to us? When they stand too far away?

8. Why is the handshake such a vital form of nonverbal communication in some countries, including the United States?

9. What facial expressions have more than one meaning? How can we determine the correct meaning?

10. What is the acceptable "looking time" among students in a classroom? Between the instructor and an individual student?

11. What kinds of noverbal signals do students send instructors during class?

12. What kinds of nonverbal signals do instructors send to their students?

13. In what ways do our voices convey a sense of confidence and control, as opposed to uncertainty and loss of control?

14. What might it mean if, during labor-management negotiations for a new contract, the main union representative loosens his tie, sits back in his chair, and uncrosses his legs?

15. How can nonverbal messages sometimes contradict what we are saying? Provide one or two examples.

16. Should we judge the person only, or the total picture that the person presents—including the home, automobile, and other material possessions?

17. What are some examples of status symbols in business, and why are they so important?

18. How would you respond to the following comments?
    a. I wonder if Greta will ever be assigned to a managerial position; she certainly dresses and acts the part.
    b. I'm not going to shave off my beard or dress any differently than I do now when I begin looking for a job. If I don't land a job on the basis of my knowledge in accounting, then I won't land a job.
    c. How could I smell of perspiration; this blouse was laundered just yesterday?
    d. When she leaned far back in her seat and crossed her arms, I knew that she was going to reject my request for a raise.
    e. He didn't say anything after I had answered his question. The silence became embarrassing, so I just rambled on about anything that came to mind.
    f. She kept on walking while I was trying to tell her about my idea for streamlining office procedures, so that I had to walk backwards in front of her.

PART SIX
BUSINESS
REPORTS

Report writing is very important to a business student's success, because administrators at many schools require students to submit at least one written report for each class taken—as a matter of policy. They don't impose this requirement as a way of creating "busywork," as students sometimes speculate; they use reports as instruments for teaching students to express their thoughts in writing.

Writing skills are likewise essential in most areas of business, because reports are the most widely used form of upward communication in business organizations. Routine reports include sales reports, production reports, quality control reports, inventory reports, shipping reports, wage-and-salary reports, insurance reports, and many types of financial reports. Such reports are prepared and submitted regularly—daily, weekly, monthly, quarterly, or yearly.

Business managers have occasional needs for special information not included in routine reports, as indicated by the comments of a key employee of Allis-Chalmers, a leading multinational corporation.

Considering the definition of a report—the conveyance of useful information—it is easy to see why in the commercial, technical, and financial environment a great deal of the average professional's and paraprofessional's time is occupied with oral and written reporting, or using the reports of others.

Reports are used to report progress, explain failure, forecast performance, analyze statistics, propose the sale of products or services, plant new ideas, evaluate equipment, and hundreds more subjects. Because various job functions traditionally employ report types peculiar to themselves, certain categories are really not commonly used.

Yet, in all reports there is a common element, which involves using common patterns for planning and structuring. This use of patterns can be learned in a classroom or by simple study. In fact, report formulas are more commonly stressed in technical writing courses than in general writing-communication courses. There has been a growing emphasis in business in making report writing a worthwhile adjunct to the success of the venture, rather than a tedious operation with high possibility of wasted time and dubious results.

Reports are a vital part of business today, and many successful people are known for the vigor and value of their reports.

Robert J. Houlehen
News Bureau
Allis-Chalmers Corporation

We will concentrate on what Robert Houlehen calls the "common element" in reports. More precisely, this section of the book deals with planning, researching and writing reports; and the procedures presented here are applicable to a wide range of academic and business reports.

22
PLANNING
THE STUDY

Do you respond negatively when someone asks you to write a report, as so many people do? Or do you view the preparation of reports as an opportunity to improve your grades or to advance yourself in business? You will be more likely to adopt a positive attitude toward report writing after you have been introduced to the five steps in report preparation outlined in Figure 22-1.

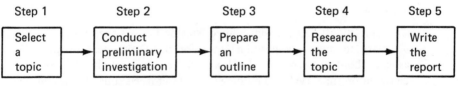

Step 1	Step 2	Step 3	Step 4	Step 5
Select a topic	Conduct preliminary investigation	Prepare an outline	Research the topic	Write the report

Figure 22-1   Key steps in report preparation

The first three steps involve subject matter, preliminary research, and outline preparation—all of which are dealt with in this chapter. Chapter 23 is devoted to Step 4, researching the topic; and Chapter 24 deals with the essential elements of a semiformal report, Step 5.

Don't cheat yourself!

DO YOUR OWN WORK

Before delving into the nuts and bolts of report writing, let's take a moment to consider the unpleasant subject of cheating. Sure, you may be able to borrow or buy a report instead of writing one for yourself, and the odds may be high that you won't be caught. But who will you be cheating: Your professor? Your employer? Yourself? Consider the following story as told by syndicated columnist Tom Braden.

Tom Braden

HONEST EFFORT:
NOT A POPULAR SUBJECT LATELY

If I were addressing a class of graduates this year, I would tell the story of Winston Lord and Henry Kissinger. I know there is a degree of cruelty to the story. But the world is not a comfortable bed. Also, the point of the story is old-fashioned. It goes as follows:

Shortly after Dr. Kissinger hired Winston Lord as one of his assistants, it became necessary to prepare a position paper for the Department of State; Dr. Kissinger assigned Lord to prepare it. Lord worked very hard at the task, and the paper was delivered on time. He heard nothing more about it. Next day he was informed that Dr. Kissinger was on the telephone.

"About this paper you've sent up," Dr. Kissinger said, "is this your best work?"

Lord's heart sank. Obviously, Dr. Kissinger had been disappointed. Stammering slightly, he replied, no, he was not prepared to say that it was his very best work, but what sections of the paper . . . ? Dr. Kissinger cut him off in midsentence.

"I want your best work. Bring it in tomorrow."

Lord went back to work. He worked all that day and half the night, and the next morning he personally delivered a second paper to Kissinger's office. Kissinger took it from Lord's hand, leafed it appraisingly, and inquired again, "Is this your best work?" "I don't honestly believe I can write a better paper on this subject," Lord answered. "Fine," said Henry Kissinger. "In that case, I'll read it."

Now you will at once agree that a story with such an old-fashioned point will be unpopular among graduating seniors. It is old fashioned these days to talk about effort. My own children talk to me of luck; of injustice; of teachers who have hang-ups; but they do not speak of trying.

They speak of cheating, too. Apparently cheating is very much in these days. At West Point, where cadets graduate into an Army stupid enough to allocate jobs and determine careers on the basis of class rank, cheating is understandable. I would think the solution would be to change the Army and not the West Point honor code.

But why cheat anyone else? Suppose Winston Lord had cheated in college. What good would that have done him on the day Henry Kissinger asked him to write a paper? Either he was able to write a good paper or he was not. What men like Winston Lord and Henry Kissinger learned early was that the most important thing in life is to try.

I would tell the graduates that if they haven't learned this, it is not too late. But it is pretty late. You can't get by on a wisecrack, an excuse and a smile forever. Eventually, somebody will ask you to write a paper, mend a pump, plot a course or make a judgment and you'll have to go back and catch up. Eventually, say, by the time you are in your late 20s, it will be too late.

The fact that you are reading this particular chapter is a strong indication you are on the right track, an indication that whatever your chronological age you have *not* yet "run out of time" in learning the intricacies of report writing.

Do you take this topic to be your lawfully wedded report?

SELECT A TOPIC

In some business situations, you will not have the privilege of selecting a topic on which to report; your superior will outline the area of study. But alert employees observe details in company operatons that should be analyzed, and they request permission to conduct studies and submit written reports on their findings. Why would people of sound mind make such offers? Because they realize that well-conceived and well-written reports impress all who read them.

Although college instructors sometimes dictate the area of study, they often leave selection of report topics to the judgment of students. In either case, in business or school, you would do well to base your choice of topics on as many of the following criteria as possible: First, make certain that the topic is directly related to a part of business in which you have a legitimate interest. If you work in the production department, for example, a report in the marketing area would probably be unappreciated. In picking a topic for an academic report, be sure that your choice relates to course content; don't submit a study about managerial accounting to an economics professor, and don't submit a political science report to a business professor.

Second, select a timely topic. A subject that has current interest will be more relevant to whoever reads your report, and the availability of current newspaper and magazine articles will make a timely subject easier for you to research.

Third, choose a topic that isn't too broad. Instead of trying to solve in a single report all the problems that are plaguing your company, your country, or the world, narrow the subject to one you can handle. Rather than preparing a report about the phenomenal growth in world population, for instance, you might focus on population trends within the United States or the effects on business of this country's declining birth rate. Rather than discussing the world energy problem, which is much too broad a report topic, you might report on the impact that OPEC (Organization of Petroleum-Exporting Countries) is having on American lifestyles. Rather than reporting on federal tax structures, which would take several volumes to treat thoroughly, you might report on the tax rebellion taking place in some parts of the country.

Fourth, pick a topic that you find interesting. If you have a genuine interest in the chosen subject, the research effort will become an enjoyable adventure. And as you broaden your knowledge of the subject, you may be able to expand the initial study into more comprehensive reports for future report-writing assignments. A student in a business-math class the author was teaching prepared a report on local property taxes. He learned so much about tax assessments and the computation of local tax rates that he became a quasiexpert on the subject. He used this knowledge to prepare several reports in his third and fourth years of college, and now has plans for using the subject area as the basis for a master's thesis.

Look before you leap.

CONDUCT PRELIMINARY INVESTIGATION

Test the topic you have chosen before fully committing yourself to it. If you plan to study a morale problem in your company, sample the feelings of several employees throughout the company to make fairly certain that a problem actually exists. If you plan to report on the adverse effects of wage legislation, locate some newspaper and magazine articles that relate to the topic, to make sure that you will be able to find sufficient data supporting this view.

Maybe you have formulated some thoughts about a subject through observation. You may have noticed over the course of several weeks or months, for example, that the movement of a certain product through the factory and the warehouse is not as efficient as it could be, or you may have obesrved that the flow of paper through an office could be improved. Regardless of the method you use, you should base your report on some prior knowledge of the subject to be studied.

Instructors in graduate schools and scientists often base their studies and the resulting reports on **hypotheses** (plural for **hypothesis**). An hypothesis is an informed guess, a guess that is based on a limited knowledge of the subject that is to be studied. In analyzing the effects of minimum-wage legislation, as previously mentioned, we might base our study on the following hypothesis: "The minimum wage requirement worsens teenage unemployment." We would then conduct a study to prove or disprove the hypothesis. Note, however, that an hypothesis is not applicable to many academic and business reports, because not all studies involve concrete statements that are to be proved or disproved.

Researchers often follow what is called the **scientific method.** Rather than approaching a study in a hit-or-miss fashion, they (1) make a clear and concise statement of the problem in writing, (2) gather and analyze all available data pertaining to the problem, (3) develop alternative courses of action on the basis of that information, and (4) choose and implement the best alternative. The scientific method of study provides the best approach for ensuring that your planning is sound, objective, and comprehensive.

Divide and conquer.

PREPARE AN OUTLINE

How do you suppose authors write books? Do you imagine that the author of this book just started writing one day with the hope that the words, sentences, paragraphs, and chapters would fall into place as he went along? Of course not; when beginning a new book, he first outlines the main divisions and chapters. Then, after planning the main parts of each chapter, he decides which points are to be discussed in each part of each chapter. Sure, this procedure consumes a lot of time, but a complete outline provides organization and direction, prevents repetition, and allows him to divide a book into manageable parts.

An outline represents the same useful tool in report writing. Once you have organized your ideas on paper, you can begin researching the topic systematically and confidently. Begin your outline by dividing the study into three to five main parts, as shown in Figure 22-2.

Advertising Is Surviving	Investing in Stocks and Bonds
I. Problems in advertising	I. Understanding securities exchanges
II. Changing image of advertising	II. Securing market information
III. Future role of advertising	III. Selecting appropriate investments
IV. Summary and conclusions	IV. Making securities transactions
	V. Summary

Figure 22-2   Main parts for two separate reports

Organize the main divisions of your report into a logical sequence:

1. *Time sequence*—going from the past to the present to the future.
2. *Cause and effect*—identifying a problem, its cause and effects, and possibly offering a solution.
3. *Level of importance*—progressing from the most important item to the least important, or vice versa.
4. *Routine procedures*—following steps normally taken in a well-established function, such as beginning a new business, opening an account with a stockbroker, and hiring new employees.

Then, to form complete outlines as illustrated in Figure 22-3, divide all but the closing parts of your main divisions into several subdivisions.

Try to maintain parallelism in outlines, because each line becomes a heading in the report. Notice in the first outline that each of the main sections has a preposition (*in* and *of*), except for the terminal (final) section, which does not need to be parallel with the others. Each of the main headings in the second outline begins with an *ing* action word (*understanding, securing, selecting, making*), except for the terminal section. Only the main parts must be parallel with one another; they do not need to be parallel with the ABC . . . F subsections.

In the same way, we consider the subsections separately from the main parts of the outline. The ABC headings in the first two sections of the first outline are parallel, and each consists of two words. Keeping the lines in each section about the same length is desirable but not mandatory. The AB lines in the third section contain the word *that,* while the C line contains the preposition *in*; we do not force parallelism in this instance because *truth in advertising* is a commonly used legal term. Each of the main parts of the second outline in

Advertising Is Surviving	Investing in Stocks and Bonds
I. Problems in advertising	I. Understanding securities exchanges
A. Excessive claims	A. New York Stock exchange
B. Child abuse	B. American Stock Exchange
C. Credibility gap	C. Over-the-counter market
II. Changing image of advertising	II. Securing market information
A. Industry self-regulation	A. Regular publications
B. Consumer pressures	B. Television and radio reports
C. Restrictive legislation	C. Financial services
III. Future role of advertising	D. Corporate publications
A. Ideas that aid consumers	III. Selecting appropriate investments
B. Advertising that adds value	A. High price or low price
C. Truth in advertising	B. Risk or certainty
IV. Summary and conclusions	C. Growth or income
	D. Value or glamor
	E. Bull or bear
	IV. Making securities transactions
	A. Opening an account
	B. Making the purchase
	C. Settling the transaction
	D. Selling the security
	V. Summary

Figure 22-3   Two completed outlines

Figure 22-3 begins with an *ing* action word, as already mentioned, but only the ABCD lines in the last section begin with action words.

Let's clarify these and other important points by analyzing the incorrect outline in Figure 22-4.

Establishing and Operating a Health Food Store

I. Choosing the best location
  A. Strategic location
  B. Provisions of the lease
  C. Demographic patterns
  D. Traffic patterns
II. The sources of financing
  A. Security deposit required
  B. Buying the necessary equipment
  C. The cost of beginning inventory
  D. Adequate working capital
  E. Securing a bank loan

(continued)

III. What are the legal obligations involved?
    A. Federal regulations
    B. State regulations
    C. County regulations
    D. City regulations
IV. Sales and service considerations
    A. Buying practices
    B. Methods of pricing
    C. Credit sales
    D. Store hours
    E. Hiring employees
    F. Advertising in local newspapers
V. Summary and conclusions

Figure 22-4   An outline that lacks parallelism

In checking parallelism, we first consider the main (Roman numeral) sections. Only the first one begins with an action word. Only the second one begins with an article. Only the third one is a complete sentence and a question. So what can we do? We can be consistent in our word choice, as illustrated by the two outlines in Figure 22-5.

I. Choosing the best location	I. Site selection
II. Locating favorable financing	II. Initial financing
III. Identifying legal obligations	III. Legal obligations
IV. Outlining sales strategy	IV. Sales and service
V. Summary and conclusions	V. Summary and conclusions

Figure 22-5   Two examples of parallel construction

The outline to the left in Figure 22-5 is parallel because each of the first four lines begins with *ing* action words. The last line in an outline usually consists of one or more of the following words: summary, conclusions, recommendations, depending on what you plan to write in that section of the report. The outline to the right in Figure 22-5 consists of two- and three-word lines. The fourth line contains a conjunction (*and*), while the first three lines do not, but this small breach in parallelism is acceptable. We don't force parallelism when the results would appear awkward.

Both outlines are correct, because the lines in each outline are fairly consistent with one another; incomplete sentences are not mixed with complete sentences in either outline, and all the lines are about equal in length. These considerations are also reflected in the completed outline presented in Figure 22-6.

**Establishing and Operating a
Health Food Store**

  I. Site selection
     A. Strategic location
     B. Lease provisions
     C. Demographic patterns
     D. Traffic flow
 II. Initial financing
     A. Security deposit
     B. Equipment and fixtures
     C. Beginning inventory
     D. Working capital
     E. Bank loan
III. Legal obligations
     A. Federal taxes
     B. State regulations
     C. County requirements
     D. City regulations
 IV. Sales and service
     A. Buying practices
     B. Pricing policy
     C. Credit card sales
     D. Store hours and employment
     E. Newspaper advertising
  V. Summary and conclusions

Figure 22-6   Example of a completed outline

Having already considered the Roman numeral (RN) lines, we turn our attention to the individual subsections, the ABC lines. We only need to make the lines under RN-I parallel with one another, those under RN-II parallel with one another, and so on. In the original outline in Figure 22-4, the I-B line included the preposition *of,* which has been removed in Figure 22-6. If one of the lines has a preposition, they all should include one, and vice versa; it is an all-or-nothing situation unless the resulting change proves awkward. Rather than repeating the word *patterns* as in Figure 22-4, we have changed the word in I-D of the corrected outline to *flow.* The action words *buying* and *securing* in II-B and II-E of Figure 22-4 have been eliminated, rather than beginning all five lines with an *ing* action word. Lines II-C and II-D in Figure 22-6 begin with *ing* words, but they are not action words. These *ing* words may be used in this manner because *beginning inventory* and *working capital* are accounting terms that are commonly used in business.

These changes and others you will notice in comparing the two examples have been made to develop a tight and accurate outline that will help us (1) organize our data and (2) provide functional and attractive headings throughout the completed report. Although none of the outlines presented here reflects a special introductory section, each report would include an unlabeled introduction. This point is explained further in Chapter 24.

If six people were preparing an outline for the same study, we would probably end up with six very different outlines. Outlining can be done in a number of ways, all of which are correct so long as the main sections are parallel with one another and so long as each line within a subsection is parallel with other lines within the same subsection. Quite a bit of effort, yes, but once you have prepared a workable outline you have progressed at least halfway toward completing the final report.

BUSINESS APPLICATIONS

1. Explain how the following areas of study do or do not meet the suggested criteria for suitable business report topics.
   a. Marketing in the United States
   b. The high rate of recalls in the automobile industry
   c. The frantic merger binge among U.S. corporations
   d. Employee polygraph tests are an invasion of privacy
   e. Fringe benefits should (should not) be taxed
   f. Stockbrokers should be required to publish their rates
   g. A comparison of the U.S. and Soviet economies
   h. Alternatives to the energy problem
   i. Compensation practices in business
   j. The use and misuse of credit cards.
   k. Starting a small business
   l. Computerized checkout systems
   m. Labor unions in America

2. If you were asked to prepare a report on registration procedures at your school, what would be the main (Roman numeral) sections of your outline?

3. Once you have developed the main sections of the outline specified in Application 2, develop at least three subsections for each main section.

4. Improve the parallelism of the following sections of outlines:

   I. Consequences of credit abuse
   II. Examples of credit traps
   III. Loan types
   IV. You can avoid the credit trap
   V. Summary and conclusions

   I. Problems advertising has created
   II. Government regulations
   III. The effects of consumer pressure
   IV. Changing the image of advertising
   V. Future prospects for advertising
   VI. Conclusions and recommendations

   I. Incoming revenues
   II. Distribution of expenses
   III. Comparing with other businesses
   IV. Future trends
   V. Summary

5. Make whatever changes you consider necessary to improve the following outline, beginning with the main (Roman numeral) sections and then considering the subsections separately. (Chrysler Corporation produces the Omni, and Ford Motor Company makes the Pinto.)

   The Chevrolet Citation

   I. Cost considerations favor the Citation
      A. Initial investment
      B. Cost of operation
   II. What about trade-in value?
      A. The small cars
      B. Large-sized cars
      C. Intermediate cars
   III. The performance of the Citation
      A. Mileage
   IV. Comparison with other small cars
      A. Pinto
      B. Mercury Capri
      C. The Omni
      D. Foreign imports
   V. Summary and conclusions

23

RESEARCHING THE TOPIC

With a clear objective in mind and a tentative outline in hand, you are ready to begin researching the topic. Before beginning the research effort, however, you should secure permission to conduct the study. Once you have been given the go-ahead, assuming that your research proposal is approved, you must decide whether you are to rely on primary data, secondary data, or both; and you should develop a card system to record your findings.

May I have your autograph, please?

RESEARCH PROPOSAL

Avoid the risk of wasted time and effort by submitting a research proposal and tentative outline to your superior (your college instructor or your boss at work). Make certain that you both agree on the type of study you have in mind, reasons the study is needed, methods for conducting the study, limitations of the study, sources of data, resources needed (if any), and estimated time of completion.

The length of your proposal will depend on the length and importance of the study; and it should be written in future tense with frequent use of the words *would* and *could*. You are requesting permission, so be persuasive rather than assuming. If you plan to study a problem, provide evidence that a problem exists, that a solution is needed, and that you can successfully conduct the study. If you plan to explore certain company expenditures, for example, provide evidence that the expenditures are disproportionately high and that you are prepared and qualified to make the needed analysis. Figure 23-1 shows a sample proposal submitted by a student in a business communications class.

```
        DATE:  February 21, 1980

          TO:  Dr. Robert E. Swindle, Instructor

        FROM:  Charlotte W. Purcell, Student

     SUBJECT:  Proposal for Term Paper

     My husband and I hope to open our own health food store.  Our interest is
     based on the knowledge of high returns in the retailing segment of the
     health food business, as reported in the December, 1979 issue of Health
     Food Monthly:

            Inventory turnover in the retailing end of the health-food business
            is low, compared to most other types of food retailing, but a
            relatively high markup on cost (ranging from 25 to 75 percent)
            results in an average return on investment of approximately 17 percent.

     We have also received favorable comments during discussions with several
     individuals who presently own and operate their own (nonfranchised)
     health food stores.

     In conducting an exploratory study to learn more about establishing and
     operating a health food store, we would secure primary data from in-depth
     interviews with operators and owners of established health food stores,
     from actually observing the procedures that employees follow at several
     successful stores, and through direct contacts with real estate agents and
     vendor representatives.  Extensive secondary data are available in the
     form of statistics developed by the City of Glendale, where we plan to
     locate the business, and from numerous publications relating to the sale,
     distribution, and consumption of health foods.

     The proposed study could be completed by the due date that you have estab-
     lished, and the primary objective would be to explore the details involved
     in establishing and operating a health food store.  More specifically, we
     hope to (1) find a suitable location for the business, (2) secure adequate
     financing, (3) establish guidelines for sales and service, (4) outline
     legal obligations of the business, and (5) make a firm decision on whether
     to proceed with the venture.  The study would not include projections
     of profit (loss) levels and cash flows; that information would be presented
     in a separate report.

     May I have your permission to conduct this rather extensive study (with
     the help of my husband) and to report our findings (without his help)?

     Attached:  Tentative outline
```

Figure 23-1   Example of a research proposal

The proposal in Figure 23-1 is in memo format, but a letter would be more appropriate if it were being mailed to someone outside the company or outside the school. The author of this proposal will be able to use it as the introductory section of her final report by changing the wording from the subjunctive mood (what she hopes to do) to past tense (what she has already done).

What? Me try something original?

PRIMARY DATA

Primary data consist of evidence that researchers develop themselves, usually through observations, interviews, experiments, and surveys.

Observations. Researchers may develop primary data through their personal observations of whatever it is they are studying. If researchers were analyzing the flow of baggage between airline passengers and airplanes, for example, they would be able to make definite statements about the existing system from having observed it in operation. Such evidence is usually very convincing to report readers, because most people attach high credibility to statements that are based on what researchers have personally witnessed.

Interviews. Most readers find data secured through interviews relevant and interesting, especially when interviewees are experts in their fields. If you are researching some aspect of the stock market, for example, an interview with a stockbroker may increase your knowledge on certain aspects of the subject, and information attributed to the stockbroker will add authenticity to your report. Try to arrange interviews in advance, so that the interviewee will allow sufficient time; and always have specific questions prepared for the occasion.

Experiments. When we hear the word *experiment,* most of us picture scientists in laboratories, but business people conduct experiments regularly. Before spending hundreds of thousands of dollars to broadcast breakfast cereal commercials, for instance, manufacturers normally conduct experiments. They show trial commercials to many children in different areas, trying to determine through the children's responses whether these commercials would motivate children throughout the country to ask their parents for the advertised cereals.

Companies also test the effects of advertising by making comparisons. Using two cities that are similar in such respects as size, population density, and per capita income, they run an advertisement in one city to see how much more or less of their product is sold compared to the other (control) city, where the advertisement is not run. They test one factor (such as advertisement, price change, or packaging) at a time, holding all factors constant in the control city. Then if they find that a particular advertisement increases sales significantly in the test city, they can be fairly certain it would be successful in other areas of the country.

Business managers sometimes conduct experiments within their own companies. By changing one factor at a time (such as an incentive system or some working condition) for the test group, while holding all factors constant for a similar (control) group, they may compare the productivity of the test group with that of the control group to see if a significant difference occurs as a result of the change.

Surveys. Surveys represent a fourth way to develop primary data. Researchers may learn how people react or might react to certain products or services simply by asking them. They may survey purchasing managers to see how they view a certain product, for example, or they may survey a group of employees to determine their views on company policies.

Surveys are usually based on carefully worded questionnaires. Consider the following questions from a questionnaire administered for a large bakery. As shoppers selected loaves of white bread (any brand) from store shelves, researchers asked them the following questions:

1. What brand of bread do you think of when I mention packaged white bread?
2. Would you please tell me what brand of packaged white bread you usually buy?
3. Which of these brands do you buy most frequently? [A list of five breads was provided.]
4. Suppose you happened to overhear two housewives in a store talking about packaged bread. Which brand of white bread would you say the women were most likely talking about if you heard the following remark: "My husband's boss is coming to dinner tonight, so I am buying this brand of white bread"?
5. What if you heard this remark: "I like white bread that's really fresh and stays fresh, so I'm buying this brand"?
6. At about this time last year, what brand of packaged white bread did you use most often?

Notice that all of these questions call for specific answers—the name of a particular brand of bread. Researchers can easily calculate the number of times consumers mention a particular brand or respond "yes" or "no" to questions, but answers to open-ended questions, ones that call for statements of personal opinion, are usually difficult to interpret. Notice also that none of these questions are "leading" questions; no question prompts consumers to respond to a particular brand of bread, because no brand names are mentioned in the questions.

Researchers concluded from the results of this study that consumers were not reacting favorably to the brand being studied, and that a large percentage of consumers had switched to competing brands during the preceding year. Correspondingly, they advised the bakery managers to improve the quality or image of their bread, or both.

It is advisable to test questionnaires before using them by administering them· to selected small groups, to make certain that the questions will be understood. Questionnaires may be administered over the telephone, in person, or through the mail. Questions that may be considered personal, such as asking a person's age or income, should be placed near the end of questionnaires, because people are more likely to answer such questions once they have already invested some time by answering earlier questions. Finally, questionnaires should be kept fairly brief to avoid exhausting interviewees to the point where they answer carelessly or stop responding altogether.

Statistical analysis. If the population (number of people or things that we are studying) is small—say, 500 or fewer—we may study each person or thing. If we are concerned with whether the morale of 250 employees of a company is high or low, for example, we can instruct each employee to complete a questionnaire. When the numbers are large, researchers sample the population. If the managers of International Telephone and Telegraph Corporation wished to survey the attitudes of their more than 400,000 employees, for example, they would administer questionnaires to a relatively few employees and project the attitudes of all employees based on the answers received from those included in the sample. Rather than checking every machine part that is produced on an assembly line, quality control personnel may check a relatively small number of them and assume with some certainty that if the samples are acceptable, all the machine parts are acceptable.

Whether the results of such samples are truly representaive of entire populations (all employees or all parts) depends on statistical analysis. Researchers may use simple formulas to (1) determine the required size of samples, that is, the number of people or things to be studied, and (2) establish a specific level of confidence in the sample results, such as 95 percent or 99 percent certainty that the results are representative of total populations. Numerous books on business statistics include detailed formulas and explanations of their applications.

But I like to be first.

SECONDARY DATA

Secondary data include facts, figures, and information recorded in books, magazines, and other types of publications. Although the subject of primary data is discussed first in this chapter, research should actually begin with a review of secondary data. If someone else has already studied the subject that you are considering, you may avoid duplication of effort by learning of their findings before beginning your own study. You may use secondary data from books and magazines that you possess, or you may use those that are available in public and school libraries.

Card catalog. To locate books in libraries, you must consult a card catalog. A set of drawers may contain cards in alphabetical order according to the names of authors, subject, and title; or, if the library is large, separate sets of drawers may be provided for each of these three categories. Some libraries also record this information on microfiche, filmstrips that may be viewed on television-type screens.

Each listing (card) includes the author's name, the title of the book, and a call number, such as HF 5381 S275. To locate the book represented by this number, you check a map or list provided by the library that shows where the HF books are stacked (shelved). Upon locating HF, you look for HF 5381 books, among which you will find the specific S275 book. If the book is missing from the shelf, it probably has been checked out by someone else, in which case the people at the service counter might permit you to reserve it for your use when it is returned.

Reference books. Librarians keep many of the current reference books at centrally located reference desks, and they stack earlier copies of reference books on nearby shelves. Reference books include atlases, almanacs, encyclopedias, certain government publications, and manuals.

Atlases don't consist entirely of maps; they also include detailed information on population, minerals, energy, and food in different areas of the United States and throughout the world.

Almanacs are an extremely valuable source of secondary data. The *World Almanac & Book of Facts* consists of almost 1,000 pages of statistics and information about cities and states in the United States and most foreign countries, providing facts and figures on subjects ranging from automobiles to zip codes and cataloging details of historical and current events. The *Information Please Almanac Atlas and Yearbook* also deals with a large array of subjects, including facts about colleges, the economy, health, law enforcement, news, religion, science, transportation, and a host of other topics. Almanacs are published annually and sold at most bookstores for a nominal price.

Encyclopedias contain a wide variety of secondary data, including such areas of business as accounting, advertising, economics, insurance, investments, labor relations, management, marketing, quality control, public relations, real estate, retailing, salesmanship, statistics, transportation, and wholesaling. Among the leading encyclopedias that you will find in the reference sections of most libraries are *Encyclopedia Americana, Encyclopedia Britannica,* and *Collier's Encyclopedia.*

Some **government publications** are kept in the reference sections of libraries, such as the annual *Statistical Abstract of the United States,* which contains a wealth of facts and figures, and *Census of Business,* for retail trade, wholesale trade, and selected service areas, which are based on the national census every ten years. Many other government publications are available, with large libraries devoting entire floors to the maintenance of government documents.

A major **financial service** kept in the reference sections of most college libraries is Moody's manuals. These manuals (which are actually large books) are published annually to cover separately the industrial, over-the-counter, public utility, bank and financial, and transportation markets. If you are interested in learning something about American Airlines, for instance, you may consult the transportation manual. If you need information on International Business Machines, you may check the industrial manual, and so on. Moody's manuals provide historical and current information—including a company's address, officers, operation, and financial condition; and they provide statistical detail for a range of several years.

Magazine and newspaper indexes are a vital part of most library reference sections, because they enable researchers to check categorized titles of articles that relate to specific topics without having to read through hundreds or even thousands of issues. The leading indexes and their uses are explained in the following section.

Magazines and newspapers. Magazines and newspapers are an important source of secondary data, especially for timely reports, and most college libraries subscribe to many of them. When you want to locate magazine articles on a particular subject, you shouldn't look through magazines randomly; instead, you should consult one or more indexes. Indexes are published annually, and supplements are issued throughout the year to index articles that have been published since the last annual edition was printed.

Readers' Guide to Periodical Literature, the most widely used index, categorizes articles according to subject area from more than 150 magazines. At the front of each index is a list of the periodicals and reports that are indexed, showing abbreviations used for each entry—such as "Bsns W" for *Business Week* and "Mo Labor R" for *Monthly Labor Review.* Consider the following typical listing, which would be found under the heading "Business Management and Organization":

Insider's view of a board room, R. Ladeau
Pop Sci 84:70–2 O 5 '79

This listing indicates that the article is about a board of directors in some corporation and that it was written by R. Ladeau and published in *Popular Science* magazine, volume 84, pages 70 to 72, October 5, 1979. Magazines are also called **periodicals** because they are published periodically—weekly, monthly, quarterly, annually.

The *Business Periodicals Index* is of special value to business people, because it deals mainly with business-related articles published in about 270 magazines. A list of the magazines indexed appears at the front of each issue, along with a list of abbreviations. Consider the following typical listing:

> Making money in high-growth stocks. W. H.
>   Rentz. Bests R 82:21-2 Jl 15 '80

This listing indicates that the article relates to profits to be made by dealing in common stocks, and that it was written by W. H. Rentz and published in *Best's Review,* volume 82, pages 21 and 22, July 15, 1980.

The *New York Times Index* categorizes according to subject area all articles that have appeared in the *New York Times,* the country's leading newspaper, since the year 1913. This index, quite properly called the "master key to the news," is an invaluable tool for tracing historical events as they were reported in headlines.

Similarly, the *Wall Street Journal Index* categorizes all articles that appear in the *Wall Street Journal,* a weekday newspaper. The *Journal,* which contains many articles on business and some on nonbusiness subjects, is the most widely read publication among business people. The *Index to the Christian Science Monitor* provides a similar service for researchers.

If you don't find the types of articles you are seeking listed under one category in an index, try others. If you are trying to locate articles about salesmanship but can't find what you want under that heading, also check under such headings as Marketing and Retailing. The people who prepare these indexes have lightened our research task immeasurably, but we still must use our imaginations occasionally to find correct categories. Also consult librarians for assistance in locating elusive articles.

Having used one or more of these indexes to identify articles of interest, you must then locate the publications that carry the articles. Librarians usually keep current and recent newspapers in special areas of libraries, where you may ask for a particular paper by name and date. They keep all copies of the *New York Times* and other selected newspapers on microfilm, but they destroy the actual newspapers as limited storage space dictates.

All but the smallest libraries maintain **alphabetical lists of periodicals** (magazines) that they carry, and in large libraries these lists consist of several books of computer printouts. One book might list the names of periodicals that begin with the letters A, B, and C; a second book might list those beginning with D through F; and so on. To locate a copy of *Industry Week* magazine, for instance, you would look under the I's and find that the call number is TS3001-745. Then, looking at a map or directory of the library, you would see that TS publications are located in a particular area of the third floor. Going to that section of the library, you find your issue of *Industry Week* bound in a large book—in date order—along with several other issues of the same magazine.

If the issue of *Industry Week* is recent, on the other hand, you would go to a section of the library called Current Periodicals, where a librarian, with knowledge of the call number that you provide, would locate the magazine and check it out to you for an hour or so—depending on the rules of the library. How recent must a magazine be to still be a current periodical? Magazines may by considered current anywhere from six months to several years, depending on library policy, before they are bound and placed in open-access stacks.

With my memory? Surely you jest.

CARD SYSTEM

If you begin recording magazine references and call numbers on one piece of paper, you will soon be going around in circles. Even when dealing with as few as ten articles, you will benefit from the use of a card system.

To begin with, therefore, record the magazine references that interest you, as you find them, directly from the indexes to small **reference cards**. Be certain to record the references exactly as they appear in the indexes so that you won't have to retrace your steps later in search of information you overlooked.

Later, as you locate and read the articles, record on large **data cards** all information that appears relevant to your study and report. Place different bits of information on separate data cards so that you can easily relate the cards to separate sections of your report; and cross-reference the data and reference cards as illustrated in Figure 23-2.

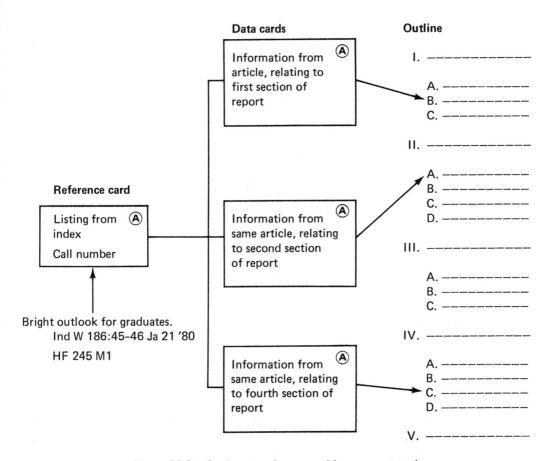

Figure 23-2   Card system for researching a report topic

Notice in Figure 23-2 that all three data cards contain information from one magazine, *Industry Week,* that is listed on the one reference card, and that the data cards and reference cards are cross-referenced with the letter A. Three data cards are necessary in this instance because all three bits of information relate to different parts of the report. You should follow this same procedure throughout your library research. The size of the cards is unimportant so long as the data cards are larger than the reference cards. And whether you cross-reference with letters or numbers is immaterial so long as you relate data cards to the appropriate reference cards.

You may use photocopies of articles in place of data cards, which can be made for as low as 2½ to 5 cents per page, depending on whether you can fit one or two pages on a single copy. Cut the copies into several parts, if different parts of an article relate to different sections of your outline and report, but be sure to cross-reference each part of the photocopy with the reference card.

Using this system, you will end up with a small stack of reference cards and a relatively large stack of data cards and photocopies. You may then arrange and rearrange the data cards and copies to fit the outline and begin writing the report. When it is necessary to give credit to someone for information you are using, you know from the cross-reference letter (or number) which reference card to use for a footnote. The following chapter contains information about footnotes, alternatives to footnotes, and other information that is essential to good report writing.

Don't try to hatch an egg with a blowtorch.

TIME SCHEDULE

Don't wait until the last possible day to begin your study. When your instructor or your boss sets a deadline for completion of a report, prepare a schedule for (1) conducting the preliminary research, (2) developing an outline, (3) completing the research, and (4) writing the report. Allow yourself sufficient time to have a rough draft on hand at least a couple of days, because when you leave a report for a while and then return to it, you will invariably see possibilities for improvement.

Another worthwhile suggestion, although you may not believe so at first, is to read the rough draft of your report aloud. Your reading will tend to falter on sentence fragments, improper grammar, mispunctuation, and illogical statements. And that is the right time to improve the report—*before* it is typed in final form.

BUSINESS APPLICATIONS

1. At the end of Chapter 22 you were asked to prepare an outline for a report about registration procedures at your school. Now prepare and submit a proposal requesting authorization to conduct the study. Mention the specific steps you will take to achieve the main objective of the study.

2. Identify some sources of primary and secondary data that might be used in researching the following topics:

   a. Raising the level of city bus service

   b. Curbing welfare abuses within the state

   c. Controlling the cost of homes

   d. Improving employee morale

   e. Increasing employee productivity

   f. Putting a stop to price fixing

   g. Curbing health care costs

3. Prepare a questionnaire for any one of the first five topics listed in Application 2 to determine whether a problem actually exists. Design the questionnaire to secure as much information about the situation and about the interviewee as practical.

4. What types of experiments might instructors conduct with their classes in an effort to improve student comprehension of the materials being taught?

5. In referring to all students in a class by their first names when conversing with them, how would an instructor know that improved learning (if it did occur) was actually the result of this personalized treatment and not attributable to some other factor such as a different textbook, superior students, or improved instruction?

6. Consult the card catalog in your library and record all information on reference cards, including the call numbers for one book from each of the following three subject areas: economics, accounting, marketing. Use each card to locate the chosen books, and record the first sentence from the first chapter of each book on the reverse side of the reference cards.

7. Consult an almanac, encyclopedia, or government publication (or more than one of these) to find the most current estimate of population in the world, the United States, and your state. Record on the front of a reference card for each publication used the name and date of the publication, and record the population figures on the reverse sides of the cards.

8. Consult the most recent edition of *Moody's Industrial Manual.* Use a reference card to record the date of the publication, and record on the reverse side of the card the company name, address of headquarters, number of stockholders, and number of employees of one of the following companies:

   a. The Procter & Gamble Company

   b. Santa Fe Industries, Inc.

   c. International Harvester Company

   d. Howard Johnson Company

9. Consult the *Business Periodicals Index* for any of the last five years and record on separate reference cards the information given for four articles of your choice from any one of the following topics:

   a. Communication barriers
   b. Business letters
   c. Word processing
   d. Telephone usage
   e. Nonverbal communications
   f. Report writing
   g. Job resumés
   h. Public speaking

10. Locate one of the articles chosen in Application 9 and summarize the main points of the article on one sheet of paper.

24
WRITING
THE REPORT

Pictures, no matter how skillfully painted, have much greater impact when placed in attractive frames. Reports also have greater impact when properly packaged, and the procedures set forth in this chapter will help you write reports that will be well received in business, government, and academic environments.

Reports consist of several parts, the number depending on the length of the report, the degree of formality involved, and the nature of the contents. When organizing the parts of your reports, place them in the following order:

> Transmittal
> Title page
> *Contents
> *Summary
> Body of report
> *Bibliography
> *Appendix

Those parts preceded with asterisks are required in some reports but not in others. Tables of contents are used when reports consist of more than ten pages. Summaries are sometimes placed near the beginning of reports that consist of more than 15 pages. Bibliographies are used when report writers must credit the contributions of others, and appendixes are useful when maps, charts, pictures, statistics, and other types of data are too voluminous to fit neatly within the related chapters.

Having established the ordering of report parts, let's discuss each of the parts in the order of preparation. The completed sample report that begins on page 360 helps to illustrate each of these parts.

TITLE PAGE

You can begin with preparation of a title page, if you have decided on a title for your report and if you know the date that you are to submit it. As illustrated in the sample report (page 360), all letters in the title are capitalized and all lines on the title page are centered. The vertical spacing of title pages for formal theses and dissertations must follow precise specifications, but there are no established guidelines for less formal academic or business reports. In the sample report (page 360), the title begins on the 10th line, the "Presented to" section begins on the 17th line from the title, and the "Presented by" section begins on the 17th line after the words "Phoenix College." You may follow these guidelines or simply use your judgment in preparing attractive title pages, so long as you include five bits of information: (1) a title, (2) the name and identification of the recipient or recipients, (3) the location, (4) your name, and (5) the date of submission.

Titles of reports should be descriptive rather than clever, to provide others with some indication of what the reports contain; and they should be brief. Titles consisting of more than 14 words are considered too long, with those of from five to ten words considered most appropriate.

BIBLIOGRAPHY PAGE

Although the bibliography is often the last page of a report, you may find it most convenient to prepare before beginning the actual writing. Rather than having students list footnotes at the bottom of report pages or on separate footnote pages, many college instructors permit the use of numbered bibliographies. A numbered bibliography like the one in the sample report (page 373) is identical to a regular bibliography except for numbers added at the left. Sequential numbering enables you to use entries on the bibliography page as footnote references. You will notice on the first page of the sample report (page 362) that the first footnote is (7:13), which refers to page 13 of the 7th entry in the bibliography (page 373), a magazine article written by Harold R. Simon. Isn't this system easy and practical? And no more *ibid, loc. cit.,* or *op. cit.* to mess with.

In preparing a bibliography, organize your reference cards according to whether they represent books, government documents, periodicals, newspapers, pamphlets, or interviews; then arrange each group alphabetically by the last name of the first author shown. If the author's name is not given, alphabetize according to the first significant word in the title of the article. You may use the illustration in the sample report (page 373) as a guide, numbering the entries at the left only if you are preparing a numbered bibliography. Notice in the illustration that the centered heading at the top is placed on the 10th line, and that each of the following centered headings is preceded by two blank lines (triple-spaced).

You may include in the bibliography any references you have consulted even when you have not used any of the information in your report. Bibliographic entries 1, 2, 5, and 6 (page 373) are included even though the student did not make specific reference to these publications in the body of the report. She consulted them during her research effort, however, so they may have contributed to the report indirectly. Although she wasn't required to include these four references, since they were not noted in the report, she did so because they made the bibliography appear more comprehensive and impressive.

We should consider the differences between footnotes and bibliographic entries because you may sometime be required to use traditional footnotes. In the following comparisons, the letters FN stand for "footnote" and the letters BIB for a bibliography entry. Notice that first letters are capitalized in the main words of titles of articles and publications, but not articles (*a, an, the*), conjunctions (*and, but, or, nor, for*), or prepositions (*at, because, before, between, by, in, on, through, to, until, with*).

Books with one author

FN   [1]John W. Mercer, How to Retail Dietetic Foods Successfully (San Francisco: Winston Press, Inc., 1978), pp. 217—18.

BIB   Mercer, John W.   How to Retail Dietetic Foods Successfully. San Francisco: Winston Press, Inc., 1978.

The FN is numbered (elevated half a line), the first line is indented five spaces, and page numbers are specified. The BIB is numbered sequentially only when it is part of a numbered bibliography; and the second line, rather than the first, is indented four spaces. Notice also that the punctuation uses periods (full stops) rather than commas.

Books with two authors

FN   [14]Sarah P. Moore and Benjamin Stewart, <u>Health Guide for Life</u> (New York: Javitts Publishing Company, Inc., 1979), p. 315.

BIB   Moore, Sarah P. and Benjamin Stewart. <u>Health Guide for Life</u>. New York: Javitts Publishing Company, Inc., 1979.

Books with more than two authors

FN   [7]Rosie S. Stein and others, <u>Marketing in the 80's</u> (Boston: Business Publishers, Inc., 1979), pp. 95—99.

BIB   Stein, Rosie S. and others. <u>Marketing in the 80's</u>. Boston: Business Publishers, Inc., 1979.

Or, if you wish, you may list the names of all authors.

Government publications

FN   [8]Interstate Commerce Commission, <u>94th Annual Report</u> (Washington: Government Printing Office, 1980), p. 82.

BIB   Interstate Commerce Commission. <u>94th Annual Report</u>. Washington: Government Printing Office, 1980.

Both the FN and BIB begin with the name of the agency that created the document, followed by the title of the publication (underscored), the name of the capital city, the name of the printing office, and the date of publication. Except for the page reference in the FN, only the indentations and punctuation differ.

Periodicals with names of authors

FN   [5]Leon T. Flood, "You Aren't What You Don't Eat," <u>The Health Food Store</u>, 181 (April, 1980), 23.

BIB   Flood, Leon T. "You Aren't What You Don't Eat." <u>The Health Food Store</u> 181 (April, 1980), 23.

The number following the underscored title of the magazine is the volume number, which, despite its lack of meaning to report writers or readers, is still in general use.

The number following the date is the page number. When a reference includes both a volume and page number, the abbreviations "vol." and "p." need not be used. When a magazine such as *Business Week* has no volume number, the page number or numbers should be preceded with the abbreviation "p." (for one page) or "pp." (for more than one page). Notice that both the FN and the BIB show page numbers. When some volume numbers in your references appear in Roman numerals and some in Arabic numbers, be consistent; convert all of them to Roman numerals or all to Arabic (Arabic is preferred).

Periodicals with author's name omitted

FN   [12]"Location Is the Name of the Game in Retailing,"
National Health Guide, 47 (December, 1979), 10—11.

BIB   "Location Is the Name of the Game in Retailing." National
Health Guide 47 (December, 1979), 10—11.

Encyclopedias

FN   [5]Encyclopedia Americana (1980), XLI, 541—45.

BIB   Encyclopedia Americana.   1980.   XLI, 541—45.

The year is used to locate encyclopedias, because they are revised continuously.

Newspapers

FN   [12]"Glendale in Rapid Growth Area," Glendale Star,
December 4, 1979, p. 5.

BIB   "Glendale in Rapid Growth Area." Glendale Star, December
4, 1979, p. 5.

Since the date is not placed within parentheses, as in footnotes for magazine articles, the only difference between the FN and BIB for newspaper articles is the footnote number in the FN, the period after the article title in the BIB, and the different indentations.

Pamphlets. If you use data from one or more pamphlets, show as much of the following information as the pamphlets provide—in both footnote and bibliographic format—in this order: title of pamphlet, issuing organization, city of publication, and date of publication.

FN   [3]A Comparison of Economic Systems, National Federation of Business, San Rafael, California, 1979.

BIB   A Comparison of Economic Systems. National Federation of Business. San Rafael, California, 1979.

Interviews. If you are using a numbered bibliography, include references to interviews; otherwise, list them only in footnotes and endnotes. Show the name of the interviewee, the person's title, and the organization with which the person is affiliated, the location, and the date.

FN   [12]Interview with Lydia Gonzales, Commercial Agent, Milt Jackson and Associates, Phoenix, Arizona, March 12, 1980.

BIB   Gonzales, Lydia, Commercial Agent, Milt Jackson and Associates, Phoenix, Arizona, March 12, 1980.

The BIB does not show that it was an interview, because the entry would appear under the heading INTERVIEWS in a numbered bibliography.

Take a moment to study these relationships in the numbered bibliography of the sample report (page 373).

And now for the main attraction!

BODY OF THE REPORT

You have already gathered and sorted the data to fit your outline, so writing the body of the report should be relatively easy. This section contains several helpful guidelines, which, after you have applied them two or three times, will become routine procedure in writing attractive reports.

Placement on page. Telling students or employees to write attractive reports is not enough; invariably, they want specifics. Accordingly, the following measurements have become standard for most types of reports:

Top of page: Begin all writing (except page numbers) on 10th line.
Left side: Allow 1½ inches (18 spaces elite, 15 pica), so that you can attach the left side of reports to folders and notebooks.
Right side: Leave a margin of approximately 1 inch (12 spaces elite, 10 pica).
At bottom: Leave a margin of approximately 1 inch (6 blank lines).

These margins are also appropriate for most letters. If you use the same type-writer regularly, make pencil marks for proper placement of the margin stops, so that you won't have to be concerned with such detail every time you type a report or letter.

Page numbers. Every page of a report has a number, but numbers are not shown on the title page or the first pages of the contents, the report, the bibliography, or the appendix. We use small Roman numerals for all pages preceding the body of the report, so that a report with two contents pages and a three-page summary would be numbered as follows:

    i   Title page (not shown)
   ii   1st page of Contents (not shown)
  iii   2nd page of Contents
   iv   1st page of Summary (not shown)
    v   2nd page of Summary
   vi   3rd page of Summary
    1   1st page of body (not shown)
    2   2nd page of body

The bibliography in the sample report (page 373) is actually page 12 (not shown); and a second page of the bibliography, if there were one, would bear the number "13." Small Roman numerals, when they are used in the front pages of reports, are placed in the center of the pages, 1 inch from the bottom; and Arabic numbers in the body of the report and subsequent pages are placed on the eighth line from the top of each page, just inside the right margin.

Introductory section. Very formal and lengthy reports usually have special sections at the beginning under the heading INTRODUCTION. Most academic and business reports also have introductory sections, but they are not labeled as such. The authors simply begin writing about the chosen topic, as shown in the sample report (page 362)—telling readers what the study is about and how the report is organized. Notice that the introductory section of the sample report is an almost exact copy of the research proposal on page 335, having been re-worded to express past tense.

Indentations. The first lines in paragraphs are indented five spaces in informal reports and from six to eight spaces in formal reports. Lists such as those shown on page 7 of the sample report (page 368) are indented the same number of spaces as the first lines of paragraphs. Notice in item 2 of the second list that when more than one line is required for an individual listing, the additional lines are begun immediately beneath the first word in the listing.

Levels of headings. Imagine trying to read this textbook if it had no headings. The headings used here, which were taken directly from chapter outlines, help you understand the organization of the book; and they enable you to locate specific materials. Similarly, the Roman numeral sections of the initial outline (page 331) become the main headings in the sample report (page 360 to 373), and the ABC subsections become subheadings. The following lists provide details of both levels of headings:

Main headings:	Preceded by two blank lines (triple-spaced)
	Placed flush with left margin
	First letters of main words capitalized
	Stands alone on the line
	Followed by punctuation only if a question
	Underscored
Subheadings:	Preceded by one blank line (normal double-spacing)
	Indented the same number of spaces as first line of paragraphs (five spaces in the sample report)
	First letter of main words capitalized
	Followed by punctuation
	Underscored
	Writing begins on same line

As guidelines to report writing, however, outlines should be flexible. Having decided on Lucky Center as the best location for opening a health food store, for example, the student wrote the entire first section of the sample report about this one shopping center. Correspondingly, she used "Lucky Center" as the first main heading in the sample report, rather than "Site Location" as shown in the original outline.

The sample report beginning on page 360 actually contains three levels of headings: centered headings for the title page, contents, and bibliography, and two levels of headings in the body of the report. This number of headings is sufficient for the large majority of formal and informal reports you may encounter in school and in business. In short reports, ranging anywhere from one to ten pages, you may find just one level of headings adequate, in which case you may choose any one of the three types of headings illustrated here.

Transition statements. Notice on pages 1 and 2 of the sample report (pages 362 and 363), that the writer includes a transition statement at the end of the introductory section, just before reaching the first main heading, telling readers what they may expect to find in the body of the report. Notice also on pages 2, 5, 7, and 8 that the writer follows each main heading with transition statements, telling readers something about the materials that follow in the subsections. Transition statements in these areas of reports enable writers to tie their thoughts together for good reading, and the statements have the added benefit of separating main headings from subheadings. Transition statements are *not* required when moving from one subsection to another.

Documentation. When we include in our reports ideas or statements by other people, we usually document the materials by referring to the sources. If we cite statistics from a textbook for example, we use a footnote, end-note, or numbered bibliography to inform readers of the source of the data.

If you must use footnotes or endnotes rather than a numbered bibliography, refer to pages 349–352 for illustrations of the different types of footnotes. Footnotes and endnotes also require the use of three Latin terms, as illustrated in the following series of footnotes:

[1]John W. Mercer, How to Retail Dietetic Foods Successfully (San Francisco: Winston Press, Inc., 1978), pp. 217—18.

[2]Ibid.

[3]Rosie S. Stein and others, Marketing in the 80's (Boston: Business Publishers, Inc., 1979), 95—99.

[4]Ibid., p. 47.

[5]Mercer, loc. cit.

[6]Stein, op. cit., pp. 105—06.

Footnote (FN) 2 indicates that the materials are from the same source as those referenced by FN 1, the preceding footnote—the same book and the same pages. FN 4 refers to FN 3, the preceding footnote, but to different page numbers. FN 5 tells readers that the materials referenced with Number 5 are from the Mercer book, *loc. cit.* indicating that other footnotes intervene between FN 5 and the Mercer reference and that the materials are from the same pages shown in the original reference. FN 6 tells readers that the materials referenced are from the Stein book, *op. cit.,* p. 105–106 indicating that other footnotes intervene between this footnote and the Stein reference and that the materials are from *different pages* than those shown in the original foot-note. Many authors now list the entire footnote in each instance, rather than burden readers with Latin terms. Entire footnotes should be listed even in very formal reports, rather than using Latin terms to refer to footnotes several pages away from the materials being referenced.

If you choose to use footnotes, you should double-space following the last typewritten line, strike the underscore key 15 times, double-space again, and enter the footnote. Footnote numbers should be elevated one-half line, in the body of the report and in the footnotes, as shown in the following example (assuming that this is the last typewritten line on a page).

---

^{3}Leon T. Flood, "You Aren't What You Don't Eat," The Health Food Store 181 (April, 1980), 23.

^{4}"Location Is the Name of the Game in Retailing," National Health Guide 47 (December, 1979), 10—11.

^{5}Ibid.

We would have to stop typing soon enough to allow five lines at the bottom of the page for the first footnote, an additional three lines for the next footnote, and an additional two lines for the last one—ten lines altogether. A guide sheet, prepared with a sheet of paper that is slightly wider than the standard 8½-inch page, can be used to indicate the number of typing lines remaining on a page, so that you can reserve enough space for the number and length of footnotes to be listed.

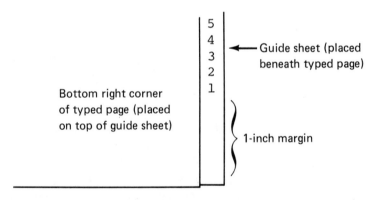

When spacing makes it difficult or impossible to complete a long footnote, you may carry forward the extra lines to the bottom of the next page, following the required underscore.

We must document all direct quotations, of course. On page 5 of the sample report, at the end of the first paragraph (page 366), the student credits a real estate agent for having used the term "strong client" by enclosing the agent's exact words within quotation marks. The footnote that follows refers not only to the term, but also to other data within the same paragraph.

When a direct quotation or part of a written document consists of more than three lines, as in the first paragraph of the sample report (page 362), the lines are set off from the regular paragraph, single-spaced, and footnoted. Notice that the quotation is indented on the left only, the first line an extra three spaces, and it is without quotation marks. Lead readers into quotations as the writer does here by providing them with some indication of the source.

Example: As the president of our company once commented, ". . .
Example: In a recent interview with the press, Henry Ford stated, ". . .

Because quotation marks are used only with direct quotations by individuals and with materials copied verbatim, many reports are written without the use of even one set of quotation marks. Instead of using the exact words of others, we paraphrase what they have said or written by stating the same information in our own words. On pages 2 and 3 of the sample report (pages 363 and 364), under the heading "Demographic Patterns," data in three separate sentences are footnoted. No quotation marks are used, because the writer stated information from the referenced articles in her own words. She followed each sentence with a footnote, however, to credit authors of the original articles for the information used.

Not all information needs to be documented. As you research a topic, you will notice that some of the information is discussed by more than one author in different books and articles. Such knowledge is general information which does not require documentation. Similarly, any knowledge of the topic that you possessed to begin with may be used without documentation.

Writing style. Although the trend in business writing is toward an informal style, in which authors write as they would talk, many people prefer a more formal approach. When writing formal reports, you must avoid the use of personal pronouns such as *I, me, we, us,* and *you.*

Informal: *I found* that working people do much of their shopping during trips home from work.
Formal: *Studies show* that working people do much of their shopping during trips home from work.
Informal: Having decided on a location for the business and the amount of rent to be paid, *I estimated* the total required investment.
Formal: Having decided on a location for the business and the amount of rent to be paid, *the writer estimated* the total required investment.

Informal writing sometimes adds life to reports, but formal writing often spares readers the tedious repetition of personal pronouns. Also, many business managers avoid personalizing research efforts and report writing as a way of stressing teamwork over individualism.

But first a synopsis.

SUMMARIES

Authors of long reports (more than 15 pages) often include a summary (synopsis) of findings near the beginning of their reports. A summary allows readers to grasp major details and important findings without having to read an entire report. This feature is an important consideration for busy people, especially when they have only a minor interest in the report topic. Many business reports consist of hundreds of pages, which makes brief summaries (one to five pages) essential.

Plus a few odds and ends.

APPENDIX

Report writers and the authors of books often refer readers to supplementary materials placed near the end of their reports and books in sections labeled APPENDIX. In fact, some reports and books contain more than one appendix, separating such materials as maps, charts, tables, questionnaires, letters, and legal documents—materials that are supportive but too lengthy to include in the main parts of reports or books.

A preview of coming attractions.

CONTENTS PAGE

A contents page like the one in the sample report (page 361) is useful when a report consists of more than ten pages, because it allows readers to grasp the organization of reports and helps them locate specific segments.

The contents page shown here is simply a copy of the outline on page 331, with the Roman numerals and subsection letters deleted and page numbers added. In lengthier reports, you may elect to show page numbers for each subsection as well as for each main part of the report.

You asked for it; you got it.

TRANSMITTAL

When you have completed all parts of the report and have combined the pieces to form an attractive package, take a moment to write an accompanying letter or memo. When students and business people submit reports, they invariably have some comments to make about the report—interesting findings, difficulties encountered, incomplete information, and so forth. You will be wise to put such comments in writing as a permanent record for all who may read the report. Keep the transmittal brief, telling the reader that you are including the report that was previously discussed or requested; add some comment about the research effort or the report itself, and offer clarification of any points that may be required. Place the letter (memo) and the report (stapled in the top left corner) in a suitable envelope or folder so that it will not be folded or soiled. Before actually releasing the report, however, review the sample report that follows and compare your report with the checklist on page 374.

ESTABLISHING AND OPERATING
A HEALTH FOOD STORE

Presented to
Dr. Robert E. Swindle
Business Communications
Phoenix College

Presented by
Charlotte W. Purcell
April 14, 1980

CONTENTS

My husband and I plan to open our own health food store. Our
decision was based on knowledge of high returns in the retailing segment of the health food business, as reported in a leading industry
magazine:

> Inventory turnover in the retailing end of the health-food
> business is low, compared to most other types of food retailing,
> but a relatively high markup on cost (ranging from 25 to 75 per-
> cent) results in an average return on investment of approximately
> 17 percent.(7:13)

We also received favorable comments during discussions with several
individuals who presently own and operate their own (nonfranchised)
health food stores.

In conducting an exploratory study to learn more about establishing and operating a health food store, we secured primary data from
in-depth interviews with operators and owners of established health
food stores, from actually observing the procedures that employees
follow at several successful stores, and through direct contacts with
real estate agents and vendor representatives. Extensive secondary
data were available in the form of statistics developed by the City
of Glendale, where we plan to locate the business, and from numerous
publications relating to the sale, distribution, and consumption of
health foods.

The objective of this expanded study was to explore the detail
involved in establishing and operating a health food store in Glendale,
Arizona. More specifically, we (1) found a suitable location for the
business, (2) secured adequate financing, (3) established guidelines
for sales and service, (4) outlined legal obligations of the business,

2

and (5) made a firm decision to proceed with the project. Not included

in this study are projections of profit (loss) levels and cash flows;

that information will be presented in a later report.

Lucky Center

Lucky Center is a neighborhood shopping center that is dominated

by a Lucky Stores supermarket, and our choice of this particular

location was based on the types of businesses that are present occu-

pants of the center, demographic patterns within the surrounding

community, traffic flows, and provisions in the lease.

Strategic Location. Lucky Center is located on the northwest

corner of 51st and Northern Avenues in the City of Glendale--just eight

blocks west of 43rd Avenue which divides the cities of Glendale and

Phoenix. As shown by the diagram in Figure 1, the mix of stores in

Lucky Center is complementary to a health food store, and the nearest

competitors are General Nutrition Centers (a retail chain) at Valley

West Shopping Center (five miles to the west) and at Metrocenter (six

miles to the northeast). Although customers of the beauty salon, sewing

center, and health spa may occupy parking spaces for relatively long

periods of time, many of these people are also regular consumers of

health foods.

Demographic Patterns. According to a recent survey, 65 percent of

all health food sales are made to working women between the ages of 25

and 45 years of age--women whose family income is significantly above

the national median.(4:30) Correspondingly, the population of North-

west Phoenix (Metropolitan area, which includes Glendale) is young

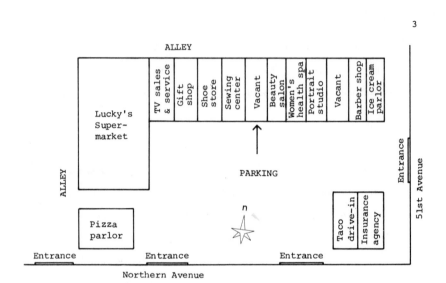

FIGURE 1

Diagram of Lucky Center
Glendale, Arizona

(median age 28), prosperous (median family income $27,150), and well-educated (65 percent of adults have had some college education).(8:22)
Also, Northwest Phoenix is the fastest-growing area in Arizona and one of the fastest-growing communities in the country.(9:5)

Traffic Flow. Studies show that working people do much of their shopping during trips home from work and that they tend to patronize businesses that are located at the right of streets, where they need not make left turns.(3:231-32) As the diagram in Figure 2 illustrates, Lucky Center is ideally situated to receive the heaviest flows of "going home" traffic from Phoenix. Of the night (P.M.) traffic in all directions, which totals 26,090 vehicles, 18,922 (70 percent) may turn into Lucky Center without having to make left-hand turns.

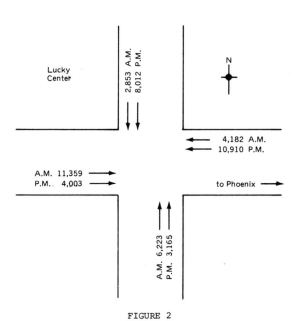

FIGURE 2

Traffic flow at intersection of
51st and Northern Avenues
Week of August 13, 1979

Source: City of Glendale, Department of Engineering

Lease Provisions. The property to be leased (see arrow in Figure 1)
is 15 feet wide and 50 feet deep, a total of 750 square feet. Monthly
rent under a five-year lease is $412.50, plus a common-area maintenance
fee of approximately $20.00 per month. The maintenance fee is subject to
adjustment each year, with any underassessments charged to occupants
at the end of the year and any overassessments refunded. The lessor
requires a security deposit of $825.00, the equivalent of two months'

5

rent, on which no interest is paid. The lessor provides fluorescent lighting (fixtures only) and an appropriate air-conditioning unit. The lessor is also willing to construct without charge a partition for a storeroom--if we can convince the agent that we will be what they refer to as a "strong client."(11)

Initial Financing

Having decided on a location for the business and the amount of rent to be paid, we estimated the total required investment and sought bank financing.

Security Deposit. As already mentioned, the landlord requires a security deposit of $825.00, the equivalent of two months' rent. The landlord pays no interest on security deposits, which effectively increases the annual lease expense by $82.50 (10 percent of $825.00).

Equipment and Fixtures. With the landlord providing a partition, the lighting fixtures, and an air-conditioning unit, only the following items are needed initially:

1.	Shelving on back wall and two side walls	$ 350.00
2.	Deep-freeze unit (6 cu. ft.)	285.00
3.	Two refrigeration units (5 feet wide)	2,050.00
4.	Six standard-sized bread racks	438.00
5.	U-shaped checkout counter	225.00
6.	Juice bar	345.00
7.	Tiled floor at entrance (installed)	450.00
8.	Wall paneling (installed)	350.00
9.	Electronic cash register	1,150.00
10.	Outside sign (installed)	475.00
11.	Miscellaneous supplies	250.00

The total cost of the equipment and fixtures needed to start the business is $6,368.00.

6

Beginning Inventory. The cost of stocking the store initially is
placed at $8,500.00. Terms (initial order only) provide for payment of
one third of this amount at the time of delivery, one third 30 days
later, and the remaining one third 60 days from date of purchase. Terms
of sale for the initial order are F.O.B. delivered, which means that
no transportation charges will be added to the vendor's invoice.

Working Capital. We will begin each month with $1,500.00 in a
checking account. We anticipate, however, that our sales volume by the
end of the third month of operation will have reached a level where
working capital of only $1,000.00 will suffice. We plan to keep this
figure as low as possible, because the bank does not pay interest on
monies deposited in checking accounts.

Bank Loan. The security deposit, equipment and fixtures, beginning
inventory, and working capital total $17,193.00. Because of our flawless
record of paying bills on time, our previous business experience, and
my husband's income from his job at a nearby electronics firm, we can
secure an $8,000.00 loan from Phoenix National Bank. We will be per-
sonally responsible for repaying the loan; and the equipment, fixtures,
and inventory will serve as collateral for the loan.

The loan agent at Phoenix National Bank advised that they will
extend to us a commercial loan for four years at 10 percent simple
interest, which results in 48 monthly payments of $233.33. Having
checked with other lending institutions and with officials of the Small
Business Administration, we found that this rate was the lowest-cost
loan available.(12)

7

Legal Obligations

The name of the business will be "Nutrition Corner," and it will be a sole proprietorship in my name. A sole proprietorship is the simplest form of business organization; the tax rate is the same as for a partnership (less than for a corporation), and my husband will inherit the company if my life should end. As a sole proprietor, I must adhere to numerous government requirements.

Federal Taxes. The federal government requires the following forms:

1. Application for Employer Identification Number
2. Employee Withholding Allowance Certificate (Form W-4)
3. Income Tax Withheld and Social Security Taxes (Form 941)
4. Final Return (Form 941)
5. Deposit of Income and Social Security Tax Withheld
6. Wage and Tax Statement (Form W-2)
7. Unemployment Tax (Form 940)
8. Unemployment Tax Deposit
9. Self-Employment Tax (Form 1040-SE)
10. Estimated Tax (Form 1040-ES)

State Regulations. The following forms must be filed with the State of Arizona:

1. Application for Transaction Privilege
2. Combined Transaction Privilege Tax and Educational Excise Tax Return
3. Application for Employer's Identification Number
4. Report to Determine Liability
5. Contribution and Wage Report
6. Quarterly Report of State Income Tax Withheld (Form A-1)
7. Fourth Quarter Report
8. Federal and State Income Tax Withheld (Form A-2 or W-2)
9. Employer's Liability Insurance
10. Income Tax Return (Form 140)
11. Business Property Statement

8

    <u>County Requirements</u>. The serving of juices for consumption in the store makes it necessary for us to comply with two county requirements:

1. Application for Health Permit
2. Health certificates for each employee who is to prepare and/ or serve food or beverages for public consumption

    <u>City Regulations</u>. In addition to federal, state, and county regulations, all businesses within the City of Glendale must submit the following forms:

1. Application for Privilege License
2. Monthly Privilege License Tax Return
3. Certificate of Occupancy

These requirements by the City of Glendale are in addition to periodic building inspections and annual sign inspections.

<u>Sales and Service</u>

    We have not yet accounted for all details of the business, but a statement can be made concerning several aspects of the operation.

    <u>Buying Practices</u>. We will purchase most of our products from Arizona Wholesalers, which is located in Southwest Phoenix, about eight miles from the store; and, except for the initial order, we will use our panel truck to pick up orders. Terms of sale after the initial order are 2/10, n/30, and delivery service is available when and if needed.

    We will place orders directly with vendors, rather than through the wholesaler, when we are able to order in a large enough volume to realize lower per-unit costs. We will also order directly from vendors in Los Angeles and pick up the merchandise ourselves when we take occasional trips to that city to visit relatives.

9

Pricing Policy. Markup will be based on cost, which is a common practice within the health food industry, and our percentage markup will be based on average markups of retailers in the Rocky Mountain area as reported periodically in Health Food Monthly. Our pricing policy will be sufficiently flexible, however, to enable us to respond to competitive practices within a ten-mile radius of the store, and we will run weekly specials on selected "loss-leader" items.

Credit Card Sales. We are almost forced to follow the practice of accepting Master Charge and Visa credit cards. The cost to us for this privilege, based on an average ticket size of $7.50 (estimated) is 5 percent of all credit sales, and this cost is in addition to any charges that the banks may assess the credit card holders. The banks charge a nominal "set-up" fee for beginning this service, plus a charge for buying an imprinter--$17 new, $10 rebuilt.(10)

Store Hours and Employment. The store will be open for business from 10:00 a.m. to 7:00 p.m. on weekdays, and from 10:00 a.m. to 6:00 p.m. on Saturdays. We will close Sundays and all legal holidays.

As store manager, I will work weekdays and Saturdays to begin with, 53 hours per week. My efforts will be supplemented by two high school students, who will work approximately 16 hours apiece each week--stocking shelves, serving juices, assisting customers, and acting as manager during my absences from the store. Part-time employees will be paid the prevailing minimum wage, but we will treat my income as withdrawals from invested capital.

10

    <u>Newspaper Advertising</u>. Except for point-of-purchase advertising
and displays, which are provided without charge by vendors, we will rely
totally on newspapers for advertising our store and our products. Most
vendors of health foods offer cooperative advertising programs,
providing mats for newspaper advertising and paying 50 percent of the
cost of local newspaper ads that feature their products.(3:441)

<u>Summary and Conclusions</u>

    We will lease a section of Lucky Center, a neighborhood shopping
center in the northwest part of Metropolitan Phoenix, under lease conditions that parallel those for similar properties. Demographic patterns
in this area and the traffic flows past the shopping center add to the
attractiveness of Lucky Center as the site for a health food store.

    Initial financing will total about $17,193, and will include a
security deposit, equipment and fixtures, beginning inventory, and working
capital. Phoenix National Bank will extend a loan of $8,000, and my
husband and I will contribute the balance from our savings account.

    Our initial order and most orders for stock replenishment will
be placed with a nearby wholesaler, under terms that are typical of the
health food industry. We will place occasional orders directly with
vendors, and we will use our panel truck to pick up most orders. Markup
will be based on our costs in relation to industry averages and competitive actions, and Master Charge and Visa credit cards will be
accepted.

    Store hours will parallel those of competing stores and other

11

retail establishments in the area, which will require, in addition to my own daily efforts as manager, the services of two part-time employees. Newspaper advertising will be our major promotional tool, most of which will be adapted to cooperative programs offered by vendors.

As a result of this study, and in consideration of favorable financial projections (separate report), my husband and I have decided to proceed with this business venture. We have signed a lease, ordered fixtures, filed the required reports with government agencies, and secured the necessary financing. The grand opening is set for June 21, a Saturday, which will allow sufficient time for arranging inventory, interviewing job applicants, ordering and shelving stock, and placing advertisements with local newspapers.

NUMBERED BIBLIOGRAPHY

A. BOOKS

1. Mercer, John W. How to Retail Dietetic Foods Successfully. San
       Francisco: Winston Press, Inc., 1978.

2. Moore, Sarah P. and Benjamin Stewart. <u>Health Guide for Life</u>. New
       York: Javitts Publishing Company, Inc., 1979.

3. Stein, Rosie S. and others. <u>Marketing in the 80's</u>. Boston:
       Business Publishers, Inc., 1979.

B. PERIODICALS

4. Binichi, Sylvia R. "Affluent Women Are Health Conscious According
       to Survey." <u>National Health Guide</u> 48 (January, 1980), 27—32.

5. Flood, Leon T. "You Aren't What You Don't Eat." <u>The Health Food
       Store</u> 181 (April, 1980), 23.

6. "Location is the Name of the Game in Retailing." <u>National Health
       Guide</u> 47 (December, 1979), 10—11.

7. Simon, Harold R. "Health-Food Retailing Brings High Returns."
       <u>Health Food Monthly</u> 34 (December, 1979), 12—15.

8. Yaw, Susan. "Some Interesting Statistics." <u>Arizona Lifestyle</u>
       143 (February, 1980), 21—22.

C. NEWSPAPER

9. "Glendale in Rapid Growth Area." <u>Glendale Star</u>, December 4, 1979,
       p. 5.

D. INTERVIEWS

10. Apley, Donald, First National Bank of Arizona, and Rose Anne Smith,
       Valley National Bank, Phoenix, Arizona, March 12, 1980.

11. Gonzales, Lydia, Commercial Agent, Milt Jackson and Associates,
       Phoenix, Arizona, March 12, 1980.

12. Moreno, Delores, Commercial Loan Officer, Phoenix National Bank,
       Phoenix, Arizona, March 5, 1980.

I am now a firm believer in checklists.

CHECKLIST: BUSINESS AND ACADEMIC REPORTS

Transmittal

☐ Does your letter
Indicate that the report is enclosed?
Refer to authorization for the study?
List all necessary comments about the study or report?
☐ Have you placed the report in a suitable envelope or folder with your name on it?

Title page

☐ Is the title concise (fewer than 15 words) and descriptive?
☐ Is the title centered on the 10th line and is it in all capital letters?
☐ Does it show the receiver's title, name, course (for academic reports), and location?
☐ Have you included your name and the date?
☐ Is the spacing attractive?

Contents

☐ Is the heading CONTENTS centered on the 10th line?
☐ Are the margins the same as those used in the body of the report?
☐ Did you leave two blank lines (triple-spaced) following (below) the centered heading?
☐ Is your vertical spacing attractive, avoiding a crowded appearance?
☐ Are the dots in each of the dotted lines even with one another?
☐ Are the page numbers accurate?

Summary

☐ If your report is more than 15 pages, did you include a summary at the beginning?
☐ Did you keep it brief? (not more than one page for a 20-page report or more than two pages for a 50-page report)

Body of the report

☐ Are the margins consistent and correct?
☐ Are the pages numbered correctly?
☐ Did you include an unlabeled introductory section?
☐ Did you indent the first lines of all paragraphs five spaces?
☐ Are the first letters of all main words in *all* headings capitalized?

☐ Are the headings underscored?

☐ Are main headings preceded by an extra blank line and flush with the left margin? Do they stand alone on the lines, and are they without punctuation at the end (except for questions)?

☐ Are your subheadings indented and followed by punctuation?

☐ Does writing commence on the same lines?

Transition statements

☐ Does your introductory section end with a transition to all main (Roman numeral) sections of the report?

☐ Have you included transition statements between each main heading and the first subheading that follows each of them?

Documentation

☐ Have you quoted other people (used their exact words) only when paraphrasing would detract from the desired impact?

☐ Did you use quotation marks only with direct quotations?

☐ Did you use transition sentences to alert readers of impending quotations and their sources?

☐ Do your footnotes or endnotes (if used) follow some prescribed format? Are they consistent with one another throughout the report?

Writing style

☐ If you adopted a formal style, did you avoid using personal pronouns?

Bibliography

☐ Does the heading BIBLIOGRAPHY or NUMBERED BIBLIOGRAPHY begin on the 10th line of an unnumbered page, and is it followed by two blank lines (triple-spaced)?

☐ Are books, periodicals, and other types of documents placed in separate categories and labeled?

☐ Is the heading for each category preceded by a capital letter, a period, and two spaces?

☐ Are the headings for each category preceded by an extra blank line (triple-spaced) and centered on the page?

☐ Are the margins consistent with those in the body of the report? Are all but the first lines of each entry indented four spaces?

☐ If it is a numbered bibliography, is each entry preceded by a number (sequentially), a period, and two spaces?

☐ If the bibliography consists of more than one page, are page numbers shown on all but the first page?

Appendix

☐ If you placed materials in an appendix, are they preceded by a page with a centered heading APPENDIX?

☐ If there is more than one appendix, do the title pages for each specify the types of materials included?

☐ Are page numbers shown on all pages in the appendix, except the title page(s)?

Package

☐ Are all pages in the correct order?

☐ Are all pages of the report stapled in the top left corner?

☐ Did you place the report and transmittal in an envelope or folder?

BUSINESS APPLICATIONS

1. Most reports contain three parts. What are they and in what order do they appear in reports?

2. List the five essential elements of a complete title page.

3. Print or type a footnote and bibliography entry for page 125 of this textbook, assuming that it is the fifth source footnoted in a report.

4. Print or type a bibliography entry for this textbook, assuming that it is the sixth entry in a numbered bibliography.

5. Janet Arner and Rod W. Marks coauthored a book that they titled THE FIVE MOST IMPORTANT RULES IN MARKETING (stated in all caps to see how you handle it). The book was published by Ramco Press, Inc., in Chicago, Illinois, in June, 1979. Print or type a footnote (referring specifically to pages 314 and 315) and bibliography entry. Assume that it is the sixth footnote.

6. Print or type a footnote to follow immediately the one in Application 5, assuming that it refers to the same book but to page 420.

7. Print or type a footnote (the second source referenced in the report) and bibliography entry for the following magazine article: The title is ECONO-MISTS ARE A VERY DIVERSE BREED OF PEOPLE, and it appeared on pages 12, 13, and 14 of BUSINESS MONTH magazine in the January, 1980 issue. The volume number is 65.

8. Print or type a footnote following the one in Application 7, assuming that it refers to the same pages of the same magazine.

9. List the ways that main headings are similar to subheadings when typing them on report pages.

10. List the ways that main headings differ from subheadings.

11. Prepare a guide sheet for typing reports. Draw vertical lines for each margin. Number the lines that are still available for typing before reaching the bottom margin, and make a mark at the top of the page for the center (the center between the two vertical lines).

12. Locate from books, magazines, or newspapers two examples of direct quotations and the preceding transition (lead-in) statements.

13. Provide two examples of material you might include in a report that would not require documentation.

14. What does the reference (7:12) mean when placed at the end of a line? When placed at the end of a paragraph?

15. Explain the spacing and punctuation required for a direct quotation that consumes five typewritten lines in a report.

16. Rephrase the following sentences, changing them to a formal style of writing.
    a. I consulted three books and several magazine articles.
    b. When we approached people with our questionnaire, most seemed pleased to provide us with information.
    c. From what I could find in our school library, those of us in the $15,000 to $25,000 income range are shouldering most of the tax burden in this country.
    d. As a regular consumer of electricity, you are probably unaware of the many types of expenditures that power companies include in the prices they charge you for their services.

17. In Chapter 22 you were asked to prepare a complete outline on a business topic of your choice, and in Chapter 23 you were asked to write a proposal requesting authorization for the study. Assuming that the proposal was approved by your instructor, prepare a title page, the introductory section, and the first main section of the report (Roman numeral I and all of the subsections under that heading). The portion of the report that you are to prepare, not including the title page or bibliography, should consist of from four to six double-spaced pages. Include the original proposal and outline, and submit the report in the type of folder preferred by your instructor. (This assignment is based on the premise that if you can prepare this portion of a report properly you will be able to prepare an entire report.)

18. Complete the report that was assigned in Application 17.

PART SEVEN
EMPLOYMENT COMMUNICATIONS

We have discussed many types of business communications in the preceding sections of this book, all of which have helped prepare you for what might be the most important communications of all—those that help you land a good job. Communication skills are an essential element in a successful employment campaign, as suggested by the personnel director at one of the country's largest and most successful corporations.

The job applicant and the subsequent employment interview both hinge on the prospective employee's communication skill. By the nature of the busy business world, the applicant typically earns but a few moments of the interviewer's time. In that condensed interval, the interviewer seeks to gain a valid impression of the long-term potential, motivation, and knowledge possessed by the applicant. Since the applicant's career is being held in the balance, the ability to communicate effectively is never more thoroughly tested.

Job applicants make numerous errors of omission and commission. Some talk too much and some talk too little. Most listen inattentively. Many come unprepared. One suggestion that I have for those facing these critical interviews it to practice beforehand on some helpful friend rather than on the interviewer. Have a friend role play various interviewers, asking a mix of job-related and personal questions. Most applicants could benefit from even a make-believe practice session of this type.

Paul Elsen
Director of Human Resources
Honeywell, Inc.

This section of the book not only deals with some of the fine points in preparing for and conducting yourself during interviews, but also shows you how to customize a resumé, write attention-getting employment letters, and follow through on job offers, rejections, and noncommittals.

25

CREATING RESUMÉS

Because you are an educated person looking for an above-average job, potential employers will expect you to present them with a functional and attractive resumé. Resumés, which many people refer to as "data sheets" and "vitas," (short for Latin *curriculum vitas,* meaning "course of a life"), generally consist of three main parts: personal data, formal education, and work experience.

You may decide on the arrangement of these three categories of information. You may elect to list your education first, for example, because it is more impressive than your work experience. You list your work experience first, on the other hand, if it relates more closely to the job you are seeking than your education does. Or you may list personal data at the beginning because it improves the overall appearance of the resumé. In addition to these three categories of information, you may include a career objective, personal references, or any other category of information that might interest employment managers in hiring you.

A resumé should provide an overview of your past, so don't try to include every little piece of information. Accentuate the positive by listing only complimentary information, and leave unfavorable details for later explanation. Remember, a resumé is not intended to reflect a complete record; that is the function of application forms provided by employers. The primary purpose of a resumé, instead, is to secure an interview.

Personal, yes, but not too personal.

PERSONAL DATA

Don't consume valuable space at the beginning of the resumé by using the title "RESUMÉ"; employment managers and their assistants know a resumé when they see one. Emphasize your name, instead, by placing it at the beginning in all capital letters, as illustrated in the sample resumés in Figures 25-1 and 25-2. Other personal data that usually appear at or near the top of resumés are your address (sometimes one for the present and another for the future) and telephone number (including the area code). Don't use the labels "Address" or "Telephone"; most people recognize addresses and telephone numbers when they see them.

You may place other personal details near the top of the page, such as your address to the left and personal data to the right; or you may follow the more current practice of placing such personal data near the bottom of the page, as shown in the sample resumés in Figures 25-1 and 25-2. Job seekers often include their birthdates (not their ages, which would soon date their resumés), marital status, physical dimensions, general health, and special interests; but there is no need to label this information.

Unnecessary labeling	*Preferred form*
Birth date: June 5, 1955	Born June 5, 1955
Marital status: Divorced	Divorced
Height: 5'5"	5'5"–135 lbs.
Weight: 135 lbs.	Excellent health
Health: Excellent	Enjoy skiing and tennis
Hobbies: Skiing and tennis	

The preferred form eliminates the superfluous, leaving more white space (space without typing) on the page and less verbiage for the reader to deal with. Notice the different ways this information is presented in the two sample resumés.

Most employment managers advise applicants *not* to include photos of themselves, but if you believe that your appearance might help you land a particular job, then by all means include a picture. Passport-type pictures are most appropriate, since they are small enough to fit in the top right corners of resumés. When having the picture taken, dress in a manner appropriate for the position that you are seeking and assume a business-like pose.

```
                    JULIA (JULIE) METZENDORF

Until May 16, 1980:              After May 16, 1980:
6035 North 21st Avenue           6395 Orange Avenue
Phoenix, Arizona  85015          Long Beach, California  90805
(602) 242-3807                   (213) 423-9427

                    Employment Objectives

Initial: Any clerical position     Eventual:  Accounting position

                      Formal Education

9/78 -        Phoenix College, Phoenix, Arizona  85013

              Accounting major (Earned A's in all accounting courses)
              Will graduate May 10, 1980, with Associate in Arts degree
              Dean's honor list two semesters

              Worked part-time (see Work Experience below)

9/74 - 6/78   Long Beach High School, Long Beach, California  90805

              Graduated in top one fourth of a class of 165
              Astronomy club three years (president, one year)
              Marching band four years (clarinet)

                       Work Experience

9/78 -        National Life Insurance Company, 1102 West Camelback Road,
              Phoenix, Arizona 85192

              Part-time file clerk in marketing department, reporting
              directly to Mr. Timothy Borman, Office Manager.

6/78 - 8/78   Desert View Resort Hotel, 1036 South Mountain Pass Road,
              Scottsdale, Arizona 85251

              Front-desk reservation clerk (full-time summer job).  Also
              handled light bookkeeping chores and routine correspondence.

                        Special Skills

              Typist (60 wpm)      Filing systems and records management
              10-key calculators   Multilith and ditto machines
              Keypunch (IBM)       TELEX and TWX machines

                        Personal Data

              Born 5/11/57         Hobbies include playing soccer,
              Single                  riding horses, and gardening
              Excellent health     Active in community social programs
```

Figure 25-1   Sample resumé

MICHAEL R. SCHULTZ
3231 North 53rd Drive
Phoenix, Arizona 85031
(602) 247-8560

career objectives	Seeking a position as data-processing manager, a position that will not only permit me to demonstrate my creative and administrative abilities more fully, but one that will also enable me to expand my knowledge of sophisticated computer systems and business management.

Data Processing Manager   Wholesale Distributors, Inc.
5/78 - present   6322 North 34th Avenue
                          Phoenix, Arizona 85005

practical computer experience

Manage the activities of five employees: two computer
   operators and three keypunch operators.
Schedule production runs and consult with the Controller and
   other key management personnel regarding current problems
   and future informational requirements.
Determine data requirements (format and timing), design forms,
   and plan file layouts and program specifications.
Write, rewrite, and test programs.
Major accomplishment: Designed and implemented programs for
   the complete automation of all inventory-control systems.

Computer Operator   J & R Electronic Systems
6/76 - 12/77   713 University Drive
                        Tempe, Arizona 85281

Ran scheduled jobs, checked validity of output, distributed
   printouts, and maintained a log of computer utilization

Business Administration Major Arizona State University
9/76 - 5/78   Tempe, Arizona 85281

related education

Strong emphasis on computerology and economics
Graduated with high distinction
Member Beta Gamma Sigma (honorary business fraternity)

General Business Major   Phoenix College
9/74 - 5/76   Phoenix, Arizona 85013

Data processing curriculum
Dean's honor list every semester
Cumulative grade point average of 3.65 (3.50=A)

personal

Born 10/3/58 . . . married, 2 children . . . 5'7" . . . 150 lbs.
excellent health . . . avid sports fan and dedicated jogger.

Figure 25-2 Sample resumé

Exactly what is it you want to do?

CAREER OBJECTIVE

A frequent complaint by the people who read resumés is that applicants do not indicate the type of jobs they desire. You may close this communication gap by stating a realistic career objective.

> Example: To obtain employment as a legal secretary with
>   a large company, where I can increase my skills,
>   efficiency, and knowledge of law.

> Example: To work for Dun & Bradstreet in the area of
>   research and development.

The first example narrows the applicant's interests to the legal field, which probably was her exact intention. The second example not only narrows the applicant's interest to a particular field of business but also to a specific company; the resumé is useful only when applying to Dun & Bradstreet. In contrast, the employment objective in the sample resumé in Figure 25-1 states the applicant's long-term objective while effectively leaving the door open for any clerical position that might now be available. If you would accept almost any type of job to begin with, don't include a career objective that is unnecessarily restrictive.

What did you do in school besides breathe?

FORMAL EDUCATION

Try to maintain the reader's interest by listing your most recent education first. Forget about grade school, unless you were some type of whiz kid, and mention your high school education only if you had an outstanding record or if you are younger than 35 years of age.

Show the dates of attendance (months and years) in a prominent place, so the reader doesn't have to search for them, along with the name and address of the institutions. Specify your major areas of study at each school, and list any accomplishments of merit, such as being included on the Dean's honor list, belonging to an honor society or fraternity, and maintaining a respectable grade average. In deciding whether to mention your grades, you should realize that employment managers hire many, many more average people than they do Einsteins. If you graduated from a school, say so; and if you ranked in the top half or higher of your graduating class, now is the time to mention it.

Employment managers are especially interested in activities that reflect an inclination and ability to get along well with people. Respond to this interest in any way possible. Did you belong to a club? The newspaper staff? A sports team? A debating team? The band? Student council? ROTC? Did you direct the activities of others in any way? Group leader? Office holder? Team captain or co-captain?

You may include separate categories such as Leadership Experiences and Honors and Awards, but only if you have rather impressive lists. Otherwise, list your educational and extracurricular activities along with other information about the high school or college where they occurred, as shown in the sample resumés in Figures 25-1 and 25-2. If you don't have much information to include under Education, you might add a list of Related Courses Taken. If you are seeking a sales job, for example, list marketing, math, speech, and other classes that reflect preparation for that type of work. If you are applying for a clerical position, on the other hand, list such courses as typing, filing, and business machines. You may also list any special education, such as training programs provided by companies where you have worked and business-related education received in the military.

"Work" is a four-letter word, but so is "food."

WORK EXPERIENCE

Outline your work history by showing your most recent experiences first. You may follow any of several formats, including those shown in Figures 25-1 and 25-2, so long as you show the names and addresses of the places where you were employed, positions held, duties entailed, and dates of employment.

One of the first details that people consider when reading resumés is the continuity of dates, so place the beginning and ending dates of employment (months and years) in prominent positions on your resumé and explain any gaps that might exist. If there was a period when you were unemployed, provide an explanation.

Example: `Attended college full time during this period.`

Example: `Devoted full time to my role as wife, mother, and homemaker.`

Unexplained gaps in employment often exclude applicants from further consideration for employment.

Many women return to school and to work following "interrupted" careers. If this is your situation, be sure to mention any involvement that you might have had in community affairs during that time—such as being active in politics, working for charitable organizations, and helping manage church affairs.

If you have worked several jobs during school or during interruptions in your career, avoid the appearance of instability by lumping the experience into a single statement.

Example: Worked in numerous part-time jobs while attending school, including employment as a service-station operator, construction worker, and salesman.

Example: My husband was transferred to five different cities in this four-year period, during which time I performed a variety of clerical duties for several manufacturing and retailing firms.

Potential employers are interested in the job functions where you are presently working and those in earlier positions. Notice in the sample resumé in Figure 25-2 that each of the statements in the first position (this applicant's current job) begins with an action word in present tense: *manage, schedule, determine,* and *write.* For the Computer Operator position (an earlier job) the applicant uses action words in past tense: *ran, checked, distributed,* and *maintained.*

List different jobs that you have held with the same company, especially when you have assumed more responsible positions with each job change.

Example: Promoted to stenographer after working just six months as file clerk.

Example: In my first position as Claim Agent, I was responsible for the compilation and presentation of OS&D claims to transport and insurance companies. After just one year in that position, I was appointed Office Manager of the West Coast division, where it was my responsibility to run the office and coordinate procedures and personnel with all other divisions.

Notice in the second example that the positions are underscored for emphasis. If you use complete paragraphs in your resumé, as in the second example, keep them brief (no longer than eight lines) and guard against overuse of the pronoun

I. Consistency in your resumé is important also; use either phrases or complete sentences, but not a mixture of the two; and maintain parallelism in your sentences and paragraphs.

Potential employers are especially interested in major accomplishments by applicants. Did you design or introduce any new procedures? Did you solve any problems? Did you establish any performance records? Were you directly involved with any special programs? Did you receive any type of recognition for your contributions? If you can answer "yes" to any of these questions, now is the time to brag a little.

Example: When my supervisor needed legal documents
             prepared right away, she routinely assigned
             them to me.

Example: The division manager frequently called upon me
             to rearrange disorganized offices and, on occa-
             sion, sent me to large offices for the main
             purpose of abolishing unneeded positions and
             reducing or completely eliminating overtime work.

Notice the "major accomplishment" listed in the sample resumé in Figure 25-2 (first computer position). This statement provides evidence that the applicant's contributions exceeded the minimum effort that his employer might have expected.

How far back should you go when listing jobs? You should account for all work-related activities for at least the last ten years, if you have worked that long. You may show positions that you held beyond a ten-year period, if you believe the information will make the record appear more comprehensive and impressive. But you should devote less space to earlier positions. Notice in the sample resumé in Figure 25-2 that the applicant has devoted five times as much verbiage to his current position as to the previous one. If you have had absolutely no work experience, on the other hand, omit the Work Experience section and dwell on your preparation for the job that you are seeking.

If early positions would emphasize advancing age, which you might see as a negative factor, don't list them. The same advice applies to your date of birth; if you believe that knowledge of your age might work against you in the employment decision, don't list it. Employers cannot legally request this information, even in employment applications or during interviews.

Do not consume valuable space or introduce negative thoughts by explaining why you left earlier jobs; save this information for the formal application form that you will be asked to complete. And don't list the salaries earned in previous positions. Employment personnel might view a high salary as an indication that you are overqualified for the position that you are seeking; if the salary appears low, they might have the opposite reaction. Also, with present rates of inflation, a salary that was impressive a couple of years ago might be very unimpressive in today's labor market.

Employment personnel talk of "creative" resumés, those in which job seekers lie. Applicants have been known to list degrees they haven't earned, positions they haven't held, and achievements that were never realized. Their untruthful resumés sometimes open doors for interviews, but the truth invariably catches up with them. Some companies automatically reject (some even fire) people they expose as having made dishonest statements in resumés and applications.

Be truthful in resumés, but not to the point of being naive. If you are trying to secure a job with an accounting firm, for example, do not mention in your career objective that you actually wanted to be a doctor but failed chemistry. If you ranked fifth in your high school graduation class, don't add that there were only sixteen students in the class; and, if you were fired from a job, even if through no fault of your own, don't even bring up the subject in your resumé. If you introduce potential problem areas in the resumé, you may never receive an interview and a chance to explain your side of the story.

Advertisers don't mention the bad features of their products unless the government forces them to do so, and neither should you. Emphasize the positive instead, including only information that might cause others to view you as a promising candidate for the type of job that you are seeking. This is the name of the game; this is the approach that business people have come to expect.

HUP, two, three, four.

MILITARY SERVICE

If you wish to deemphasize any military service you have had, simply enter under Work Experience the dates of service, branch of service, terminal rank, and the fact that you were honorably discharged. You may devote a separate section of your resumé to your military background, on the other hand, if it was extensive or if you have several experiences to list that in any way relate to the type of job that you want.

If you directed the activities of others, be sure to provide details. Also provide details of any foreign travel that may be relevant to the target position. If any of the knowledge that you received through military training programs

can be transferred to business situations, relate the experience in a way that
will help the reader make the connection. Also list any honors and awards
received.

Do not list your draft status or go into great detail about your military
experiences unless they are directly related to the particular job that you are
seeking. Avoid the use of military jargon and any mention of retirement
status. Even more important, perhaps, do not use the guidelines that the military
provides for resumé preparation, because they are widely recognized as "military." Many employment managers are unreceptive to people with extensive
military backgrounds, on the theory that such people have never had to assume
responsibility for earning profits, so plan your resumé to establish yourself as
a business-oriented person.

What about witnesses?

PERSONAL REFERENCES

Most employment managers, the people who actually read resumés, advise
against listing references on resumés. To do so is redundant, because most
companies have job seekers complete application forms before they actually
begin checking references; and all standard application forms have sections for
listing several personal references. Besides, if potential employers should check
references from the information provided in resumés, the people listed would
soon tire of responding to requests for information. Knowing this, most applicants add one line to their resumés indicating that references will be provided
on request, or they simply avoid mentioning references altogether.

You will want to show references on your resumé, however, if you have
friends in high places; but be sure to secure their permission beforehand. Also,
if you are without extensive education or work experience, you may add from
two to four references to help balance your resumé on the page. Type the
references at the end of the resumé exactly as they would appear on envelopes
so that employment managers won't have to search for street addresses or zip
codes.

Example:

Dr. Willie Minor, Professor
Department of Business
Phoenix College
1202 West Thomas Road
Phoenix, AZ 85013

Example:

Ms. Maria Gonzales, Manager
Tempe Shoe Center
1210 Mill Avenue
Tempe, AZ 85281

References should *not* include previous employers; if you want the people who are analyzing your resumé to contact a particular person at a company, list the person's name under Work Experience as illustrated in the sample resumé in Figure 25-1 (in the current position). You should also distinguish the references as educators, business people, government officials, or clergy—not just pals of yours. Without this clarification, references are valueless.

Please ignore the coffee stains.

GOOD APPEARANCE

Employment managers claim that a resumé has only 30 seconds or so to bring success or failure to the applicant. Because of the hundreds of resumes received each day, they must select promising candidates through process of elimination. In other words, they look for reasons to exclude applicants from consideration. And an unattractive appearance can eliminate a resumé from the game before they even begin to read its contents.

So how can you create an attractive resumé? Begin by planning an appealing layout. When the people at advertising agencies create advertisements, they place parts of ads on separate pieces of paper and then position the pieces (pictures of products and printed matter) in different arrangements on a page of paper until they identify the best arrangement. You should take the same approach with your resumé, determining whether to center your address at the top with your name or place it alone to the left, whether to use centered headings for each category of information (Figure 25-1) or side headings (Figure 25-2), whether to show personal data at the beginning of the resumé or at the end, and to answer a host of other questions concerning indentations and spacing.

Although you should leave sufficient white space to avoid a cluttered appearance, most people with fewer than ten years of work experience can easily confine their resumés to a single page. If you must use a second page to include essential information, rearrange your information to balance it evenly on both pages. Don't use a three- or four-page resumé, unless you are a very high-level employee with extensive managerial experience, because most busy employment managers will not take the time to read it.

Employment managers can usually recognize professionally prepared resumés clear across the room, and they respond more favorably to resumés that have been prepared by the applicants themselves. So plan your own resumé. Type it, too, if at all possible. High-quality paper, a good typewriter, clean type, and a fresh ribbon will contribute significantly to the appearance of your resumé. Properly spelled words and good grammar are essential also, so check and doublecheck your wording before typing; and have a knowledgeable friend or an instructor appraise the final product before actually putting it to use.

No, you do not need to prepare a separate resumé for each potential employer, because resumés are relatively difficult to type. Instead, take the original to a local duplicating service, where they will use a multilith or regular copy machine to produce copies that will be difficult or impossible to distinguish from the original. The cost will depend on the number of copies ordered. Do *not* use resumés that have been reproduced with a ditto machine or carbons.

The information in your resumé will change from time to time as you acquire more education and work experience, but it is much easier to update a resumé than it is to start from scratch, especially at a time when you are under pressure to secure a job. As you put forth the considerable effort that is required to develop a functional resumé, therefore, remember that a resumé is not just another page of information; it is a document that is likely to influence your business career and life for many years to come.

Have I touched all bases this time?

CHECKLIST: RESUMÉS

Personal data

- ☐ Did you avoid use of the word "resumé"?
- ☐ Did you include your name, address, and phone number near the top of the page?
- ☐ Did you include in a separate place on the page your birthdate and marital status?
- ☐ Did you decide to add or omit a photograph or any reference to your health, physical dimensions, or hobbies?
- ☐ Did you avoid the use of unnecessary, space-consuming labels?
- ☐ Did you exclude any reference to your social security number and draft status?

Career objective

- ☐ If you included a career objective, is it sufficiently broad to encompass a wide range of potential jobs?
- ☐ Is the statement appropriate for more than one company?

☐ Is the objective realistic in terms of your preparation and experience?

☐ Did you consider a two-part objective, one for your initial objective and another for long-range goals?

Formal education

☐ Did you begin with and emphasize your most recent education?

☐ Did you show the dates of attendance, names of schools, their locations, and your major areas of study?

☐ Did you list any honors and awards received? Your grade average? Honorary groups? Social groups?

☐ If you had difficulty completing a full-page resumé, did you consider listing classes taken that relate to the type of job that you are seeking?

☐ Was there a need for separate categories such as Leadership Experience, Honors and Awards, and Special Skills?

☐ Did you list school activities in which you participated?

☐ Did you identify any leadership roles that you fulfilled?

☐ If you are under 35 years of age, did you include information about your high school education and related activities?

☐ Did you mention that you worked part-time while attending school?

Work experience

☐ Did you begin with your most recent job?

☐ Did you show the beginning and ending dates, the names and addresses of companies, and the positions held?

☐ Did you list your duties and accomplishments?

☐ Did you emphasize the positive, omitting any detail that might cause employers to question your attitudes and abilities?

☐ Did you use action words to describe your duties and accomplishments, using present tense for current activities and past tense for previous activities?

☐ Did you use short phrases (the preferred form) or complete sentences and paragraphs, avoiding a mixture of the two forms and avoiding or minimizing use of the word *I*?

☐ Did you include part-time and summer employment, if any?

☐ If you held many jobs during high school or during interruptions in your career, did you avoid the appearance of instability by grouping them?

☐ Did you provide an employment record for at least the last ten years, omitting any earlier references that would emphasize advancing age?

☐ Are your comments truthful, but not to the point of naivete?

Military experience

☐ Did you use a separate section (if your military service was extensive) or place this information under Work Experience?

☐ Did you show the branch of service, your terminal rank, and the fact that you were honorably discharged?

☐ Did you outline your activities, if business related, and especially those involving leadership roles?

☐ Did you avoid the use of military jargon, any mention of retirement status, and the military format for dates and resumés?

Personal references

☐ Did you include references only of people with recognized and impressive positions or titles?

☐ Did you avoid using previous employers as references?

☐ If you listed references, did you place them in mailing-address format, showing each person's position or title?

Good appearance

☐ Did you place all parts of your resumé in the most attractive arrangement possible?

☐ Does the resumé contain a liberal amount of white space?

☐ Did you confine your resumé to one page (if fewer than ten years' work experience) or two pages at most?

☐ If you used two pages, did you balance the information evenly on both pages?

☐ Is the resumé well typed?

☐ Is the paper of high quality and without smudges?

☐ Are all words correctly spelled?

☐ Is your grammar in good form?

☐ Are the copies clear and on high-quality paper?

☐ Does the finished product represent you accurately and positively?

BUSINESS APPLICATIONS

1. Arrange the following information into phrases beginning with action words, for inclusion in the Work History section of a resumé:

   As a retail sales clerk at Sears, Roebuck and Company from June, 1977 to May, 1979, Rosemary Cohen was responsible for counting all inventory in the housewares department; and it was her responsibility to order merchandise from the warehouse when stock needed replenishing. During exceptionally busy periods, she helped with customer sales. She was promoted to the position of Credit Interviewer in May, 1979, where she still works. Responsibilities in the new position involve interviews with people seeking to make credit purchases at Sears for the first time and the final approval or rejection of all credit applications for $500 or less. She also counsels young applicants on the uses and abuses of credit cards.

2. Place the information of Application 1 in paragraph form as though you were writing about your own experiences.

3. During his last two years in high school and first two years in college, Marty Robbins held the following positions:

6/77–9/77	Summer job as a dishwasher at a plush Mexican restaurant
9/77–12/77	Part-time after school as service-station attendant
3/78–6/78	Delivered papers (morning route)
6/78–9/78	Lifeguard and swimming instructor at city pool
11/78–6/79	Busboy at the same Mexican restaurant (part time)
6/79–9/79	Lifeguard and swimming instructor
9/79–6/80	Part-time keypunch operator at electronics firm
6/80–9/80	Assistant computer operator at same company (full time)

   Group this experience for entry in a resumé as two separate statements. The last two jobs were at Reuter Electronics, Inc., in Chicago, Illinois (zip code 60607).

4. Make a list of all bits of information that could possibly be included in your resumé under Personal Data.

5. List all your educational experiences (including high school, if you are younger than 35), including all of your activities and leadership roles.

6. List all the companies or organizations you have worked for, positions that you held, immediate superiors, functions, and accomplishments.

7. Compose separate lists, if needed, for such categories as honors and awards, related classes taken, military experience, special skills, general information, and personal references.

8. Using the lists you have developed in the four preceding assignments, check those items that you consider useful to your resumé, taking space restrictions into consideration and eliminating all superfluous and negative elements.

9. Decide on the best arrangements of the information retained, and prepare a rough draft of your resumé.

10. After having others appraise the rough draft, and after having reviewed it yourself, use the rough draft (with any necessary alterations) to prepare a final resumé for submission to your instructor.

26
WRITING
APPLICATION LETTERS

If you decide to approach companies directly by showing up at their employment offices and asking for interviews, it won't be necessary for you to write application letters. You will simply present your resumé in person. Many people have landed their present jobs this way, knocking on one business door after the other until the right one opened for them.

Realizing that the direct approach requires a lot of time, effort, shoe leather, and gasoline, and knowing that employment managers don't always respond positively to unannounced visits, you may decide to rely on the U.S. mail. Rather than actually knocking on doors, you may decide to mail copies of your resumé to several companies, briefly describing your potential contributions to each company and requesting interviews. But which companies should you contact? What should you include in your letters? How long should your letters be? What should they say? These next few pages will answer these questions and others that you may not have considered.

For which of the millions of companies
would you like to work?

TARGET COMPANIES

You may select companies randomly in your search for employment, but the chances of finding the "right" job through such a hit-or-miss approach are not favorable. The probability of your finding a suitable job will be much greater if you respond to the challenge systematically.

Campus services. Check with the placement office at your school to see what jobs are available and which companies have scheduled interviews. Most placement offices use bulletin boards to post information about local job offers. They also invite students to complete standard application forms and to submit letters of recommendation (from instructors) and personal resumés. They present this information to representatives of companies in which students express interest before the representatives grant interviews to the students during their scheduled visits to the campus.

Also take the time to inform business instructors of your search for employment. Many companies contact business faculty directly rather than relying on placement offices. When an employment manager is seeking recruits for an accounting position, for instance, he or she might telephone an accounting instructor. Although faculty members generally pass such information to placement offices, they might give you a running start toward the job by telling you about it first. And such a recommendation from an instructor, a person who is personally aware of your performance record and abilities, often results in employment.

Employment agencies. Local governments in large cities provide employment services without charge to applicants or employers, but many are understaffed and most focus on the placement of unskilled labor. You will also find many private employment agencies listed in telephone directories. Private agencies usually specialize in stenographic, secretarial, and relatively low-level clerical positions; and their fees range anywhere from 10 to 25 percent of the annual salary earned in the new position.

Newspapers and trade journals. Many employers place employment ads in the classified sections of city and neighborhood newspapers, and they usually invite those who are interested to respond by submitting resumés to listed box numbers. Many employers also advertise in nationally distributed newspapers such as the *Wall Street Journal* and the *Christian Science Monitor.* Other popular vehicles for employment offers are **trade journals**—magazines directed at specific segments of society such as people who work in the food, electronics, aviation, and auto industries; and there are tens of thousands of such publications.

Yellow pages. If you are interested in working locally for a specific type of company, you should "let your fingers do the walking through the yellow pages." These annual publications place local businesses in categories ranging from accounting to insurance and heavy machinery to X-ray equipment. And with the use of maps at the front of the directory, you can avoid running from one side of town to the other on the same day by categorizing the target companies geographically. For a broader approach, you may visit the telephone company and consult the yellow pages for other cities.

National directories. Assuming that your search for employment is national in scope, a visit to your school or city library will enable you to consult one or more national directories:

1. *Dun & Bradstreet Million Dollar Directory*
2. *Poor's Register of Corporations, Officers, and Directors*
3. *Thomas Register*
4. Moody's manuals

These directories differ in amount of information provided, but they all list companies alphabetically, geographically, and by product line or services offered. Looking in the alphabetical section under C, for instance, you will find a listing for Coca-Cola. You will also find Coca-Cola listed under Atlanta, Georgia (and many other geographic locations) and in product classifications under "Soft Drinks." These directories provide the name, address, and telephone number for each company—along with the names, functions, and backgrounds of key management personnel. As you know from our discussion in Chapter 23, Moody's manuals are published annually for industrial, financial, transport, and other categories of business activities; and they include extensive biographical and financial information for each company listed.

If you are interested in working in a particular industry (advertising, cosmetics, grocery, marketing research, soft drinks) in a specific area (Chicago, Denver, Los Angeles), you can use directories to pinpoint target companies and to learn something about the companies and their managements. Consult the contents pages at the front of these directories for details about the specific types of information included and methods of locating the information.

Government publications. The federal government issues three directories that may assist you in your search for a specific type of employment. The Department of Labor publishes the *Dictionary of Occupational Titles,* which groups occupations into occupational classifications (based on job tasks and requirements) for nearly all jobs in the U.S. economy. Included also are comprehensive descriptions of job duties and related information for more than 20,000 different occupations.

The Department of Labor's *Encyclopedia of Careers and Vocational Guidance* catalogs opportunities in major industries such as advertising and retailing, and includes detailed information about the nature of work in different occupations—educational and special requirements, methods of entry, conditions for advancement, employment outlook, earnings potential, working conditions, and additional information concerning the social and pyschological factors involved. You may also study the current and projected demand for employees in different employment categories by consulting the *Occupational Outlook Handbook,* an annual publication by the Department of Labor.

Personal leads. Many jobs, perhaps most of them, are found by word of mouth. Before going to the trouble and expense of advertising new or vacant positions, many employment managers first make the information known to their own employees. Rather than keeping your search for employment a secret, therefore, ask friends, relatives, and acquaintances to inform you of any job leads they encounter. Provide them with copies of your resumé, and keep in touch.

The S★T★A★R approach revisited.

PSYCHOLOGICAL CONSIDERATIONS

The S★T★A★R (service, time, audience, reason) approach presented in Chapter 7 is extremely important in all types of employment communications.

Service. Employment managers are human, just like the rest of us, and they often identify with job seekers—remembering when they, too, were mailing resumés, knocking on doors, and being interviewed. But these people who do the hiring, if they are doing their jobs correctly, strive to employ people they believe will contribute more to the welfare of their companies than they will cost the companies in wages, salaries, and fringe benefits. Correspondingly, self-centered statements about the applicant's personal goals and ambitions generally make an unfavorable impression.

When applying for a job, therefore, dwell on the employer's interests and the welfare of the companies they represent. Adopt a service attitude by outlining those aspects of your education and experience that will make you a valuable employee—an employee who will make a greater contribution to the company than other applicants would be able to do. Such an approach will enable you to minimize use of the self-centered pronoun *I*, as illustrated in the following examples:

Self-centered   I read your advertisement in the paper on July 5, and am interested in such a position because I like the benefits, the pay, and the chance for advancement that your company offers. I am seeking a job with a future.

Service-
oriented
The position that you advertised in the *Denver Star* on July 5 seems to match my qualifications exactly. My typing speed and knowledge of legal terminology, as outlined in the enclosed resumé, should enable me to complete all types of legal documents for you with only a minimum of on-the-job exposure.

On the basis of these two statements alone, can there by any doubt about which applicant will capture the interest of the people who placed the ad in the newspaper?

Time. As with all types of communications, pay close attention to the time element when you are writing employment letters. If you mention your activities at a previous job, keep your writing in **past tense** (*performed, directed, participated, handled, improved*). Use **present tense** (*perform, direct, participate, handle, improve*) when discussing your current activities. Use **future tense** (*will, plan to, expect to, going to*) when discussing events that are yet to occur, and use the **subjunctive mood** (*would, could, should*) when dealing with uncertainty (events that you hope will take place).

Audience. Before you begin writing an employment letter or any other communication, identify your audience. Do you consider it best to direct your remarks to one person (the employment manager, the personnel manager, the vice-president of marketing) or to more than one person (all persons involved in the hiring process)? If you are addressing just one person, is the individual a male or a female? By identifying your audience, you will find the correct choice of words almost automatic.

Reason. Identifying and remembering the main reason for your communication will help you keep your thoughts on track, and the main reason for writing application letters is to secure interviews which might lead to employment. Correspondingly, you should phrase every statement in your employment letters to persuade readers that you are a likely candidate for the position you seek. Such an orientation will help you write concise and convincing letters.

Ms. who?

UNEXPECTED LETTERS

Many job seekers mail copies of resumés each week to several companies, hoping that at least a few will result in interviews. These unexpected letters, the ones that businesses have not solicited from applicants, should follow a three-part format: attract attention, provide evidence of qualifications, and request action.

You are trying to sell a product that is dear to your heart (your own services), and, in a very real sense, you are competing with many other products (the qualifications of other applicants seeking the same job). To compete successfully, you must phrase the opening statements in your application letters so that they will capture the attention of employment managers. Try to arouse their interest in the letter, the resumé, and (eventually) the person.

> Example: WORK WANTED!   ONLY COMPANIES SEEKING SOMEONE
>   WITH MIDDLE MANAGEMENT EXPERIENCE NEED APPLY.

> Example: Is your company in need of a competent, mature
>   secretary? A person who has the ability to
>   follow instructions, as well as exercise good
>   judgment in independent work?

Be sure to indicate the type of position you desire, and do not overstate your qualifications. Don't apply for a high position if you are without experience, for example, and don't suggest that all their problems will disappear soon after your arrival.

Another effective way to begin an unexpected employment letter is to indicate that some recognized person has suggested that you apply. If trying to secure a job as ticket agent with an airline, for instance, drop by a ticket office or the airport and talk with a company employee. Make a note of the individual's name and learn the name, position, and address of the person who hires ticket agents. This information will enable you to begin employment letters with attention-getting statements.

> Example: Margaret Jones at your Rosemead office
>   suggested that I write directly to you con-
>   cerning employment as a ticket agent.

> Example: After discussing my ticket-selling experience
>   with me at some length this morning, Mr.
>   Beech at your Palm Springs office recommended
>   that I submit a resume for your consideration.

Such opening statements imply that a company employee has seen and talked with you and was favorably impressed. Accordingly, recipients of these types of communications tend to be receptive to what applicants have to say about themselves.

Once you have attracted the attention of readers, you must maintain their interest by presenting evidence of your qualifications.

Example: A glance at the enclosed resume will reveal
           that I have had five years experience as
           Operations Manager for a medium-sized dis-
           tributor of air-conditioning units and
           replacement parts. This experience included
           regular participation in new-product
           workshops presented by the company each month.

Example: As shown in the accompanying resume, my
           academic training and actual work experience
           have provided me not only with knowledge of
           standard accounting procedures, but has also
           given me a comprehensive overview of an
           entire manufacturing operation. Don't you
           agree that this experience, coupled with the
           business courses that I have taken in college,
           qualifies me for a clerical position with
           your firm?

When writing application letters, don't just copy a lot of information from the resumé. Call attention to specific highlights of your background instead, making sure to mention the accompanying resumé at some point in your letter.

End your application letters with appeals for action. If you want an interview, ask for one. Phrase your request as a question, rather than giving the impression that you *expect* a positive response.

Example: If you are favorably impressed with my qualifications, Ms.
           Teng, will you please call me for an interview?
Example: May I have an interview, please?

Don't detract from your request for action by tacking on an afterthought or a plea for consideration. End your letter with the question; and if you have not mentioned the person's name elsewhere in the letter, include it in the closing sentence as shown in the preceding example.

Sample application letters. Having considered the three parts of unexpected application letters, let's put the pieces together to form two completed letters. The following letter is related to the sample resumé in Figure 25-1.

Attract attention	Several accounting courses in college and some actual work experience! Would a young person with these qualifications be able to make a positive contribution to your clerical staff this summer?
Provide evidence	In addition to outlining my formal education and work experience, the enclosed resume lists several skills that I possess which may be directly applicable to your office procedures. Notice also that I am seeking any type of clerical work to begin with, even though my greatest contribution will eventually be in the area of accounting.
Ask for action	If you have a need for such a person, Mr. Reuter, will you please invite me in for an interview?

As a second example, the following letter is based on the sample resumé in Figure 25-2, and was written by an applicant who has considerable experience in data processing.

Attract attention	DATA-PROCESSING PROBLEMS? Are there obvious gaps in your information system? Are you paying too much money for the information you are receiving? Are you experiencing recurring problems in the data processing area? If you answer "yes" to any of these questions, you should consider my application for employment as Data Processing Manager.
Provide evidence	The enclosed data sheet presents evidence of my qualifications as an experienced and creative data processing manager. You will notice, for example, that I write and test my own programs-- including the designing and implementation of a sophisticated inventory control system for my present employer.

| | My managerial potential with your company is further enhanced by several academic achievements. My education has continued following graduation, moreover, because of an insatiable desire to continue learning as much as I can-- not just in the field of data processing, but about all areas of business management. |
| Ask for action | Shall we discuss my potential contributions to Westco Corporation? |

Brevity is essential in unexpected application letters, just as it is in advertisements. Two paragraphs were judged necessary in the middle section of the second letter, because more explanation was called for in connection with this managerial position. Both letters are sufficiently brief, nevertheless.

Oh, hello again.

EXPECTED LETTERS

Expected letters are those that potential employers have asked you to submit. Maybe you have talked with employers in person or on the telephone, and they have asked you to submit a resumé. Or maybe you are responding to a help wanted ad in the local newspaper.

Expected letters differ from unexpected ones in one major respect: The attention-getting statement at the beginning of the letter is replaced with a reference to the employer's request for information.

Example: The enclosed resume is in response to your ad in today's Washington Post.

Example: Here is the resume that you requested during our telephone conversation this morning.

One other way that expected letters sometimes differ from those not expected by employers is that they are longer. When an employer has requested job-related information, you may include a considerable amount of data in your letter without risking a loss of interest. You must still exercise good judgment, however, avoiding the temptation to include every little bit of available information and, in most cases, confining your letters to a single page. A good rule of thumb concerning the length of application letters is to include just enough information to arouse the interest of employers, but withhold enough information to cause them to want to learn more through interviews.

The sample application letter in Figure 26-1 is "expected," since the campus recruiter for the company asked Roslyn Petre to write to R. Ronald Becker, the employment director. In fact, the recruiter probably submitted a report to Becker, presenting his impressions of the applicant from having interviewed her. Correspondingly, Roslyn begins the letter with a reference to the interview rather than an attention-getting statement. She then interprets her training and experiences by relating them to the needs of the company—rather than repeating what has already been stated in the accompanying resumé.

She does not include her address in the letter (above the date line), because to do so would repeat information that is prominent in her resumé. She uses a modified block format, as described on pages 153–154, and she notes at the bottom of the page that two items are being enclosed with the letter (a resumé and a list of courses and grades).

When preparing application letters for yourself, follow the same advice that was given about the appearance of resumés: high-quality paper, a good typewriter, clean type, and a well-inked ribbon. Unlike the resumé, however, you should not send the same letter to more than one company. If you are writing to similar companies (15 oil companies, for example), you may use similar wording; but each letter should be an original, and each should be addressed to a specific person. You are using the same resumé for all companies; your application letter customizes each presentation.

February 6, 1980

Mr. R. Ronald Becker
Director of Employment Services
Melbourn Industries, Inc.
3546 N.W. 58 Street
Oklahoma City, OK 73112

Dear Mr. Becker:

At the conclusion of a very informative interview yesterday with James
Mason, your campus representative in this area, he asked that I write
to you concerning my interest in your management training program.

If you will take a moment to consider the enclosed resume, Mr. Becker,
you will see that my academic achievements in high school and in college
reflect a capacity to master complex materials. Just as important,
perhaps, the nature of my participation in extracurricular activities
throughout school is indicative of a strong leadership potential and
an ability to relate well to diverse groups of people.

The part-time job that I have held for the last two years has enabled
me to apply several of the managerial concepts that I studied in college,
and my personal supervision of several people for three months this
last summer provided me with additional leadership experience.

From what I learned of your training program from Mr. Mason, and based
on information about your company that is available in our school
library, it appears that much of my curriculum is closely related to
the type of merchandising that is your specialty. In addition to the
accompanying resume, therefore, please see the attached list of related
classes taken, and the grades earned.

I believe that I could do well in the Melbourn environment, during the
training program and in the field, and would welcome an opportunity to
discuss that possibility with you.

                          Sincerely,

                          Roslyn W. Petre

                          Roslyn W. Petre

Enclosures (2)

Figure 26-1   Sample of an expected application letter

So that's how I was supposed to do it.

CHECKLIST: APPLICATION LETTERS

Target companies

☐ Have you checked all employment possibilities?
- Campus employment services?
- Employment agencies?
- Newspapers and trade journals?
- Yellow pages?
- National directories?
- Government publications?
- Personal leads?

Psychological considerations

☐ Did you apply the S★T★A★R approach?
- Adopt a service attitude?
- Maintain consistent time frames?
- Communicate with specific audiences?
- Focus on the primary objective?

Unexpected letters

☐ Did you open with an attention-getting statement?
☐ Did you identify the type of work wanted?
☐ Are your objectives and claims realistic?
☐ Did you follow with evidence of your qualifications?
☐ Did you refer to the enclosed resumé?
☐ Did you refer to the addressee by name?
☐ Did you end with a request for action?

Expected letters

☐ Did you open with a reference to their request for information?
☐ Did you identify the type of work you want?
☐ Are your objectives and claims realistic?
☐ Did you follow with evidence of your qualifications?
☐ Did you refer to the enclosed resumé?
☐ Did you provide sufficient information, without trying to include every detail?
☐ Did you refer to the addressee by name?
☐ Did you end with a request for action?

Other considerations

☐ Did you use your own words, rather than copying?
☐ Did you keep a file copy of each letter?
☐ Did you enclose a copy of your resumé?
☐ Did you attach sufficient postage?
☐ If writing to more than one company, did you type a separate letter for each? Did you doublecheck to make certain that you placed the letters in the correct envelopes?
☐ Did you confine your letter to one page?
☐ Is your letter attractive (see Chapter 9)?

BUSINESS APPLICATIONS

1. Using any one of the national directories available to you, record the names and addresses (including zip codes) of five companies located in the state of Kentucky and five companies in the city of Denver.

2. Again referring to national directories, record the names of the key manager (president or chief executive officer) of the following companies:

> Aluminum Company of America
> Home Oil Company, Ltd. (Canada)
> The Procter & Gamble Company
> Santa Fe Industries, Inc.

3. Use any of the available directories to identify one company (name of the company only) in each of the following product categories: aluminum, engineering services, machinery, petroleum, textiles.

4. Record the names, addresses, and telephone numbers of five manufacturing companies located in your state.

5. Record the names, addresses, and telephone numbers of the five employment agencies nearest your school, noting the types of employment in which they specialize. Telephone them if necessary.

6. Using one or more newspapers, find two help wanted advertisements of jobs for which you may be qualified.

7. Comment on the following statements:
   a. I would like nothing better than to start off my accounting career with a topnotch organization like Reynolds Corporation. When may I expect to hear from you?

b. I am currently a typist, and I would like to advance to a secretarial position as quickly as possible. When may I come in to fill out an application or set up an appointment for an interview?

c. Although I didn't do too well with my studies during high school, I played football all four years and was captain of the football team my senior year. I ranked in the lower fourth of my graduation class.

d. In my first position as inventory clerk, I counted all inventory, submit daily product orders, and maintenance duties. In my current position as assistant store manager, I am responsible for five employees, making certain that waiting lines do not become too long at checkout counters, and post all price changes on the products and shelves.

e. Having worked two years as a sales clerk and having just earned a two-year degree in fashion merchandising, I believe that I am well qualified to direct your national marketing magazine.

8. Choose a local company that appeals to you as a potential place of employment and write an "unexpected" application letter to the employment manager. Relate the contents of your letter to the resumé that you prepared earlier.

27

PREPARING FOR INTERVIEWS

Okay, an employer is favorably impressed with your letter and the qualifications outlined in your resumé and has asked you to come in next Tuesday for an interview. Now what?

After first learning as much as possible about the company, identify elements in your education and work experience that relate to company operations. Prepare answers to probable questions and plan ways to support your statements. You should then approach the interview with a high degree of confidence that what you are selling (your services) is what they are seeking.

What kind of outfit is this?

ANALYZE THE COMPANY

One sure way to please interviewers is to demonstrate extensive knowledge of company organization and operations. If you are to be interviewed for possible employment at The Greyhound Corporation, for example, you can use a Moody's manual to learn that this business is now much more than a bus company; Greyhound is a holding company with controlling interest in or full ownership of over 100 subsidiary companies. You would also learn that Greyhound employs nearly 55,000 people, divides operations into six distinct product or service groups, and generates sales in the billions of dollars each year. Notice that the correct name of this company, as shown in Moody's, is "The Greyhound Corporation," not just "Greyhound Corporation"; such detail is important to the people who would be interviewing you.

411

A glance at a Moody's manual or *Standard & Poor's* (two leading financial publications that are available at most brokerage offices and libraries) will also give you an indication of the financial condition of the company. You may learn, for instance, that the company you are considering is very profitable or, at the other extreme, is on the verge of bankruptcy. Knowledge of such conditions is essential before the interview rather than after the fact—after you have already accepted employment.

But what if the company is not listed in either of these publications? You may approach the company directly for information by simply writing or telephoning and requesting a copy of the most recent annual report. Annual reports usually include financial data and summary statements about the firm's plans, profitability, products, and services; but the information will probably be less objective than the coverage by Moody's or *Standard & Poor's.*

A company's suppliers, customers, employees, and even its competitors often represent candid sources of information. Ask anyone who relates to the company in any of these capacities what they think of the company and what kind of place it would be to work. You may find that the company is known for excellent employee relations or, conversely, that it is not what you would consider an acceptable work environment.

Why do they need a wonderful person like me?

RELATE YOUR BACKGROUND TO THE JOB

It isn't enough to be a well-qualified person; you must demonstrate that you are qualified for the specific job you are seeking. Having learned as much as you can about the company, therefore, identify those parts of your education and work experience that relate to the type of work that you would be performing as a newly hired employee.

Next, try to anticipate questions that interviewers may ask. Using your resumé as the basis for their questions, they may suggest that you elaborate on your major areas of study: Why did you decide to major in marketing? What type of marketing position would you eventually like to hold? Which college courses did you enjoy the most? Which ones did you like the least?

Interviewers often ask very direct questions about past employment: Are you still employed at National Insurance Company? Why are you thinking of changing jobs at this particular time? How do you like working for the people there? Why did you leave your job at Desert View? Would the people there be willing to provide you with a letter of recommendation? What made you look to us for employment?

If you already have a job, try to hang onto it until you find a better one, because it is widely accepted knowledge that employment managers prefer to hire people who are presently employed. The implication seems to be that the employed are ambitious people who are probably seeking employment as a way of improving their situations; those who are unemployed, by this way of think-ing, probably experienced difficulty in their previous positions and are more apt to represent future problems.

After questioning applicants about their education and work experence, interviewers often discuss the applicant's preparation for the job at hand: In what ways has your education prepared you for this job? Did any of your tasks with other employers involve this type of work? What makes you think that you can relate well to our customers? These are the types of questions that will enable you to tie your specific skills and knowledge directly to the position being sought, providing you are well prepared with answers.

If the job involves some degree of teamwork with other employees, cite evidence from your past that illustrates an ability to perform well in group efforts. If the job calls for leadership ability, mention any leadership roles that you played in school or at work. If the job involves clerical work, call atten-tion to your knowledge of office procedures.

As a very young man being interviewed for his first clerical position, the author was just one of many people seeking the job—until he mentioned that he could type extremely fast. As it turned out, the job didn't involve much typing, but the mere mention of this one skill gave him enough of an edge over other applicants that he landed the job. Such skills as typing and the operation of various office machines, no matter how basic they may seem to you, often gain important points with employment managers.

After you have practiced answering questions that interviewers are likely to ask (in front of a mirror, perhaps), ask someone to role-play an interview situation with you. Have the person sit on the opposite side of a desk or table, the usual setting for interviews, and assume the role of interviewer. Direct the surrogate interviewer to ask questions from the list of probable questions that you have prepared and to interject unplanned questions during the role-playing session. Although the sessions may seem strained (even a little corny) at the beginning, the experience can add significantly to your confidence when you engage in actual interviews.

May I borrow your pen again, please?

GO PREPARED

Now that you have your thoughts organized for the interview, begin organizing the materials that you are to take along. Don't take just one pen; ballpoints seem to run out of fluid at the times you need them most. Equip yourself with two pens and two or three well-sharpened pencils and some paper.

When employment managers decide that you are a likely candidate for employment, they usually have other managerial personnel interview you, so take along additional copies of your resumé for their use. Also prepare a list of important personal data so that you will be able to complete application forms accurately and quickly:

1. Details of your education (including dates, courses, and extracurricular activities)
2. Names and addresses of previous employers
3. Dates of employment
4. Beginning and ending salaries
5. Reasons for leaving earlier jobs
6. Addresses and dates of previous residences
7. Social security number (self and spouse)
8. Marriage and divorce dates
9. List of references (including their titles, addresses, and phone numbers)
10. Financial data

Some application forms request financial information such as additional sources of income, lists of debts and assets, and insurance coverage—information that may be impossible for you to provide if not included in the type of data sheet recommended here.

You want to convince interviewers that you did more than just "float along" during your schooling and work experience, so include samples of your work—copies of reports that you prepared in school or at work, letters and other documents that you wrote, computer programs that you designed. And be sure to include copies of any commendations received from college instructors and employers.

Where will you put all these materials? Place the samples of your work and letters of commendation, if any, in a separate folder, so that you can easily find them to present to interviewers at opportune times during interviews. Place this folder, along with your pens and pencils, resumés, data sheets, and other materials in some type of small case. A briefcase would appear too formal unless you are applying for a position as middle manager or higher.

What you see is what you get.

SELL YOURSELF

You've gone to a lot of trouble so far—developing a resumé, writing an application letter, researching the company, preparing a personal data sheet, role-playing. With the interview now at hand, put the finishing touches on the package by presenting a favorable appearance, being punctual, and conducting yourself properly during the person-to-person exchange.

Check your appearance. Numerous studies have shown that interviewers tend to make up their minds about applicants during the first two or three minutes after meeting them—often using the time remaining in the interviews to justify their first impressions. Cater to this tendency by playing the part; dress at least as well as they would expect for the type of work you are seeking. Strive for a businesslike appearance by avoiding extremes in dress and hair styles, and make sure that your shoes are clean, that your clothes are fresh and well-pressed, and that you are well-groomed. Remember, companies hire people, not resumés or application letters. The main purpose of interviews, in fact, is to provide employment personnel with opportunities to observe applicants before deciding which ones will "fit in" best with the people who already work there.

Arrive ahead of time. Don't arrive on time; arrive at least 30 minutes before the scheduled interview. Allow time for traffic delays, mechanical failures, and parking hassles. If everything goes smoothly en route to the interview, use the extra time to organize your thoughts and to observe as much of the company facilities and as many employees as possible.

Be pleasant to the help. Be courteous to all employees that you encounter. While waiting for the interviewer, you may have an opportunity to converse with a secretary or receptionist; pleasant exchanges at this time might bring important rewards later. These are the people you may later be telephoning to check on the status of your application. Also, interviewers often ask assistants for their impressions of certain applicants. In other words, people other than the interviewer may be interviewing you without your even realizing it.

Make an impressive entrance. Those critical first impressions do not depend entirely on your appearance; behavior is equally important. If you are sitting when the interviewer approaches, rise and prepare yourself for the traditional handshake—a custom discussed at some length in Chapter 21. Respond to an offer to shake hands by looking the interviewer directly in the eye and shaking hands firmly. If the interviewer doesn't initiate a handshake, which is sometimes the case, you must decide if you are to take the initiative. The best advice for this situation is to do what seems natural to you at the time.

Be yourself. During the initial encounter, and after the interviewer has offered a chair to you, be pleasant and courteous. And if at all possible under these trying conditions, try to smile a little. Interviewers expect a certain amount of nervousness from applicants, even experienced ones, because they realize that anxiety is a natural reaction to having other people analyze your background, preparation, and potential. So relax and act natural. Keep reminding yourself that these people believe you to be the right person for the job or they wouldn't have called you in for an interview in the first place. This outlook should allow you to contribute to an intelligent discussion of the job you are seeking and your qualifications for it, to reinforce their belief that you are the best possible candidate for the job.

Be responsive. As stressed throughout this book, the ability to communicate well is very important in business. Employment managers at one or more companies have already observed samples of your written communications by reading your resumé and application letters; interviews will now enable them to judge your ability to communicate orally.

They usually begin interviews by engaging in small talk. Sure hot out today, isn't it? Did you find our building without too much difficulty? Can I offer you a cup of coffee? Try to relax and be friendly during these first few moments, realizing that interviewers generally do not spin their wheels long before delving into the topics that you are so eager to discuss.

Interviewers not only seek answers to specific questions; they also want to hear how you convey the information. So don't be reluctant to talk; answer each question as accurately and tactfully as possible, keeping your answers brief and to the point. Try to respond naturally—not as if you were on a witness stand in a court of law, but as though you were engaging in cordial conversation with a respected friend. If you realize at any point that you do not have an acceptable answer to a specific question, admit your lack of knowledge in that area. Interviewers generally react better to candid responses than they do to bluffers and "know-it-alls."

But don't talk too much. Talk freely, but don't overdo it. Come up for air occasionally to give the interviewer an opportunity to control direction of the discussion. Be sensitive to the other person's wishes; if the interviewer appears to be losing interest in what you are saying, pause and seek new direction: Do you want me to comment further on this subject? Does that answer your question, Mr. Green? I never tire of discussing frazitts, but maybe you are eager to move on to another question? Such comments gain a lot of points, because they demonstrate a high degree of tact and empathy.

Be positive. The dialogue in interviews typically centers on past inter-relationships of applicants with other business people. No matter how frustrating your experiences with other employers might have been, do not dwell on the negative. Negative comments imply not only that you have experienced difficulty with others, but that other people have also experienced difficulties in their relationships with you; and your main objective during interviews should be one of demonstrating your ability to relate well to people.

Postpone discussions of money. Don't bring up the subject of money during the initial interview. A direct question about salary will typically result in a counterquestion about how much money you expect to earn, and expectations that are either too low or too high will have an adverse effect on your chances of landing the job.

But what if the interviewer introduces the subject? Try to postpone any discussion of money at the beginning of the interview with statements such as, "I believe that I will be in a better position to discuss salary after learning more about the job," and "Can't we talk about money after we determine that I am the right person for the job?" The risk of blowing a job opportunity will be reduced considerably if the discussion of money is postponed until later in the hiring process, when you begin to sense that you are the chosen candidate.

Interview the interviewer. After preparing and mailing many resumés and application letters, the name of the game by the time you reach the interview is "Land that job." Such an orientation often causes applicants to overlook valuable information during their visits to companies. When the author was being interviewed for an office position with a food-processing company, for example, he was so intent on securing the job that he might as well have been blindfolded during his entry and exit to the interview.

Try to avoid being so goal oriented or self-conscious that you stop seeing or hearing what is going on around you. Take an inquiring look at the facilities and the people, and keep asking yourself if it is a working environment in which you could be reasonably content and productive. Go one step further by interviewing the interviewer. Ask questions about company operations, programs, and products. Ask for a look at the department where you would be working and, if practical, a tour of related facilities. Such an introduction to the company isn't too much to expect, considering the fact that you might end up spending 250 working days each year at the company for the rest of your productive life. Moreover, interviewers are usually favorably impressed with applicants who have the knowledge and foresight to ask discerning questions.

Watch nonverbal clues. Employment interviews offer excellent opportunities for you to apply your knowledge of nonverbal communications (see Chapter 21). Try to read the feelings of interviewers by observing their facial expressions, voice inflections, and posture. Comment favorably on items in their offices that appear to be cherished status symbols. Monitor their body movements for signs of interest, acceptance, rejection, and impatience. When you respond to nonverbal cues by altering the length or content of your responses, your success ratio should increase significantly.

But there is another person at every interview that you should watch even more closely—yourself. Broadcast the desired signals of interest, honesty, reliability, and intelligence by monitoring and controlling your own nonverbal behavior. Arrive at the interview freshly groomed and in appropriate clothing, as advised earlier, and make certain that your body language conveys the intended messages. This advice includes several no-nos such as not picking at or biting your nails, not chewing gum, and not smoking (unless the interviewer lights up and invites you to join in).

Exit strategically. When the comments or nonverbal activities of an interviewer suggest that the interview is nearing an end, tactfully interject any points that you consider relevant to your chances of landing the job. This moment may represent your final opportunity to sell the interviewer on the importance of your potential contributions to the company.

Try to extract a commitment from the interviewer at this time, or as you both rise and prepare to end the conversation. If the interviewer does not provide such a commitment but does indicate that you are still in the running for the job, ask when you may telephone for a progress report. Thank the interviewer for having taken the time to visit with you, and, if you truly want the job, say so.

I was only rejected 16 times today.

PERSEVERE

Many applicants express shock and dismay when employers do not respond warmly to their initial efforts to find employment. But wouldn't it be unusual for applicants to land the desired jobs on the first try—or even the second, third, or fourth try? The job market doesn't even become aware of their presence until they begin introducing themselves with resumés, application letters, and interviews.

So keep trying until the right door swings open. You may do poorly the first few interviews; most people do. But the only way to improve your performance during interviews is through more interviewing. Accept every interview that is offered to you, therefore, by on-campus recruiters and by employment managers in their offices. Your feelings will not be so easily bruised after a few rejections, and you will learn to settle down during interviews and do a better job of selling yourself. Remember, you are not alone in this endeavor. Almost everyone, even the people who will be interviewing you, have experienced a similar scenario at least once in their lives. This year just happens to be your turn.

BUSINESS APPLICATIONS

1. Research a nationally known company of your choice, a company that you might someday contact for employment, learning as much as possible about the company's history, current operations, and plans.

2. Learn as much as you can about the financial situation of the company chosen in Application 1. If necessary, because of a limited knowledge of accounting and finance, you may seek help from others in completing this assignment.

3. Consulting one of the financial services recommended in the chapter, briefly summarize in writing all business activities of the following companies:
   a. The Budd Company
   b. Consolidated Freightways, Inc.
   c. RCA Corporation
   d. Pennzoil Company

4. Research a local company of your choice, a company you might someday contact for employment, learning as much as possible about its history, current operations, and financial condition.

5. Write a brief paragraph describing the type of job you would like to have. Then identify those aspects of your education and work experience that can be related to the job.

6. Make a list of all possible questions that interviewers might ask about your educational, occupational, and personal background.

7. Prepare and rehearse answers to all questions, and then ask someone to assume the role of interviewer in a role-playing session.

8. Prepare a list of personal information—including the types of data that were recommended in this chapter.

9. Include in a folder copies of your resumé, personal information sheet, samples of your work, and any letters that you may possess relating to commendable performance.

10. Try to arrange an authentic interview. If you don't have a job, try to secure one; if you already have a job, try to secure a better one. Follow all the guidelines presented in this chapter, and rate your performance on the basis of the following criteria:
   a. Arriving ahead of time
   b. Being pleasant to the help
   c. Making an impressive entrance
   d. Being yourself
   e. Being responsive
   f. Not talking too much
   g. Being positive
   h. Avoiding discussions of money
   i. Interviewing the interviewer
   j. Watching nonverbal cues
   k. Exiting strategically

11. Relate the details of your interviewing experience to your classmates, adding any ideas that you may now have for improving your performance and soliciting any suggestions that they may wish to contribute.

28
FOLLOWING UP

Don't just fade away after an interview, no matter how well or how poorly you may have presented your case. Follow the interview with a letter, a telephone call, and maybe another visit to the company. A job offer, when it comes, usually requires a letter of acceptance or rejection; and, if you take the job, you should present a letter of resignation to your current employer and send brief notes of thanks to those people who provided references for you.

It was love at first sight.

FIRST A LETTER

You've been interviewed and have put forth your best effort in relating your qualifications for the job. But don't stop now! In your competition with other applicants who are seeking the same job, a follow-up letter might be the extra input that tips the employment scales in your favor.

Send a letter to the interviewer within the first day or two following the interview. As illustrated in the following example, express your gratitude for the time taken to interview you, mention your qualifications for the job, and ask for further consideration.

Express gratitude	Our discussion on Monday was very interesting, and I thank you for the time that you spent with me.
Allude to qualifications	After hearing your description of the duties of an inventory clerk, I am even more certain that my qualifications match the position. Correspondingly, another glance at my resume (copy enclosed) may convince you that I am well prepared to undertake this type of work.
Request further consideration	I will appreciate any further consideration that you may give me for this position, Ms. Jones, because I am more eager to work for Bell Enterprises than before talking with you.

Notice that the applicant is including a copy of the resumé, making it very convenient for the interviewer to review the mentioned qualifications.

I'm still interested; how about you?

THEN A PHONE CALL

When four or five working days have passed with no word from the company, give them a call. Beginning a telephone conversation with the interviewer is especially easy if you mentioned such a follow-up during the interview.

> Example: Good morning, Ms. Jones, this is Ron Cox. You suggested that I phone you a few days following the interview last Monday— about the position in inventory control.

When Ron Cox has introduced himself and the situation in this manner, the remainder of the conversation will depend largely on Ms. Jones's response. At some point in the conversation, however, he should seek a commitment on the current status of his application and when the employment decision is to be made. He should briefly restate his interest while avoiding any indication of desperation.

If you are unable to get through to the interviewer in your follow-up call, attempt to question whoever answers the telephone. Try to coax as much information from the person as possible, using all the tact and persuasive abilities at your command. A good impression on the office help often results in favorable comments passed to the interviewer about your continuing efforts to land the job. And at this point in the employment process, you need all the help you can get.

But how long should you wait before abandoning the effort as hopeless? If two or three weeks pass with no encouragement, telephone and ask for a status report.

Example: Am I still being considered for the job?
Example: When is a decision to be made?
Example: May I provide you with additional information?

Your patience may be nearly exhausted at this point, because days often seem like weeks when you are waiting for job offers, but don't be too demanding. The wheels of business turn slowly sometimes, and you may still be a prime candidate for the position.

Maybe a bouquet of forget-me-nots.

A TIMELY VISIT

While you await the employment decision, consider the practicality of dropping by the company on your own volition. If you judge the interviewer to be fairly accessible, go directly to his or her office. The people there may consider this action a little atypical, but they will probably admire your initiative and perseverance. Just tell the interviewer or the assistant that you are concerned that you haven't heard from them and that you want to do everything within your power to secure the job.

The final decision about hiring you is usually left to the person who would be your immediate supervisor. If you have already been interviewed by this individual, consider a follow-up visit. You may catch the person at an inopportune time, but you can always offer to come back at a time that *is* convenient. A visit of this type will not cause them to label you as a nuisance but instead will make them realize that your interest in the job is sincere; and employers would rather hire people who are eager for employment than those who are lackadaisical about the whole process.

Also consider the possible benefits of talking with rank-and-file employees, the people you would be working with if hired. Upon learning of your plight, they might be able to provide you with insight into the hiring process. You might learn, for example, that the best approach in dealing with the employment people at this particular company is to keep bugging them. Conversely, you might discover that a more subtle approach will be more effective. Of course, the amount of time and effort you expend on this type of follow-up depends on how badly you want the job.

You surely don't mean that I have a choice?

ACCEPTANCE OR REFUSAL

Sooner or later you are bound to hit the jackpot; *someone* will offer you a job. But an offer that comes early in the search, especially if it is of only marginal interest to you, can present problems. Do I really want this job? Could I command a higher salary elsewhere? Should I wait until I hear from all those other companies?

Don't panic and accept the first offer that comes along, unless you are convinced it is a good one. If the company directs you to respond to the offer by a certain date, you might be able to delay acceptance (or rejection) until you receive responses from other companies where you have applied. This is also the time to mention a higher salary if you plan to, and to discuss reimbursement for moving expenses and other conditions of employment, because you will have much less leverage in such negotiations once you accept the job offer.

Because of the federal laws that now regulate their actions, most employment managers present job offers in writing to establish a record of when and to whom the offers are made. If you receive an offer that is satisfactory, you should respond with a written response—a letter or a telegram, whichever they sent to you. Begin your communication by indicating your acceptance of the job. Continue with a discussion of the starting date and other relevant detail, and end with a "thank you" and an optimistic comment about the future.

| Accept the offer | I am very pleased to accept your offer of employment with Amack Corporation. |

Include relevant detail	Allowing a two-week notice to my present employer and about five days for traveling and locating an apartment, I will be prepared to begin work on November 6; and, unless you instruct differently, I will report directly to Mr. Hedges at 8:30 a.m. on that date.
Express gratitude and optimism	Thank you for selecting me from among the several applicants for the job, Ms. Jawarski. I will do my best to prove that your choice was a wise one.

Although most acceptance letters are brief, like this one, you may find it necessary to extend the middle paragraph (or add another paragraph or two) to include additional information. If you could not begin employment at the agreed date, for example, you should include a detailed explanation of your circumstances. Employers seldom resent delays that result when employees continue in their old jobs until replacements can be found, because they realize that such employees may some day extend them the same consideration.

If you receive a job offer after already beginning work at some other company, tactfully refuse the offer in a brief letter. Use the deductive approach by stating your refusal in the first paragraph. Provide some detail in the middle paragraph, and end with an expression of gratitude.

Decline offer	Although I appreciate the chance to work for Esquire Sporting Goods, I must decline your job offer.
Provide details	Since discussing the clerical position with you last month, I have accepted employment with a canning firm on the West coast.
Express gratitude	Thank you for the time that you spent with me, Mr. Lyons. I enjoyed talking with you and was very impressed with your new office building.

Avoid any temptation to brag about the position you did accept, and do not burden the reader with excessive detail about your employment decision. Be brief, courteous, and appreciative. If you are upset with the offer or their delays in making the offer, do not express your true feelings, because you may knock on their door for employment again someday.

Working for you has been a real pressure . . . er, pleasure.

LETTER OF RESIGNATION

Once you have the new job well secured, present your present employer with a letter of resignation. This communication establishes a permanent record of the fact that you resigned, rather than being fired, and it sets forth the conditions of your departure. The most frequent pattern, and probably the best one, is to (1) break the news in the first sentence, (2) provide some detail in the middle paragraph, and (3) express appreciation in the final paragraph.

Break the news	The main purpose of this letter is to inform you of my impending departure.
Provide details	I have accepted employment with Rodgers Manufacturing Company as a Data Processing Supervisor--an opportunity that is too attractive to pass up. I am prepared to continue working here until November 10 or to assume the new job immediately, whichever arrangement you prefer.
Express appreciation	The experiences that I have gained with this company contributed greatly toward my preparation for the type of work that I will be doing in the new position, and I am very appreciative of the fine treatment that I have received from Mr. Lambert and all of my coworkers.

Don't gloat over your success in landing a better job, and don't tell anyone off. You may succeed in making other employees envious and in humiliating your superiors, but they will have the last and loudest laugh if things don't go well for you in the new position. Many employees leave companies each year to take "better jobs" only to return a few months later in pursuit of their earlier positions. So don't slam the door too abruptly or too permanently upon your departure.

Thanks a trillion.

INFORM REFERENCES

When friends, relatives, or business acquaintances have provided references or assisted you in any way, be sure to notify them promptly of your successful conclusion of the job search. Send them an informal letter, but one that is attractive and well written. Begin by conveying the good news. Provide some details in a middle paragraph, and end the letter with a direct expression of gratitude.

Convey the good news	SUCCESS AT LAST! I finally landed the job that I have been pursuing so diligently.
Provide some detail	Thanks to you and others who helped me, I am now the Data Processing Supervisor at Rodgers Manufacturing Company. This job suits me perfectly, and I am certain that my letters of reference (like the very impressive one that you wrote) were an important consideration in the selection process.
Express gratitude	I thank you very much Clarence, and look forward to taking you to lunch sometime soon for a minicelebration. Okay?

Rewarding the people who helped you secure employment is good business, because you never know when you may need their support again. A luncheon at a fancy restaurant, a family get-together, or some type of small gift will help to maintain these invaluable relationships.

BUSINESS APPLICATIONS

1. Assume that you have just returned home from an interview at National Publishing House, 111 West Clarendon Street, Monterey Park, California (zip 91754). You and two other applicants were interviewed separately by Maria Rodriguez, Personnel Manager, for a clerical position in the production department. A brief tour of the main building left you highly impressed with the facilities and the people. The way employees dressed and acted seemed so informal and pleasant; no one seemed to work very hard. Consequently, you have decided that you do want the job (if you can get it), which involves the operation of several office machines that you haven't worked with before, some light bookkeeping, and a limited amount of typing. Write a follow-up letter to the interviewer. Today's date is October 16 (current year).

2. Having just received a written job offer from National Publishing House (Application 1), write a letter refusing employment. Almost four weeks have passed since the interview without your having received one word of encouragement, during which time you have accepted a job as relief teller with Arroyo Savings & Loan Company. You have been working at the bank for more than a week, and you are earning $50 per month more than offered by National Publishing House. Today's date is November 15 (current year).

3. The job that you are seeking at Crestwood Cable Company, 1601 West 47th Street, North Chicago, Illinois 60064, involves the filing of OS&D (over, short, and damage) claims involving shipments of company products. You have had some experience in processing OS&D claims in a summer job with the Illinois Central Railroad. In the railroad job, you processed claims for both rail and truck shipments, either denying the claims or approving them for payment. The job involved a lot of correspondence, and, since you had no secretarial help, it also required a lot of typing. You explained all of this information to Wayne Braddock, Personnel Manager at Crestwood, and to Joyce Anderson, Traffic Manager, in separate interviews yesterday. Ms. Anderson will be your immediate superior if you are hired as an OS&D Clerk. You liked what you heard and saw during the interviews, and both people seemed favorably impressed with your background and enthusiasm. Write a follow-up letter to the personnel manager. You will be available for full-time employment the middle of next month, upon graduation from college, and today's date is April 17 (current year).

4. After one telephone call to Wayne Braddock, and another to Joyce Anderson (Application 3), and a trip to Ms. Anderson's office to check on the status of your application, you have just received an offer of employment dated April 26. The letter from Braddock specifies a starting date of May 8, just one week from today, but the 8th is the first day of final exams week. Accept the position, explaining your reasons for wanting to begin work a week later—May 15. Date your letter May 1 (current year).

5. You have been employed at Three Diamonds Corporation for two years now as a clerk in the product distribution department the first year and as assistant traffic manager the second year. The company is located at 1600 East 10th Street, Wilmington, Delaware 19899, and the name of the personnel manager is Judith Presley. You have learned a lot about product distribution and traffic management during the past two years, especially from the traffic manager, Ted Macky; and you have enjoyed your working relationships with all employees. Write a letter of resignation, giving the company a two-week notice in connection with your having accepted a job as traffic manager at Dressor, Incorporated, a major producer of pollution-control equipment.

6. You have just accepted a job with Adams-Hoyt Associates, a brokerage firm that deals in securities transactions. You are to participate in a three-month training program to prepare you as an account executive, a sales job. The program begins two weeks from today (August 20 of the current year). You would like to have at least a one-week break between jobs, but are willing to work the full two weeks if your present employer so desires. Write a letter of resignation to Citizens Central Bank, explaining the circumstances and resigning your job as teller. Although you have applied yourself at the bank during the past four years, striving for a promotion to head teller, your extra contributions have apparently gone unnoticed. From the very beginning, you considered the head teller incompetent and unfair, and, compared to other jobs in the area with similar responsibilities, the pay has been ridiculously low. Address your letter to William F. Bussy, General Bank Manager. The mailing address is P.O. Box 3591, Dallas, Texas 75221.

7. Marva Goulder works at Gorton Ashton Company, 15 California Street, San Francisco, California 94119. Marva was the one who told you that a job was available at Adams-Hoyt Associates. As a business acquaintance with the people at Adams-Hoyt, and having known you on a personal

basis for the past ten years, Marva wrote a recommendation that probably helped cinch the job for you. Write a "thank you" note, expressing your gratitude and inviting her and her husband (Delbert) over to your home for an outdoor barbeque next weekend. Date your letter August 10 (current year).

8. Ronald Price, your accounting professor in college, was considered by most students to be a very demanding instructor—always expecting a little more than most students thought they could deliver. After having completed his courses, however, you realize that he prepared you well for employment as a junior accountant—a position that you accepted just two weeks ago (September 11 of the current year) with Metcalf Industries, Inc. Professor Price was also one of three people who sent letters of recommendation to Metcalf. Write a letter to Price at Lakeside Community College, 1114 North Darlington Road, Tulsa, OK 74135, thanking him for all he has done for you.

INDEX